I0824921

# BOTANI
# CAL
# REVOLU
# TIONS

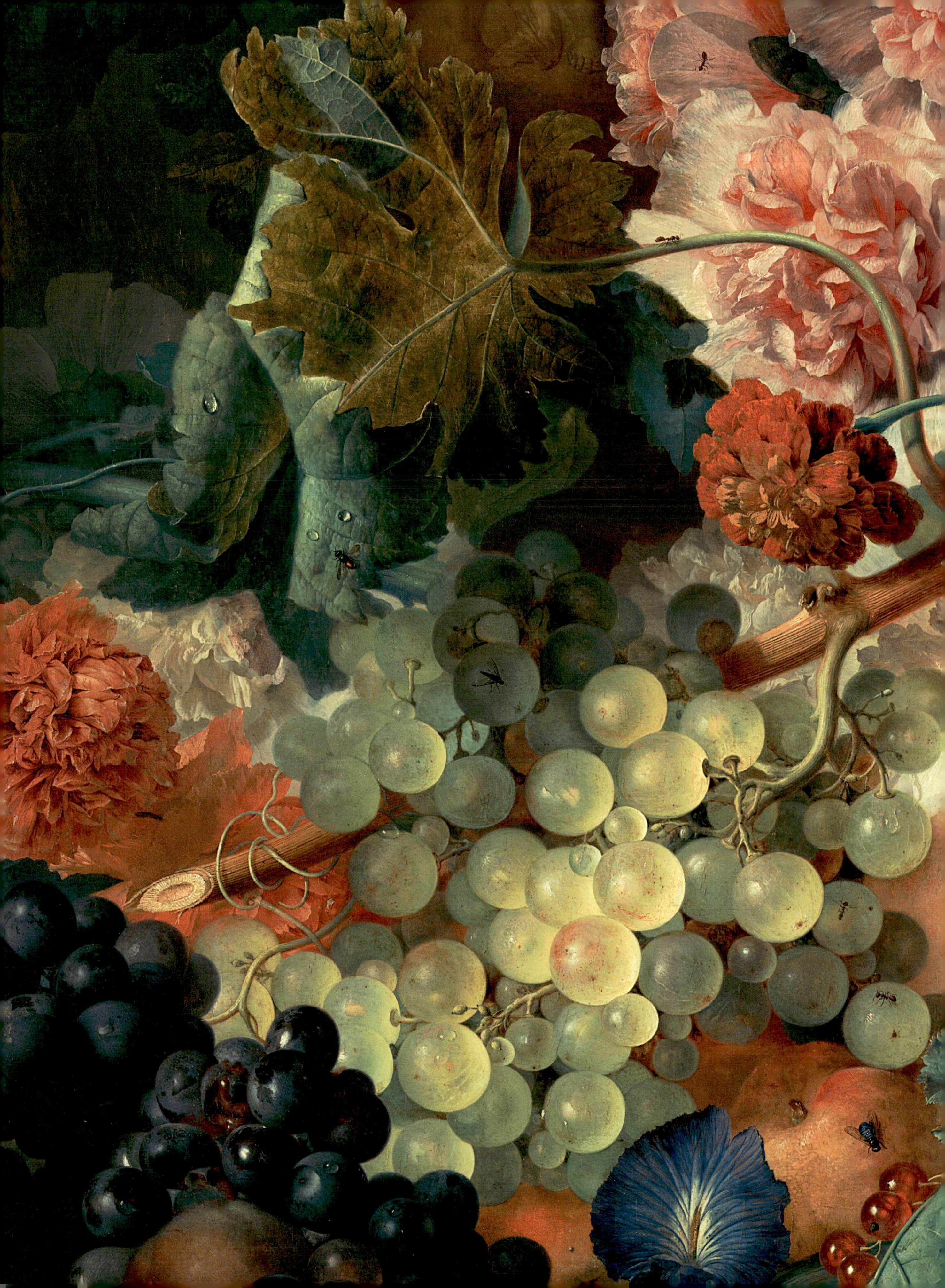

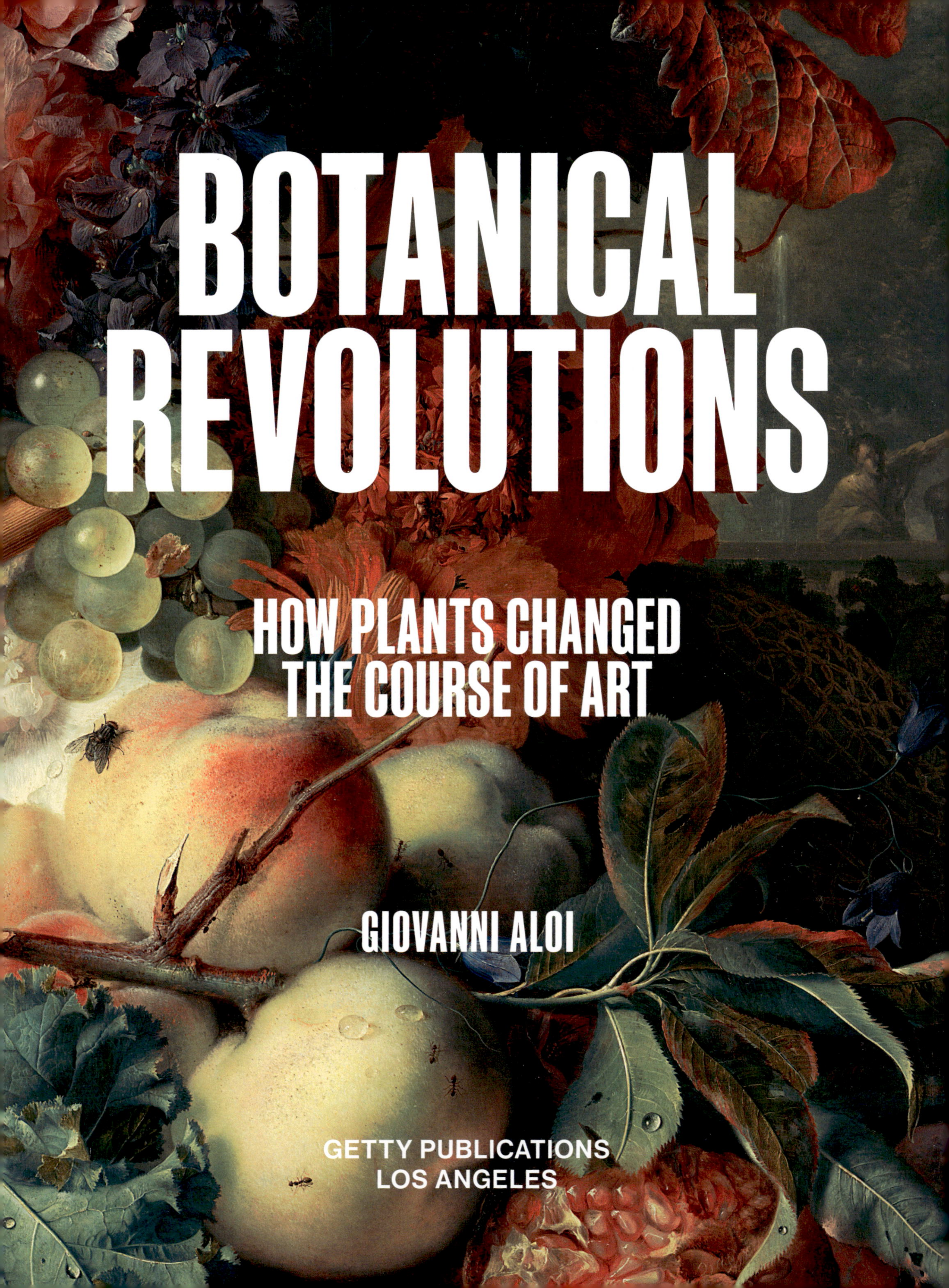
BOTANICAL REVOLUTIONS
HOW PLANTS CHANGED THE COURSE OF ART
GIOVANNI ALOI
GETTY PUBLICATIONS
LOS ANGELES

# INTRODUCTION

# CREATIVE GERMINATIONS

Plant life is not a fixed category, but rather an ever-evolving constellation of alignments binding our lives to those of other animals, the soil, fungi, bacteria, water, air, and light. In their branchings, fibers, textures, and colors, plants embody a wholesome sense of imperturbable presence and continuity between the living and the dead. Inscribed in their roots are blueprints of ancestral knowledges and promises of sustainable futures.

Plants are intimately and indissolubly bound to the earth from which they emerge. It is tempting to believe that their lives might be limited by this, that they are simpler and hence less fascinating than those of humans. But much of what plants are and do stays invisible to us, or simply eludes our perception. The shortcoming is all ours, of course. Humans and plants live on the same planet but exist in different worlds—ours dependent on theirs—only in part overlapping. The apparent simplicity of plants is deceptive; their character is the sum of all natural forces. Plants are crystallizations of material discourses that can only deposit and grow over time, bloom after bloom, season after season.

When our joint evolutionary history parted one and a half billion years ago, the eukaryotic division into plants, fungi, and animals entailed a radical shift in everyone's relationship with the soil. Plants and fungi opted to stay close, gripping tight to the earth. But animals chose to flee; some, following desire, leaped into the sky. It is from this evolutionary divergence that plant wisdom emerged as an art of restraint—a skill most animals have learned to forget. This vegetal art has something to teach us about tenacity and conviction; making the most of, and thriving with, what is at hand; withstanding prolonged adversity; persevering at all costs. It is a learned form of wisdom that requires patience, resilience, adaptability, and determination. No two plant species—or even two plants of the same species, for that matter—master this form of wisdom in the same way. Much depends on where they grow and how they respond to challenges—how they problem solve.[1]

It is from this evolutionary divergence that our opportunity to learn from plants as kin also stemmed. Over time, some cultures seized this opportunity, making plant wisdom central to their beliefs. Others took them for granted and became blind to the beauty of their intelligence and the complexity of their being. In taking so many wondrous forms, plant life is persistently elusive and indecipherable, neither fixed nor exhaustible. Its laconic essence can seem equally awe-inspiring and unnerving.

Acknowledging that the otherness of plants is truly valuable and must be respected as a genuine type of diversity can assist us in returning to that slow, vegetal, discursive process that was already ingrained in our evolutionary history but that colonialism, capitalism, and the anthropocentric philosophies of the West have taught us to disregard, or even reject, as signs of weakness. This form of miseducation has dramatically impoverished our world, culturally as well as ecologically.

As a species, humans are by nature profoundly anxious and insecure—perhaps the price we've paid for the evolutionary conquest of mobility. The invention of deities is an artifact of our perpetual sense of precariousness, our dread of the future, our ultimate fear of death—a characteristic of the human condition. Disoriented and burdened by an all-pervading sense of meaninglessness that relentlessly carves our very being, we have fashioned benevolent guardians and unforgiving masters to justify our existence. Every civilization has dealt with this existential unsteadiness in a unique way. In the West, our blind ambition to position humankind at the center of the world has for centuries served as an antidote—or, more precisely, a palliative. Around twelve thousand years ago, the introduction of agricultural practices marked a significant shift in the dynamics of human-plant interactions. Domestication rapidly dissipated the sacred aura of animals and plants: they were swiftly replaced by humanoid gods. Aristotle developed his theorization of the vast "chain of beings," *scala naturae*, during the fourth century BCE. It established a hierarchical structure of life on Earth, with vegetation occupying the lowest level and humans, supposedly the most intelligent and complex species, at the apex.[2] This biological, cultural, and affective chasm between humans and plants soon widened into an insurmountable abyss. Christianity's view of humanity as masters of the natural world, a conception largely inspired by Aristotle's argument, bolstered a convenient form of anthropocentrism in the centuries that followed.[3]

The rise of humanism—the fifteenth-century revival of classical Greek culture in Italy—reinvigorated forms of plant reductionism. Humanism was a response to the immense devastation inflicted by the Black Death, a widespread epidemic that resulted in the loss of as many as two hundred million lives throughout Eurasia and North Africa between 1346 and 1353.[4] This catastrophic event forced humankind to grapple with an existential crisis of unparalleled magnitude. Why would God punish his most valued creation in such a heinous way? In the aftermath of this tragedy, humanism emerged as a formidable remedy: a philosophical system of thought that reaffirmed the supremacy of human intelligence above that of all other earthlings. Humanity needed its self-confidence restored, and as the artistic output of the Renaissance amply demonstrated through its victorious aesthetics of positive grandness and stability, it served us well until it devolved into outright hubris. Astonishing architectural and artistic marvels; the flourishing of literature, music, and science; the transatlantic slave trade; relentless fighting among counties, cities, and kingdoms; looting, burning, raping—the sheer sense of protagonism that pervaded Western civilization also defined the optics of natural history. Under the false guise of purity, perfection, and progress, humanism eventually gave us a patriarchal world order that enabled colonialist atrocities, genocide, irreversible ecological damage, racism, misogyny, and endless conflict.

Over the course of five hundred years, the unrelenting anthropocentrism that characterized Western thought naturalized itself. This sense of absolute protagonism has carved our identities—we have convinced ourselves that our presumed exceptional intellectual abilities are the sole and unique tools responsible for every cultural expression stemming from our imaginative faculties. Throughout it all, we have also miseducated ourselves into believing that everything around us is passive—that materials are lifeless and that the distinctiveness of being human rests in our ability to breathe life into them.[5] Many art history books still support this view as a mark of human exceptionalism over plants and animals. This ill-conceived idea has also had a major impact on our relationship with art and art making.

But as any dedicated artist who spends time experimenting in the studio knows, materials are always alive, never inert. Materials have characters, behaviors, identities, histories, voices. Materials indulge, provoke, engage, and seduce. And most importantly, they resist—they'll bend, twist, crush, mix, and flatten for us only so far. They at once expand and set the boundaries for our expressive desires. They help us to conceptualize our creative potential and often inspire us to achieve feats that would have been unimaginable without them. They extend the limits of our cognition beyond our human remit. Where does our thinking end, and that of the material begin? In order to see how closely these are linked, one must be brave enough to rethink the very idea of thinking, and make the leap from René Descartes's 1637 "I think therefore I am" to a worldview in which everything can co-represent and co-create—where everything can think.[6] More than ever before, artists actively participate in a collaborative creative process known as plant-thinking, which transcends Cartesian binaries, the illusory assumption of a self-contained brain, as well as obsolete notions of consciousness, like the very idea that humans alone are conscious.

Recent years have witnessed the growth of art practices that rethink our interactions with plants in ways that do not fall into the logical and mental pitfalls of anthropocentrism.[7] Today art allows us to take productive risks in the reconfiguration of our reality and the world we coproduce, as well as build visions of futures in which the human species is less lonely and alienated.

The turn of the new millennium was characterized by an exciting cultural fervor that in the humanities was labeled the ontological turn.[8] Inclusivity, diversity, agency, and interconnectedness quickly became the guiding principles around which thinking and making practices sought to reconfigure the epistemological domain of creativity. New fields of inquiry such as post-humanism, animal studies, new materialism, queer ecologies, Anthropocene studies, and, more recently, critical plant studies have actively engaged with ecological themes in order to craft ethical frameworks for coexistence. This transition, strengthened by the emergency generated by the current climate crisis, has had far-reaching ramifications for how we critically evaluate older conceptions of humanness and how these need to be altered in order to support a sustainable future for an inclusive web of life on Earth.[9] It is in this context that plants have finally begun to gain true visibility in art.

As botanists James H. Wandersee and Elisabeth E. Schussler put it in 1999, we have become blind to plants. "Plant blindness," as they call it, essentially is a cultural condition that prevents us from recognizing plant life's complexity beyond the realm of curiosity or specialist knowledge.[10] In their vegetal gifts lies the burden:

plants' profound malleability and versatility sometimes make them invisible. We take them for granted. But without them, the vast majority of the art we love would have never been created. Papers, canvases, boards, brushes, pigments—these are the vegetal gifts all art made across the world has depended upon for millennia. To make matters worse, a substantial internalization of the Aristotelian *scala naturae* has meant that even when plants appear in the picture, they most often serve as backgrounds, are cast as marginal, or are smothered by symbolism. Whether subject or material, plants' contribution to art has, over time, remained mostly silent and unacknowledged. Just as we take for granted the important roles plants play in supporting ecosystems, we likewise forget how they manifest, support, and expand our creativity. Or, to put it differently, we far too frequently forget that our creative inventiveness is rarely the consequence only of human brilliance, but far more likely the outcome of an intimate and passionate negotiation and coauthoring with vegetal collaborators. One could rightly argue that animals and minerals have played similarly important roles, and while I cannot agree more, this book focuses on plants for the sake of coherence.

*Botanical Revolutions* employs principles central to the ontological turn in the humanities to recover and link past moments, fragments, and relations in which plants have enabled us to express our creative potential or changed the course of art by playing important roles in the advancement of movements and styles, or the invention of new media. This alternative history of art, by nature incomplete and fragmented, foregrounds the indispensable contributions plants have made through multispecies co-creative engagements. It is indisputable that the power relationships involved often remain unbalanced, inevitably leaning toward the human side. Ultimately plants do not care about art as we do; it is we who bring them into that context. But once in, their agency is undeniably all-encompassing and world-forming. If we have not noticed this yet, it is simply because we have been blinded by the monolithic, romantic figure of the artist as undisputed genius creator, whose intellect bestows meaning on an otherwise empty or meaningless creation. Becoming aware of the contributions plants have made to the history of art also helps us to replace that tired narcissistic stereotype with new and humbler models of creativity based on mediation, attentiveness, reciprocity, engagement, entwinement, and empathy.

Furthermore, *Botanical Revolutions* also contextualizes plants in art as malleable collaborators in multiple and layered ways. Via example after example, this book shows how plant-derived matter helped us ground our knowledge so that it could grow; how the complexity of plant forms allowed us to co-envision patterns of meaning and codevelop aesthetic vocabularies that would not exist without vegetal intervention; and how the wisdom of plant-thinking brought us to invent new media together. Over and over, plants have subtly restructured our thinking trajectories, offering rooted convictions, branching departures, and rhizomatic thought networks through which our intuitions could bloom, reaching beyond the immediacy of the now and outlining constellations across time and space. For better or for worse, plants have made us humans. It is now time to give them credit for the immense role they have played in our creative evolutionary journey. At stake is the invaluable opportunity to change the course of art once again, for future generations and for the planet.

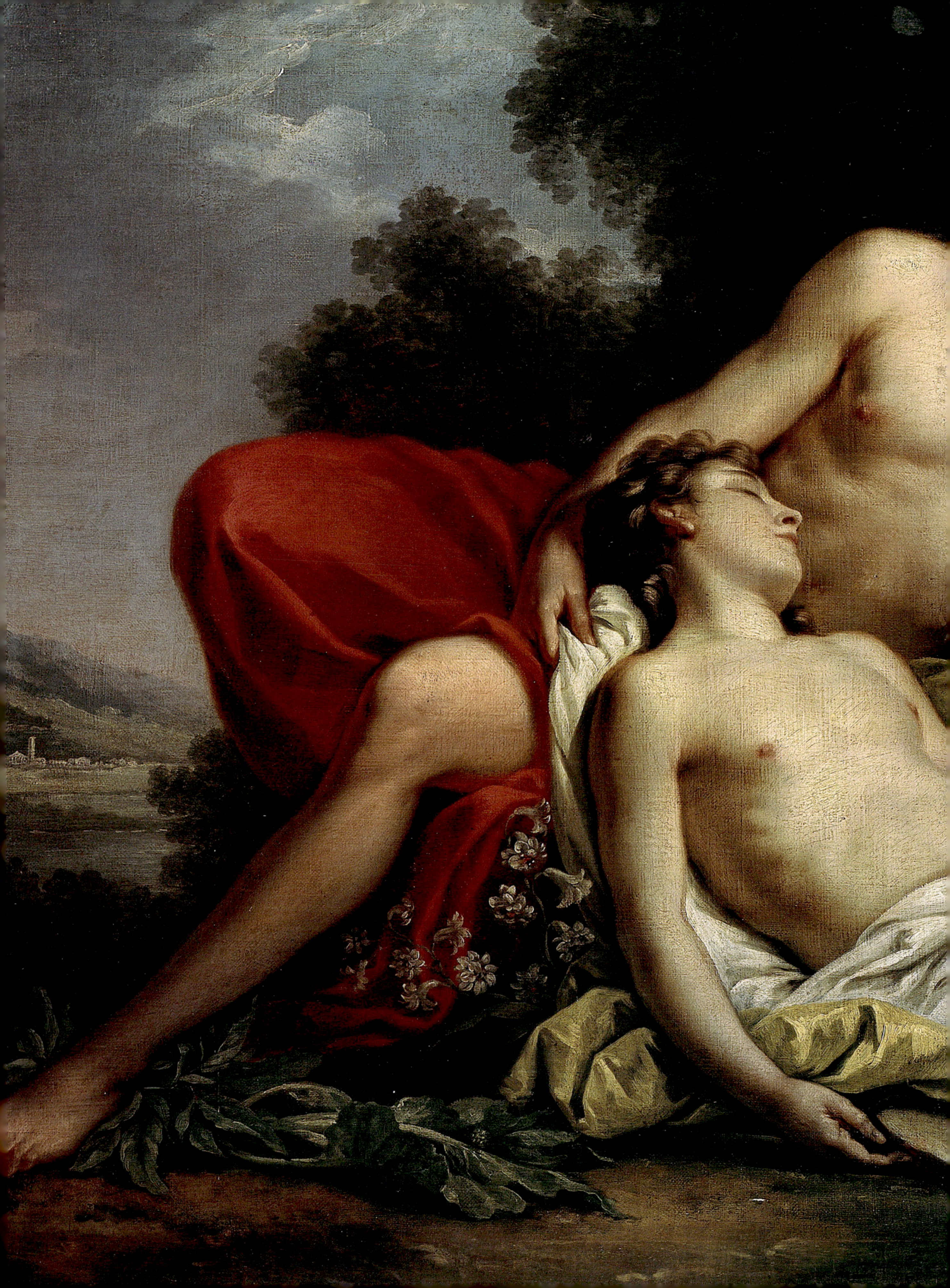

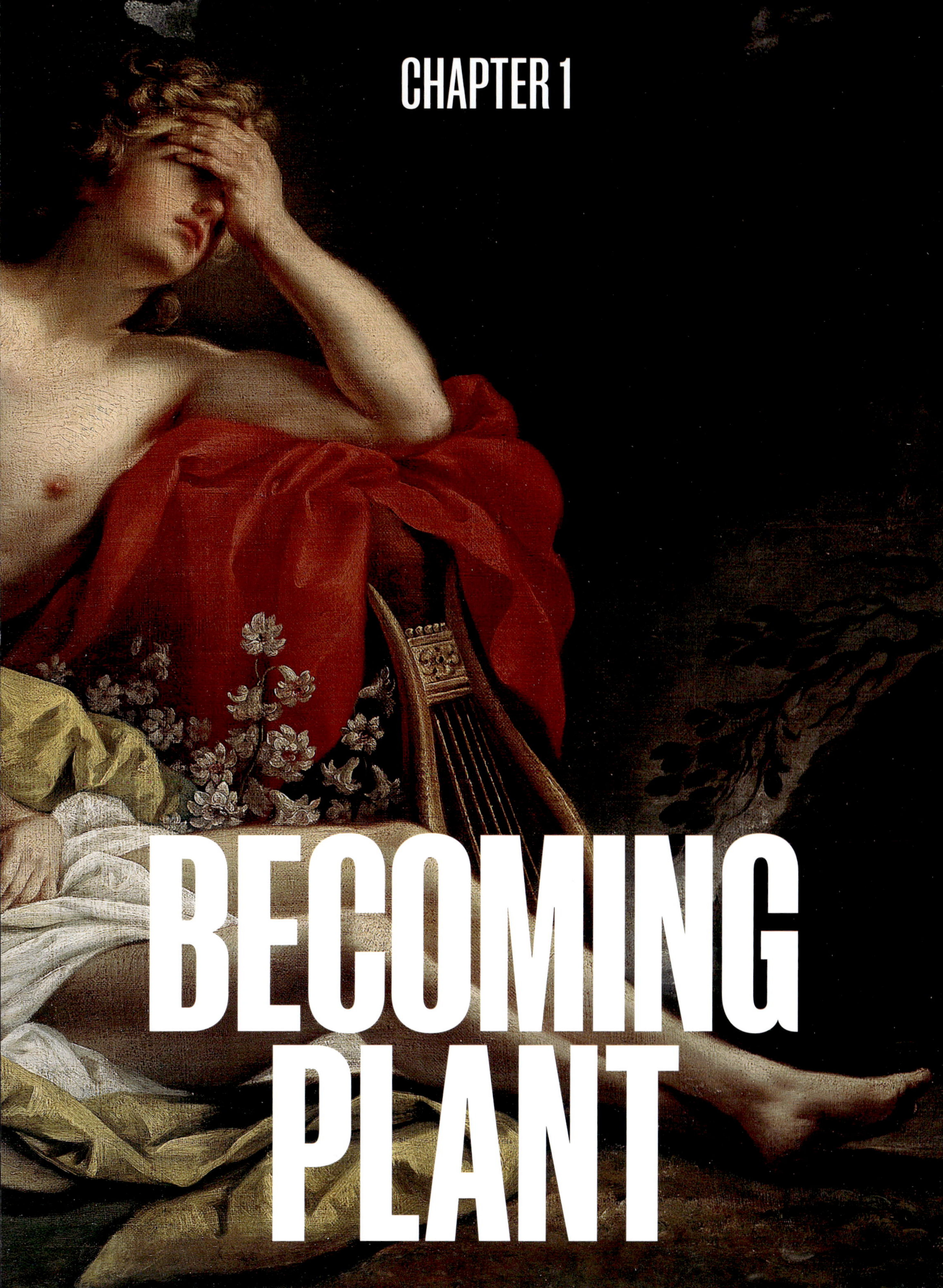

CHAPTER 1

# BECOMING PLANT

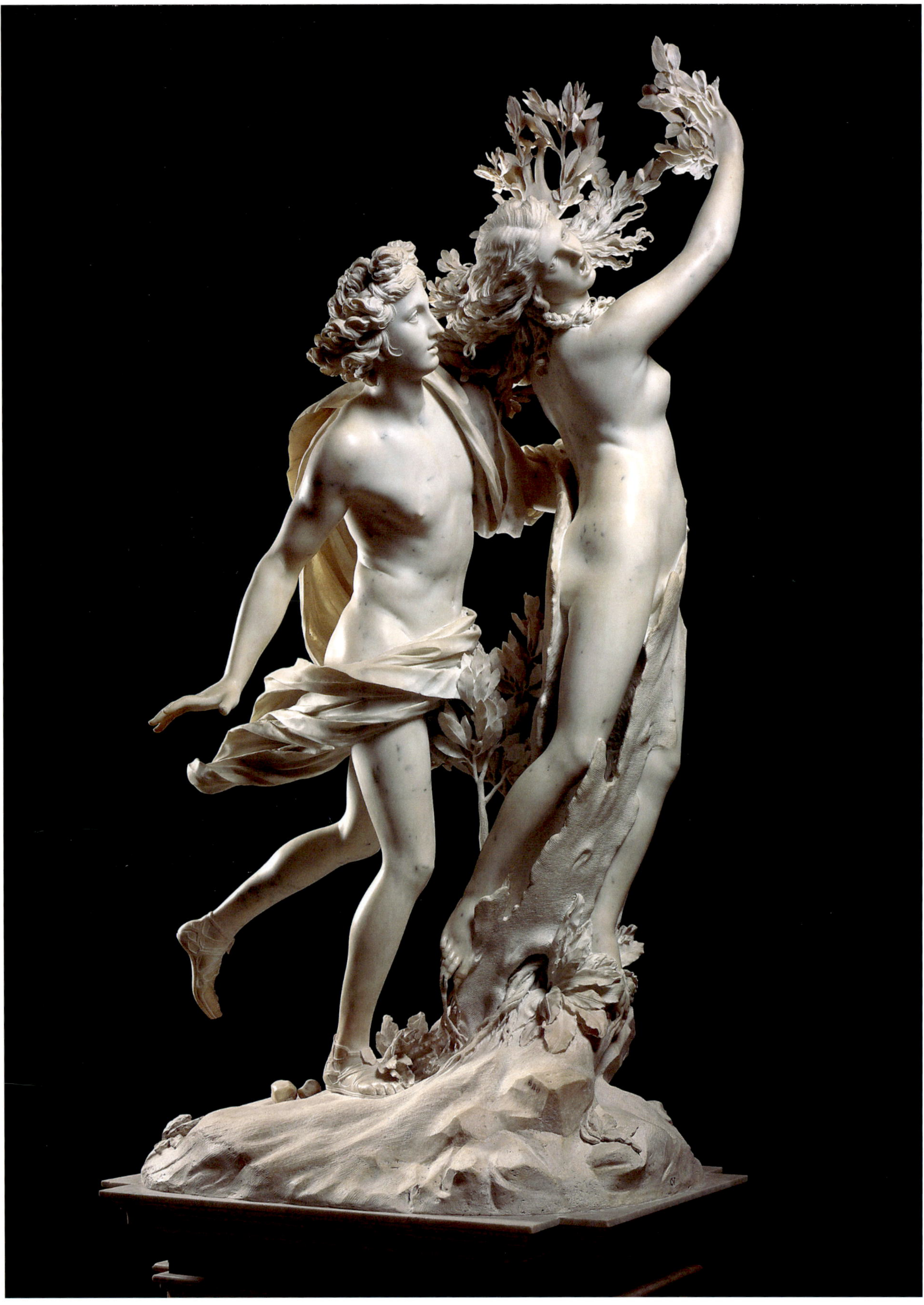

Gian Lorenzo Bernini, *Apollo and Daphne*, 1622–25, white Carrara marble

> Daphne's "soft white bosom was ringed in a layer of bark, her hair was turned into foliage, her arms into branches. The feet that had run so nimbly were sunk into sluggish roots; her head was confined in a treetop; and all that remained was her beauty."[1]

Gian Lorenzo Bernini's Baroque sculpture *Apollo and Daphne* (1622–25) masterfully crystallizes the pathos that seeps through Ovid's verses. Painstakingly detailed and delicately intricate, each marble twig and leaf is an extension of Daphne's veins and bones—her human fragility carved into the austere resilience of vegetality. Daphne, a water nymph and daughter of the river god Peneus, is being transformed into a laurel tree by her father so that she will not fall prey to Apollo's undesired and unrelenting pursuit. In the story, Apollo strokes the rough bark and kisses it in a last attempt to satisfy his longing, but the wood shrinks away. Screams, tears, rushing, panting—then it's all over, everything is silent. Bernini chiseled Daphne's lips as slightly parted—a hint of stupor, or the last gasp of a human breath? The recalcitrant nymph has not vanished, but she now belongs to a far and distant kingdom from which there is no return. Her stillness and imperturbable vegetal silence deeply anguish Apollo:

> Since you cannot be mine in wedlock, you must at least be Apollo's tree. It is you who will always be twined in my hair, on my tuneful lyre and my quiver of arrows. The generals of Rome shall be wreathed with you, when the jubilant paean of triumph is raised and the long procession ascends the Capitol. On either side of Augustus' gates your trees shall stand sentry, faithfully guarding the crown of oak-leaves hanging between them. As I, with my hair that is never cut, am eternally youthful, so you with your evergreen leaves are for glory and praise everlasting.[2]

In a desperate attempt to bridge the physical and emotional abyss that now separates them, Apollo fills Daphne's silence with his triumphant voice—one that can't echo in her throat. Daphne's bid for freedom is thwarted. Violence upon violence—her vegetal escape is co-opted. Apollo takes possession of Daphne by turning her into an emblem. His words reduce her to an effigy of something she was never meant to be. In a cruel twist of fate, the independent woman who wished to remain a virgin forever succumbs to the all-pervasive grip of patriarchy.

Ovid's ancient mythology portrays the intricate interconnections between humans and plants as simultaneously challenging and awe-inspiring. Desired for their aesthetic beauty, sought after for their medicinal properties, harvested for their scents and flavors, or grown as indispensable material resources, plants are indissolubly entwined with our existence. All life on this planet depends upon them, and yet over millions of years, evolution has made us strangers to them. More than any other animal species, we gaze at plants but no longer really see them because we have simply forgotten how to look.

Animals among animals: our perception has evolved to help us avoid predators who move more quickly than we do. When life gets dire, animals flee in search of shelter or greener pastures. Plants instead stay rooted—for life committed to their place of birth, their bodies relentlessly shaped by the endurance of their fibers and the elements that nourish and batter them. Over time, far too reliant on the superiority complex that characterizes our species, we began to read the stoic demeanor of plants as a deeply ingrained inferiority. In our eyes, vegetal silence became dumbness, and plant stillness nothing more than inadequacy. We turned blind to plants' awesome complexity and lost sight of their wisdom.

It is no coincidence that across the mythologies and folklore of different cultures, it is only humans who aspire to become invisible. Whether cloaked in a magical cape or wearing an enchanted helmet, we dream of hiding our identities so as to wander unseen. But in Western cultural narratives, plants can't possibly covet invisibility simply because they already are invisible—never brimming with individuality, in art plants fade into the insignificance of backdrops. They seem staunchly indifferent to the sufferings and joys of others, as when Daphne's metamorphosis into a tree—a piece of cold, hard wood—comes to represent the ultimate deterrent to Apollo's relentless desire. The tree embodies the muting of human expressiveness, the grave of sensuality.

There is no scenario in which Apollo's loss of interest in Daphne's new arboreal form could be

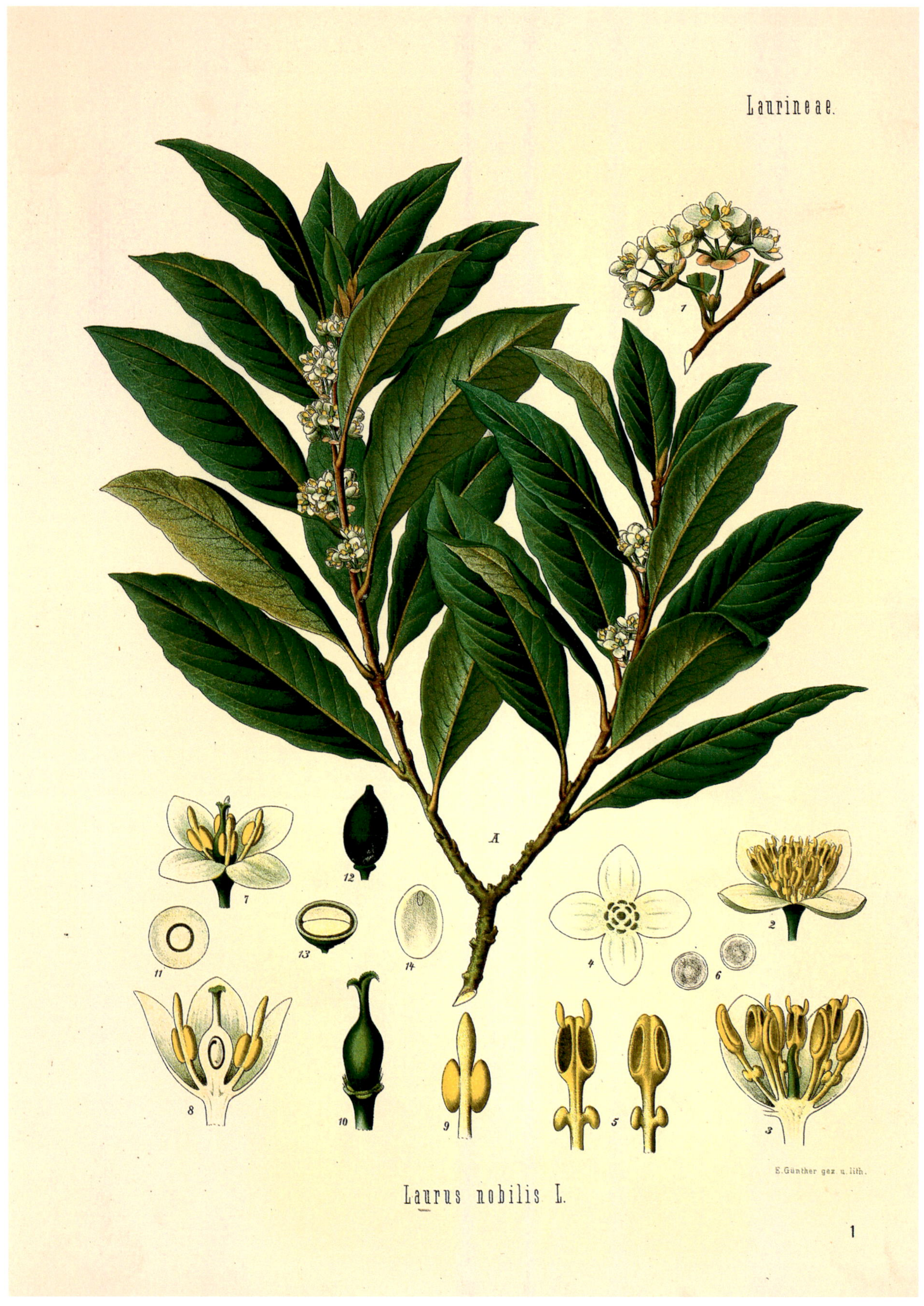


K. Günther, Bay laurel or sweet bay tree, *Laurus nobilis*, 1887, in Hermann Adolph Köhler, *Köhler's Medicinal Plants*, chromolithograph

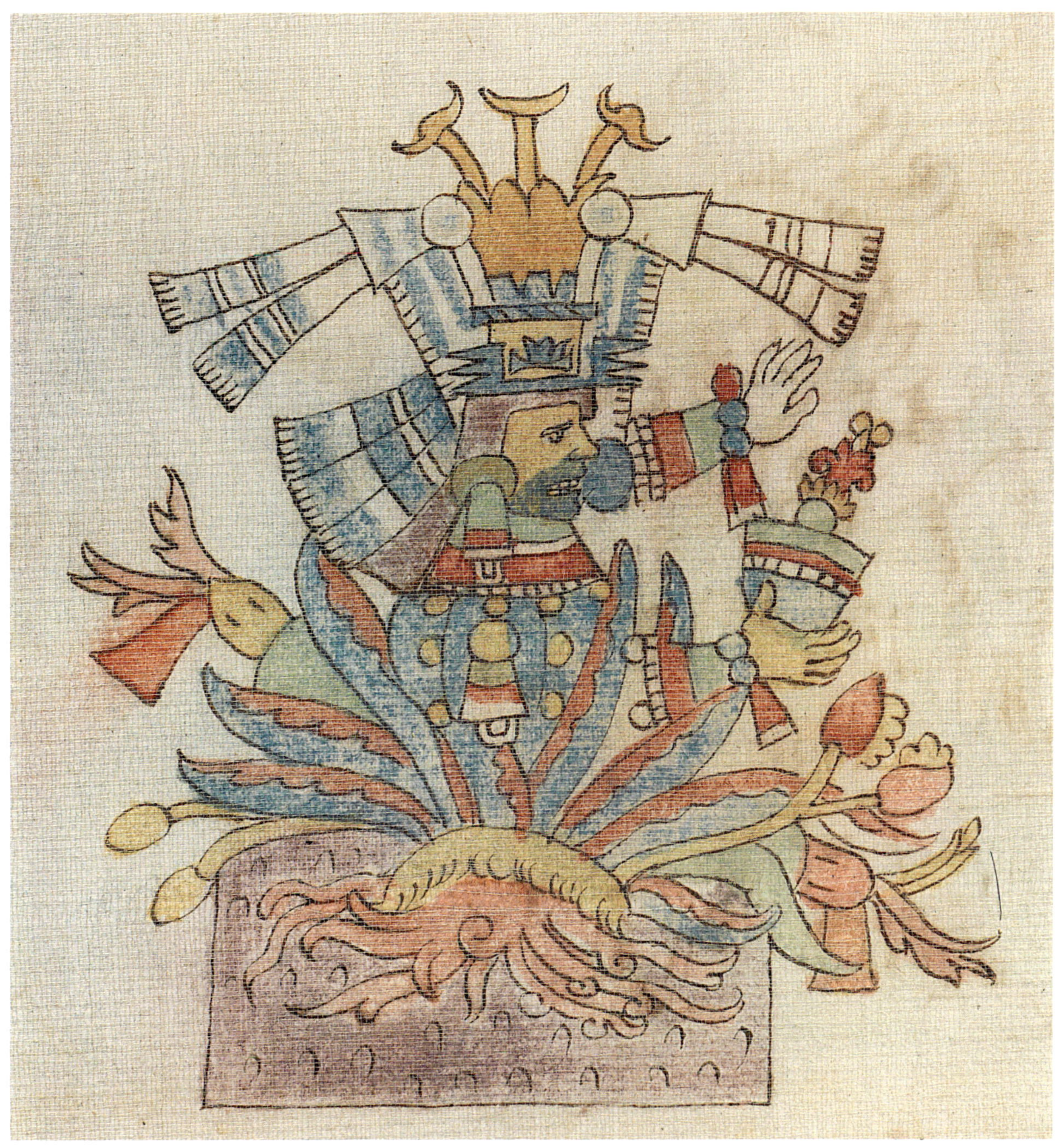

Illustration of Mayahuel (detail), in *Codex Ríos*, Italian, sixteenth century

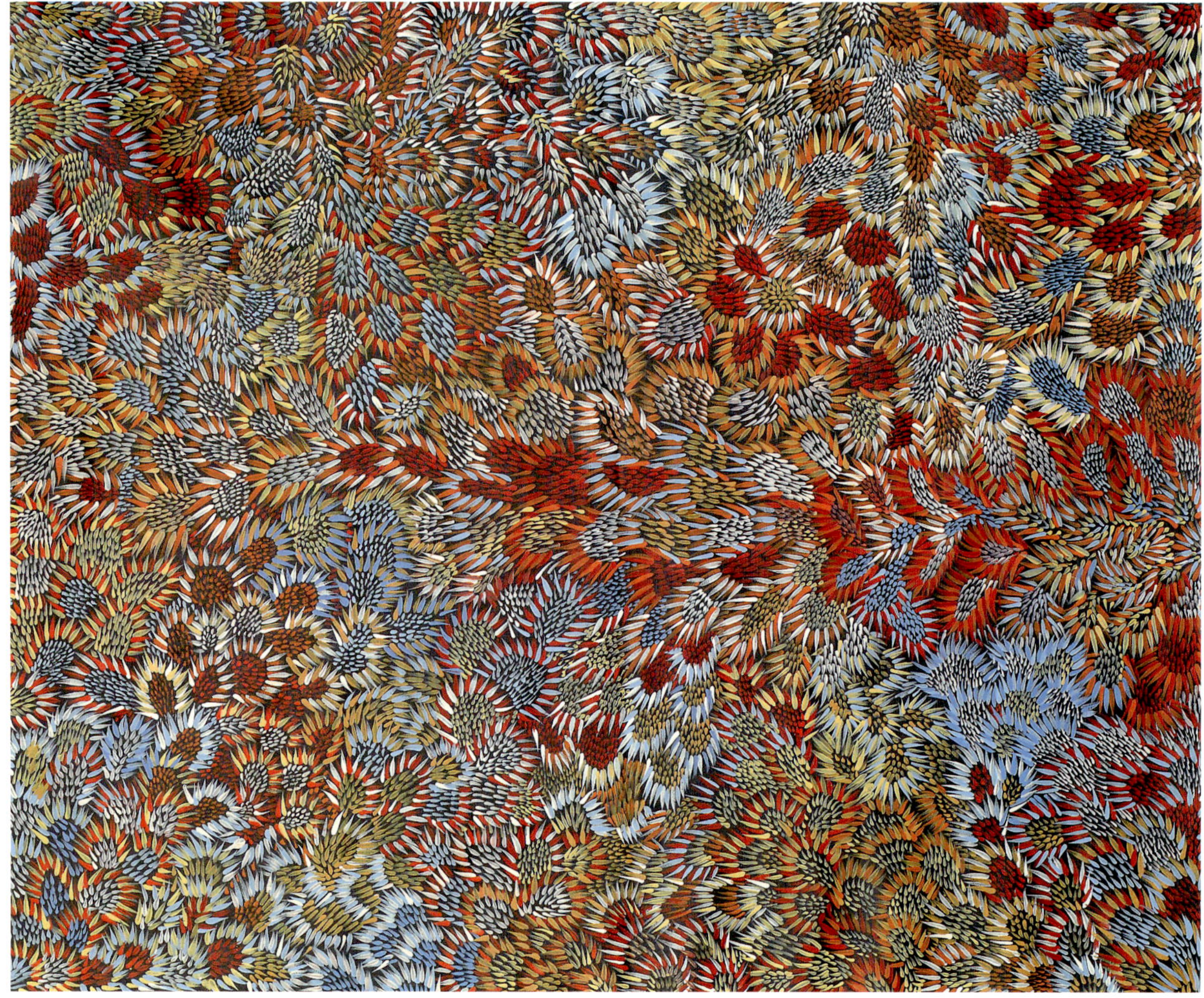

Abie Loy Kemarre, *Bush Medicine Leaves*, 2020, acrylic on linen

framed as a matter of personal preference. In the context of Western culture, a metamorphosis from human to tree simply implies degradation. But in others, human-to-plant transformations have often brought about enrichment. An example can be found in the Toltec-style rock paintings at Ixtapantongo, Mexico. Among other mythical figures we find Mayahuel, an Aztec goddess of fertility.[3] According to Mesoamerican mythology, Mayahuel was banished to the darkest corner of the universe by her wicked grandmother Tzitzímitl—a skeletal demoness, enemy of the sun. Quetzalcoatl, the god of wind and knowledge, falls in love with Mayahuel and takes her away to Earth, where she can hide and be safe. Aware of Tzitzímitl's impending wrath, the two entwine and transform into a tree to hide from her. But she finds them, destroys Mayahuel's side of the tree, and feeds the broken parts to her horde of demons. Quetzalcoatl, heartbroken, buries her corpse and weeps on her grave until, by heavenly intervention, a magnificent spiky plant—an agave—breaks through the earth. The swordlike leaves, towering toward the sky, represent Mayahuel's celestial essence; the sharp darts at the end of each will forever guard her from Tzitzímitl.[4] Her sweet white sap will bring Quetzalcoatl eternal consolation.

In precolonial depictions, Mayahuel is frequently seen sitting at the center of an agave plant, the leaves stylized to suggest a continuity between the goddess's body and that of the plant.[5] The agave is sacred to the peoples of Mesoamerica and for thousands of years has been an important source of sustenance. The resilient and adaptable fibers can be manipulated into textiles and cords, and the spiny tips serve as stitching needles. The antiseptic property of the sap—often associated with maternal milk—has made it a staple in traditional medicine. Fermented, it is the essential ingredient of pulque, an alcoholic drink deemed sacred prior to the Spanish conquest of the Aztec Empire in the sixteenth century.[6]

Plants are regarded as world-forming allies in other cultures as well, where plant-human entanglements are firmly established on profound and inseparable fluidities anchored in primordial kinships. First Nations artist Abie Loy Kemarre lives in the community of Utopia, in Central Australia in the Northern Territory. Her *Bush Medicine Leaves* (2020) captures an intense swirl of minute, multicolored feather-like leaves seemingly converging at the center of the canvas. The artist's abstract-leaning aesthetic approach reflects the Aboriginal notion of plants as mystical partners, profoundly entwined in lifesaving interactions and codependency. The specific plant represented here is *Acacia tenuissima* (narrow-leaved wattle), whose leaves, according to tradition, are crushed and mixed with animal fat into a medicinal ointment, or soaked in water and distilled to produce an antiseptic tincture. Aboriginal tribes across Australia know that snakes mate, and are therefore more aggressive, at the same time of year that the acacia flowers fall to the ground, and in this seasonal vegetal message they read a warning. The plant is a benevolent guardian who reminds them to remain vigilant while hunting.[7]

Kemarre's depictions of flora are recognizable but deliberately nonrealistic, as the objective of Aboriginal art does not involve replicating the precise form and hues of leaves as perceived by the human eye. Rather, these images of plants and landscapes are repositories of coevolution and energies that pervaded the Dreamtime—the foundation of Aboriginal religion and culture underpinning the ancestral interrelations of all living beings, time, and land. Aboriginal artists depict celestial life forces that permeate the Dreamtime through whirling patterns and motifs reminiscent of currents and natural flows. This indivisibility between humans and other beings is central to the stories passed down from generation to generation. In this dimension, plants are neither reducible to a resource to exploit nor an emblem of power.

For Aboriginal populations and other Indigenous peoples around the world, plants can be simultaneously past and present—living custodians of identities and heritage, indispensable protectors, and benevolent guardians. Thus, the ecological erosion we are witnessing in the Anthropocene also means cultural oblivion in a world where tales are woven through grass blades and tree branches. With every species of native plant lost, stories and traditions also vanish, in most cases forever. Deforestation, fires, agricultural monocultures, blights—the ecological dismantling of Native lands perpetrated by capitalist forces has, over the past two hundred years or so, irreparably impoverished our planet. It is in stories from the past that we can reconnect with plants and the natural world in ways that might support more sustainable futures. It is from these stories that we might learn to see plants again.

Plants have been drawn, painted, and sculpted in many ways throughout history, and how we portray them can be more than just an effort to express their beauty. Every image of a plant is an inscription of ideologies, conceptions, and beliefs that may remain invisible, or forgotten, and yet define our perspectives and relationships with plants, with the rest of the planet, and with each other. The history of plants in Western art has been marked by a pervasive marginalization and omission that closely parallels the power dynamics and hierarchical conceptions of colonialism and capitalism. It is by reconsidering how and why we have represented plants throughout time that we may lay the groundwork for new, richer, more complex plant philosophies for our era.

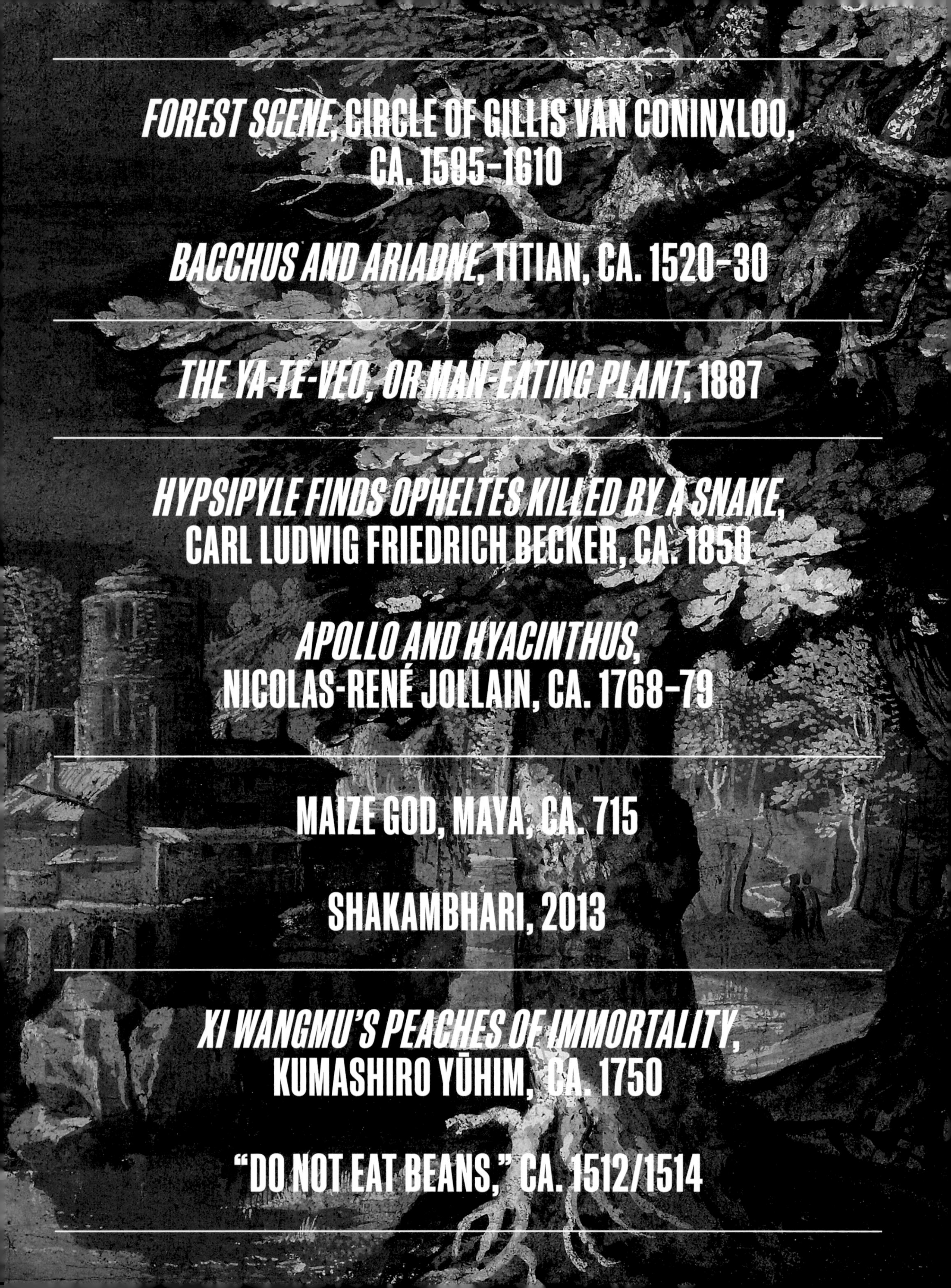

*FOREST SCENE*, CIRCLE OF GILLIS VAN CONINXLOO, CA. 1595–1610

*BACCHUS AND ARIADNE*, TITIAN, CA. 1520–30

*THE YA-TE-VEO, OR MAN-EATING PLANT*, 1887

*HYPSIPYLE FINDS OPHELTES KILLED BY A SNAKE*, CARL LUDWIG FRIEDRICH BECKER, CA. 1850

*APOLLO AND HYACINTHUS*, NICOLAS-RENÉ JOLLAIN, CA. 1768–79

MAIZE GOD, MAYA, CA. 715

SHAKAMBHARI, 2013

*XI WANGMU'S PEACHES OF IMMORTALITY*, KUMASHIRO YŪHIM, CA. 1750

"DO NOT EAT BEANS," CA. 1512/1514

*METAMORPHOSIS OF NARCISSUS*,
SALVADOR DALÍ, 1937

*CASSAVA ROOT WITH GARDEN TREE BOA, SPHINX MOTH AND TREEHOPPER*,
MARIA SIBYLLA MERIAN, 1705

---

*ABIMELECH GATHERING SUPPORT; JOTHAM'S COMPARISON; THE TREES CHOOSING A KING; TROOPS LYING DOWN UNDER THE TREES*,
UNKNOWN ARTIST AND RUDOLF VON EMS. CA. 1400–1410

*DRUIDS BEING CONVERTED TO CHRISTIANITY*, 1758

---

MAIN PANEL AT CROW CANYON ARCHAEOLOGICAL DISTRICT, NORTHWEST NEW MEXICO, SIXTEENTH–EIGHTEENTH CENTURIES

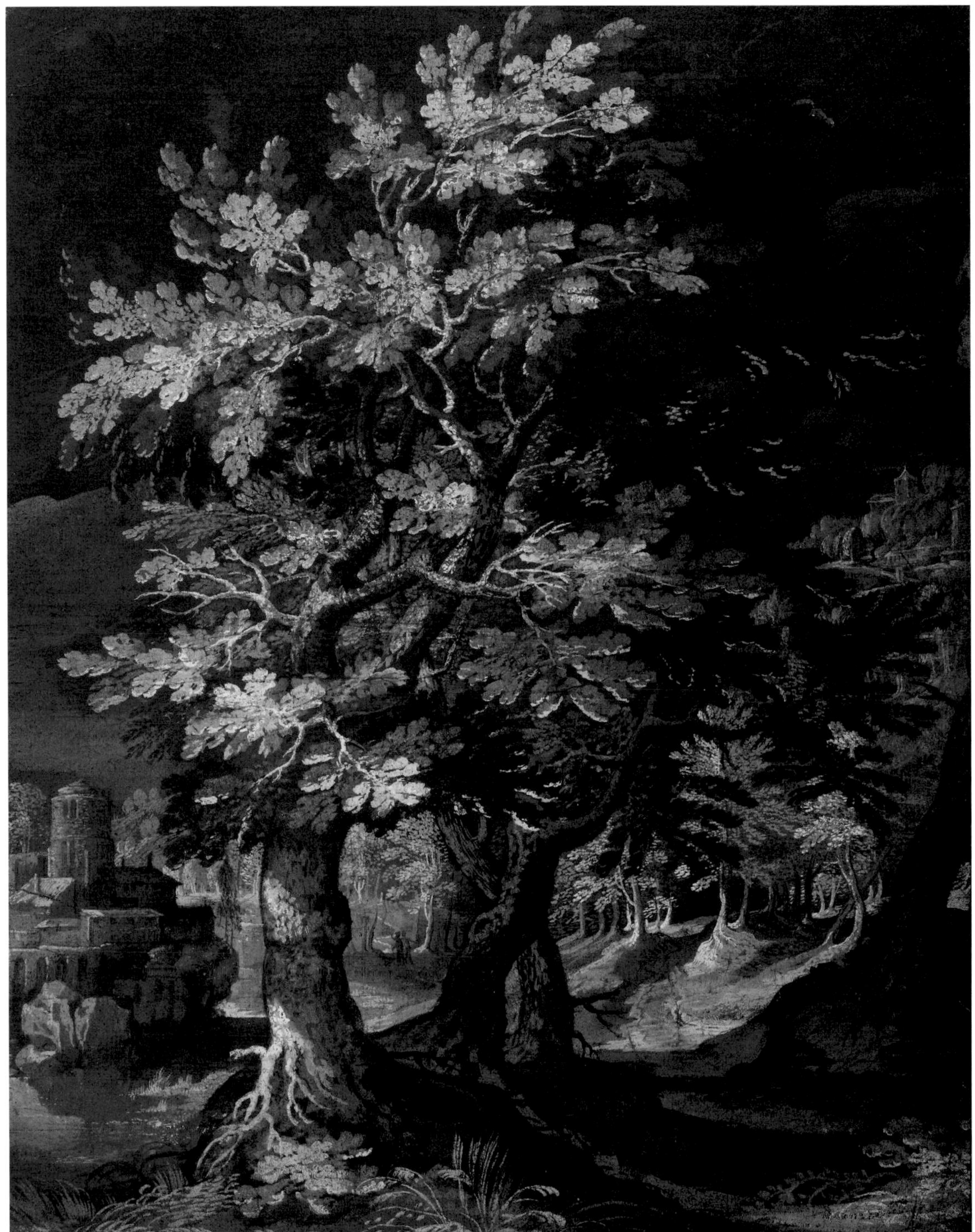

**Circle of Gillis van Coninxloo, *Forest Scene*, ca. 1595–1610, brush and gouache on toned paper on prepared paper**

In the Western imaginary, forests have for centuries symbolized the darkness of human unreason and the abandonment of ethics and morals. The nearly impenetrable vegetation, the risk of losing one's way to the point of no return, the threatening beasts, witches, and monsters, and the absence of human-made reference points are all brutal reminders of our vulnerability. The forest has lent itself to metaphorical representations of the unconscious—the uncontrollable, unpredictable, irrational, and unscripted. In its darkness, human rationality is haunted by bestial instincts, such that the risk of evolutionary reversal becomes dangerously palpable. The forest is the quintessential plant and animal domain—

# FOREST SCENE

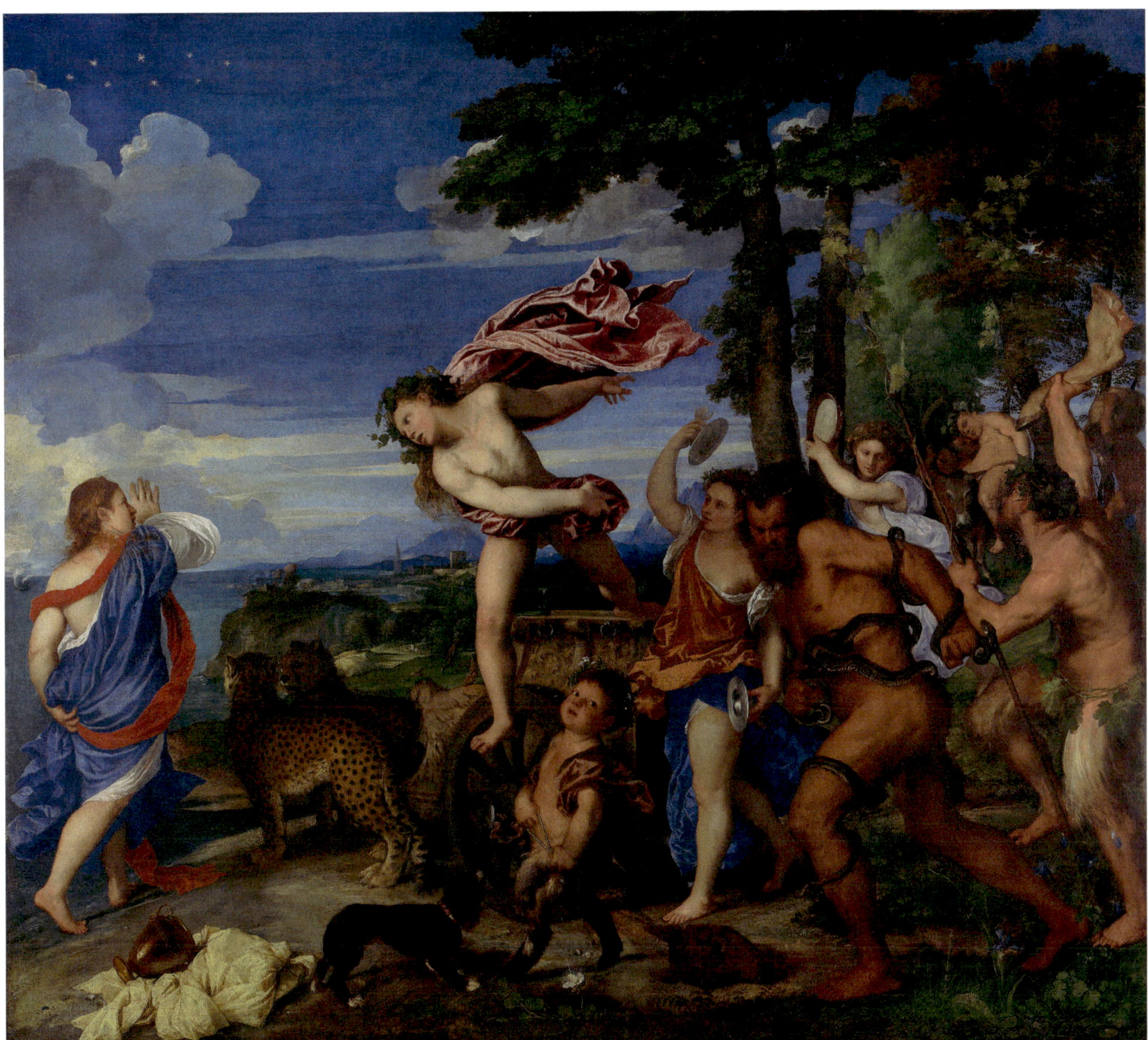

Titian, *Bacchus and Ariadne*, ca. 1520–30, oil on canvas



nature—while in opposition, the deforested urban reality emblematizes culture. These ideas are perfectly encapsulated in the myth of Bacchus, the Greco-Roman god of wine and vegetation who held boisterous, alcohol-soaked celebrations in the depths of the forest. Wine and animal blood were mixed, smeared, and drunk; inhibitions were lost and morals forsaken such that naked bodies blindly followed their desires. In the anonymity afforded by the trees, the bacchanalians (the revelers) relinquished language and reconnected with the world on otherwise forbidden sensuous and carnal planes.

## BACCHUS AND ARIADNE

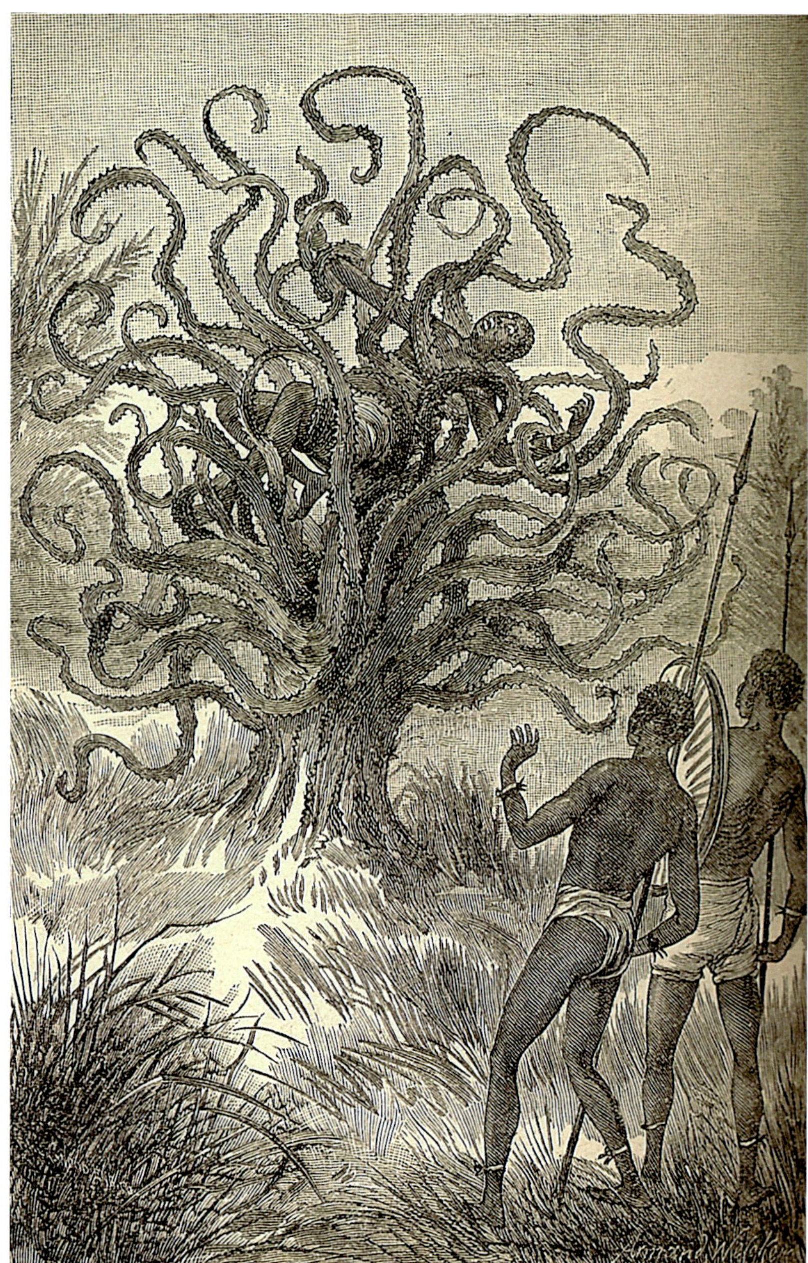

**Unknown artist, *The Ya-te-veo, or man-eating plant*, in James William Buel, *Sea and Land*, 1887, engraving**

By the second half of the nineteenth century, Western popular culture was rife with legends of human-eating vegetation. Colonialist narratives of monstrous and mysterious far-off lands, stories of fatal encounters with carnivorous trees, perpetuated a conception of African and South American cultures as primordial and uncivilized. (In comparison, Old World plants seemed tame, domesticated, even benevolent, offering beautiful flowers and fruits.) The fantasized existence of wild vegetal ferociousness in colonial lands also implicitly justified the intervention of white settlers as necessary eradicators of devilish creatures such as the Ya-te-veo: a tree with tentacle-like branches that, according to myth, grew in Central and South America, with subspecies in Africa and the coastal regions of India. Its name, which in Spanish means "now I see you," derived from the hissing sound its leaves allegedly produced when agitated by the wind. The plant was first described to English-speaking audiences by James William Buel in his 1887 book *Sea and Land: An Illustrated History of the Wonderful and Curious Things of Nature Existing before and since the Deluge.*

# *THE YA-TE-VEO, OR MAN-EATING PLANT*

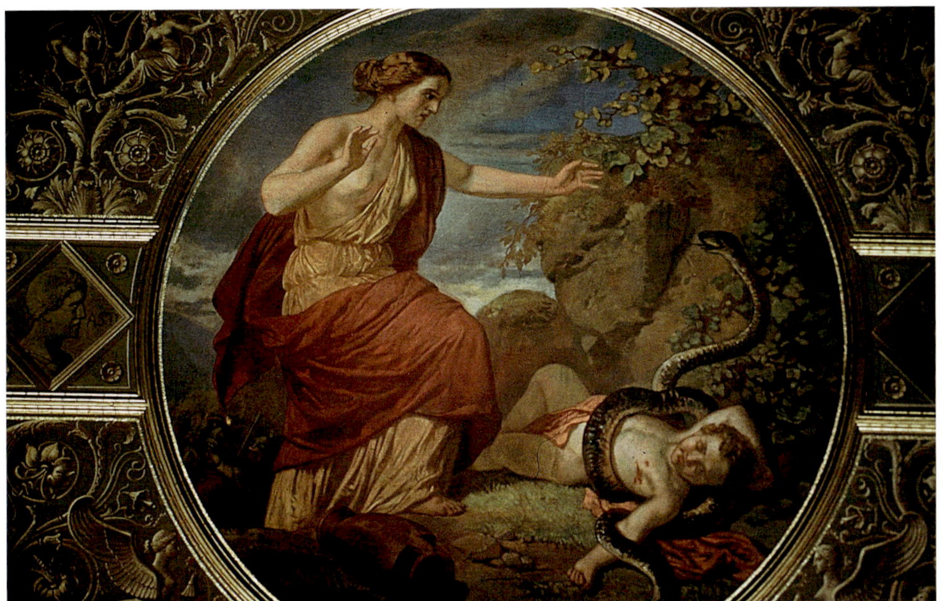

Carl Ludwig Friedrich Becker, *Hypsipyle Finds Opheltes Killed by a Snake*, ca. 1850, photograph of mural (since destroyed)

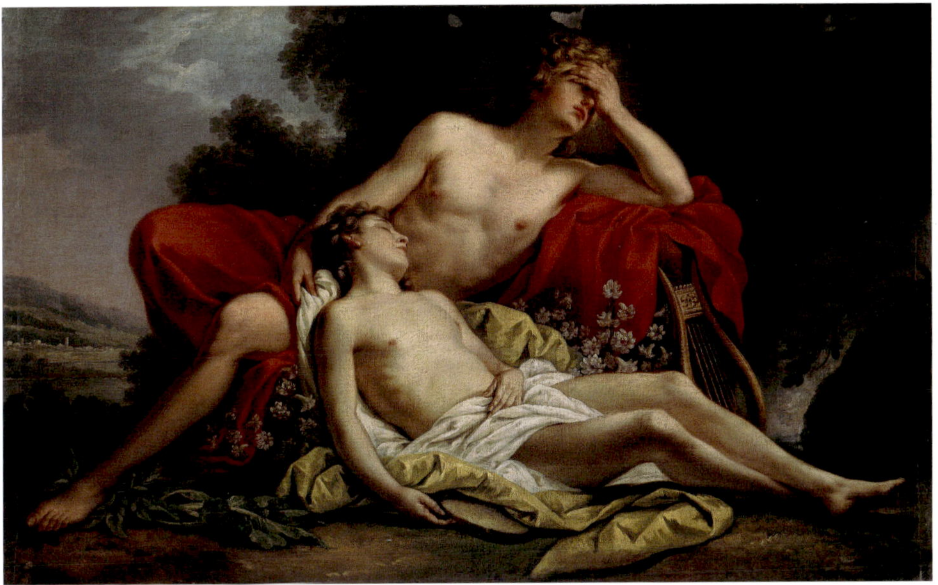

Nicolas-René Jollain, *Apollo and Hyacinthus*, ca. 1768–79, oil on canvas



In mythologies across the world, plants with portentous qualities emerged from the blood or dying corpses of heroes. In such miraculous instances, the living plant perpetuates and memorializes the heroic powers of the deceased. Either used as an amulet or ingested, the plant that sprouted from heroic blood grants access to the supernatural. According to classical myth, parsley, the herb commonly used to garnish savory dishes in many gastronomical cultures, sprang from the blood of Archemorus. It was subsequently dedicated to Persephone, queen of the afterworld. Because of this association, for centuries the Greeks wove parsley into funerary wreaths and applied it to dead bodies.

While the most famous transformation story in Ovid's *Metamorphoses* certainly is that of Apollo and Daphne, the narrative poem also recounts a homosexual love story between the god of sun and light and the breathtakingly beautiful Spartan prince Hyacinth. Many variations of the myth exist. In the most widely circulated, the lovers were playing a game of disc throwing, when Apollo threw his disc so high and far that it slashed the clouds. Hyacinth attempted to surpass his feat, and threw his own disc so fearlessly into the wind that it flew back and killed him instantly. Unable to revive Hyacinth, Apollo made the flower of the same name sprout from his lover's spilled blood.

## HYPSIPYLE FINDS OPHELTES KILLED BY A SNAKE

## APOLLO AND HYACINTHUS

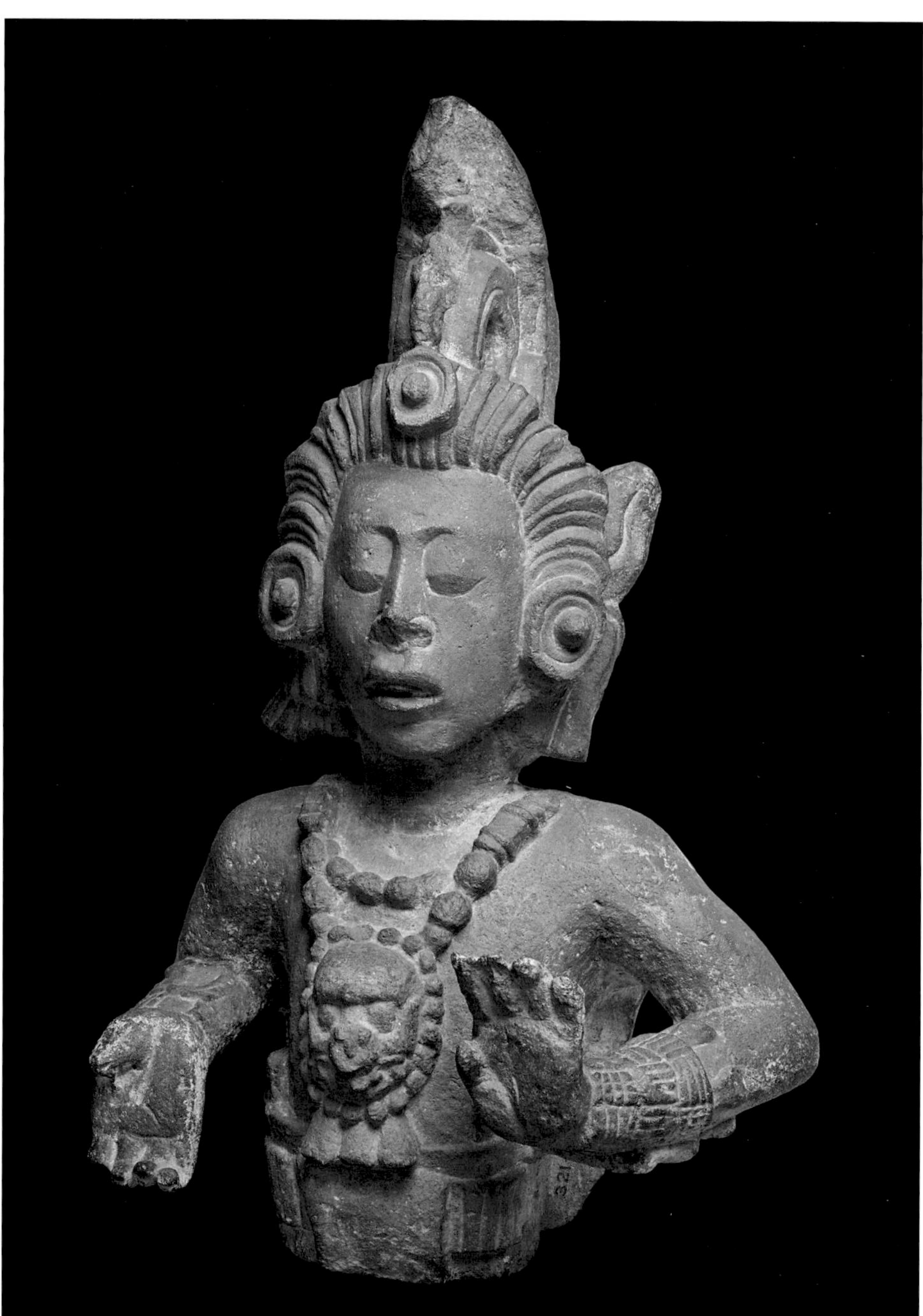

**Maize god, Maya, ca. 715, limestone**

In ancient cultures, plants are often seen as generous sources of sustenance. In Maya mythology, Hun Hunahpu was one of the most important gods—that of maize. Often shown in sculptures as a handsome young man, Hun Hunahpu is linked to a sacred history of creation. The Popol Vuh, a Maya mythological and historical text, describes how gods made humans out of yellow and white maize paste after attempts with clay and wood failed. This intimate connection between humans and plants is central to an understanding of vegetality as the root of creation. Maize plants not only generously support human and animal life, but also provide a cyclical model from seed to flower to harvest that the Maya recognized as the blueprint of their existence. For this very reason, Hun Hunahpu was also a god of rebirth. Like maize, which dies upon being harvested, the god of maize is decapitated at the end of the growing season and reappears the following spring with ears of

# MAIZE GOD

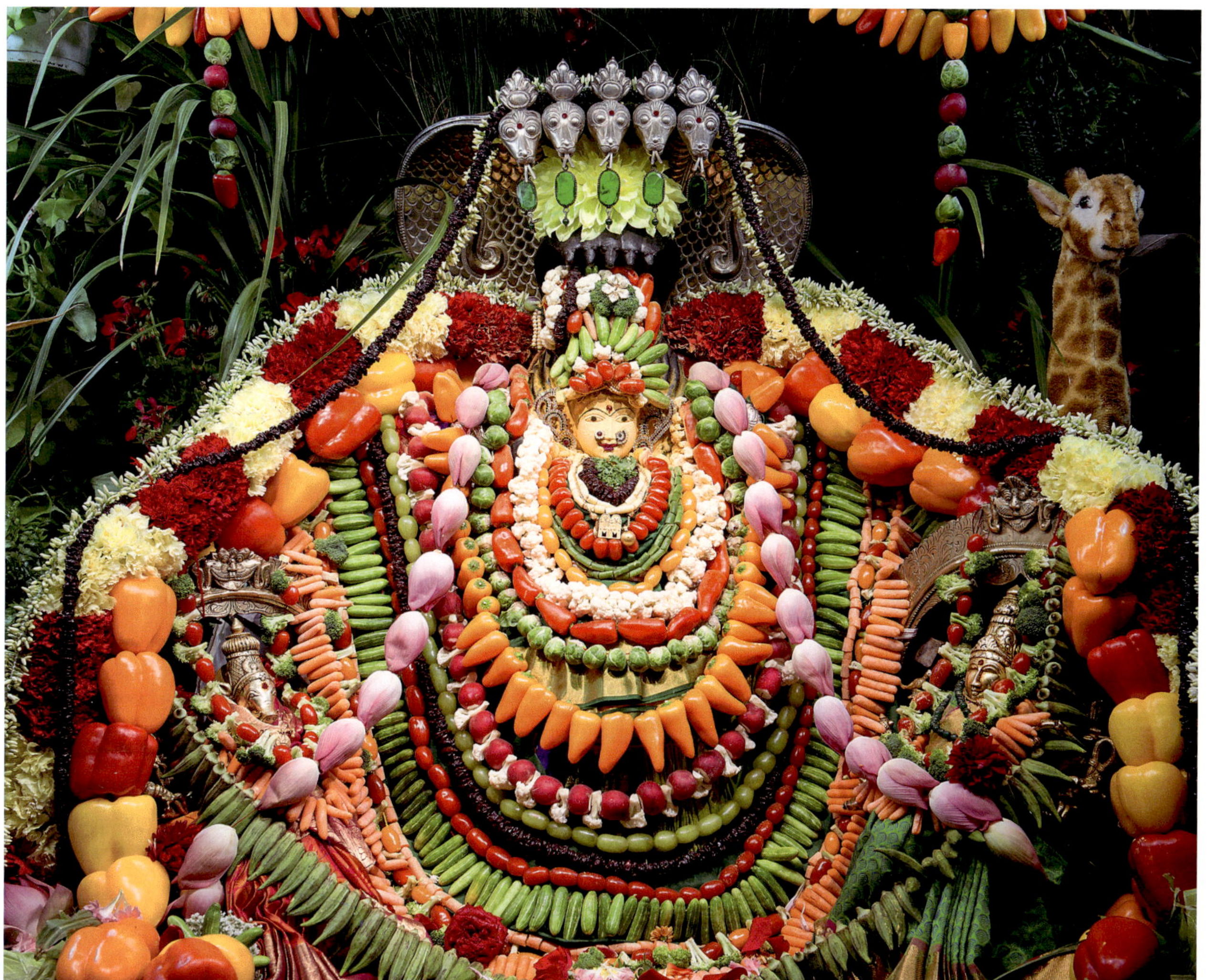

Shakambhari, *Navaratri Grand Celebrations at Sri Parashakthi Temple*, Friday, October 4, 2013, photograph



corn as headdress and hair made of the plant's silk.

Another otherworldly example of unreserved vegetal generosity is found in the Indian goddess Shakambhari, whose name literally translates as "she who brings vegetables." The goddess saved the Earth from the malevolent attack of King Durgamasura, who had caused ruinous droughts. Shakambhari appeared in the sky, as the darkest blue of rain-heavy monsoon clouds, and flooded the land with her tears while bestowing fruits and vegetables upon the starving. It is still today the custom to adorn sculptures of Shakambhari with vegetables as offerings.

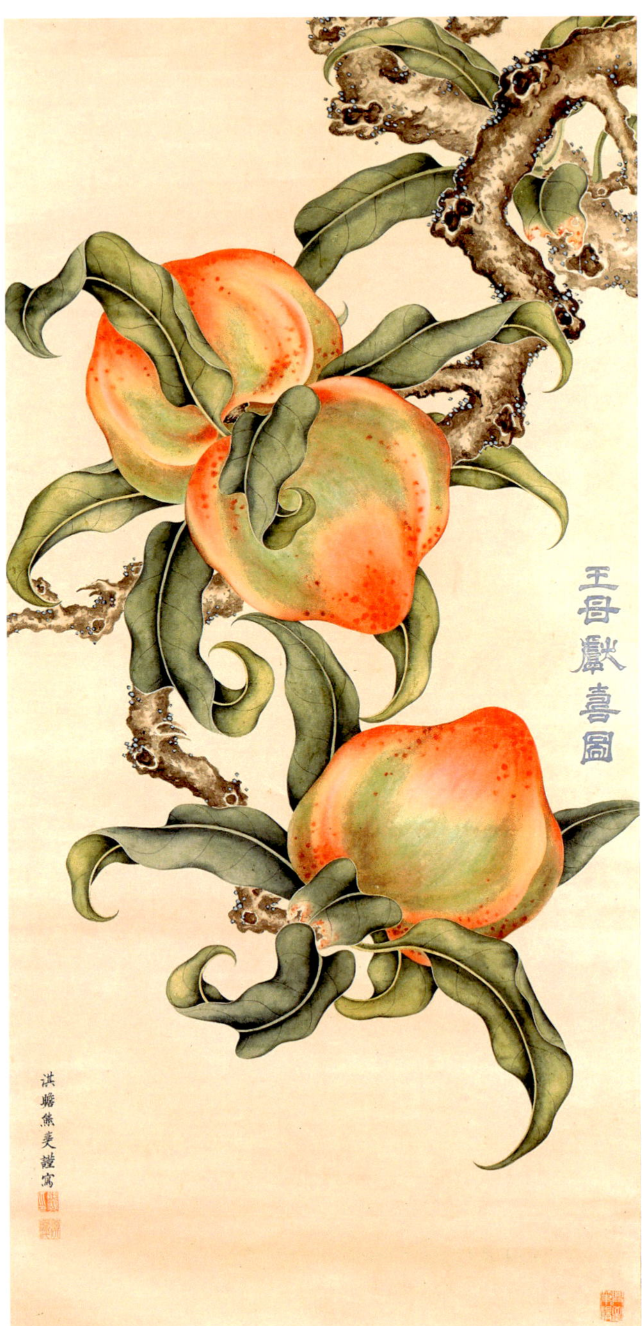

**Kumashiro Yūhim, *Xi Wangmu's Peaches of Immortality*, ca. 1750, hanging scroll**

On the third day of the third moon month, after a six-thousand-year wait, the deities residing in the palace of the Jade Emperor and his wife, Xi Wangmu, feast on the peaches of immortality. The peach tree grows in Xi's garden, in China's fabled Kunlun Mountains, and it only leafs once every thousand years. The fruit takes roughly three thousand years to ripen. Everyone who eats the peaches lives for at least three thousand years and their bodies become weightless and strong to an otherworldly degree. For this reason, members of the Eight Immortals are often represented holding a peach, while the white-bearded god of longevity emerges from a peach. These mythical attributes have persisted for millennia in Chinese culture. Peach stones carved in the shape of locks were traditionally worn by children to scare off disease-carrying demons. Peach branches placed above a home's main door were thought to prevent malevolent ghosts from entering. And the sacred wood of peach trees was made into lethal swords that Daoist masters used to kill demons.

# XI WANGMU'S PEACHES OF IMMORTALITY

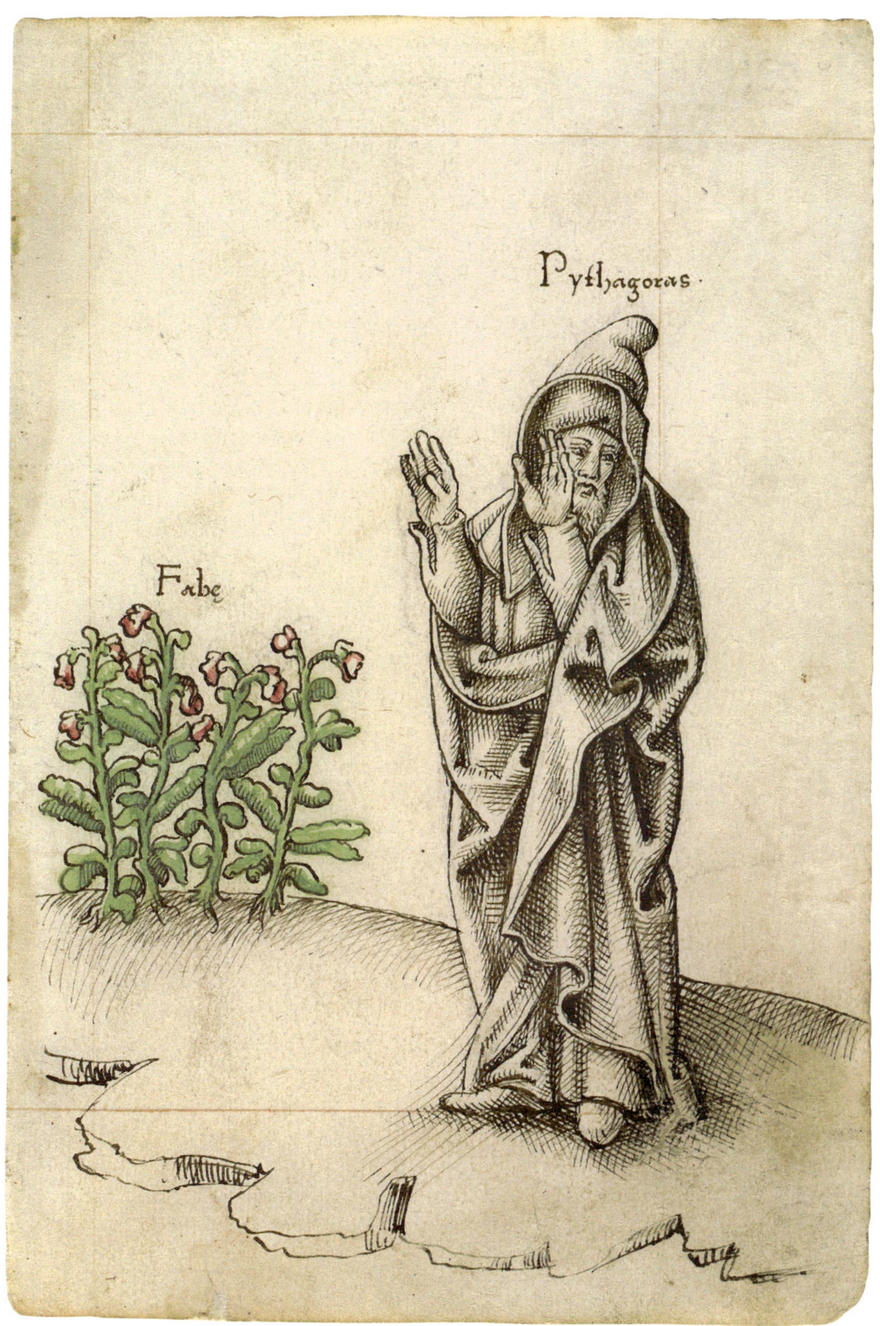


**Unknown French artist, "Do Not Eat Beans," ca. 1512/1514, pen and brown ink with watercolor on laid paper**



Sometimes it is the particular consistency of a plant or fruit, and other times its shape, that carves a special place in the human imagination. This is the case with one of the oldest known cultivated crops, *Vicia faba*, the broad bean. Pythagoras, the famous Greek philosopher and mathematician, is said to be solely responsible for mythologizing the plant based on its unique characteristics. He was apparently fascinated by its structure and the firm but tender texture of its seeds. His observations led him to believe that the plant's hollow stems may serve as a conduit between the worlds of the living and dead. As a result, he advised against eating broad beans, to allow human souls unimpeded movement. Pythagoras tied his belief—that the air was filled with souls—to the way fava beans often cause people to get gassy. According to him, expelling gas took away the breath of life. In the end, Pythagoras's intricate consideration of fava beans may have led to his demise. According to legend, he perished at the border of a field of fava beans, unwilling to trample the plants in order to escape pursuers.

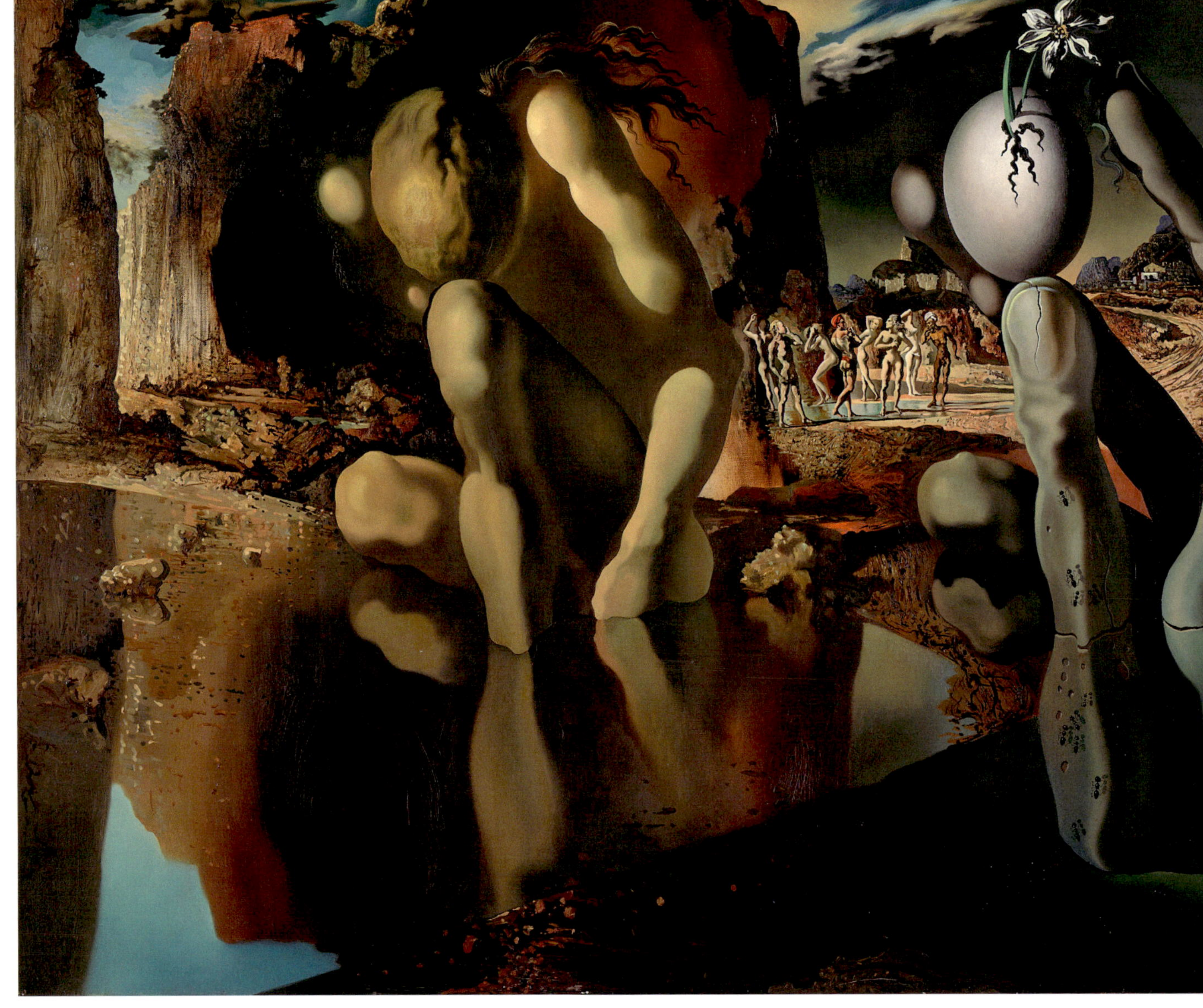

Salvador Dalí, *Metamorphosis of Narcissus*, 1937, oil on canvas

In Western classical mythology, plants sometimes immortalize and remedy tragic loss. Two such tales are rooted in the admonition that mortals should never endeavor to overshadow gods, regardless of their attractiveness. In the well-known myth of Narcissus, the gorgeous young man after whom the spring plant is named grew arrogant and cruel because of his fetching looks. His rejection of the mountain nymph Echo drew the vengeance of the gods. To punish Narcissus, they led him to a body of water where he gazed at his reflection. Irremediably infatuated, Narcissus reached into the water to embrace himself and drowned. Relenting, the gods decided to immortalize him in a beautiful spring flower, which in this Surrealist painting by Salvador Dalí is seen emerging from an egg—a symbol of nascent life. In the distance, the image repeats as an echo of itself—a nod to the jilted nymph.

To the Indigenous Tupi people of Brazil, the root of the cassava plant is sacred for similar reasons. According to their legends, the daughter

## *METAMORPHOSIS OF NARCISSUS*

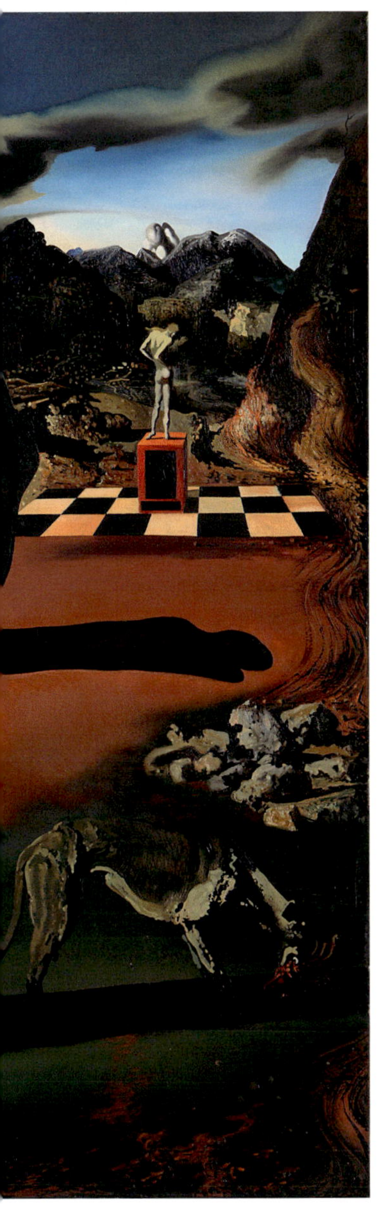

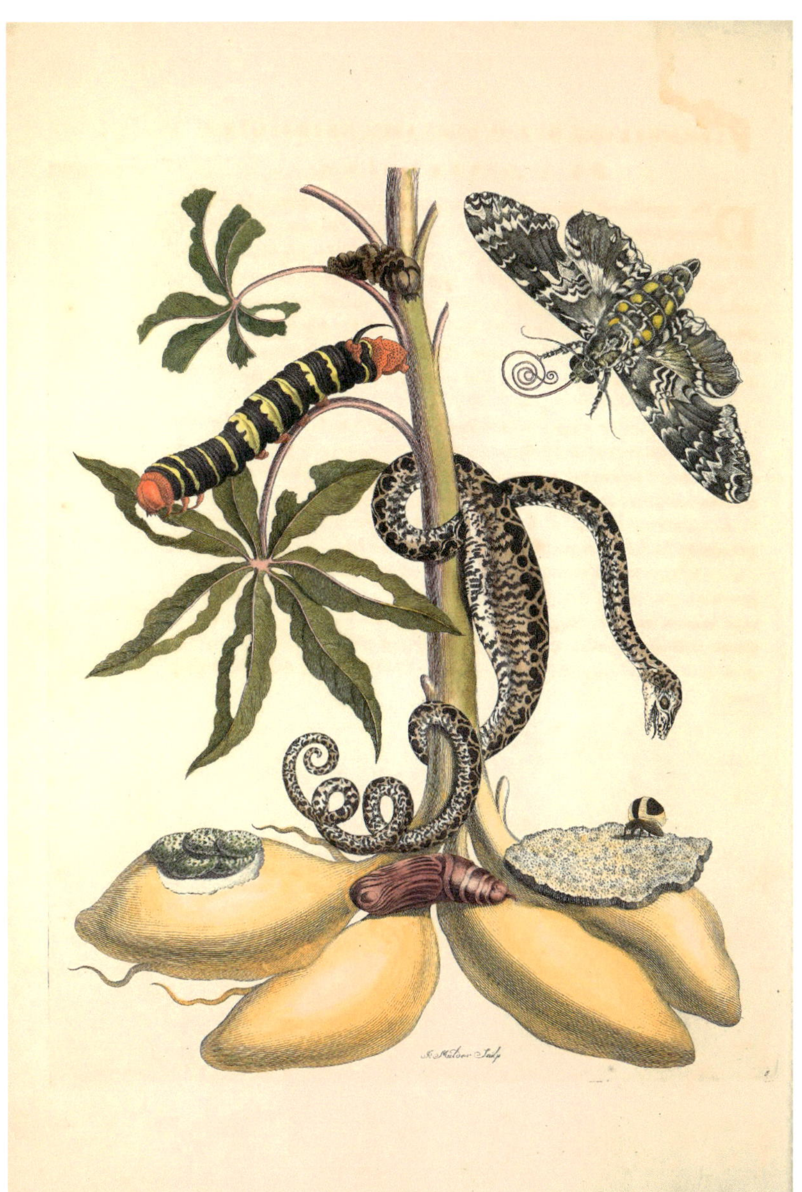

Maria Sibylla Merian, *Cassava Root with Garden Tree Boa, Sphinx Moth and Treehopper*, 1705, engraving



of a village chief became pregnant without intercourse. Her father at first did not believe her, and in an effort to protect his family's name, he threatened to have her killed. Then one night, he had a dream in which the ghost of a white man confirmed the girl's honesty and revealed that she would bring the tribe a great gift. Nine months later, the girl gave birth to a white-skinned child whom she called Mani, who unfortunately prematurely died. According to their custom, her mother watered Mani's grave every day until a new plant no one had ever seen before sprang from it. This was the cassava. Through a crevice in the earth, tribal members discovered a tuber as white as the youth's skin and proceeded to prepare and consume it, creating manioc, a food that gave them exceptional strength. Cassava has since become a staple in their traditional foods as well as a much-sought-after superfood across the globe.

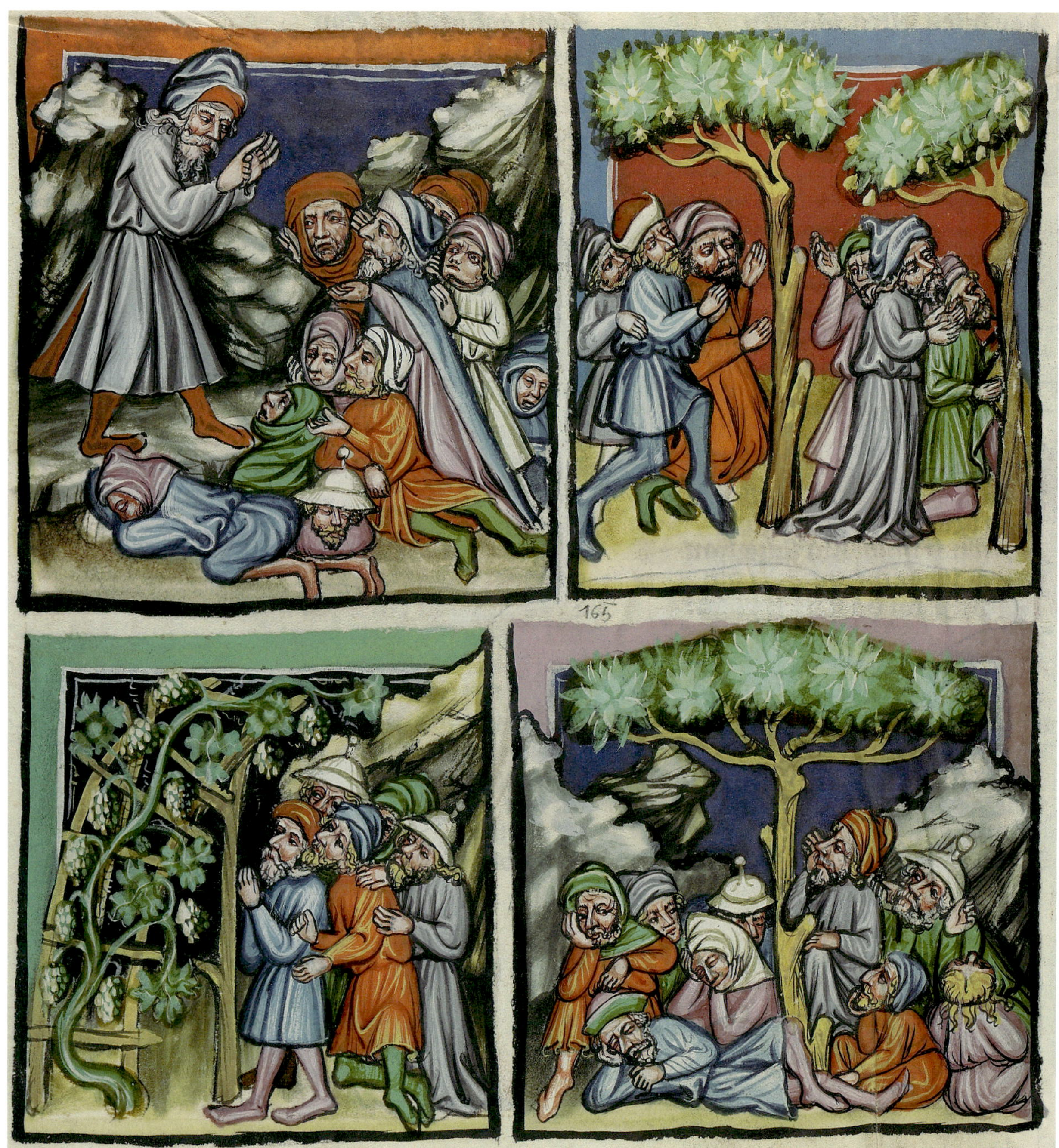

Unknown artist and Rudolf von Ems, *Abimelech Gathering Support; Jotham's Comparison; The Trees Choosing a King; Troops Lying Down under the Trees*, ca. 1400–1410, tempera colors, gold, silver paint, and ink

Trees have played important roles in Western lore. Their verticality, tallness, and longevity have for centuries inspired us to see them as resourceful and resilient figures of natural wisdom. Often cast as benevolent intermediaries, trees have provided shelter, remedies, and (more mythologically) passageways connecting multiple dimensions. In the parable of Abimelech, the son of biblical judge Gideon, the tree stands as a metaphor for the people of Shechem, who implored fig and olive trees, some of the most important and productive, to give up their gifts and spend their energies ruling the kingdom. They refused. Nor was the grapevine so inclined. Thus, the Shechemites turned to the thorny bramble, which symbolized Abimelech. The bramble replied: "If you want me as your king, come and take refuge in my shade. But if you won't choose me as your king, then let fire come out of the thorn bush and consume you."

## *ABIMELECH GATHERING SUPPORT; JOTHAM'S COMPARISON; THE TREES CHOOSING A KING; TROOPS LYING DOWN UNDER THE TREES*

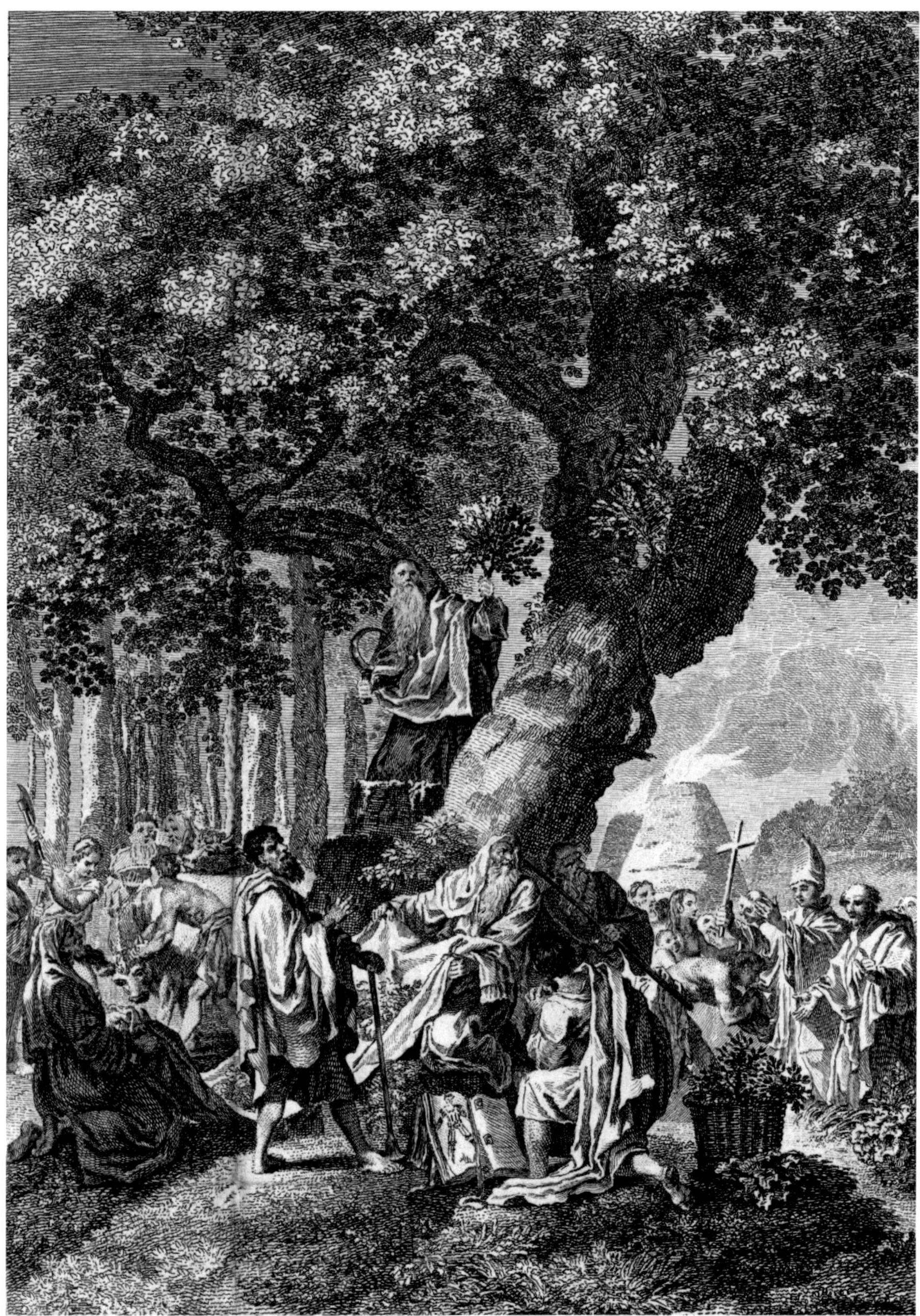

*Druids being converted to Christianity*, 1758, in David Hume and Tobias Smollett, *Complete History of England*, 1758–60, engraving



Three years later, dissatisfied with their choice, the Shechemites revolted against Abimelech, who, as promised, fought them to death with fire.

The oak frequently appears in Western lore. Considered sacred because its roots reach deep into the soil and its branches far toward the sky, the oak tree was associated with Zeus. The term "druid," designating those who know the secrets of the oaks, might have derived from the Irish word *daur* or the Welsh *derw*, meaning oak. The ritual of the oak and mistletoe that druids regularly practiced entailed the sacrifice of a white bull and was believed to cure infertility in animals. Christianity sought to systematically eradicate pagan worship and fiercely fought the druids, relegating their beliefs and traditions to the stuff of legends.

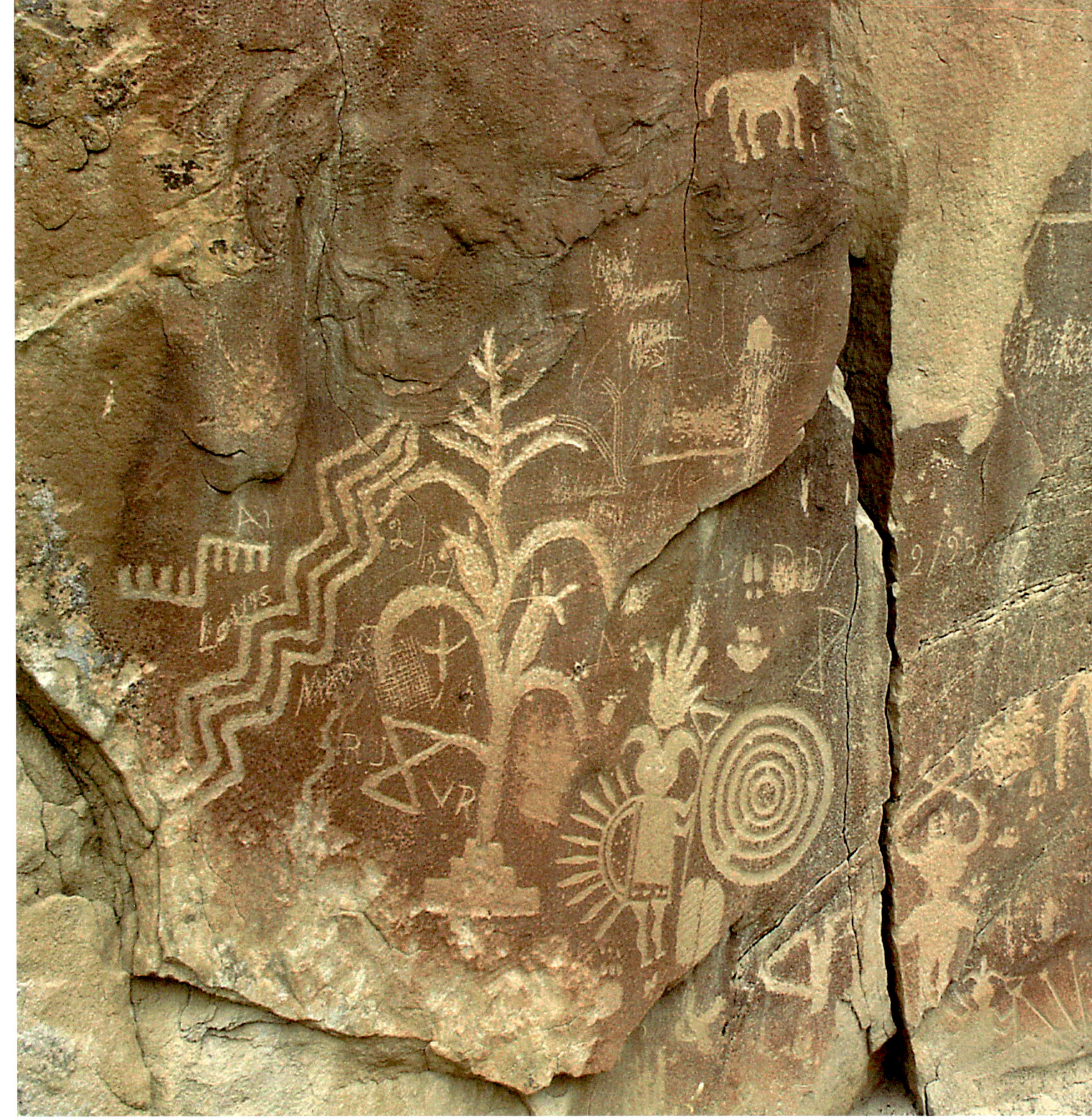

**Main panel at Crow Canyon Archaeological District, northwest New Mexico, sixteenth–eighteenth centuries, petroglyphs**

In North American Indigenous cultures, agricultural practices and mythologies have been intertwined for millennia, fostering sustainable relationships of respect and reciprocity with plants as well as the lands they grow upon. Indelibly etched on cliffs and boulders in the heart of Dinétah, the ancestral home of the Navajo people, are petroglyphs from the sixteenth, seventeenth, and eighteenth centuries representing corn (*naadą́ą́*) in a highly realistic manner. Stalks, flowers, arched leaves, and cobs, all unmistakably rendered, immortalize the most sacred plant in their creation story. According to myth, white corn emerged along with First Woman (*Áłtsé asdzą́ą́*) and yellow corn with First Man (*Áltsé hastiin*). A life-giving symbol of fertility and generosity, corn pollen—a sweet-tasting yellow powder—has been cherished as a blessing in ceremonies.

# MAIN PANEL AT CROW CANYON ARCHAEOLOGICAL DISTRICT

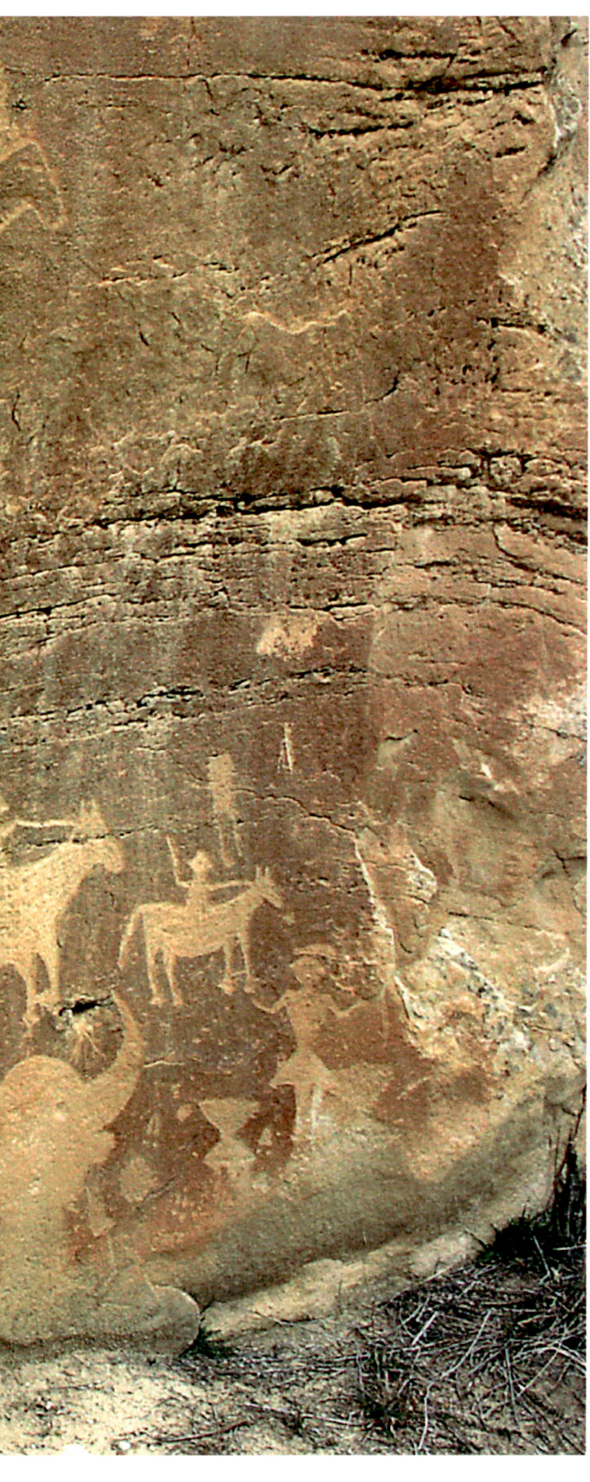



Corn seeds provide essential nourishment, and dried leaves and stalks give shelter.[8]

In Navajo culture, the four directions—north, east, south, and west—are associated with corn, beans, squash, and tobacco. From the US Northeast and the Plains to the semi-desert areas of the Southwest, corn, squash, and beans have traditionally been grown together by many Indigenous peoples. The Iroquois and the Cherokee call them the Three Sisters because they nurture one another like a family: beans climb the cornstalks, and squash leaves shelter the ground, retaining humidity and keeping weeds at bay.

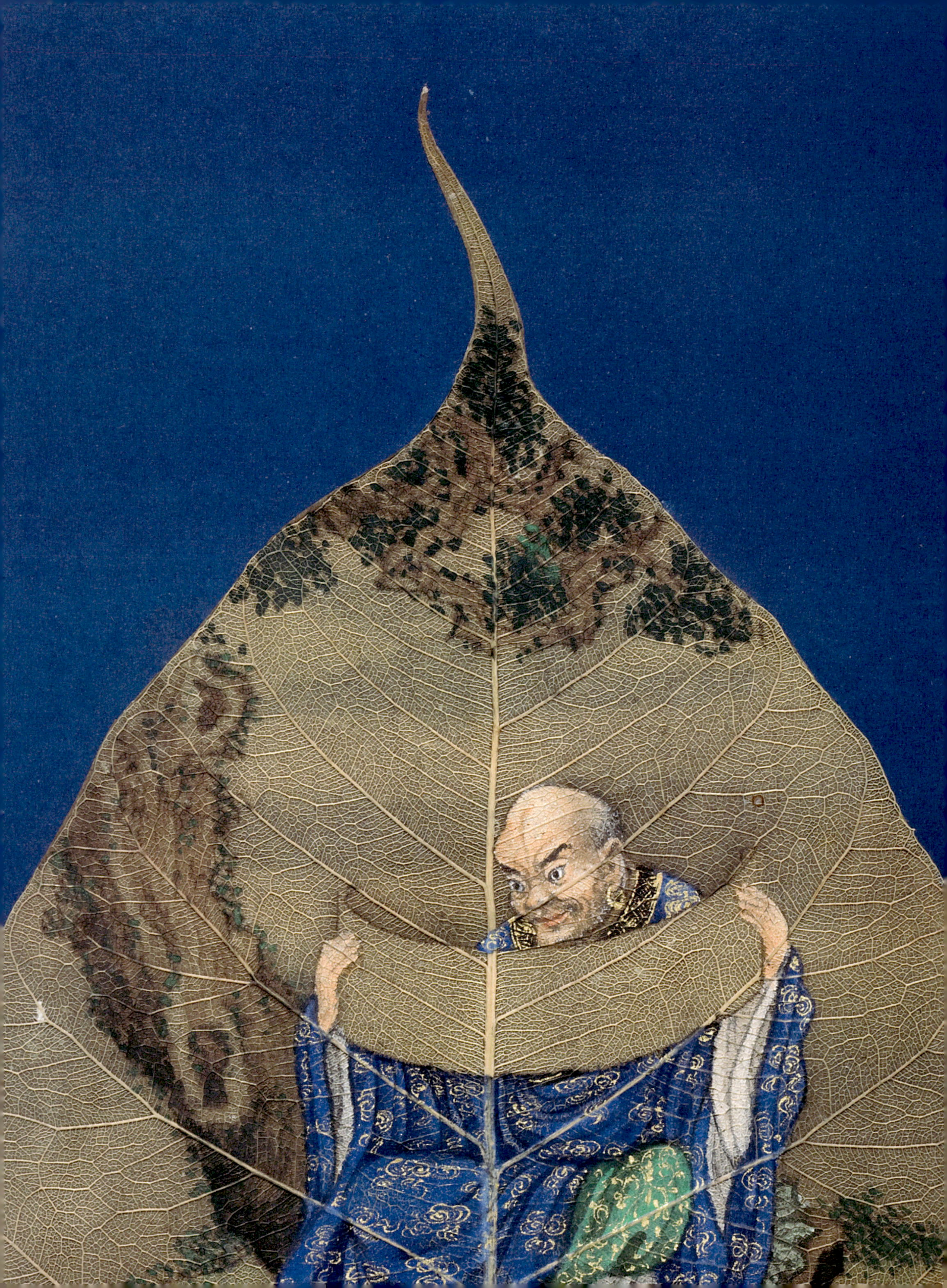

CHAPTER 2

# PLANT MATTER AND THE EDGE OF KNOWLEDGE

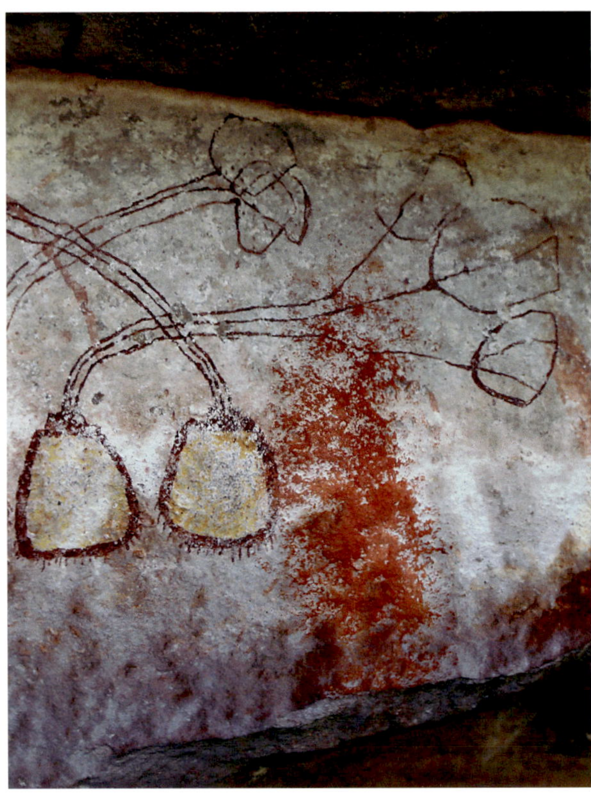

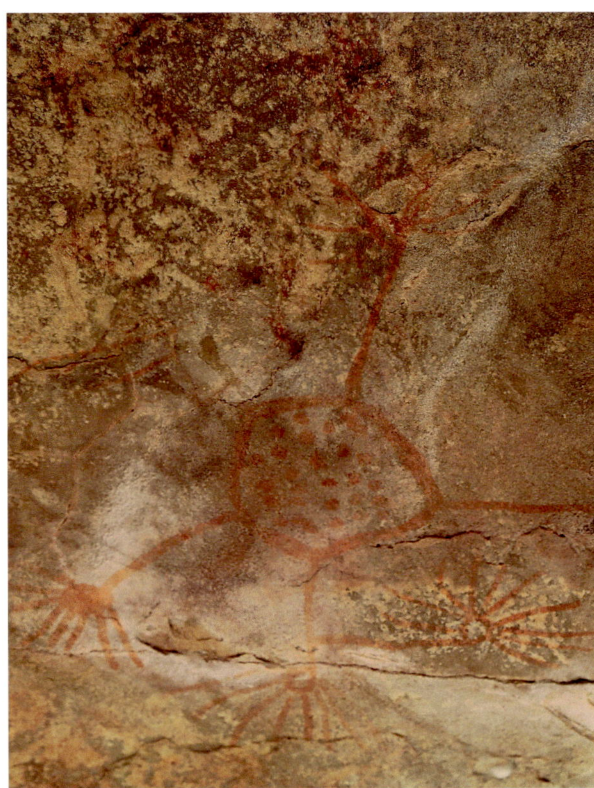

**Plants depicted in rock art of Australia's Kimberley region: Water lilies (possibly), Drysdale River, Balangarra Country (left); Wandjina-style water lily, King George River, Balanggarra Country (right), approximately 50,000 years old, petroglyphs**



Contrary to popular belief, a finished work of art never resembles its original conceptualization that emerged in the mind of the artist. Mental images are crafted in the deeper portions of the brain, below the neocortex, by neurons and electrical impulses.[1] As a result, it is only natural for these visions to be strongly impacted by the character, potential, and constraints of materials as they are externalized and translated.

Artists engage in material dialogues with the world—complex and subtle exchanges that can be observed in cave paintings, as they depict an extremely rich convergence of vegetable, mineral, and animal influences. Charcoal—often produced by slow-burning wood in kilns, sometimes mixed with charred bones and animal fat—seems to have been among the very first art materials. Black lines of charcoal traced fundamental distinctions between inside and outside, human and animal. They materialized trajectories of longing, and immortalized the living into a set of reference points around which our nascent identities could be pieced together. Vegetal extracts, plant oils, and tree sap proved valuable as pigment binders. Mosses were among the first paintbrushes. Crushed berries produced intensely saturated hues of red. Fifty thousand years ago, these vegetal gifts were used to draw highly realistic images of plants in caves at Carpenters Gap in the Kimberley, Western Australia's sparsely settled northern region. A string of yams, lilies, fruits, and ferns—the oldest plants ever to be painted—may point to the very origins of agricultural practices.[2]

The earliest forms of written language—signs impressed on tablets, petroglyphs adorning cave walls, chiseled words on cliffsides—aided *Homo sapiens* in materializing their thoughts. But plants made those thoughts portable, movable, extensible, and rearrangeable, triggering a monumental shift in our ability to express human creative potential.[3] The invention of papyrus rolls traces back to ancient Egypt, approximately 2900 BCE. *Cyperus papyrus* grew plentifully along the Nile's banks. Stalks were harvested and peeled, the pith extracted and thinly sliced. Horizontal and vertical layers of neatly arranged strips were dampened and pressed, and up to twenty sheets could be joined into a roll.[4] Papyrus served as the medium for a wide range of literary and administrative purposes, including hymns,

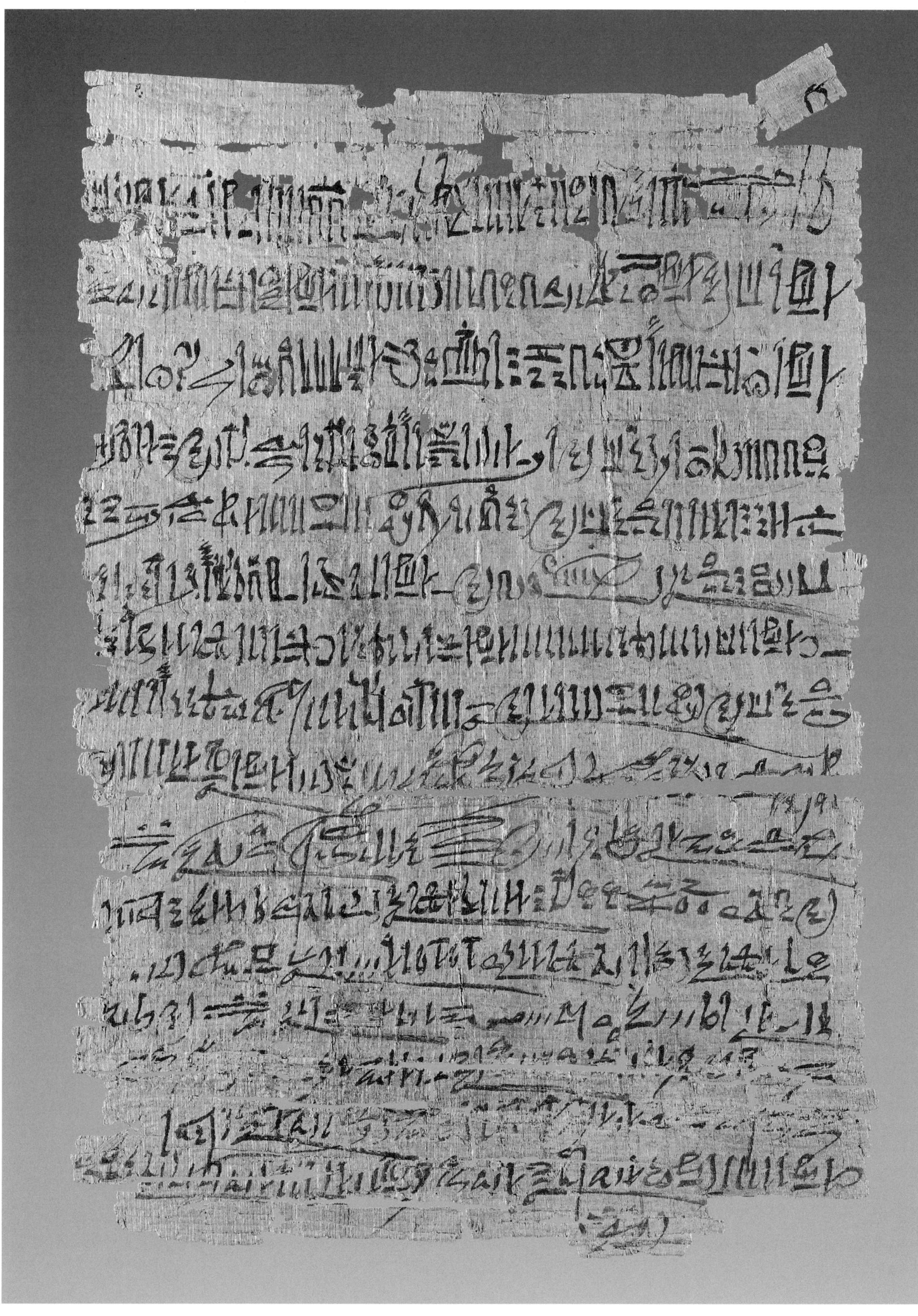

Fragmentary hieratic letter, Egyptian, ca. 1200–1085 BCE, ink on papyrus

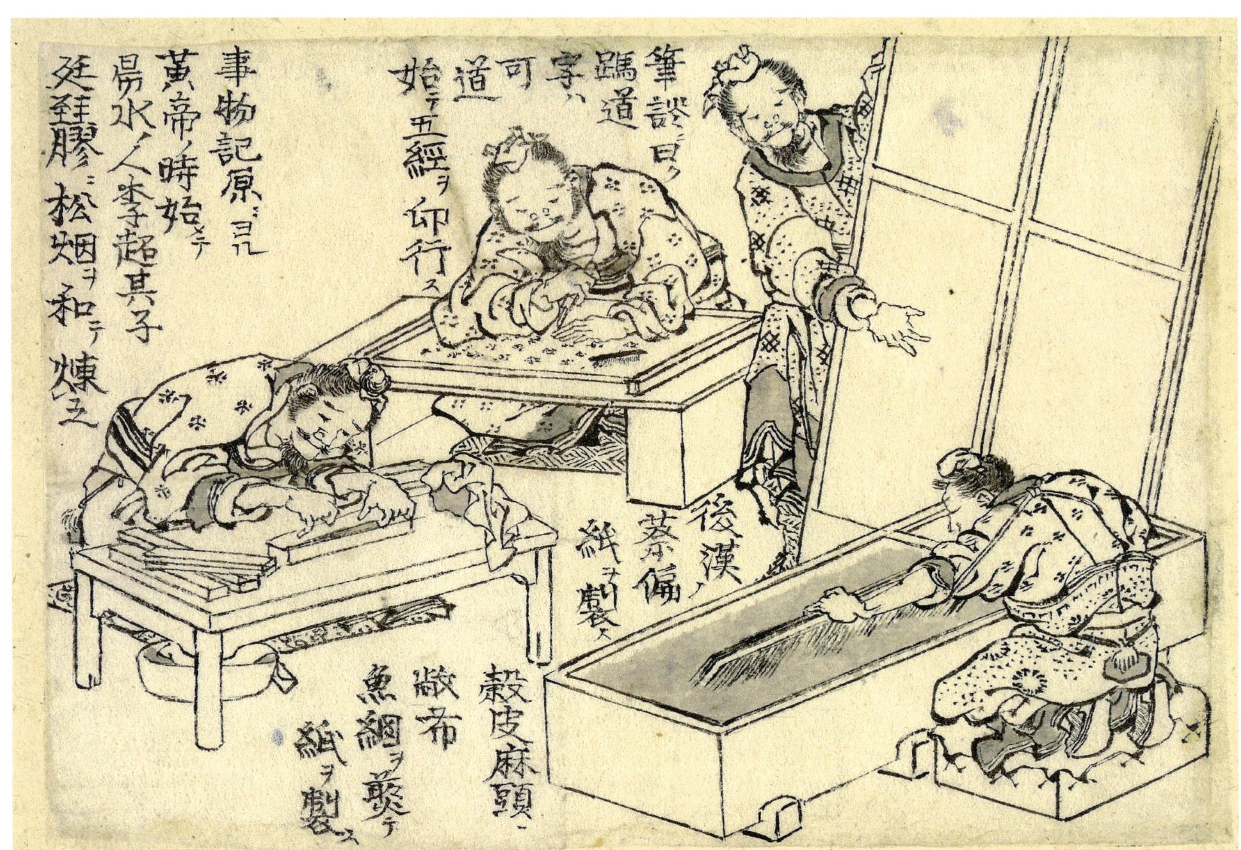




Katsushika Hokusai, *The Invention of Paper, Publishing and Ink*, ca. 1820s–1840s, ink on paper

correspondence, official records, proclamations, religious scripture, medical texts, romantic poetry, scientific and technical manuals, recordkeeping, and storytelling. This iconic plant was so much more than what the Roman senator Cassiodorus acknowledged: “a faithful witness of all human actions” and “sworn foe to oblivion.”[5] Papyrus laid the foundations for Egyptian society, and it fostered cultural identity. Scrolls could be archived, ordered, and systematically retrieved to build on preexisting knowledge—their flexibility and durability enabled the kind of knowledge stratification upon which human civilization could thrive.

It was during the fifth century BCE, if not earlier, that in South India, Nepal, Sri Lanka, Burma, Thailand, Indonesia, and Cambodia, banded palm leaves of *Borassus flabellifer* (palmyra palm), *Corypha umbraculifera* (fan palm), and *Corypha taliera* (tali palm) provided a new medium that would further stretch our imaginative realm. Half-opened young shoots were boiled, dried, pressed, and polished into narrow blades. Pungently fragrant herbs like sweet flag (*Acorus calamus*) helped keep insects at bay, while citronella and lemongrass oil softened the leaves.[6] Thyme vapors prevented fungal growth.[7] Aligned, stacked, collated, and bound into book form, palm leaves extended the linearity of thought beyond the expanses already mapped by papyrus rolls. Their thinness made the stratification and accumulation of complex content possible; their lightness made knowledge portable.

In 105 CE, the most significant botanical revolution in the early history of art materials occurred. Chinese court official Cai Lun soaked old fishnets and cloth scraps in a vat of water and added the uniquely fibrous inner bark (bast) of *Broussonetia papyrifera* (paper mulberry) to the mix. Suspended from the ground by a bamboo frame, the resulting sludge was then poured onto a stretched cloth to drain and dry in the form of a thin sheet. The invention of paper was a vegetal-human collaboration born out of Cai Lun’s observation of wasp behavior—the insect is known for chewing and mixing water with cellulose extracted from plants to build its nest.[8] The paper mulberry forever changed how we record, disperse, and access knowledge.

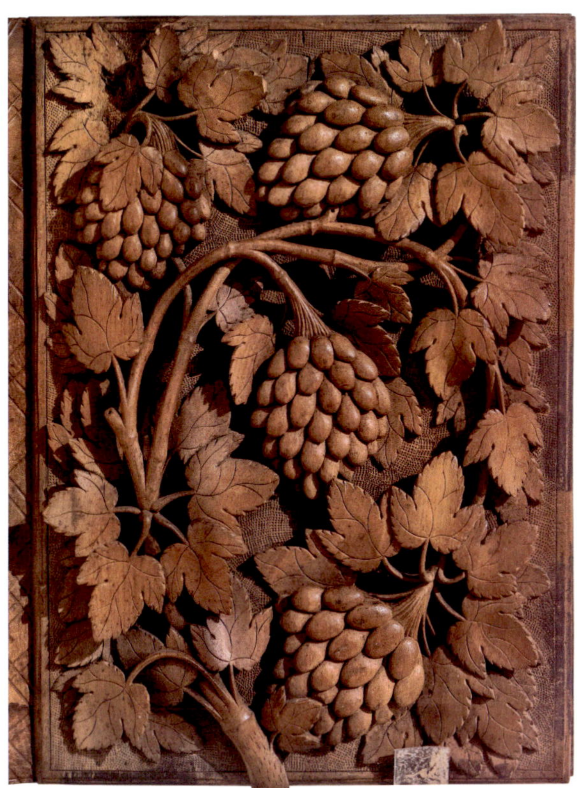

**Walnut wood carving from Kashmir, nineteenth century**

Cheaper and faster to process than silk, light but durable, large sheets of paper proved extremely versatile. Venetian merchant and explorer Marco Polo remarked on the fine summer clothing the Chinese crafted out of thin paper as well as the effigies that were constructed and burned at funerals along with the bodies of the deceased. Paper thus changed the history of fashion and expanded the range of important performative expressions central to cultural traditions and identities.[9]

By 610 CE, Chinese papermaking methods had been introduced to Korea and Japan. A century later, paper reached the Middle East.[10] Its even surface became a raw field of *naturecultural* potentiality.[11] In addition to facilitating the preservation of what had previously been oral culture, the act of recording enabled the standardization, systematization, and translation of languages. Thus, the development of human language and its subtleties was the result of a mutually reinforcing interaction between plant matter—its intrinsic qualities—and human intellect. The histories of drawing and writing, interwoven as they are by an unbreakable vegetative relationship that unleashed imagination beyond the bounds of our thoughts, are examples of this.

During the fourteenth century, in the Kashmir region of northern India, a team of seven hundred craftsmen from Iran led by scholar and religious leader Ameer-e-Kabeer Mir Syed Ali Hamdani taught local villagers the art of walnut wood carving. Only three-hundred-year-old walnut trees were deemed appropriate because the tight grain and homogeneous texture of their hardwood allowed for an exceptional degree of detail and complexity in portrayal. The *khokerdar* (undercut) style involves up to seven layers of wood, sometimes more, often adopted to great effect in the representation of forest thickets. This creative dialogue between sculptors and the walnut (*Juglans regia*) remains confined to this region, the only place where the tree still grows.[12]

In northern Europe, artists turned to limewood (*Tilia platyphyllos* and other linden tree species) for its softness, strength, crispness, tight grain, and resistance to warping.[13] Perhaps even more than in their painterly tradition, it was through the carving of limewood that German artists achieved an unprecedented level of realistic pathos and realism. The meticulous attention to detail and highly ornate imaginings made possible the aspiration to materialize the magnificence of the divine. Consequently, wood underwent a complete transformation in the collective imaginary, assuming a spiritual nature detached from its previous association with the physical realm.

Recourse to vegetal materials has been traditionally bound to an existentialist desire to connect with ancestral pasts and spiritual dimensions. Beyond the well-documented use that shamans make of hallucinogenic substances derived from plants like jimsonweed (*Datura stramonium*), peyote (*Lophophora williamsii*), and morning glory (*Ipomoea*),[14] wood, straw, and pigments extracted from a variety of plants also invited us to perform. The lightness and versatility of many different kinds of wood, from balsa (*Ochroma pyramidale*) to mangrove (*Xylocarpus moluccensis*), have for millennia enabled different cultures to transcend and transfigure reality by carving masks and costumes designed to express the depths of spiritual longing. In a sixteenth-century statue unearthed more than a hundred and fifty years ago on the side of the volcano Popocatépetl, southeast of Mexico City, Xochipilli, the Mesoamerican god of flowers, wears a mask while seated with his legs crossed upon a throne decorated with jimsonweed and other psychotropic plants. Among the Aztecs, ritual masks held significance as transformative artifacts that facilitated connections between various realms. Gazing upward toward the celestial sphere, captivated by its heavenly influence, Xochipilli is essentially heliotropic—his mask teases to the surface his vegetal soul so that it can be empowered by sunlight.[15]

Among the Ketu, Shaki, Anago, Ifonyin, Dogon, and Egbado Yoruba peoples of West Africa, wood-carved Gelede masks are complex, intricate headpieces often featuring multiple sophisticated sculptural motifs as well as fabric, beads, seeds, and bones. Exclusively worn by men at the annual Gelede festival, these ceremonial masks celebrate matriarchal powers. Their composed, assured facial expressions immortalize the modesty, poise, endurance, and tenacity of the community's female role models, also known as "our mothers," or *awon iya wa*. Honoring elderly women is a way to channel their benevolent powers toward the fertility of plants. It is no coincidence that the Gelede festival always takes place at the beginning of a new agricultural cycle—a propitious time of awakening.[16] The masks are often carved as one single block out of the light but dense *igi omo* (*Cordia millenii*), *igi arère* (*Enantia chlorantha*), or *igi ire* (*Holarrhena floribunda*). The wood is always worked fresh, immediately after felling. Rubbing leaves of *ewe eepin* (*Ficus asperifolia*) over the surface before painting grants a smooth finish. Raffia, palm, and banana tree leaves often accompany the masks as costume elements.[17]

Masks have been worn in supernatural communication and spiritual transformation ceremonies, performances, and dances. It is a common fallacy to believe that masks tend to be created out of whatever is readily available, as traditional anthropological descriptions have claimed. The use of vegetal (and also animal) matter in the making of masks and other artifacts is reflective of a holistic conception of kinship between humans and other earthlings.[18] It is the manifestation of a universe in which the Western concept of species has not yet divided reality into categories or hierarchies, and in which the numinous penetrates the cosmos and rules over all living things. In the stillness of plants, humans found the possibility of arresting the passing of time through sculptural form. Wood's adaptability and durability (as opposed to bronze, or harder-to-find materials like marble) have enabled the human imagination to materialize incredibly intricate, complex, and transportable creations, including wearable extensions of our bodies.

Faithful to their plant origin, African wood sculptures do not tend to disown the nature that makes their material presence possible. The wood of trees like iroko (*Chlorophora excelsa*), mahogany (*Swietenia macrophylla*), and ebony (*Diospyros crassiflora*), varieties suitable to the creation of extremely delicate carvings, have for millennia fomented a spectacularly rich sculptural tradition that spans the African continent.[19] African carved sculptures express a highly creative and vivid relationship with the transcendental—natural forms are reinterpreted, merged, and abstracted through geometric patterns and rhythms that transfigure the subject into timeless ideas or concepts. Trees determine not just the substance and the colors of African artworks, but also their shapes. Oftentimes, across cultures, sculptures in the round begin with the cylindrical shape of a tree trunk. Retained as an archetypal root, this natural form is regarded as nurturing an internal, indissoluble bond with the vegetal realm. A tree chosen for sculptural purposes is deemed sacred, the abode of a spirit. Sacrificial rituals often precede the felling of the tree to pacify its spirit.[20]

Similar conceptions of trees as sacred kin are present in the aesthetics of totem poles carved by Northwest Coast Indigenous peoples like the Haida, Nuxalk (Bella Coola), Kwakwaka'wakw, Tsimshian, and Łingít. The red cedar, traditionally the wood carved to make totem poles, has cultural and spiritual significance for the Cherokee and other Native American peoples. It is regarded as an ancestor tree, believed to house the souls of ancestors and provide protection as well as spiritual and medicinal healing. It demands respect. In some cases, cedar is the only wood from which any everyday object in Indigenous communities can be made, including providing fibers for baskets, ropes, and textiles. The close connection that unites many Indigenous tribes like the Kwakwaka'wakw and the Cherokee—some of whom identify as the "cedar people"—with these particular trees has thoroughly shaped their respective cultural practices.

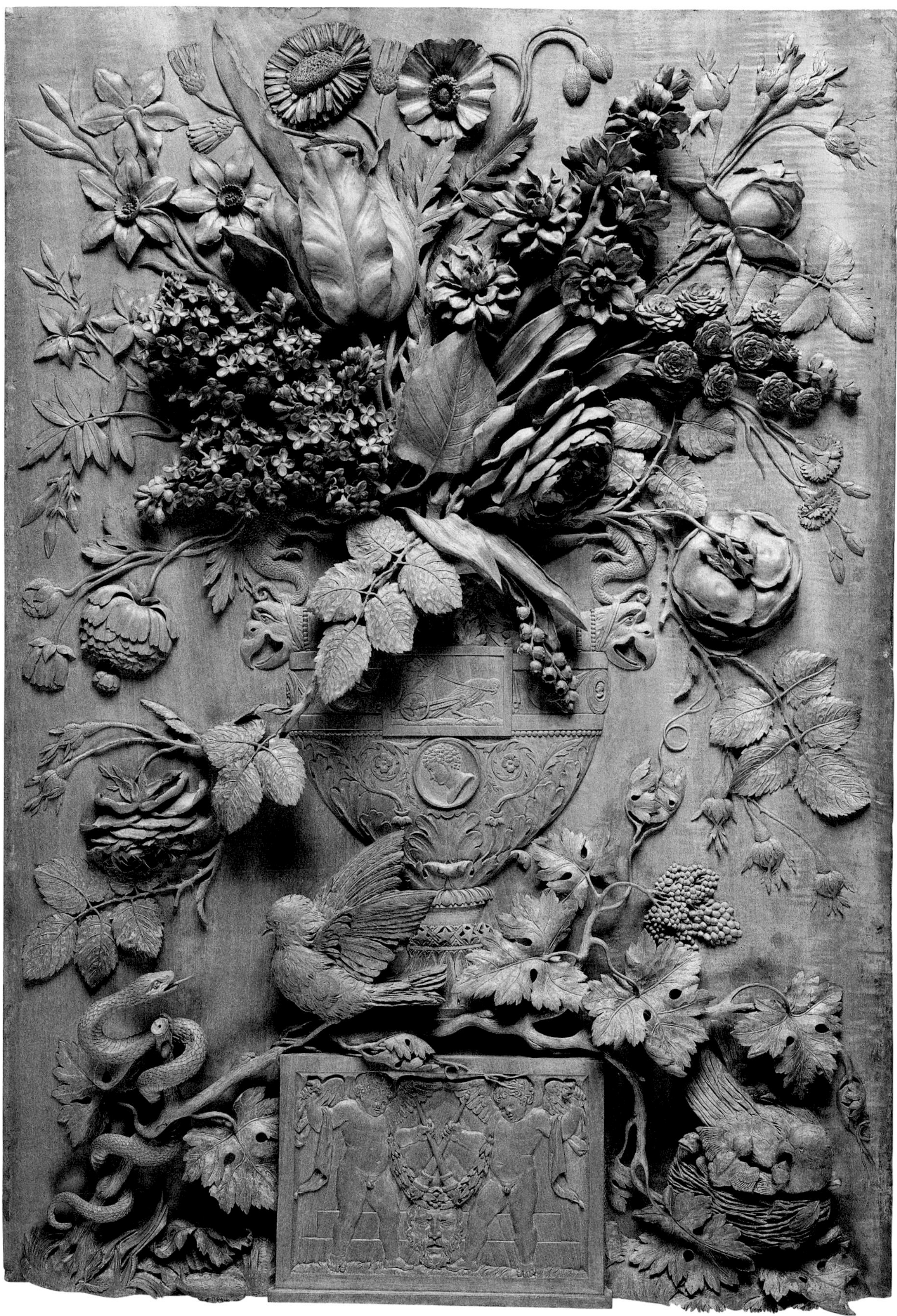

Aubert-Henri-Joseph Parent, Carved relief, 1789, limewood

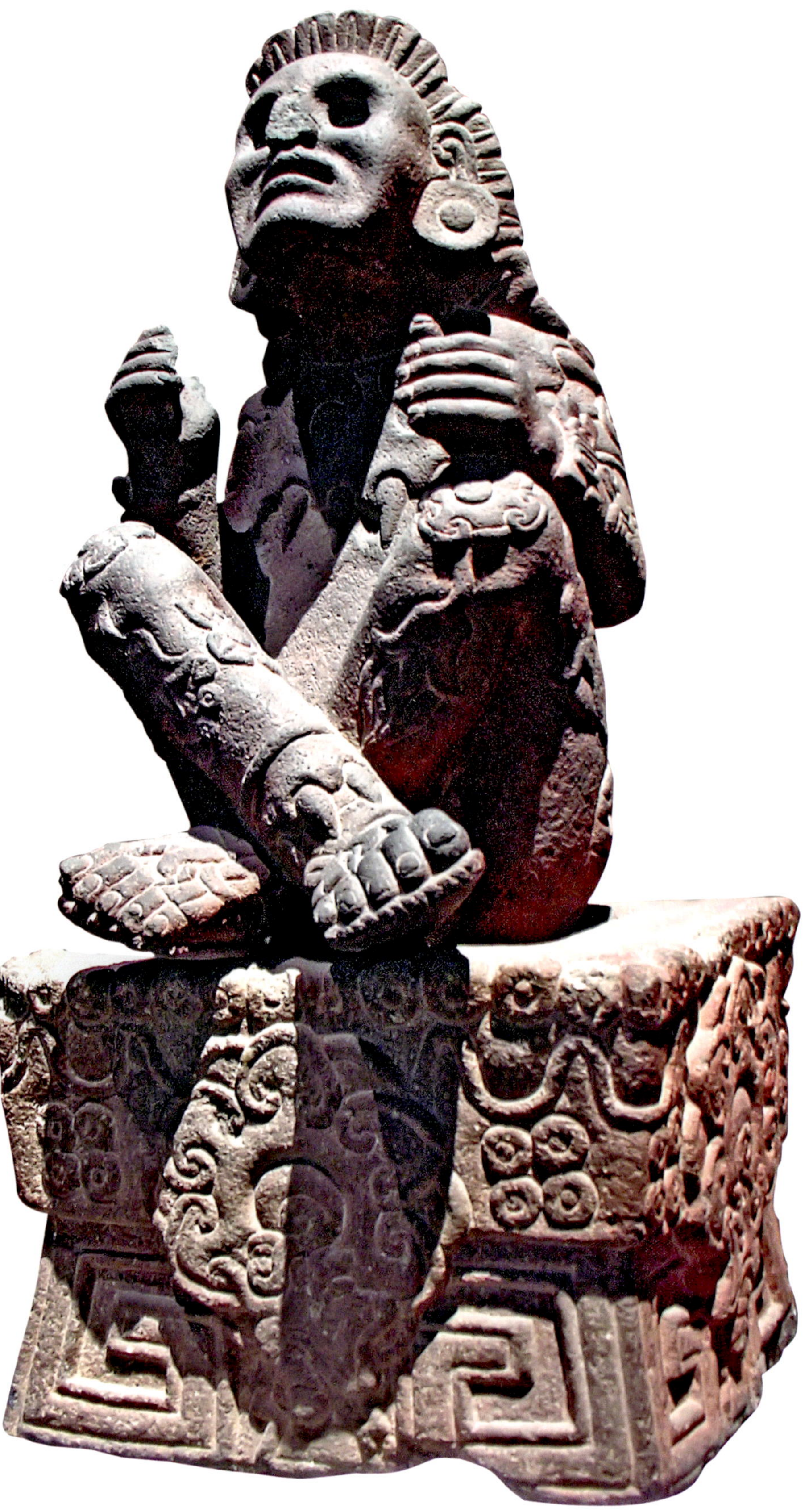

Xochipilli, “God of Flowers,” Aztec, ca. 1450–1500, pigment on volcanic rock

Carvers are particularly aware of the enormous cultural meaning of the heritage they perpetuate. Mindfulness and responsibility guide their practices. Felling a tree is often preceded by a prayer and an offering. The conversation between the carver and the tree is grounded in deep respect. The tree says to the carver, "Stand back, and I shall see what I will be." Another tree is often planted nearby to reassure the spirits that the life of the one being taken is valuable and will not be squandered.[21] The carving process that follows is rooted in this deep sense of respect and pride that intimately entwines plants and humans.

Totem poles emerge from this tradition. They essentially are autobiographical monuments—a life story, carved and coauthored—written into and with the cedar tree. Each carving represents a landmark event or key to someone's life. At times standing up to sixty-five feet in height, a carved totem pole is an indelible inscription binding human and tree into wooden memory.

While trees have influenced sculptural development throughout history, several species have also had a significant impact on the development of painting. Wood panels were prized in ancient Greece and Rome for their density and sturdiness. Specifically chestnut, walnut, and oak were among the most popular woods for this purpose. Next to none of these ancient works have survived, but some wood panels that served as substrates for artworks in the High Middle Ages (1000–1300 CE) have. Coniferous wood, especially fir, provided painting boards across Europe at this time, and poplar, a hardwood with a delicate, more homogenous texture, fewer knots, and straight grain, gained popularity at the start of the Renaissance. The relative absence of tannins in poplar also aided the adhesion of glue and plaster, while its resistance to humidity minimized the danger of warping.[22]

During the Renaissance, artists' trade secrets were gathered for the first time in Cennino Cennini's *Libro dell'Arte* (Treatise on Painting, ca. 1437). While Flemish artists preferred to work with oak,[23] Cennini recommended fourteen different tree species, including chestnut (*Castanea sativa*), fig (*Ficus carica*), plum (*Prunus domestica*), and willow (*Salix*). As a rule of thumb, and to keep costs low, artists tended to source wood locally. Flat sections could be glued together into a board, but the most sought-after large panels were cut from right across the heart of the tree. Treatment involved leaving them for extended periods under running water to eliminate resins and tannins.[24] A large cloth of cotton (*Gossypium hirsutum*) or linen (*Linum usitatissimum*) soaked in plaster and glue would then be applied to one side. Cennini recommended the application of nine layers of plaster and that the surface then be burnished to a finish resembling ivory. Artists would normally draw upon it with charcoal made from slow-burned willow twigs as the first step in the planned composition.

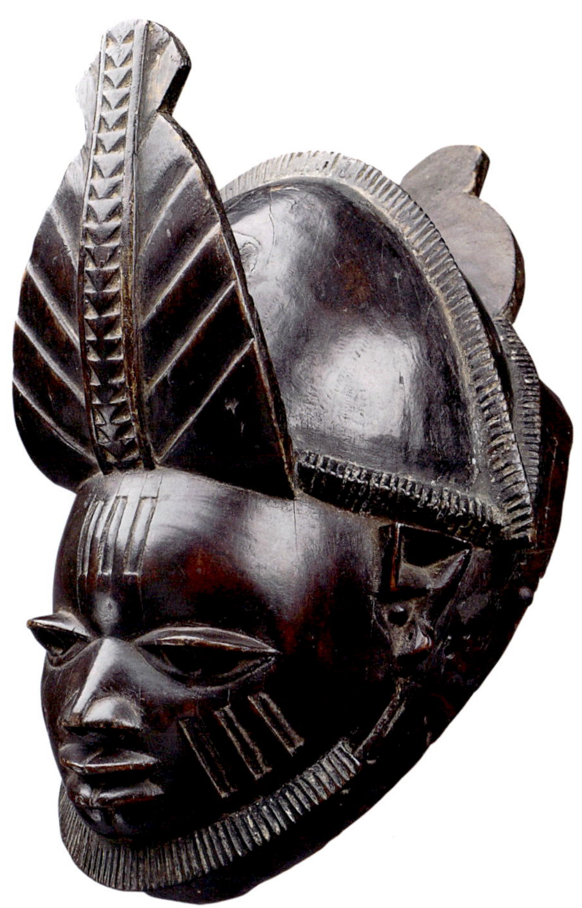

Yoruba Gelede mask, Republic of Benin, Anago Region, early twentieth century, wood, pigment

The manufacture of Byzantine icons in Eastern Europe and Russia was significantly dependent on several types of trees including linden, fir, larch, cedar, pine, and oak. The preparation of icon boards was similar to that of Renaissance panels in the West, and has remained so to this day.[25] This long-standing tradition was interrupted in the West by the mid-sixteenth century, when in Italy wood

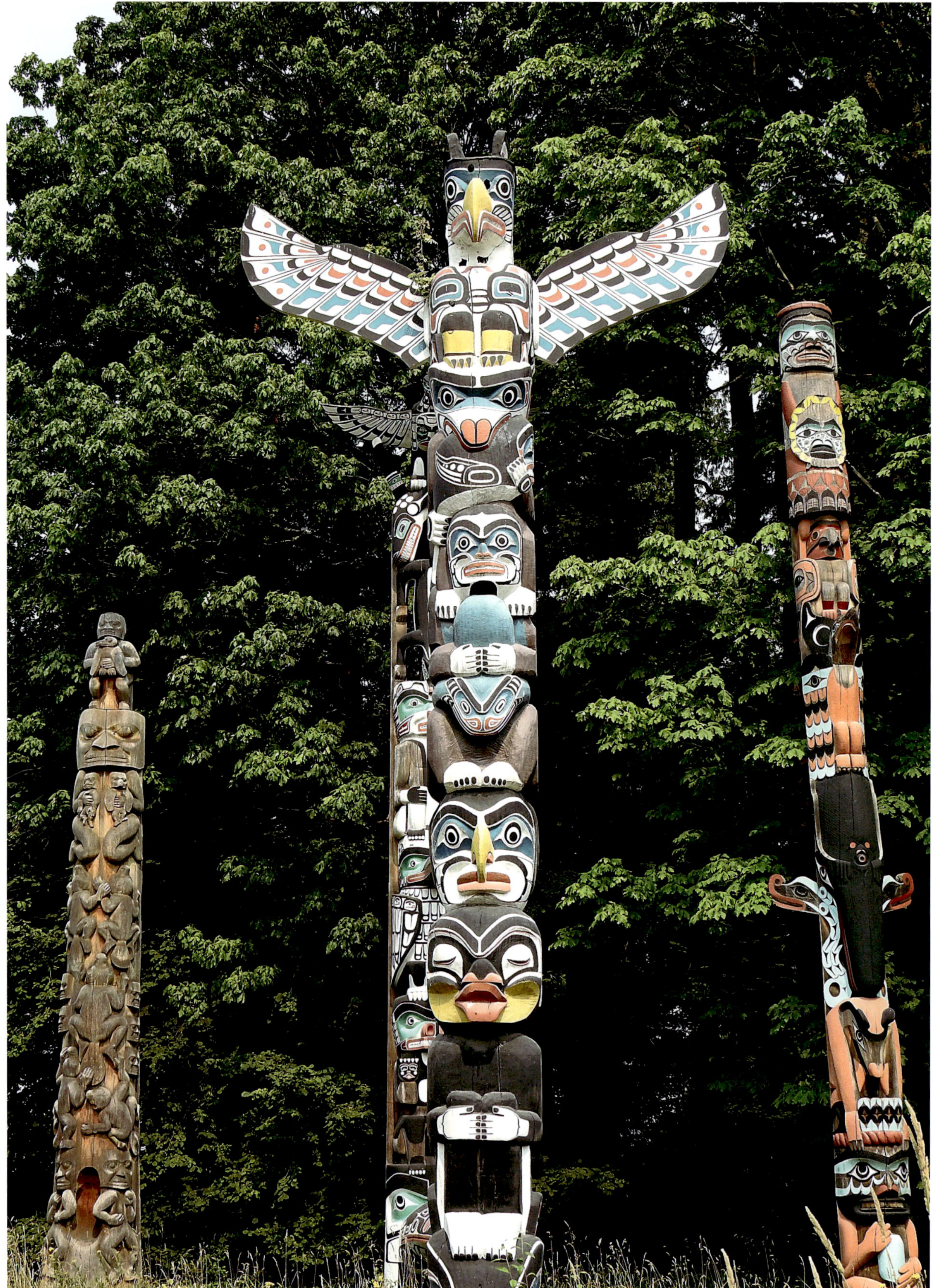

Totem poles in Stanley Park, Vancouver, British Columbia, Canada, photograph 2017

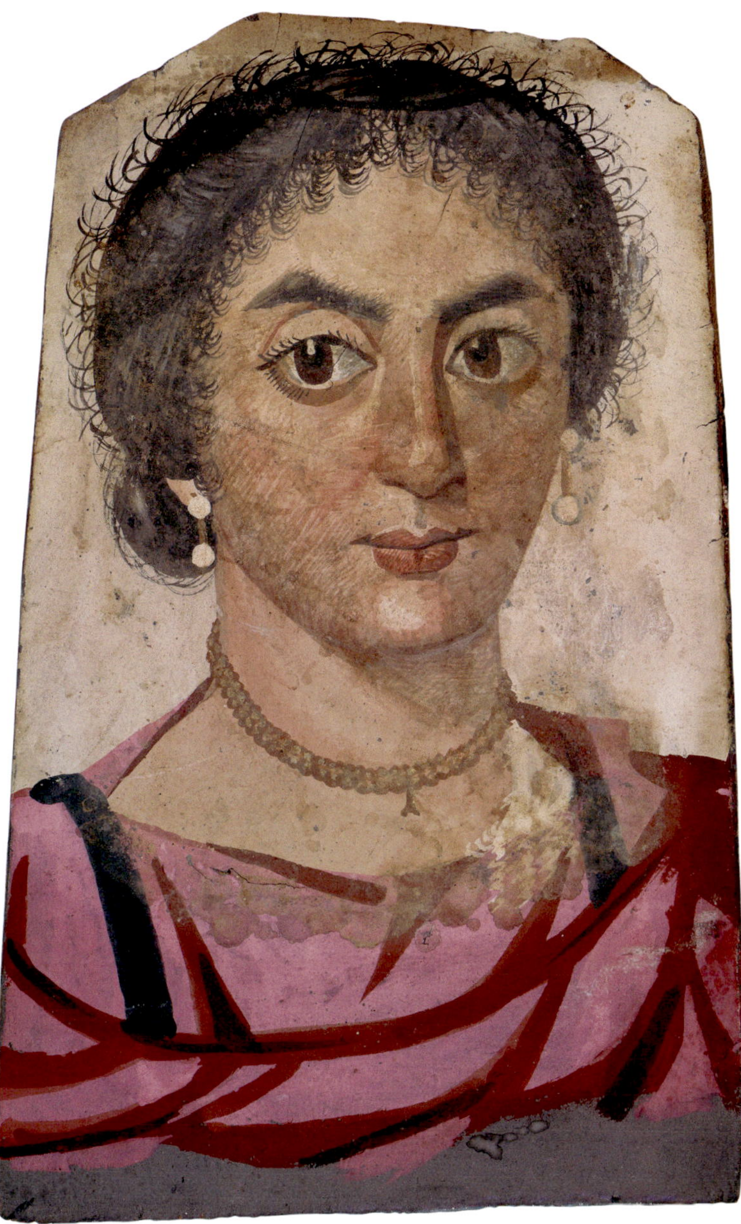

**Mummy portrait of a young woman, Romano-Egyptian, ca. 170–200 CE, tempera on wood**



panels were replaced by canvases made of hemp (*Cannabis sativa*)—one of the most significant botanical revolutions in the history of art.

While painting on loose fabric had taken place in different forms across the globe, painting on silk canvases became common in China during the fourth century BCE.[26] By the fourteenth century, this tradition might have reached Venice, a city open to many types of inventions due to its history of trade with the East. Silk was, however, replaced with hemp fiber, a durable and flexible material. Artists were no longer limited to the size of wood panels. The Venetians were expert sailmakers, and so knew how to handle large expanses of cloth. Canvas was also less prone to warping and cracking. It wasn't long before its popularity traveled to Spain, as evidenced by the significance given to the back of a big canvas filling the left side of Diego Velázquez's royal masterwork *Las Meninas* (1656). Canvases made art far more portable, facilitating exhibiting and collecting. Without hemp canvases, Canaletto would have never made a fortune from his Venetian vistas that wealthy travelers loved to ship back home as souvenirs, and John Constable would have never sketched clouds in oil pigments while painting outdoors. By the beginning of the nineteenth century, linen made

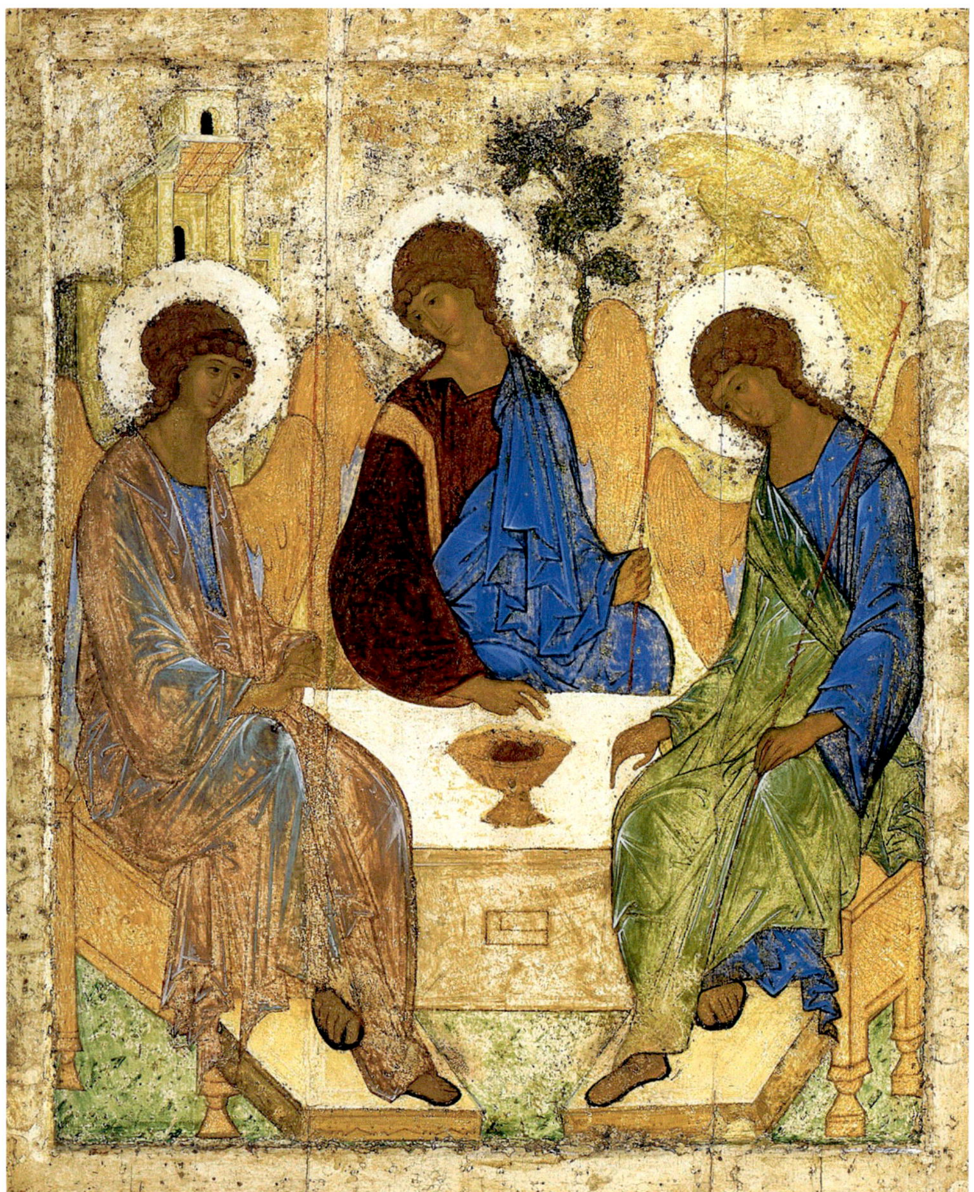

Andrey Rublyov, *Trinity*, ca. 1411/1425–27, tempera on wood

of *Linum usitatissimum*—which provided a finer and smoother surface—rose in popularity.[27] Without linen canvases, the Impressionist movement never would have happened.

Lastly, plants—sometimes blended with animal oils to enhance the brilliance of color, improve malleability, or increase durability—were the primary sources of artists' colors and dyes. To identify and extract pigments, artists had to develop an intimate knowledge of many plant species. It is often the case that the pigment in question is not evident in the flowers or leaves of the plant but only surfaces through laborious processing. *Rubia tinctorum*, or rose madder, native to Greece and other southern Mediterranean areas, is an unassuming herbaceous perennial plant distantly related to coffee, with bright green leaves and small, bright yellow flowers. But it is the red extracted from its fibers that became one of the most important pigments in the intertwined histories of art and fashion, thanks to its vibrancy and intensity.[28] Brazilwood (*Paubrasilia echinata*), safflower (*Carthamus tinctorius*), and dyer's alkanet (*Alkanna tinctoria*) also produce vibrant reds. Dragon's blood, a very intense red, is extracted from the unripe fruits of the rattan palm (*Calamus*).[29] Quercitron, a yellow-greenish pigment, is derived from

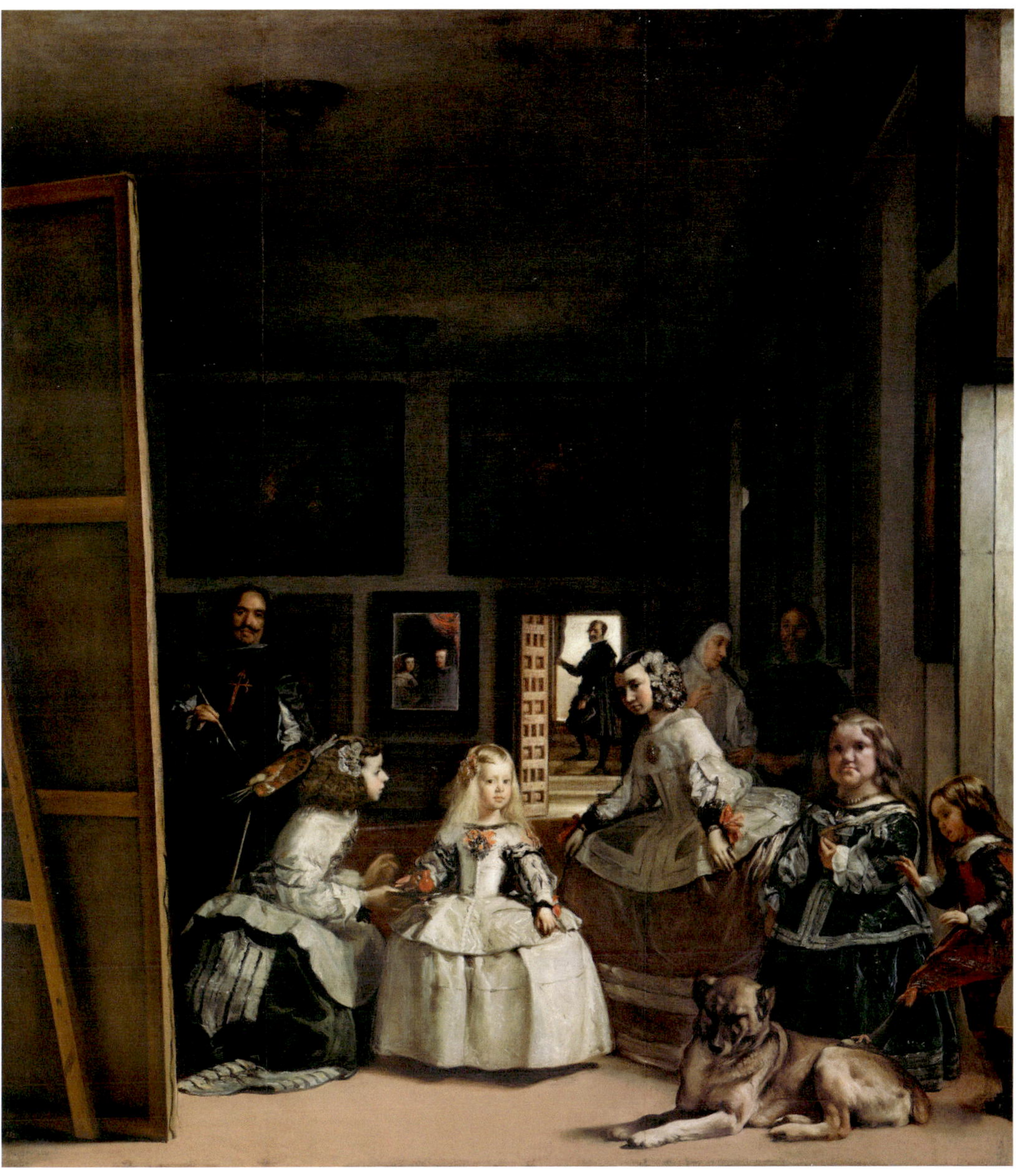

Diego Velázquez, *Las Meninas*, 1656, oil on canvas



the black- and brownish-gray bark of the black oak (*Quercus velutina*). At times it is the sap that produces the pigment, as is the case with the yellow tint made from Siam gamboge (*Garcinia hanburyi*). Commonly used in Japanese and Malaysian painting since the eighth century, it subsequently became popular in Europe as a watercolor pigment.[30] Rich shades of golden yellow may also be extracted from the root of *Curcuma longa*, the Southeast Asian plant known as turmeric, from the pollen of saffron (*Crocus sativus*), and from the Madonna lily (*Lilium candidum*). Deep shades of blue-green in Chinese paintings have been obtained from the leaves of the lokao (*Rhamnus globosa*). Among the plants from which blue can be extracted, woad (*Isatis tinctoria*) was once one of the most popular, since it was the only lightfast blue in Europe until indigo (*Indigofera tinctoria*) was introduced from Asia in the sixteenth century.[31] As it will be seen in chapter 5, woad and indigo not only exerted a huge impact on the history of Western art by making the color blue a coveted status symbol, but also dramatically redistributed wealth, reconfigured social classes, and fueled the slave trade for more than three centuries, all while wreaking environmental havoc across Europe and the Americas.

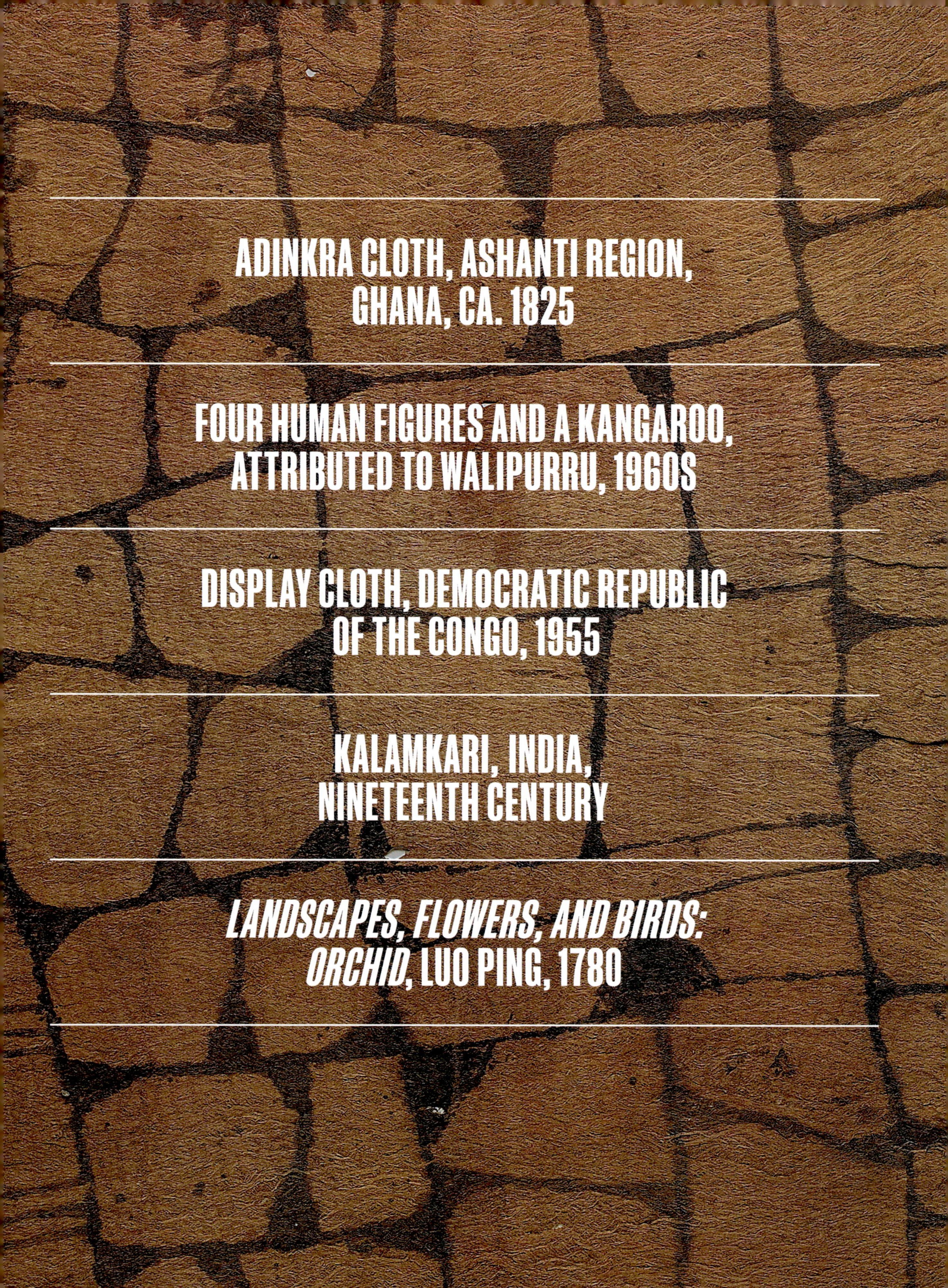

ADINKRA CLOTH, ASHANTI REGION, GHANA, CA. 1825

FOUR HUMAN FIGURES AND A KANGAROO, ATTRIBUTED TO WALIPURRU, 1960S

DISPLAY CLOTH, DEMOCRATIC REPUBLIC OF THE CONGO, 1955

KALAMKARI, INDIA, NINETEENTH CENTURY

*LANDSCAPES, FLOWERS, AND BIRDS: ORCHID*, LUO PING, 1780

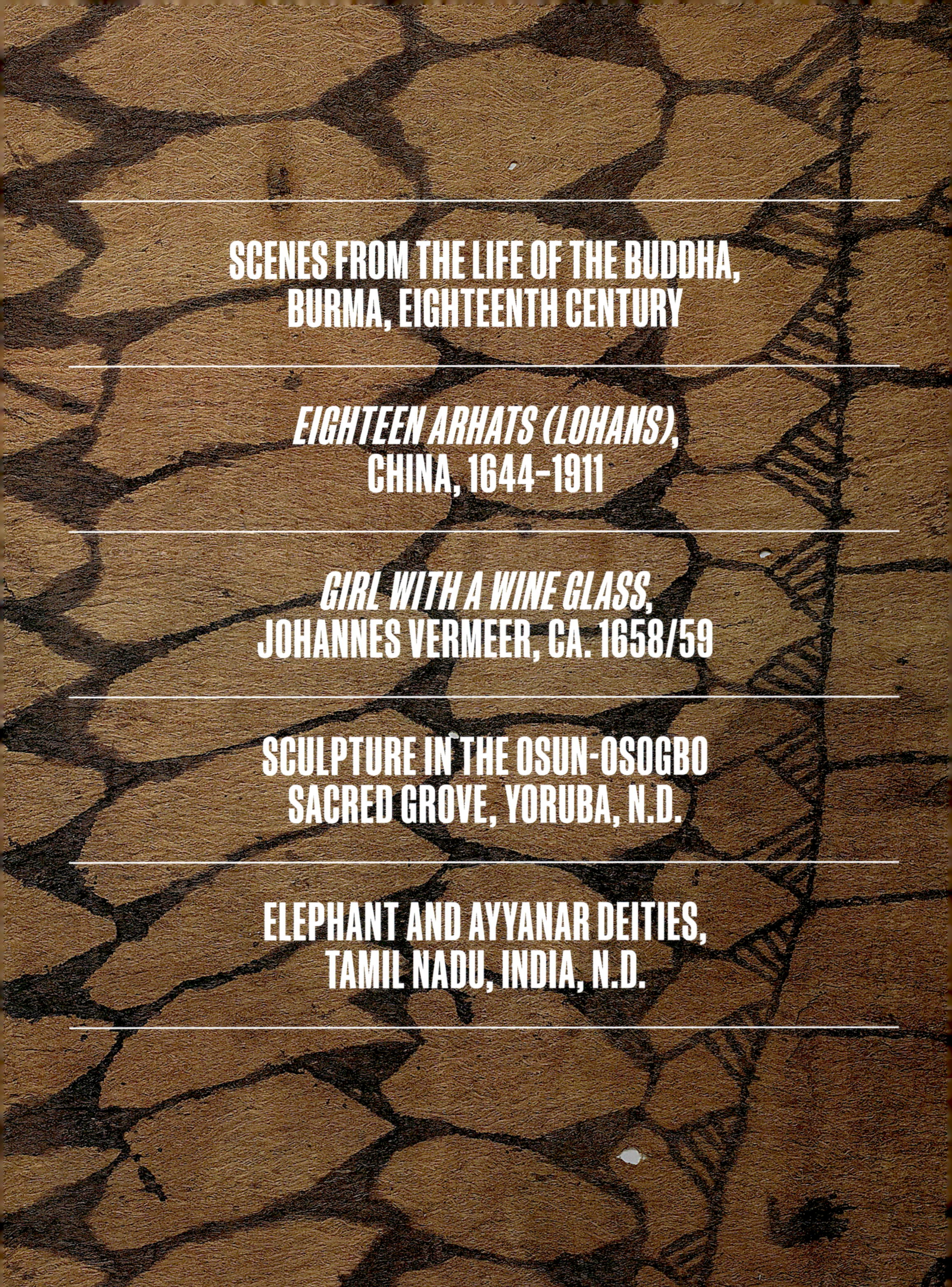

SCENES FROM THE LIFE OF THE BUDDHA, BURMA, EIGHTEENTH CENTURY

*EIGHTEEN ARHATS (LOHANS)*, CHINA, 1644–1911

*GIRL WITH A WINE GLASS*, JOHANNES VERMEER, CA. 1658/59

SCULPTURE IN THE OSUN-OSOGBO SACRED GROVE, YORUBA, N.D.

ELEPHANT AND AYYANAR DEITIES, TAMIL NADU, INDIA, N.D.

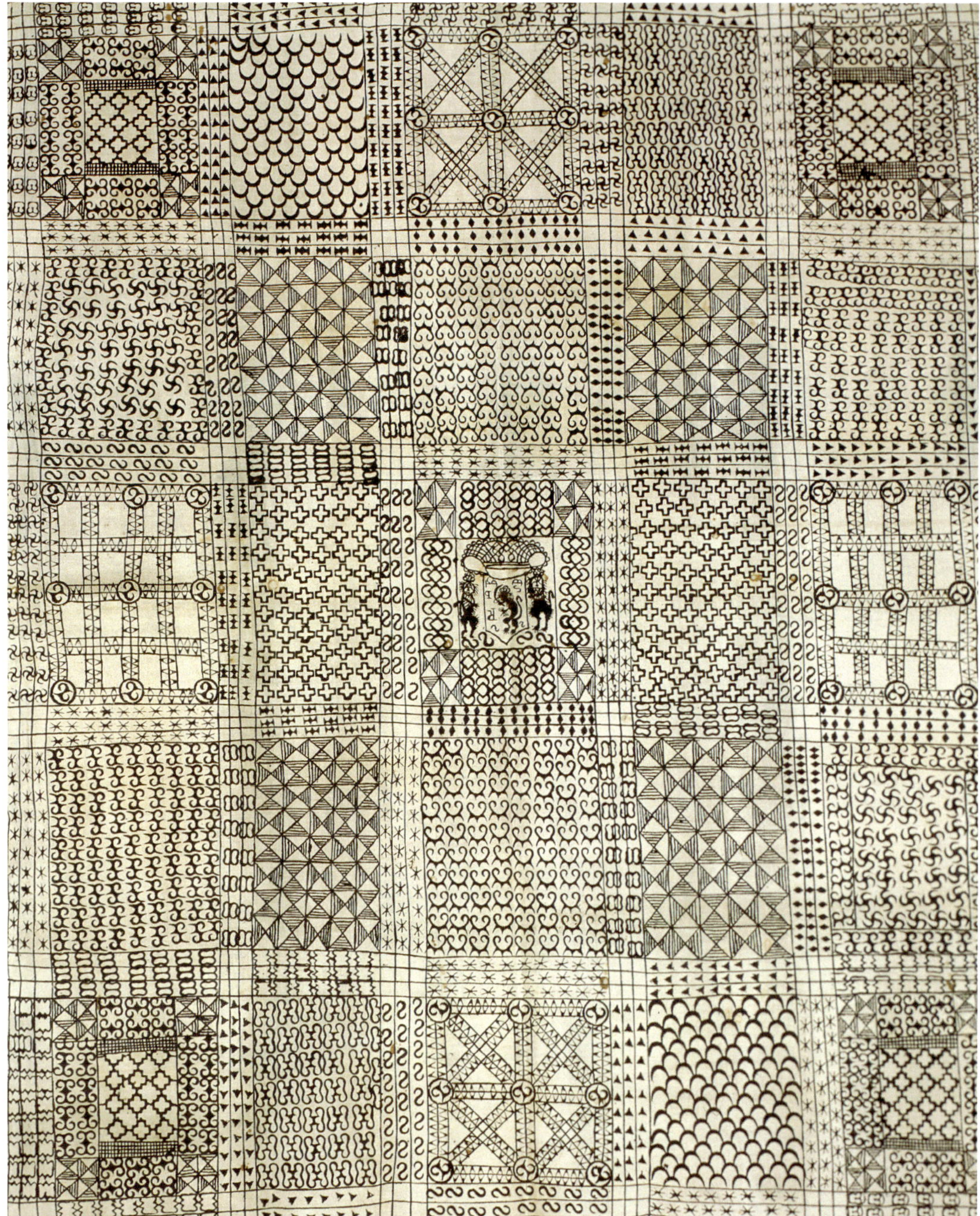

**Adinkra cloth, Ashanti region, Ghana, ca. 1825, cotton and dye**

Adinkra fabric, historically reserved for spiritual leaders and royalty to wear to funerals and other such significant events, has long been the product of a collaborative relationship between plants and humans. The fabric has for centuries been made out of cotton, often dyed in pigments of red, brown, and black extracted from the boiled roots and inner bark of the badie tree (*Bridelia ferruginea*). The stamps are crafted from a dehydrated calabash (*Lagenaria siceraria*), a durable and resilient material that allows for repeated printing. Originally created by the Bono people of Gyaman, these mesmerizing patterns became a staple among the Ashanti in Ghana and the Baoulé in Côte d'Ivoire. Today, adinkra cloth has been commercialized and is mass-produced for the international market. More than one hundred recurring symbols have been identified in the original adinkra production. They embody traditional wisdom, often including proverbs and preserving traditional belief systems.

# ADINKRA CLOTH

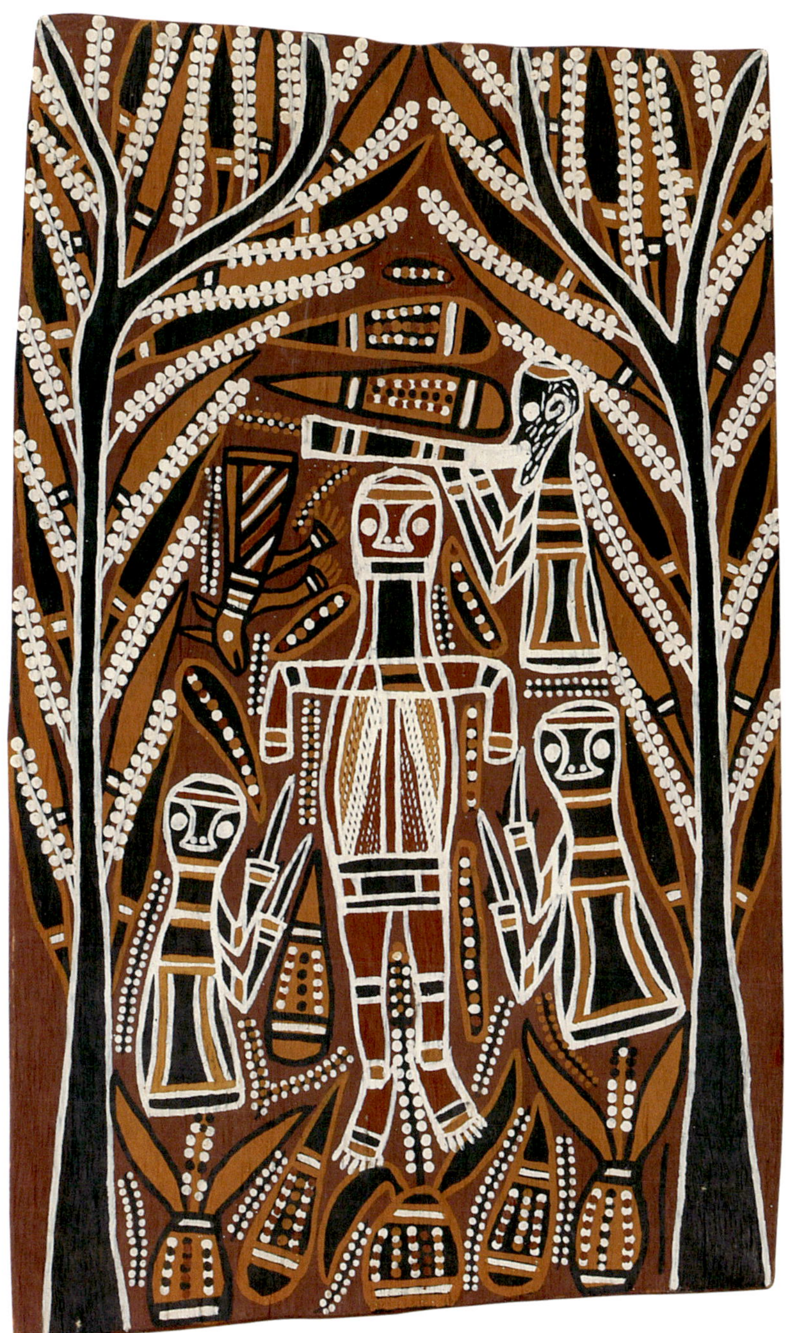

**Attributed to Walipurru, Four human figures and a kangaroo, 1960s, bark painting**



For centuries, the Aboriginal tribes of Arnhem Land—a vast wilderness area in the northeastern corner of Australia's Northern Territory—have produced complex images on the inner faces of flattened eucalyptus (*Eucalyptus tetrodonta*) bark. The bark is harvested during the rainy season, when the sap makes the fibers supple. The inner layers are heated with fire, then pressed flat under heavy weights. These paintings serve important ceremonial and instructional purposes. The material resilience and smooth surface of eucalyptus bark made it possible for the intricate social relationships that bound tribes across the northern regions to develop, disseminate, and flourish over time. In West Arnhem Land, artists deploy aesthetics more closely resembling the figurative motifs seen frequently in ancient rock art. Geometric compositional patterns have been preferred in the Eastern regions, while in the central lands, a combination of the two styles was often the norm. Original patterns and designs are identitarian; they belong to particular artists and their families, and cannot be painted by other artists.

## FOUR HUMAN FIGURES AND A KANGAROO

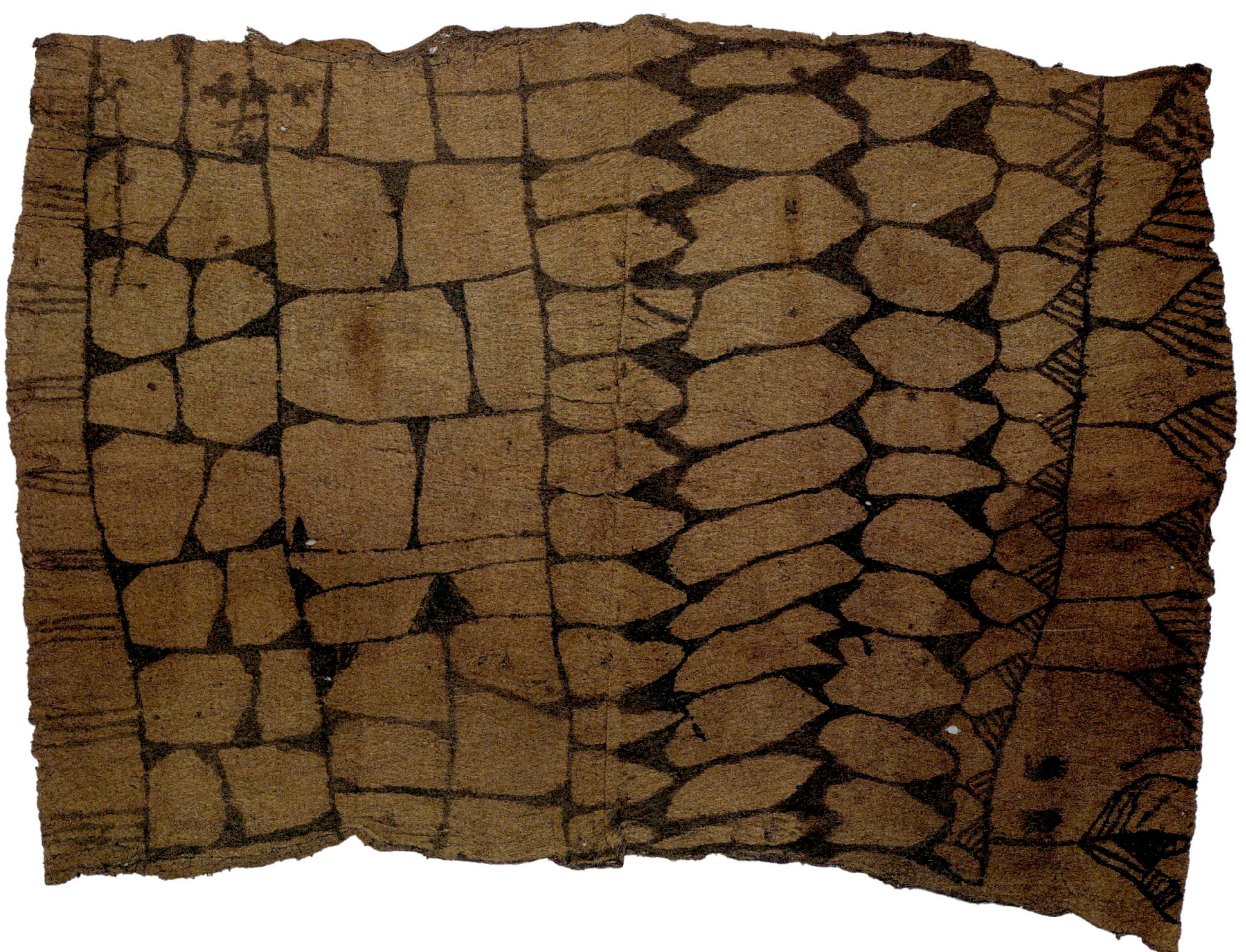



**Unknown Mbuti artist, Democratic Republic of the Congo, Display cloth, 1955, bark cloth, raffia cloth, and dye**

Across the globe, from the Pacific Islands to Africa and Asia, for millennia the bark of trees like elephant jack (*Artocarpus tamaran*), breadfruit (*Artocarpus altilis*), and paper mulberry (*Broussonetia papyrifera*) was beaten into sheets of non-woven fabric called bark cloth. Dating back to the Neolithic period, this material is extremely durable and versatile, and is believed to have originated in southeastern China, in a region adjacent to Vietnam. The oldest known surviving example of bark cloth dates back to 5900 BCE. As with the adinkra cloth, the original motifs are culturally and spiritually meaningful to particular tribes. The patterns are often block printed and feature a number of recurring symbols. In southern Uganda, where bark cloth is still produced today, the locals carefully strip only narrow sections of bark at a time from the Mutaba tree (*Ficus natalensis*) and cover the exposed live wood with large banana leaves for nine months in order to protect the tree from attack by fungi or insects. This practice of care allows the trees to live healthily thereafter.

# DISPLAY CLOTH

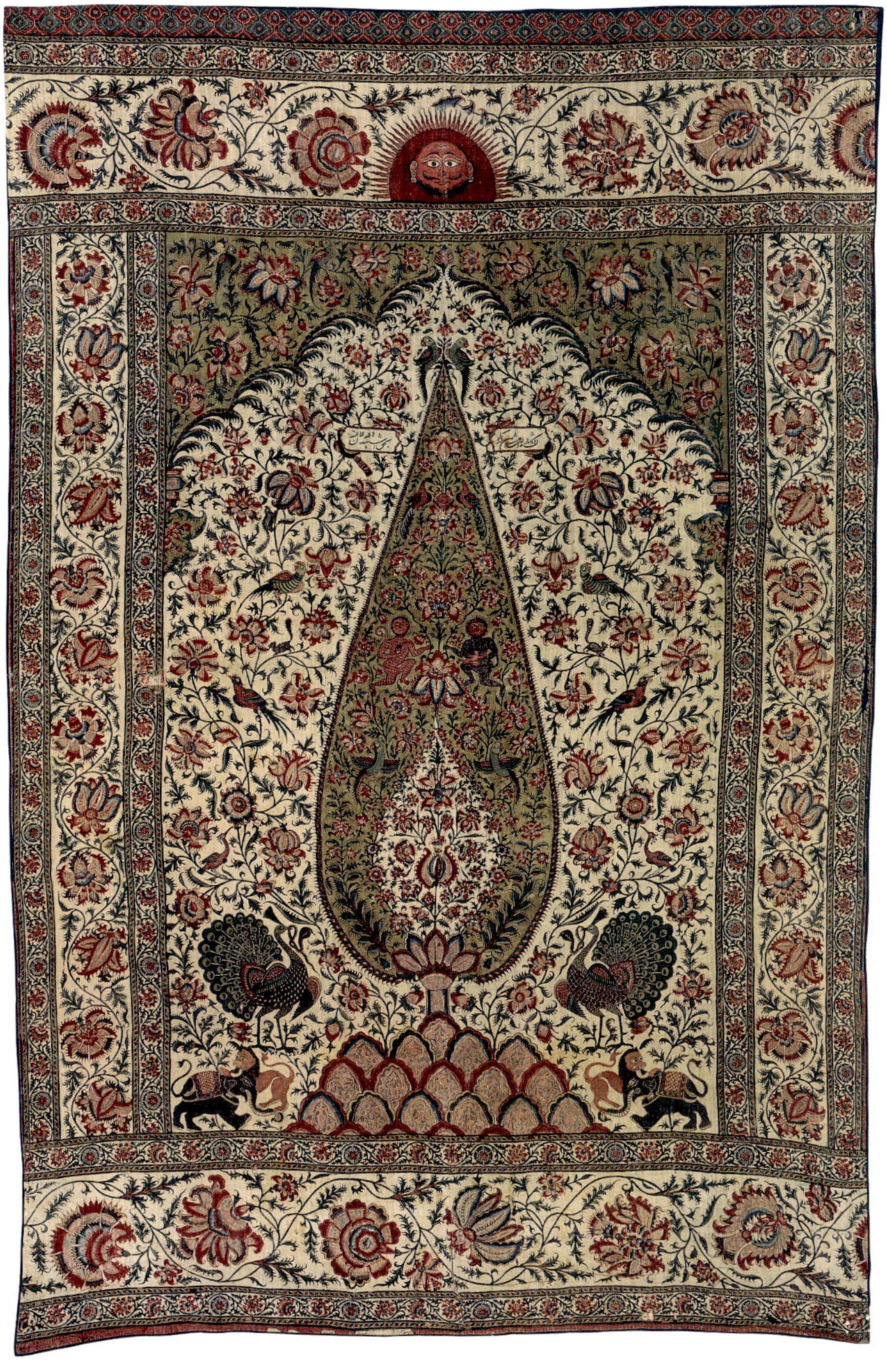

Kalamkari, attributed to India, nineteenth century, cotton textile

Produced in the Deccan region of India since the eighth century CE, a kalamkari is a cotton-based textile requiring twenty-three steps of production. A sophisticated procedure involving natural materials and wax allows for the precise application of indigo dye, while the remainder of the motifs are typically patterned using woodblocks or traced by hand with bamboo or date palm sticks. Vegetable dyes and cow dung are significant elements in the composition of the vibrant and balanced color palette commonly utilized, which includes deep hues of indigo, mustard, rust, black, and green. The Tree of Life is a recurring motif, representing the marriage between the earthly and the divine. Oftentimes, animals are represented feeding on or taking shelter under the tree—a metaphorical reminder of the common descent of all life on Earth.

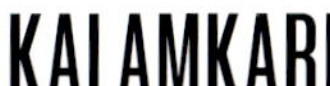

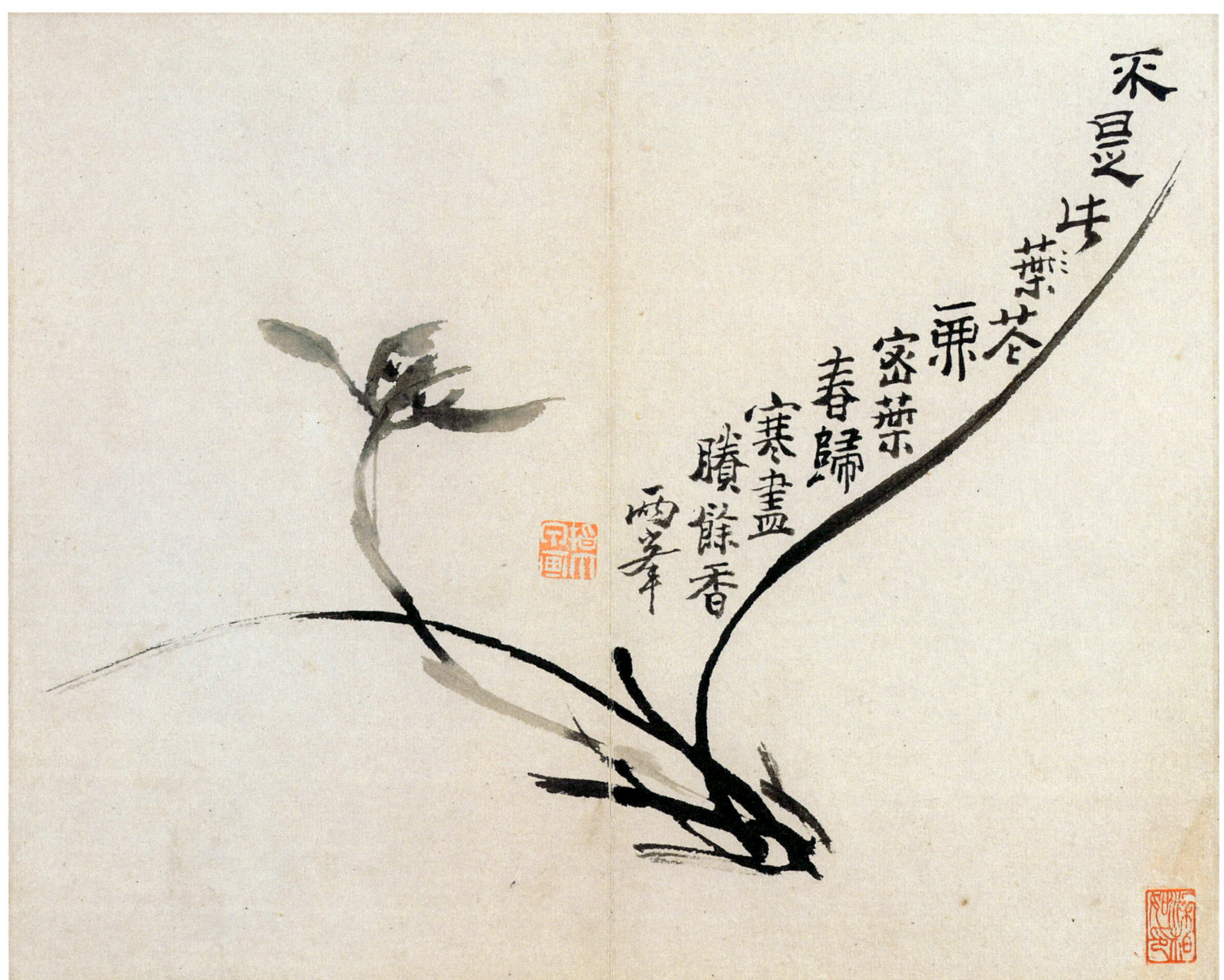

Luo Ping, *Landscapes, Flowers and Birds: Orchid*, 1780, ink on paper

For nearly two thousand years, in Chinese culture, court professionals—the literati—explored the intimate poetic relationships that bind painting and calligraphy. Images on scrolls were referred to as *wu-sheng-shih*, meaning "silent poetry." The same brushes that traced pictograms also outlined the delicate contours of branches, petals, and feathers. Calligraphic brushwork molded the aesthetic flair of painterly compositions upon the flat smoothness of thin paper. Very few other works express the delicacy of this material complicity that binds words and icons and in which language seamlessly wraps every aspect of human perception. In this wonderful painting by Luo Ping, the pictograms flow alongside the shape of the leaf, outlining a sense of harmonious material and conceptual continuity—a desire to arrest the fleeting and delicate essence of plant life without smothering it. The poem loosely translates as: "Orchids lack lush foliage; as the winter passes and the spring arrives, only the scent of the orchid lingers."

# *LANDSCAPES, FLOWERS AND BIRDS: ORCHID*

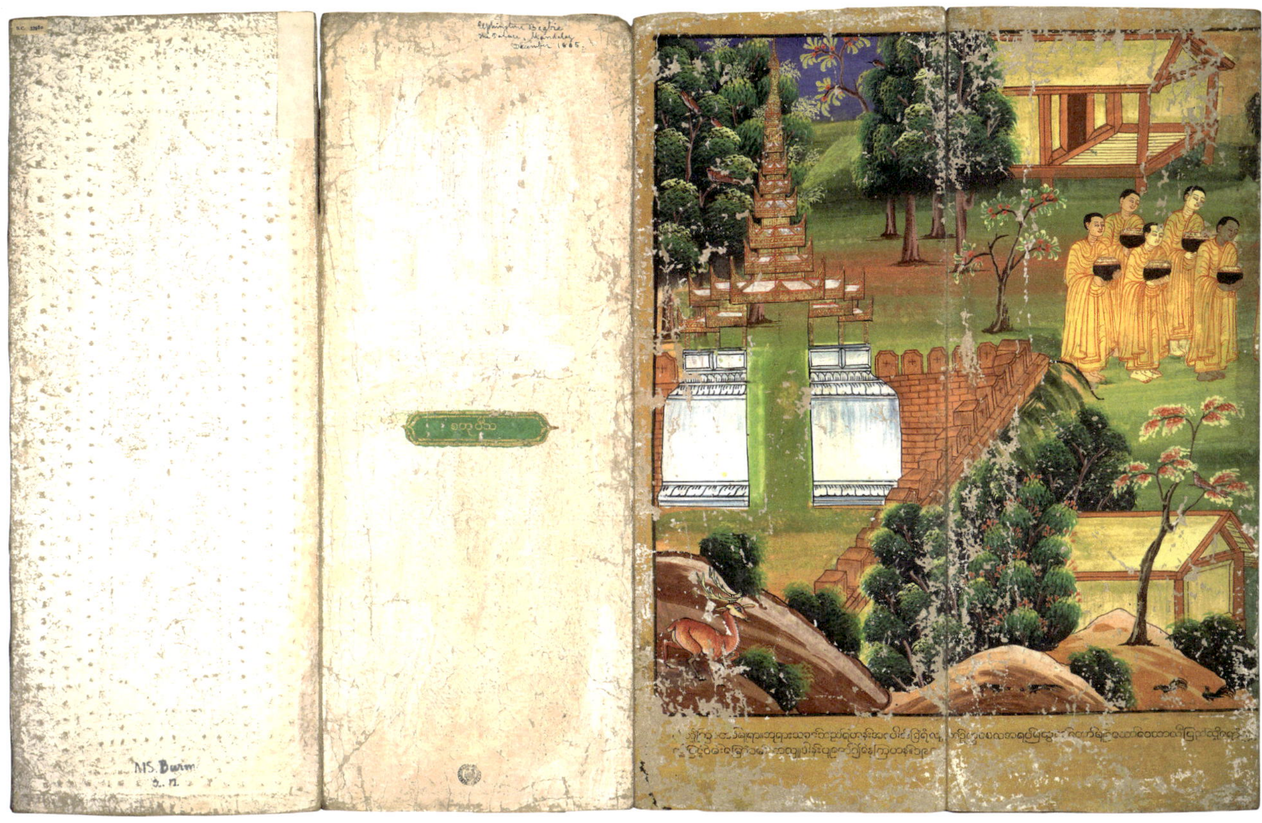

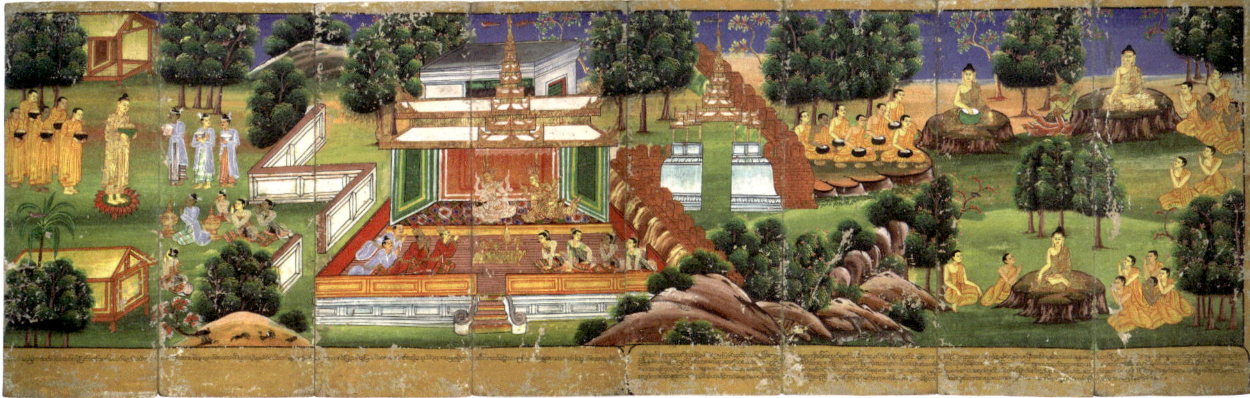



**Unknown Burmese artist, *Parabaik* illustrating scenes from the life of the Buddha, eighteenth century, watercolor on paper**

Folding-book manuscripts have been popular in mainland Southeast Asia for centuries. Made of paper derived from the Siamese rough bush tree (*khoi* in Thai and Lao) or paper mulberry (*Broussonetia papyrifera*), the manuscripts are unbound—a single, long, rectangular strip of paper folded concertina style, oftentimes two-sided, and supported at both ends by protective lacquered panels. This is typical of Burmese crafting, where the manuscripts are called *parabaik*. The paper thickness may vary, but a certain toughness is needed for the support to absorb the thick watercolor and ink. Undyed paper was traditionally used for illustrated *parabaik*, while blackened paper was preferred for other cultural or scientific texts. The earliest known *parabaik* date to the mid-eighteenth century and might have originated from Mandalay, in Myanmar.

## SCENES FROM THE LIFE OF THE BUDDHA

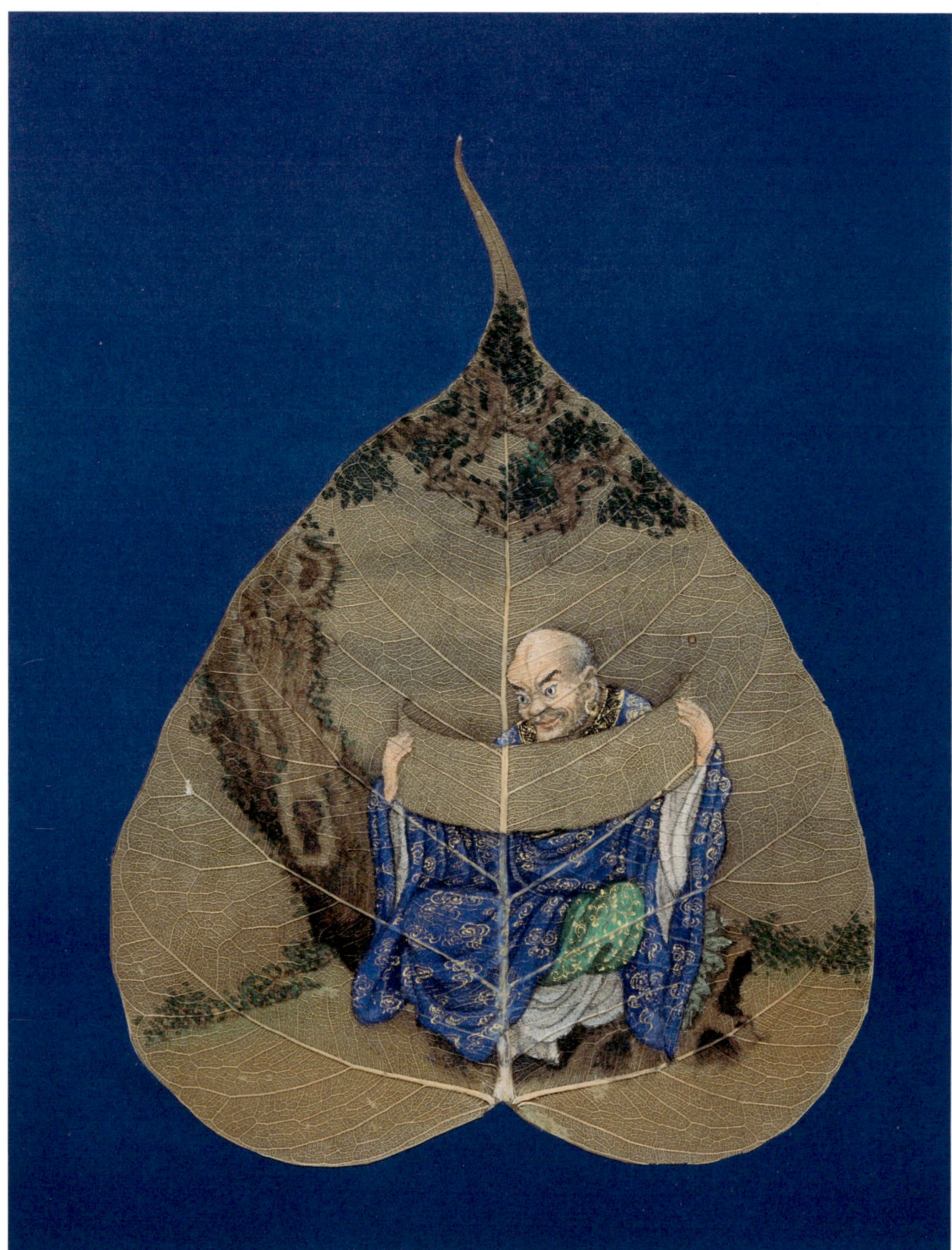

*Eighteen Arhats (Lohans)*, Qing dynasty, China, 1644–1911, ink and colors on eighteen Bodhi leaves

Remarkable for its large size and longevity, the bodhi tree (*Ficus religiosa*), native to the Indian subcontinent, is regarded as sacred in Hinduism, Buddhism, and Jainism. It is believed that the Buddha attained enlightenment while meditating under a bodhi tree. For centuries, the heart-shaped leaves have been fundamental to holy iconography. They are harvested in late spring and summer, when freshest, and soaked in vats of water for up to a month. This maceration period softens the green tissue, exposing the harder vascular system. A flattening and drying process follows. A range of permanent pigments are then applied, and the leaves are sold to pilgrims as souvenirs. This leaf is part of an extremely high-quality set of eighteen representing the arhats—Buddha's disciples—in the collection of the Asian Art Museum in San Francisco. The disciple reads a scroll that the artist has astutely represented by leaving the leaf surface unpainted to evoke the earthy color of paper.

# EIGHTEEN ARHATS (LOHANS)

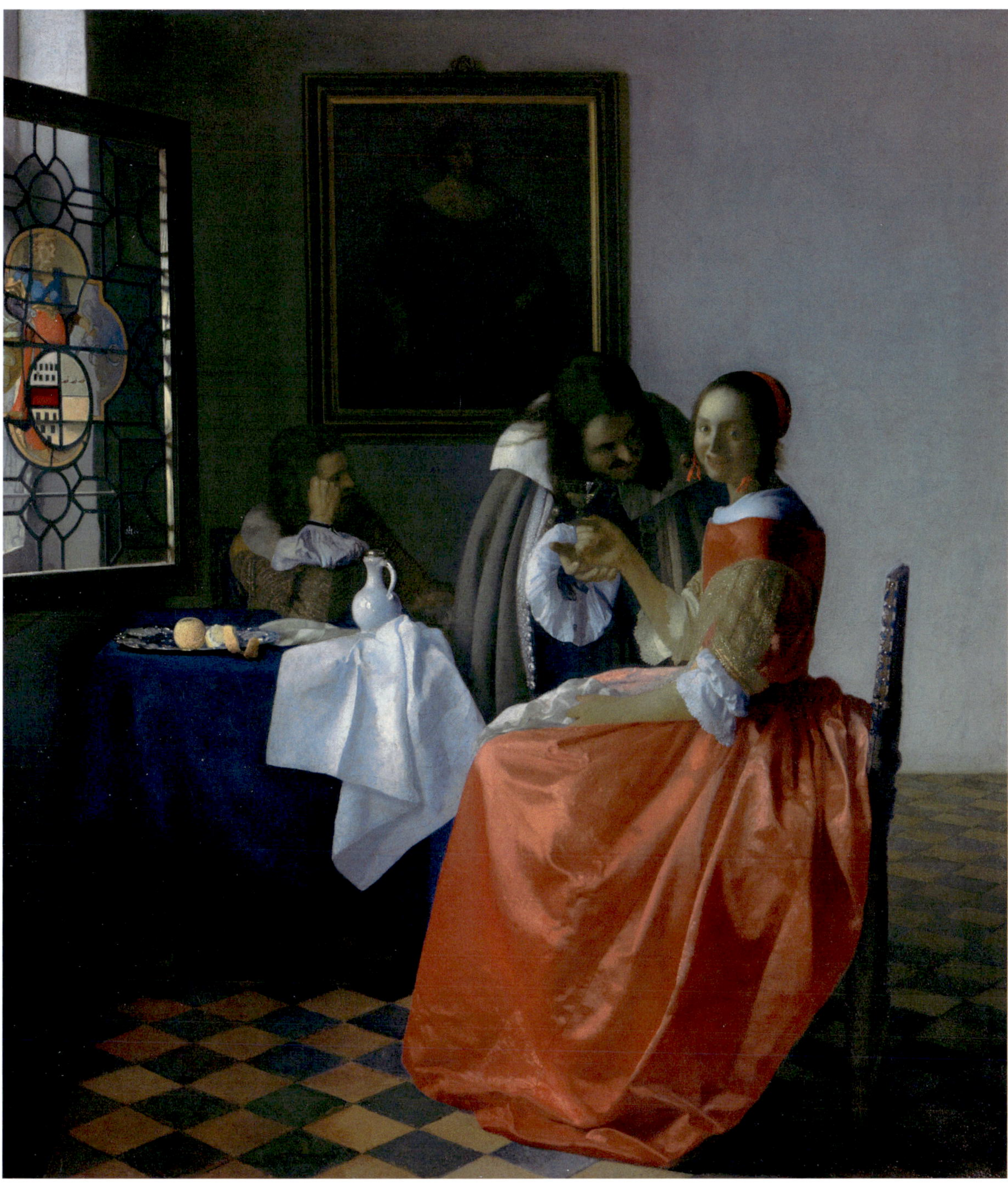

Johannes Vermeer, *Girl with a Wine Glass*, ca. 1658/59, oil on canvas



When the Dutch painter Johannes Vermeer painted *The Girl with a Wine Glass*, intense red hues were commonly extracted from the root of rose madder (*Rubia tinctorum*). Its brilliance and durability, which had been put to the test by the Egyptians and Romans thousands of years previously, contributed to its enduring popularity among painters; Vermeer frequently applied it not just to garments, but also to the cheeks and lips of his female subjects. The pigment was extracted through a lengthy process involving drying and powdering the root of the plant. The best-quality rose madder was produced in Holland, where Vermeer lived and worked.

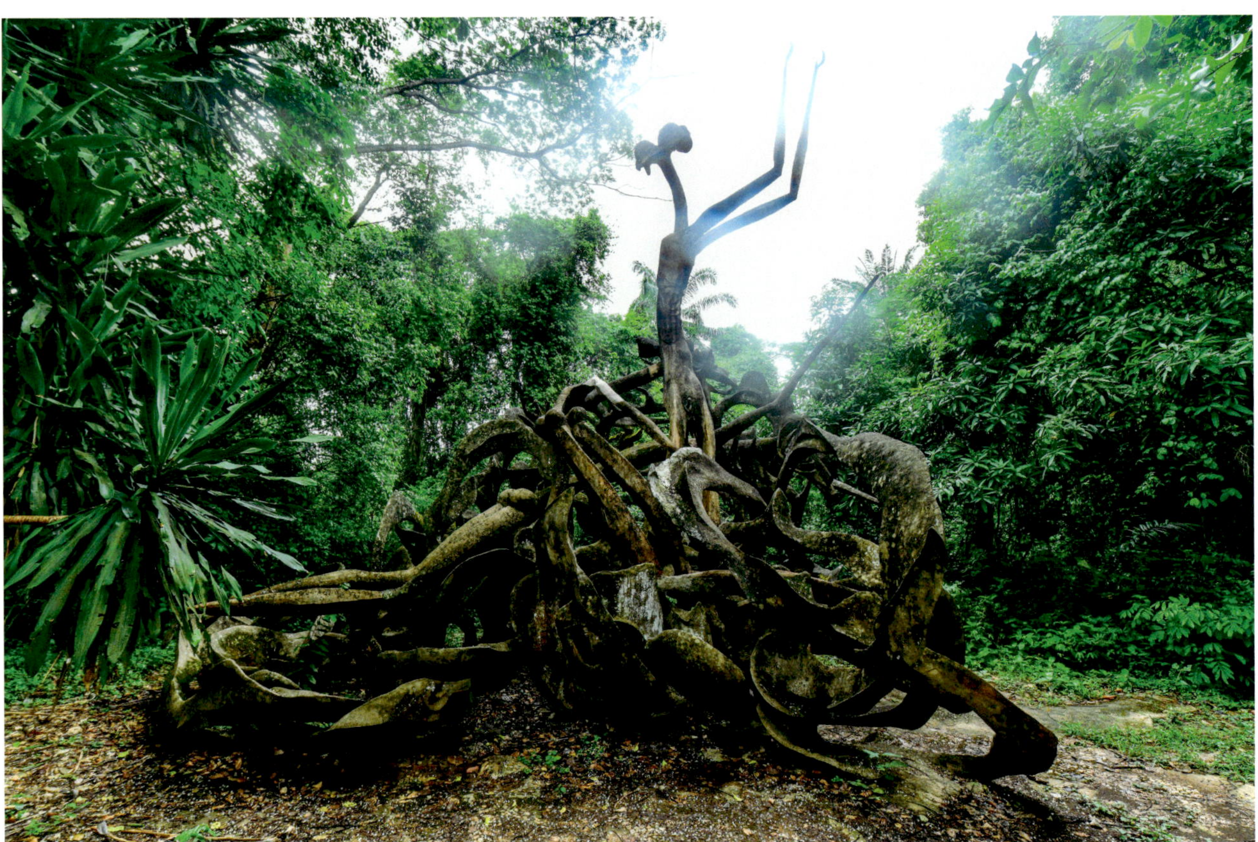

**Sculpture in the Osun-Osogbo Sacred Grove, Yoruba, n.d., iron and mud**

According to Yoruba traditions (present-day Nigeria) all plants embody a power (*ashe*) that can be negative or positive and that only Ọsanyìn, god of herbal medicine, herbalists, and healing, knows and, through his priests, can appropriately dispense. Like a plant, the god is born from the ground. He only has one leg, one arm, and one eye. Ọsanyìn has a massive ear, from which he hears nothing, and a small one, which can detect the minutest sounds made by insect feet. He is the most important of the orishas, the emissaries of the god Olodumare. Without the correct ritualistic engagements with herbs, the orishas cannot be summoned, and so plants are the foundation of Yoruba religion and spiritual life. There exists a shrine dedicated to Ọsanyìn in the last surviving sacred grove in Nigeria, along the Osun River in the town of Osogbo. Dedicated to goddess of fertility Osun, the grove is believed to be roughly four hundred years old. Today it is listed as a UNESCO World Heritage Site for both its great cultural relevance and botanical biodiversity—it is home to more than four hundred species of plants, half of which are of medicinal interest—but also because it is home to more than forty spectacular large-scale sculptures made by contemporary local artists.

# SCULPTURE IN THE OSUN-OSOGBO SACRED GROVE

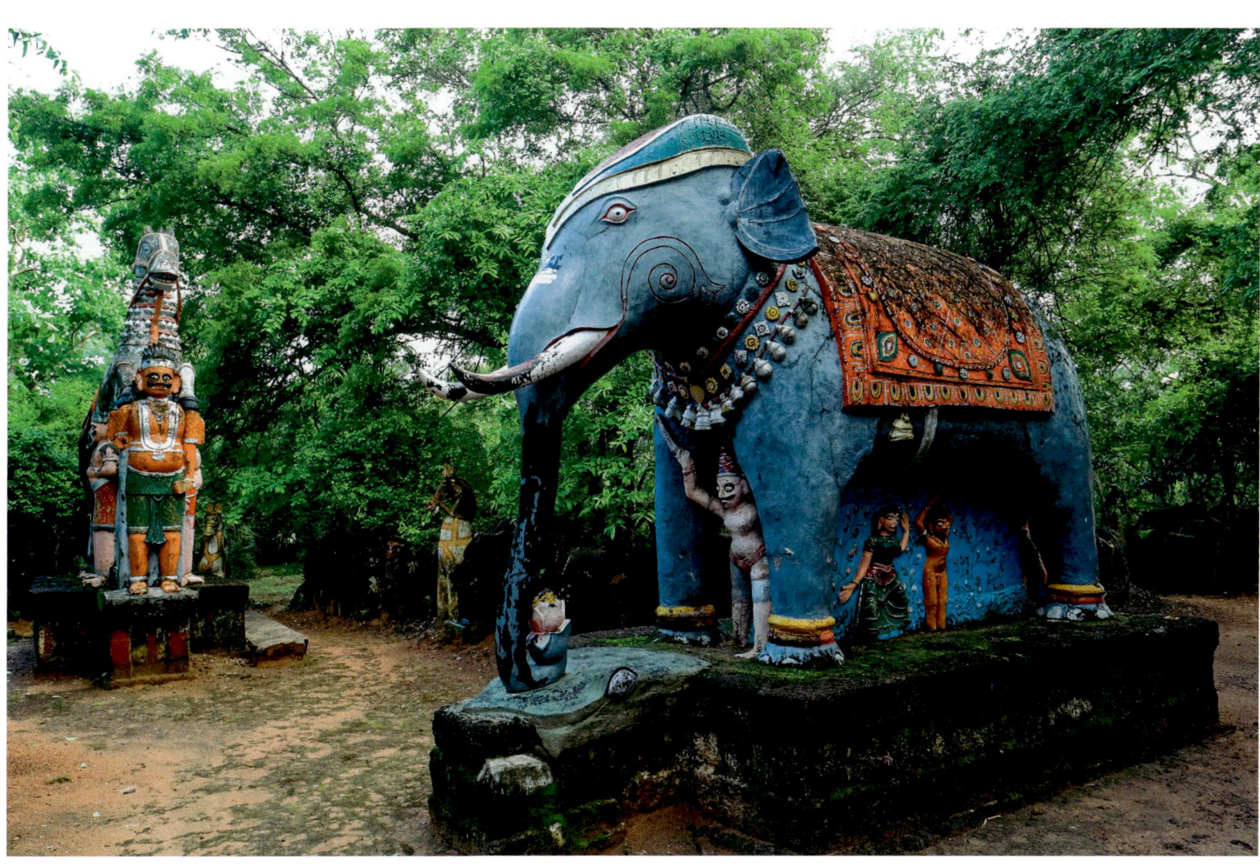



**Elephant and Ayyanar deities, Ilangudippatti village guardian temple near Pudukkottai, Tamil Nadu, India, n.d.**

The recurring motif of the sacred tree across many world religions—the Tree of Knowledge in Judaism, the sacred fig in Hinduism and Buddhism, various trees populating Celtic polytheism and Germanic mythology, African baobabs, the colossal Yggdrasil tree of Norse cosmology—symbolizes the mystery of life and celebrations of its uncontainable force, resilience, and generosity. Arboreal verticality connects earth and sky, and its silence is the sum of all life voices enveloping our planet. In India, sacred groves are actively preserved by the local communities that guard them. It is estimated that as many as fourteen thousand exist today. Some are associated with Hindu and Buddhist deities like Nagaraja, Durga, Yakshi, Chithrakoodam, and Muthappan. At times the groves surround a temple; other times, they are places of pilgrimage in their own right. Rituals that take place in the groves often involve displaying abstract drawings of intertwined snake gods on the forest floor. The ancient tribes living in the forest village of Mendha, India, see themselves as an integral part of the natural world they share with plants, animals, and the land. Reciprocation and parsimony govern day-to-day interactions with the sacred groves. As a result, these undisturbed swaths of forest have over time become extremely rich pockets of biodiversity, including an enormous wealth of medicinal plants indispensable to local communities.

## ELEPHANT AND AYYANAR DEITIES

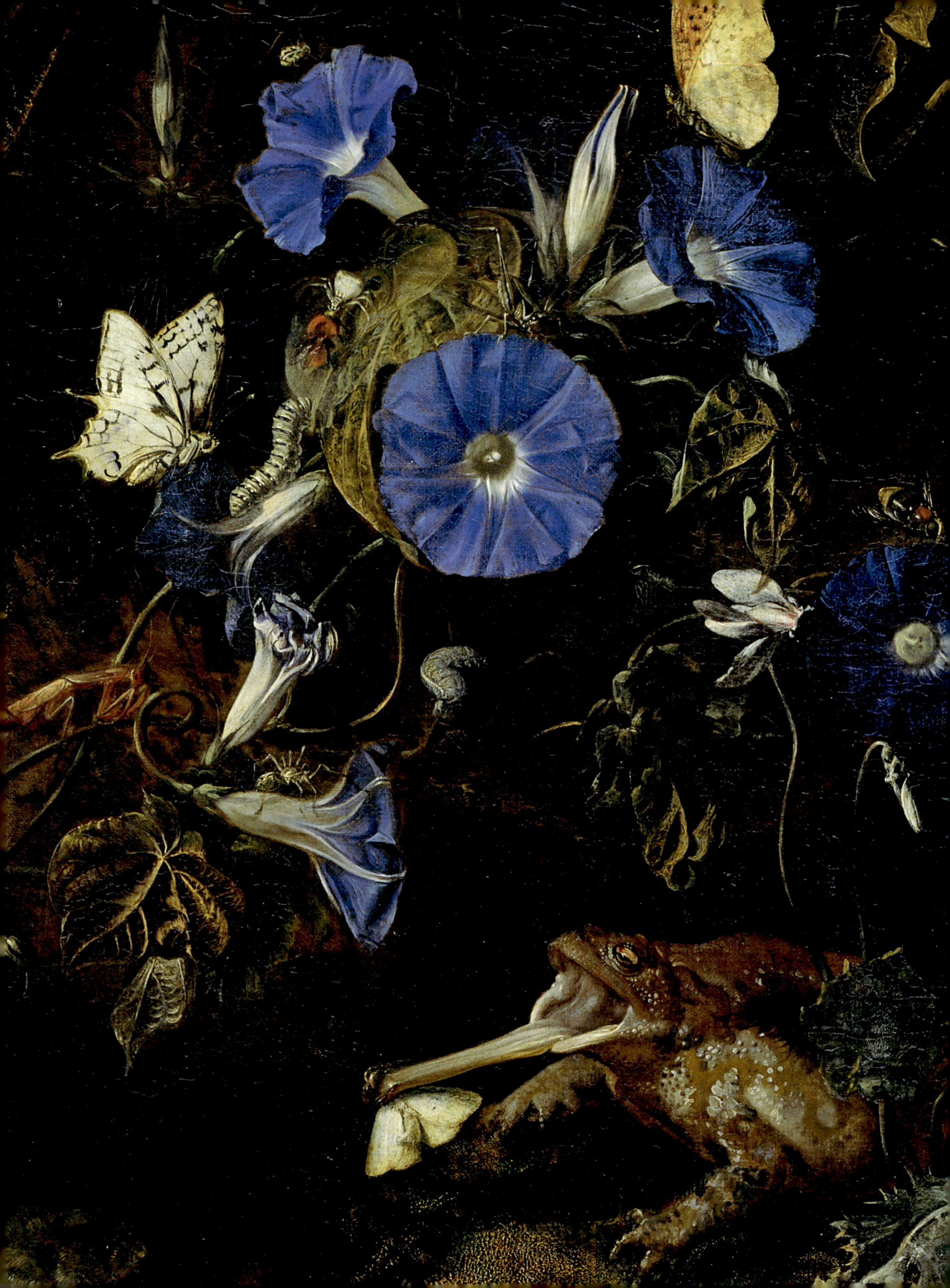

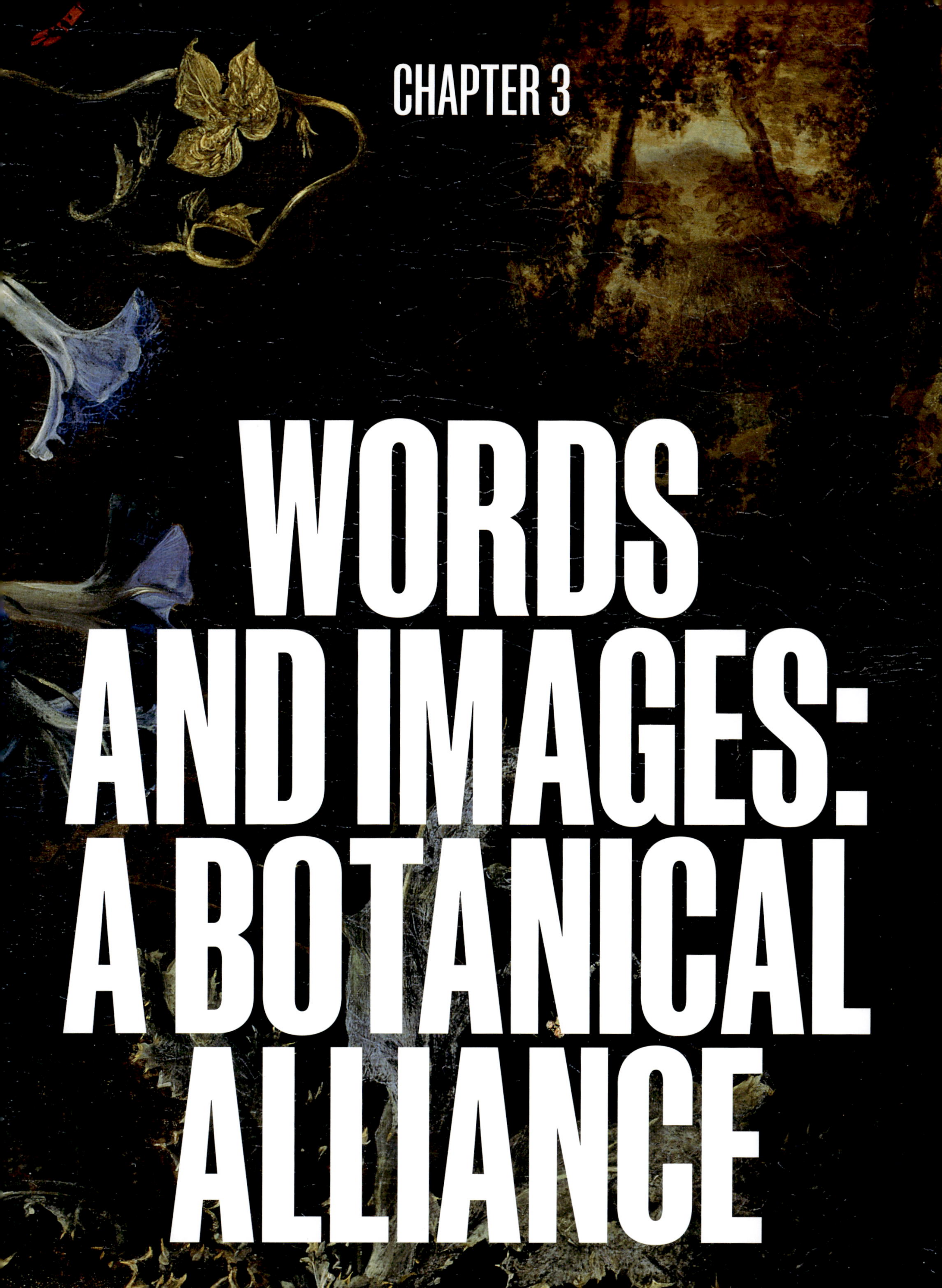

CHAPTER 3

# WORDS AND IMAGES: A BOTANICAL ALLIANCE

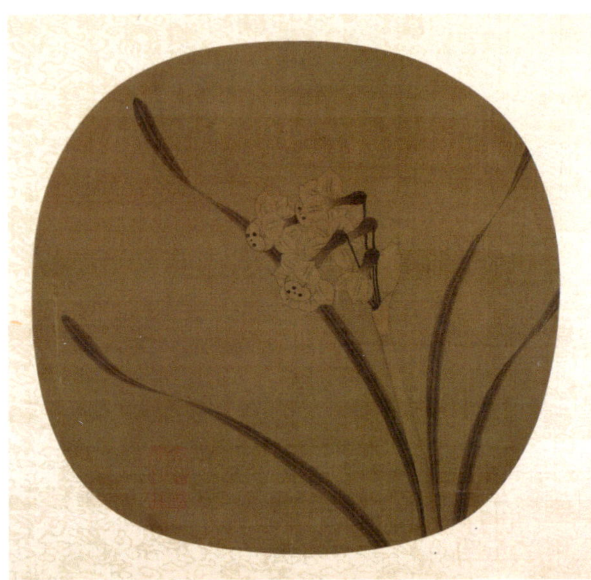

Unknown artist, *Narcissus*, Southern Song Dynasty, 1127–1279, fan mounted as an album leaf, ink and color on silk

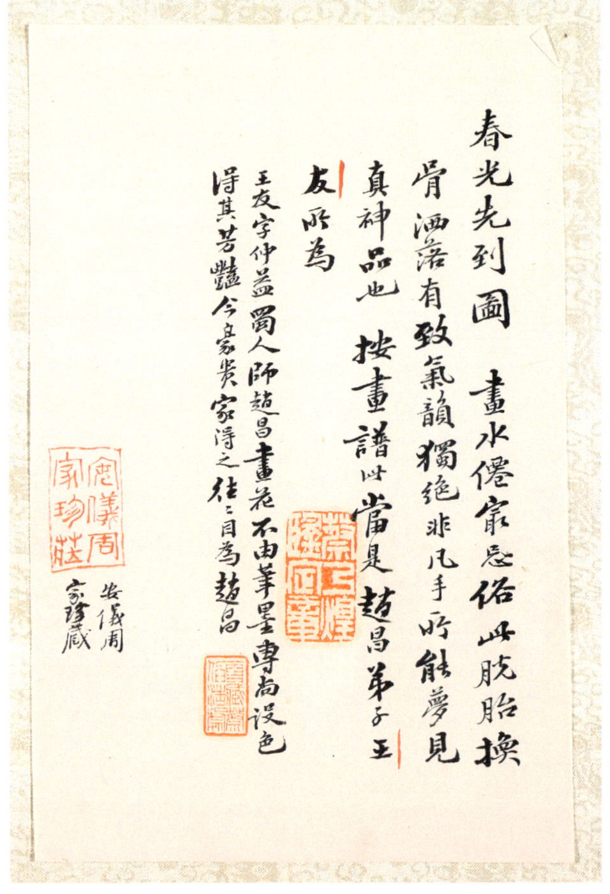

*Narcissus*, verso

A book is a very special kind of object. The apparent simplicity of its material form belies a tremendous vastness—unfathomable journeys across unmapped territories and narrow introspections plummeting deep into the crevasses of the human mind. In books, time and space are infinite dimensions constantly folding, collapsing, and unraveling. Stories ebb and flow. Knowledges are threaded; line after line, they shape patterns around and through which we attempt to make sense of more-than-human encounters.

Historians have traced the origin of books back to the fourth millennium BCE—a time when commerce in Egypt, India, China, Mesopotamia, and Central America flourished. Keeping precise track of transactions became increasingly important as the complexity of bureaucratic administration outstripped the capacity of human memory.[1] But it would be reductive to say that books were invented simply as a means of streamlining government business. The significance of the written word has always been much greater. Words are the descendants of lines drawn on cave walls by our ancient ancestors. All kinds of representation, whether outlined as pictograms, conveyed in mimetic form, or invoked by the alignment of graphic symbols, bear the imprint of a profound existential longing. They manifest a desire to piece together what was once whole, and to preserve that blueprint for eternity.

Nowhere is this ancient relationship between writing and drawing more evident than in Chinese art and cultural history. During the Song dynasty (960–1279), the same brushes that outlined the crests of mountainous ranges, that followed the zigzagged contours of twisted cypresses, that accentuated the dignified verticality of bamboo, also elegantly articulated calligraphic characters. On paper, the juxtaposition of the two was known as *wu-sheng-shih* (silent poetry), a longing for a kind of harmony with nature that resounds and echoes through the drawn line and the pictogram that reverberate in the human soul. The careful combination of charred pinewood and resin produced ink of the blackest color. Rice, wheat straw, sandalwood bark, hibiscus stalks, and seaweed fibers, macerated and pressed, made paper.[2] The silence of plants pervaded the very substance of Chinese painting and incarnated the focus and restraint that characterized Buddhist philosophy.[3] Drawings and words quickly forged a powerful alliance.

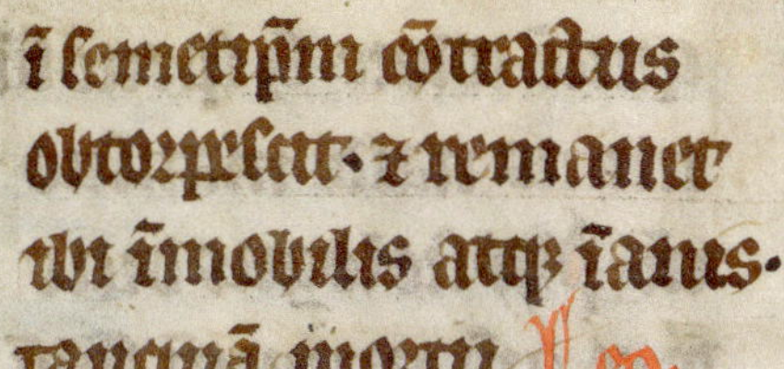

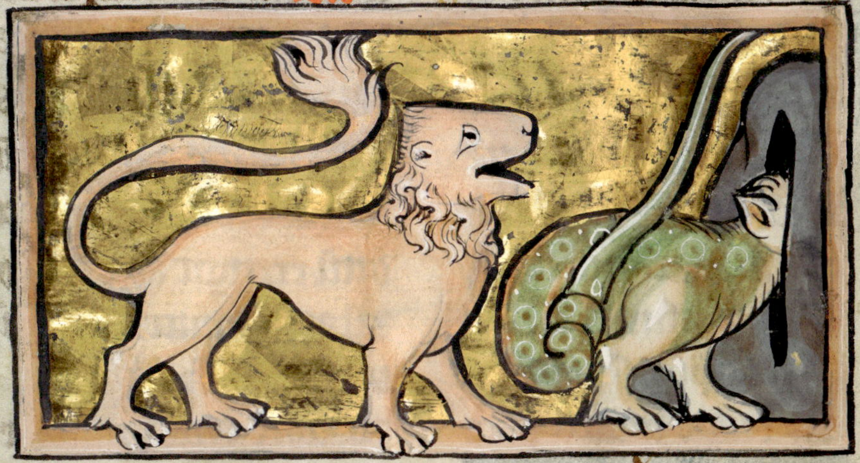

Unknown Franco-Flemish artist, A Lion (Panther) and a Dragon, ca. 1277 or after, tempera colors and ink

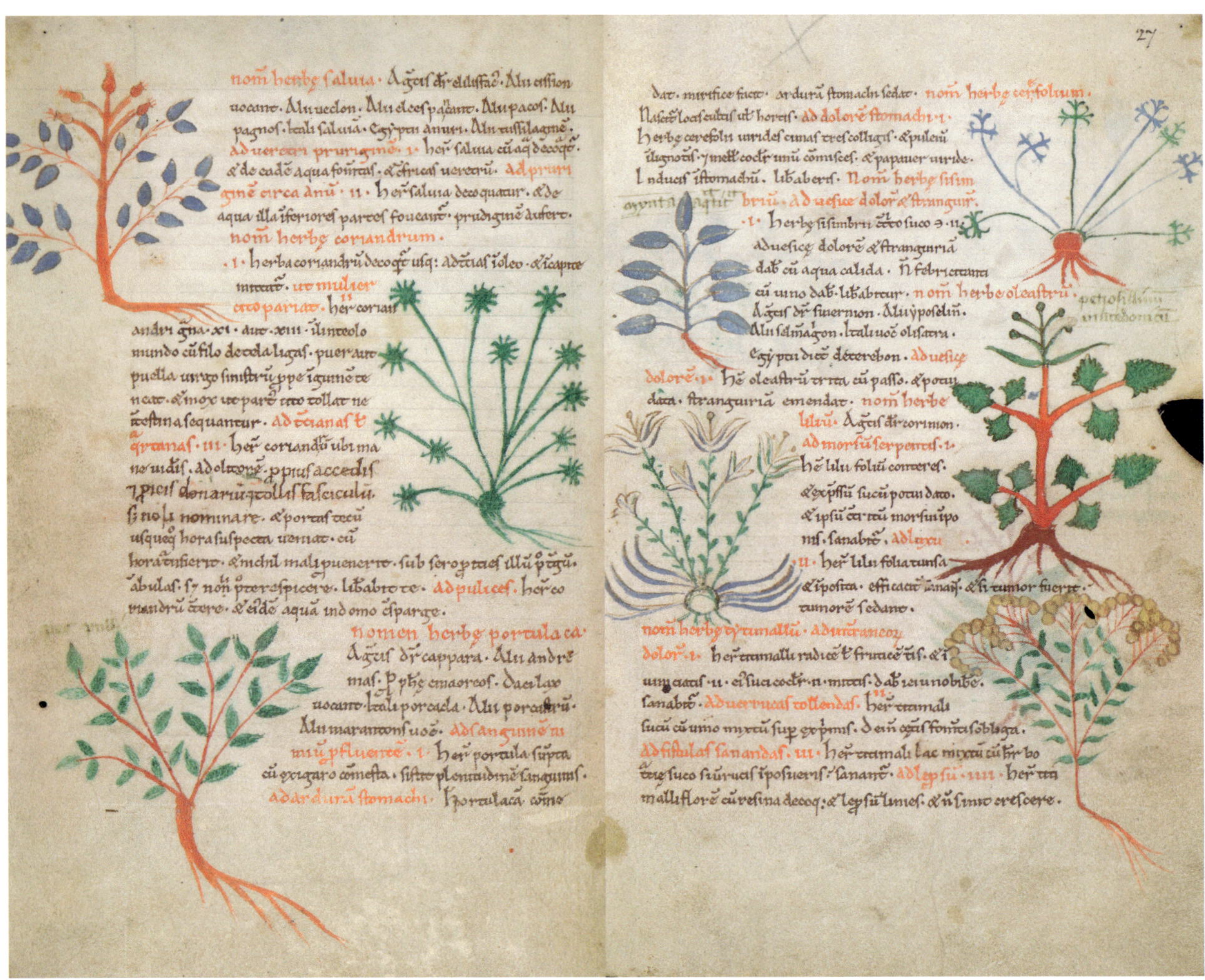

***Salvia*** **(sage),** ***Coriandrum*** **(coriander),** ***Portulaca*** **(purslane),** ***Cerefolium*** **(chervil),** ***Sisimbrium*** **(water mint),** ***Oleastrum*** **(alexanders),** ***Lilium*** **(lily),** ***Tytimallum*** **(spurge), ca. 1070–1100, colored drawings on parchment**



The healing powers of plants became central to human survival, and this further strengthened the entwinements between plants, words, and images. Plant healing has for millennia been indissolubly enmeshed with magic and mythology. Forty thousand years ago, shamans drew images of nature on cave walls to tell stories from the otherworld, communicate with animals, heal, and accompany the spirits of the deceased on their last journey. Sacred herbs transported shamans to far spiritual worlds during their hallucinogenic trances and euphoric mystical experiences. They colluded with the greater power of plants to transcend the confines of their human bodies and trigger a level of cosmic connection, allowing them to recognize diseases and find cures. Empowered by psychotropic plants, shamanic artistic expressions—whether through dance, performance, or painting—penetrated reality beyond the surfaces of things and across time.[4] It has been claimed that ingestion of psychotropic substances from plants or mushrooms may have deeply impacted our ability to form social bonds, something that accelerated and expanded language development.[5] Plants—along with mushrooms, their closest allies—might have played a key role in shaping human brains and thinking structures.

Much shamanic ancient knowledge is now lost, but some can still be found in early medicinal treatises. A five-thousand-year-old Sumerian clay tablet from Nagpur, one of the oldest documents in the history of medicine, features twelve recipes involving more than 250 species of plants—many alkaloid-based and thus important as pharmaceuticals, narcotics, and stimulants.[6] Among the most expansive medicinal collections is the Papyrus Ebers, dating to ca. 1500 BCE, which features eight

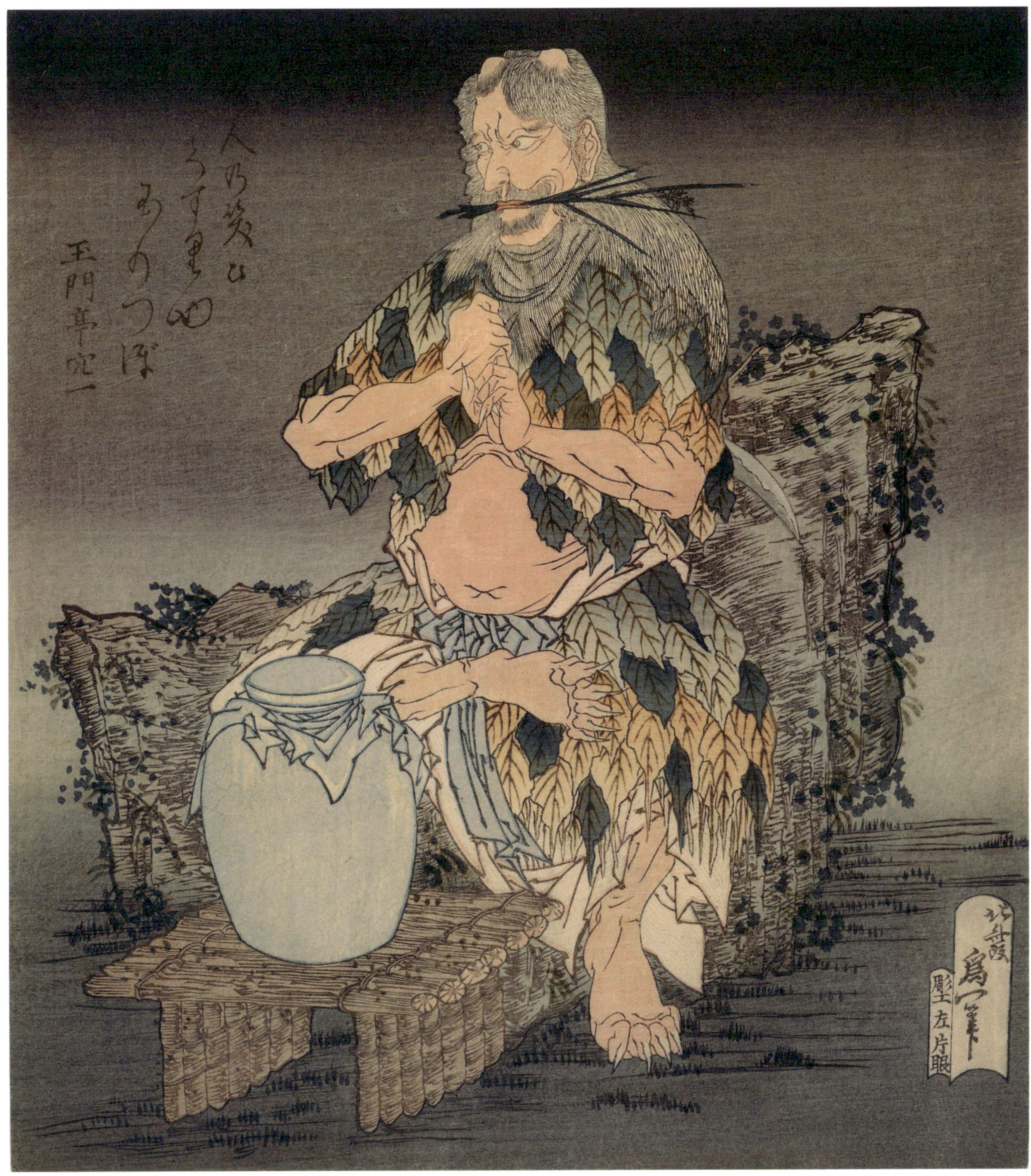

Katsushika Hokusai, *Shennong in a coat of leaves with blades of rice in his mouth, seated on a rock, his* takara-no-tsuba *(treasure jar) before him*, ca. 1820s, woodblock print

hundred prescriptions involving seven hundred different species of plants, many of them still popular today in homeopathic medicine, for instance aloe, garlic, and willow.[7] Ancient classical treatises like the Rigveda, the oldest of the sacred books of Hinduism (ca. 1500–1000 BCE), as well as the Atharvaveda, the Charaka Samhita, and the Sushruta Samhita, also feature a wealth of plant-based remedies still in use today.

A lengthy oral Chinese tradition of plant medicine was transcribed in the Daoist Huainanzi (Book of Huainan) during the second century BCE. According to this text, the legendary Chinese Yan Emperor Shennong instructed individuals to observe

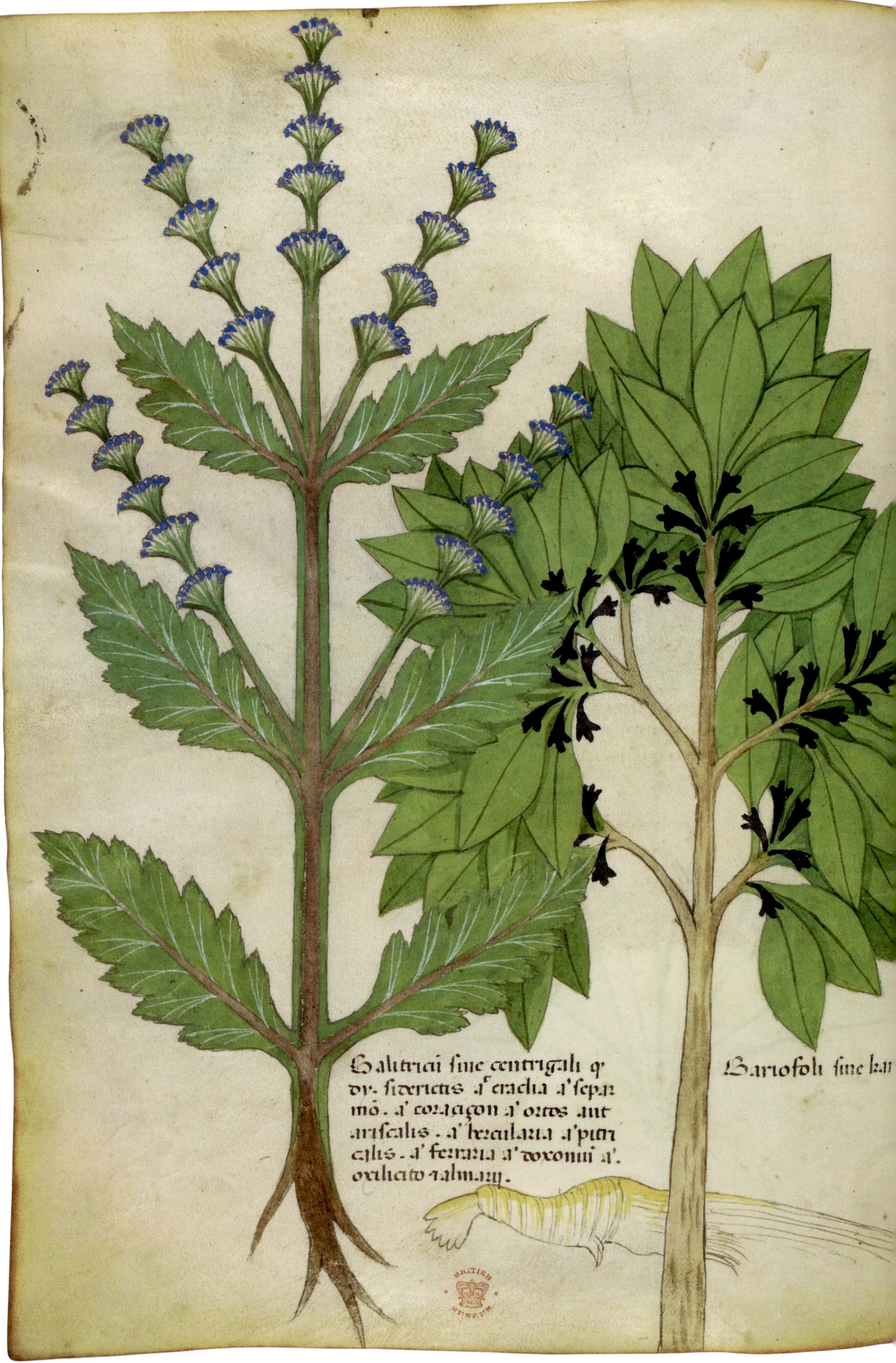

Unknown North Italian artist (Lombardy), Illustration in *Tractatus de Herbis*, ca. 1440, parchment

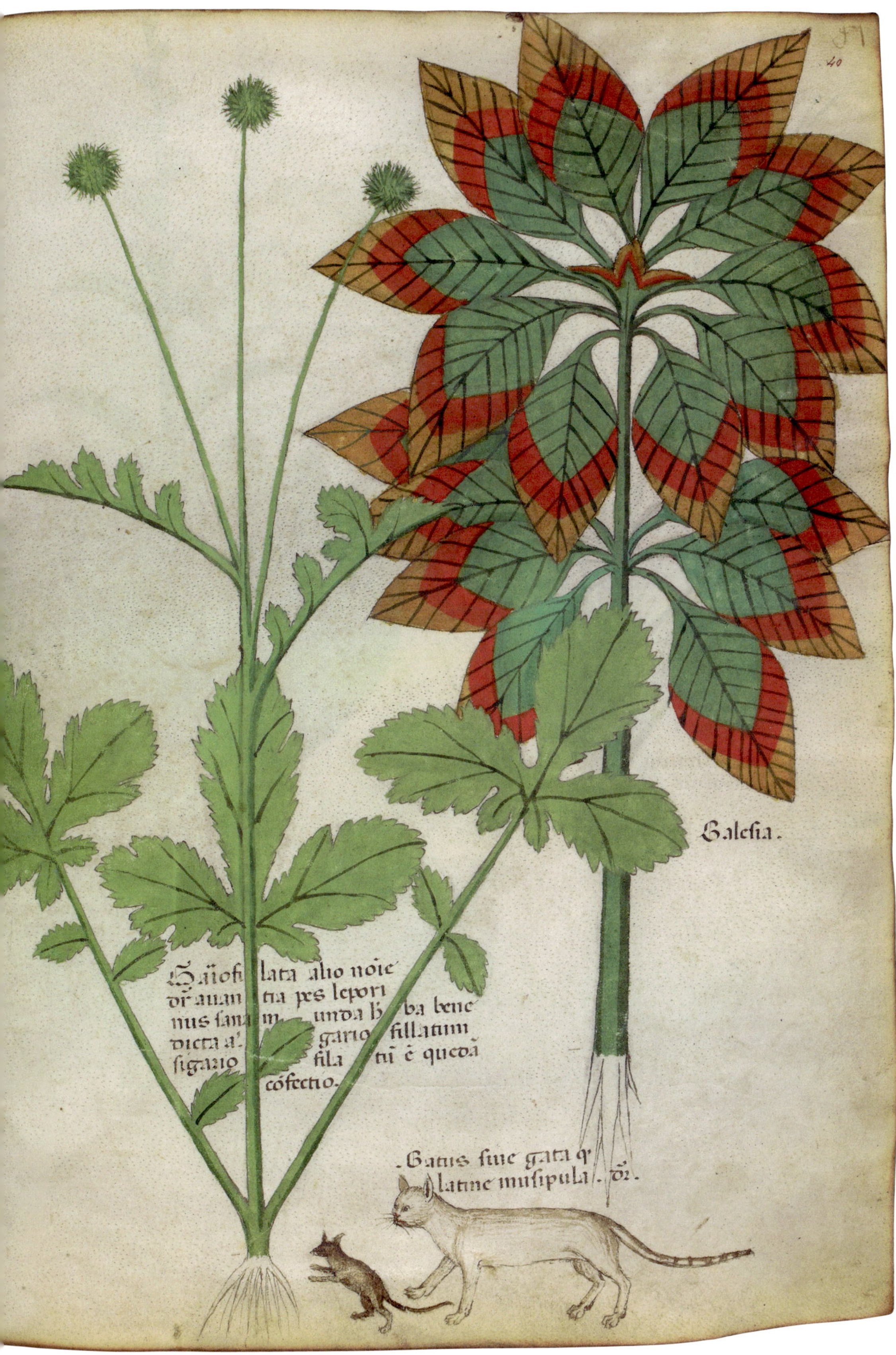


67

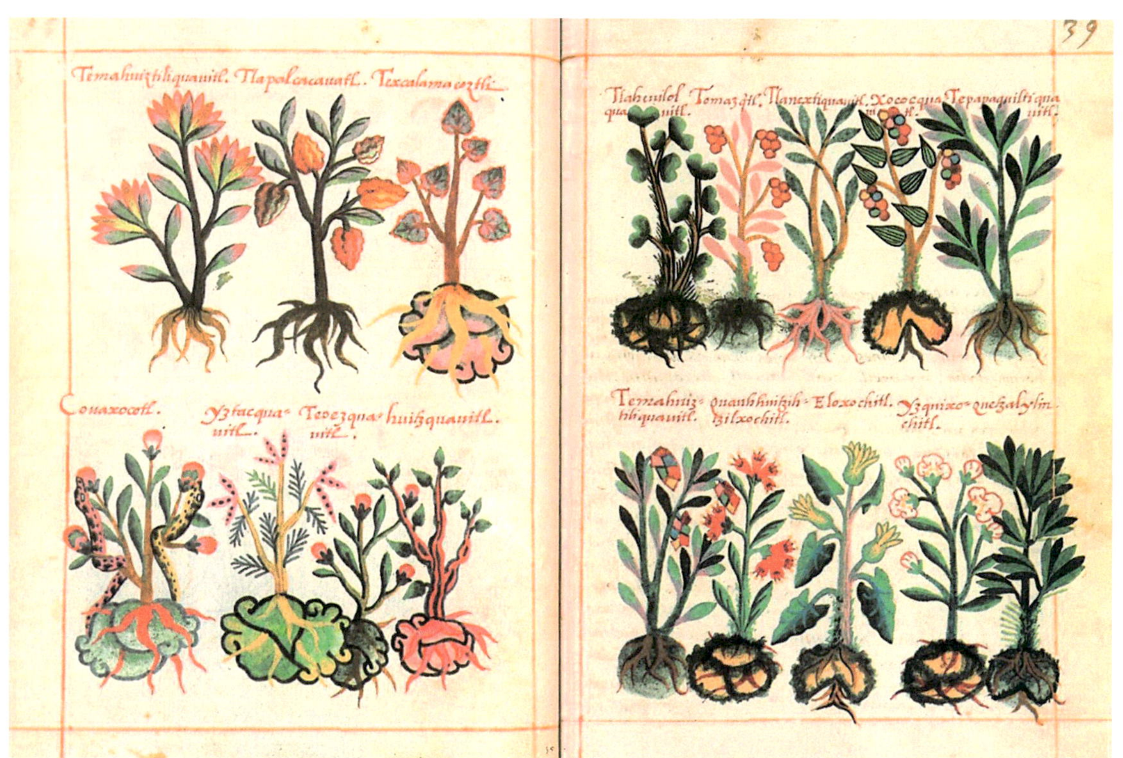

Martín de la Cruz, Illustration in *Libellus de Medicinalibus Indorum Herbis*, 1552, Aztec manuscript



plants with the intention of enhancing prosperity and well-being.[8] By the first century BCE, the complicity between images and words strengthened further. Pliny the Elder mentions that Crateuas's herbal, known as *Rhizotomica*, was the first to feature hand-colored images of plants: the first illustrated book might have been a botanical treatise. This became a model for the authors of sacred manuscripts as well as bestiaries.[9] One of the most popular illustrated books of the Middle Ages, the bestiary blended paganism-influenced animal tales with Christian moral principles. Realism wasn't the point of such books. Rather, animals played pious or monstrous roles in a morality play that saw plants relegated to the backdrop. But despite this, the success of bestiaries across Europe helped reignite interest in ancient herbals.

Illustrated versions of Dioscorides's *De materia medica* (On Medical Matters, ca. 50–70 CE) were among the very earliest herbals to circulate again during the Middle Ages. Another very early title was the *Herbarium Apulei Platonici* (fourth century CE), credited to Apuleius Platonicus. A medieval naturalist was essentially a theologian, since knowledge of the natural world was produced in monasteries. Hildegard of Bingen, a musically accomplished abbess who oversaw the large herb garden at Rupertsberg abbey in Germany, was among the first to systematize a wide knowledge of therapeutic plants in her seminal *Physica*, published between 1151 and 1158. Many of the treatments it contains are still regarded as beneficial today.

At this time, plants were represented in rather crude manners—stylized and oversimplified—so using herbal illustrations for identification in the wild proved difficult. And when nuns and monks reproduced texts and images, they often applied changes that, from copy to copy, made the depictions appear less and less like their live referents. Then in 1440, a copy of a copy of an older herbal was expanded with new illustrations made, for the first time, from life studies. Even though *Tractatus de Herbis* was not scientifically accurate by today's standards, the pictures' enhanced realism helped to establish and formalize the discipline of botany.

It took twenty-four years to finish one of the most exquisitely illustrated herbals ever created. Starting in 1545, it was sourced and assembled in Mexico City. Titled *La Historia General de las Cosas de Nueva España* (today known as the Florentine Codex), the book features more than two thousand illustrations made by twenty-two Indigenous Nahua artists working under the guidance of Spanish Franciscan friar Bernardino de Sahagún. Written in Nahuatl and translated into Spanish, the book contains the most comprehensive firsthand accounts of Aztec life and culture as well as a sizable herbal section.[10] In 1552, Nahua sages Martín de la Cruz and Juan Badiano, along with a team of local artists (most likely still working under Sahagún), produced the *Libellus de Medicinalibus Indorum Herbis*, the first true herbal in the history of the Americas. The growing influence of Christianity might account for the omission of mythological and mystical narratives in *Libellus*, a text that focuses predominantly on medicinal knowledge.[11]

At the same time, in Europe, the resurgence of optical realism, which gave Renaissance art its distinctive stylistic accuracy and solidity, owed its impetus to the study of botany just as much as to the renewed admiration for classical Greek and Roman art. The rise of empirical Aristotelian approaches that ultimately bolstered realism as the essence of Renaissance art compelled artists to relentlessly refine their vision and concentrate on the smallest of details—a transition that instigated a revolution in representation and culture.[12] To the early Renaissance naturalist, truth lay unequivocally in the details. According to the mindset of the time, the greatness of God's creation was encoded in the minute, particular features distinguishing one plant from another. A closer examination of vegetation encouraged the development of optical sciences; the more people observed, the more they were compelled to describe. Vocabularies rapidly expanded to map new visual territories, thus magnifying the ability to express and thereby master reality. Medieval Islamic botanists, including Al-Dīnawarī, Ibn Juljul, and Ibn al-Bayṭār, who were originally motivated to study plants evoked in the Qur'an's description of paradise, carried out important—and until recently, overlooked—pioneering work in this field of study.[13] By the second half of the eighth century, this original purpose had been supplanted by a desire to attentively observe and systematize plants beyond the religious context. The anonymous *ʾUmdat al-tabīb fī ma'rifāt al-nabāt li-kull labīb* of the twelfth century set the groundwork for a taxonomy of plants organized by genus (*jins*), species (*naw'*), and variety (*sanf*), predating Carl Linnaeus's nomenclatural system by nearly six hundred years.

Muslim botanists were also pioneers in understanding the role of topography, climate, and soil in plant development.[14] Their holistic approach greatly influenced, among others, the work of sixteenth-century Italian botanical master Gherardo Cibo, whose astute observations and original iconographical creations shifted plants from the background to the foreground of representation, casting them as protagonists of new vegetal narratives. Roots, pistils, stamens, trichomes—Cibo's extremely detailed images revolutionized the way Westerners looked at the natural world. Given their natural stillness, which eminently lent itself to drawing, plants became the ideal subject through which the shift from mythology to science could unfold. In their natural state, they were more easily observed and investigated than animals, which often had to be killed to be precisely described.

In early illustrated herbals, artists typically allowed the flatness and rectangular shape of the page to guide the composition, occasionally twisting the natural forms of branches and leaves in an effort to fill it. Instead, Cibo gave each depiction the solemnity and boldness of a Renaissance altarpiece, with the plant effectively usurping the heavenly ascent of a saint. Grandiose, often floating in midair, roots exposed: each of Cibo's specimens is unequivocally glorified, not as an otherworldly deity but as a living, earthly miracle. Vastly improving on the rudimentary and often awkward juxtapositions of human and plant forms typical of early herbals, Cibo framed his vegetal subjects in vividly three-dimensional, painterly backgrounds, accurately describing their habitats. In addition, he depicted laborers whose survival was dependent on that specific plant. Women kneeling in the field are seen collecting crocus flowers early in the morning before the petals unfurl and disperse the precious rust-colored pollen known as saffron. The botanist was meticulous to the point of fastidiousness, and his dedication to fieldwork was unparalleled. He keenly recorded what at first might seem wholly irrelevant—each plate included the location, day, and hour in which the plant was collected, as well as the names of the naturalist's

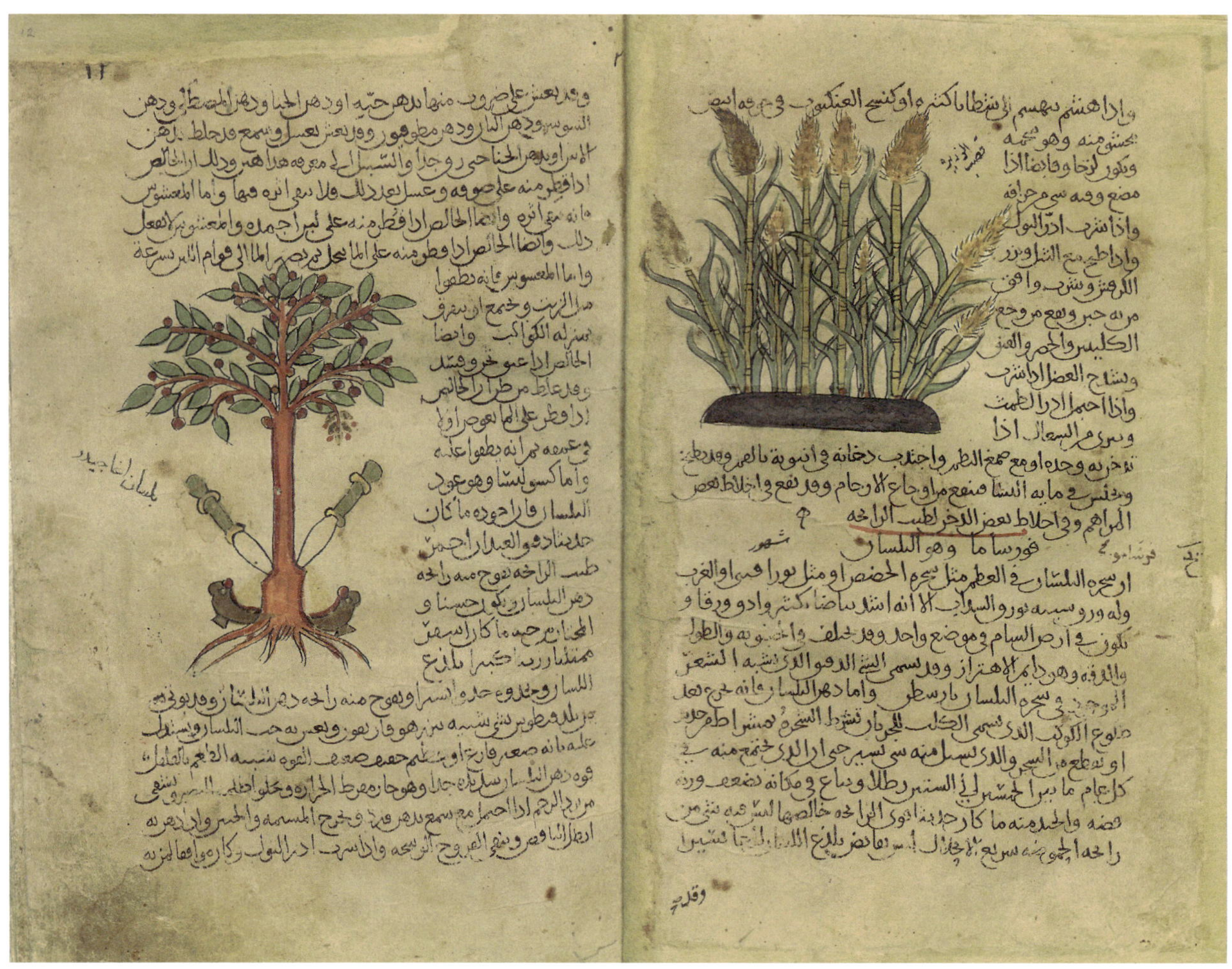

Ḥunayn b. Isḥāq al-ʿIbādī, Abū Zayd and Stephanus b. Bāsīl, Illustration in *Kitāb al-Ḥašāʾiš fī hāyūlā al-ʿilāǧ al-ṭibbī*, ca. 847–861 CE, Arabic manuscript on paper



helpers.[15] His practice set disciplinary standards and protocols that are still followed today, from archaeology to anthropology.

A major influence on Cibo's work was also that of Albrecht Dürer, one of the most inventive artists of the Northern Renaissance and a contemporary of Leonardo da Vinci. Dürer believed that

> the more precisely the forms in your work are compatible with life, the better it will appear. That is the truth. So never imagine that you can or should attempt to make something better than God has allowed his created nature to be. For your ability is impotent compared to God's creativity.[16]

The artist's most eloquent manifestation of this belief was his groundbreaking watercolor of a chunk of meadow titled *The Great Piece of Turf* (1503). The impeccable attention to detail in the representation of each minute plant part was unprecedented. From cock's-foot to creeping bent, smooth meadow-grass, daisy, dandelion, germander speedwell, greater plantain, hound's-tongue, and yarrow, nobody had previously dedicated so much attention to weeds, the absolute underdogs of the botanical world. Intricate and lush, these unremarkable plants not only challenge our gaze and ability to focus, but also drastically shift our point of view from that of a human to that of a small creature—a mouse, a lizard, perhaps a frog. Dürer's weeds, devoid of any symbolic value, likewise ask us to forgo prevailing cultural hierarchies in order to perceive the awesome complexity of these plants on their own ground. Its intimacy, delicacy, and accuracy make this image one of the earliest and most modern attempts to combat plant blindness in the history of Western art. Keenly observed from life, Dürer's study set a new

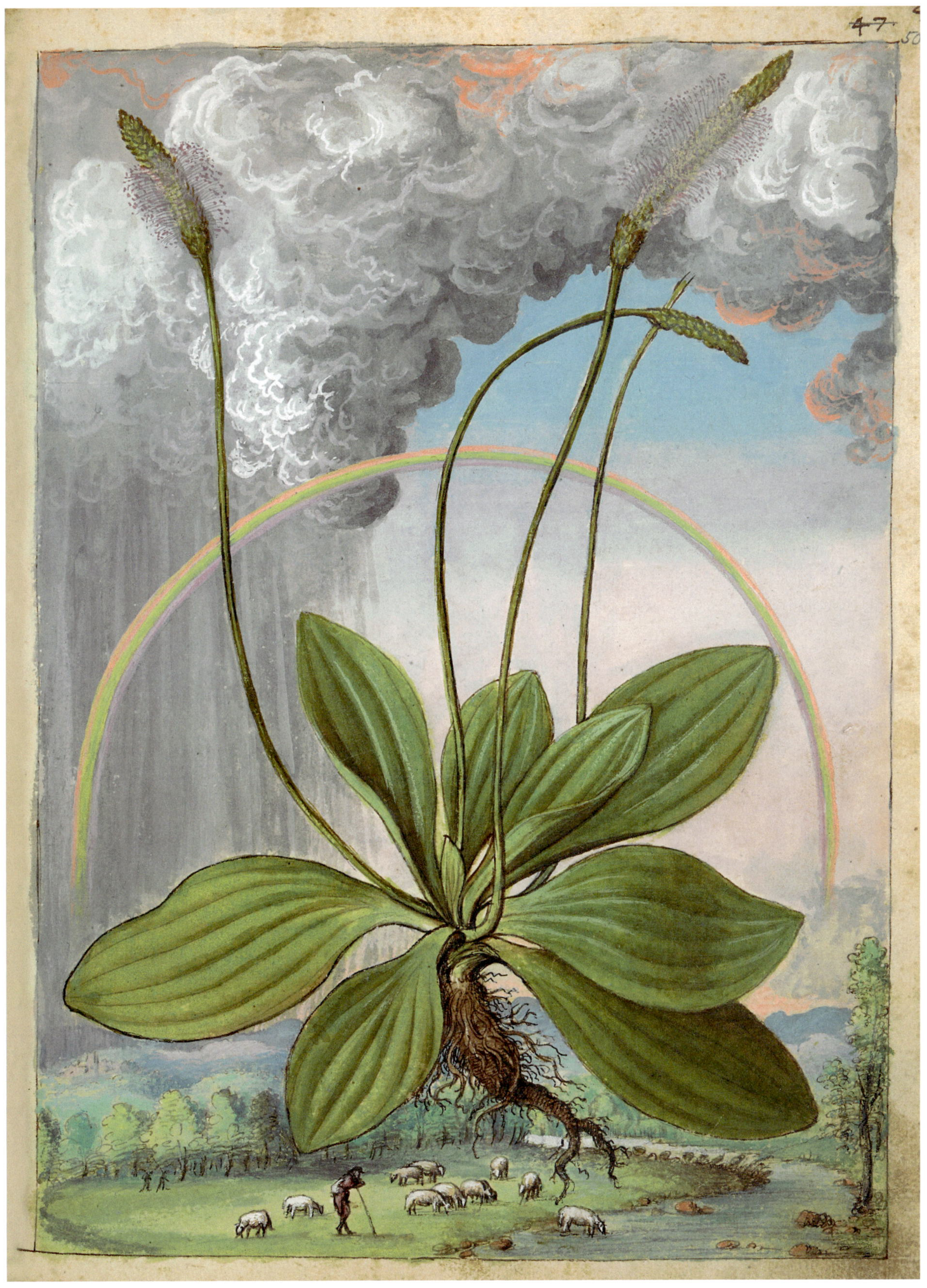

Gherardo Cibo, *Plantain*, in *Extracts from Dioscorides's De materia medica*, ca. 1564–84, watercolor and gouache on paper

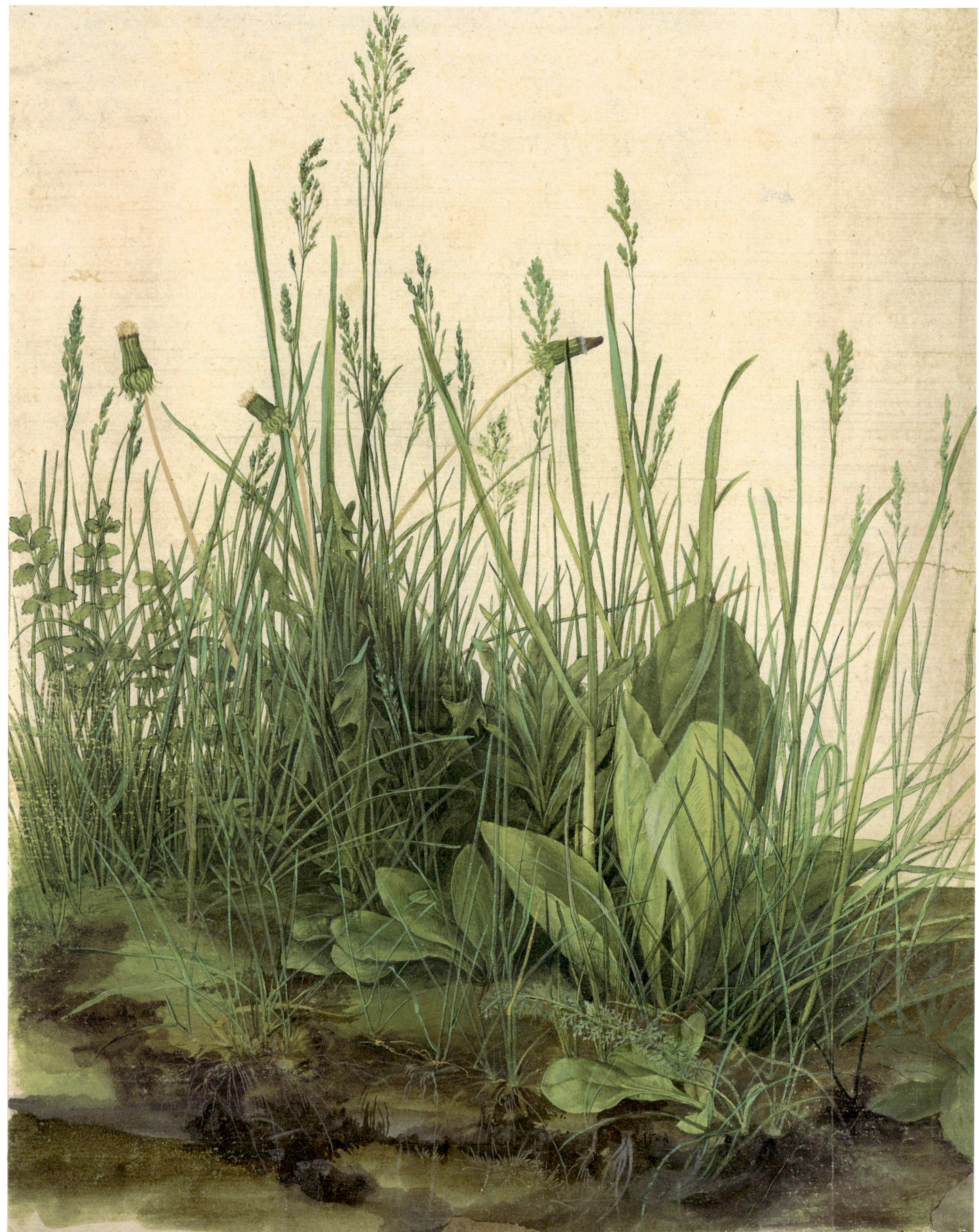

Albrecht Dürer, *The Great Piece of Turf*, 1503, watercolor

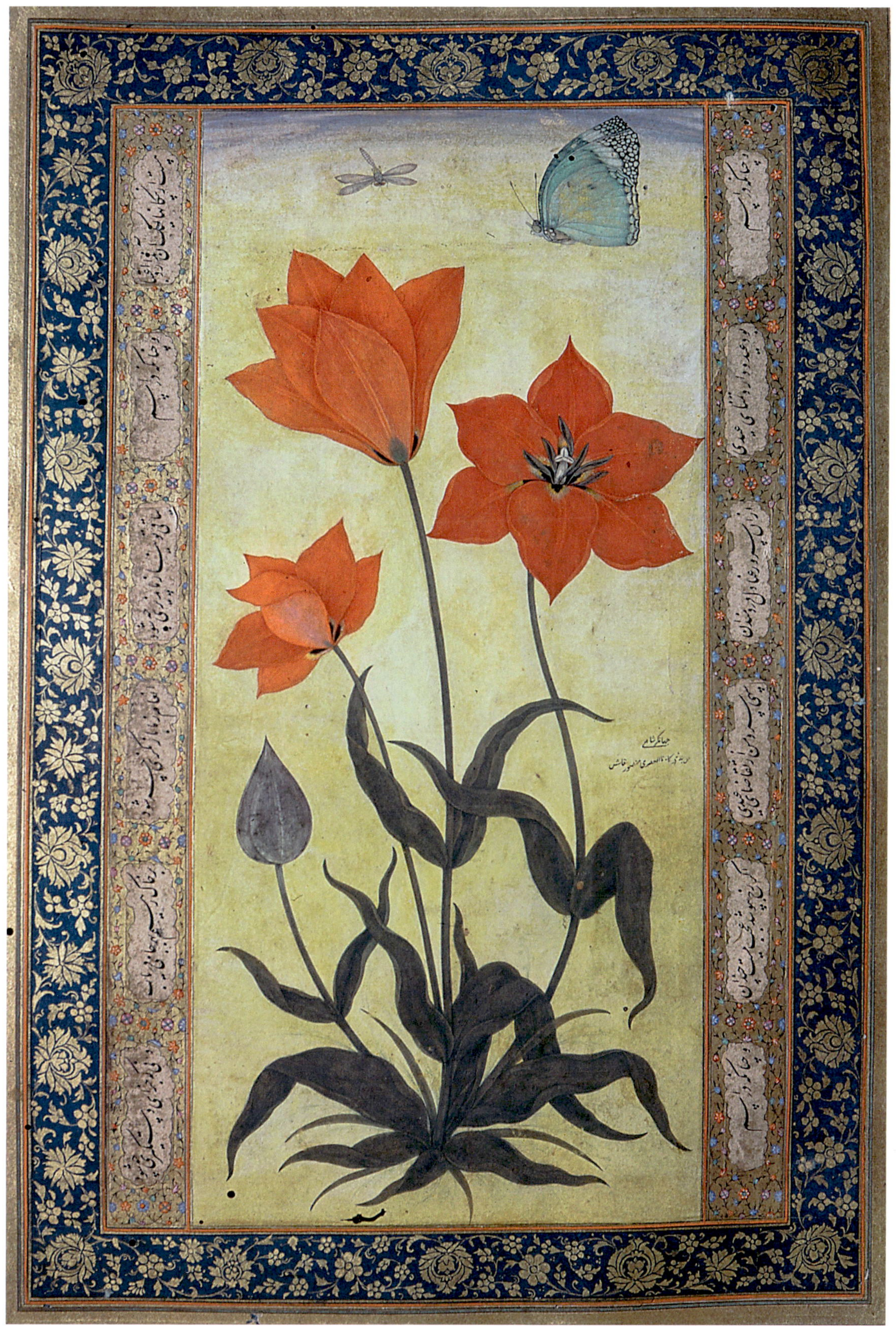

Ustad Mansur, *Red Tulip*, ca. 1620–21, opaque watercolor, gold, ink, and paper

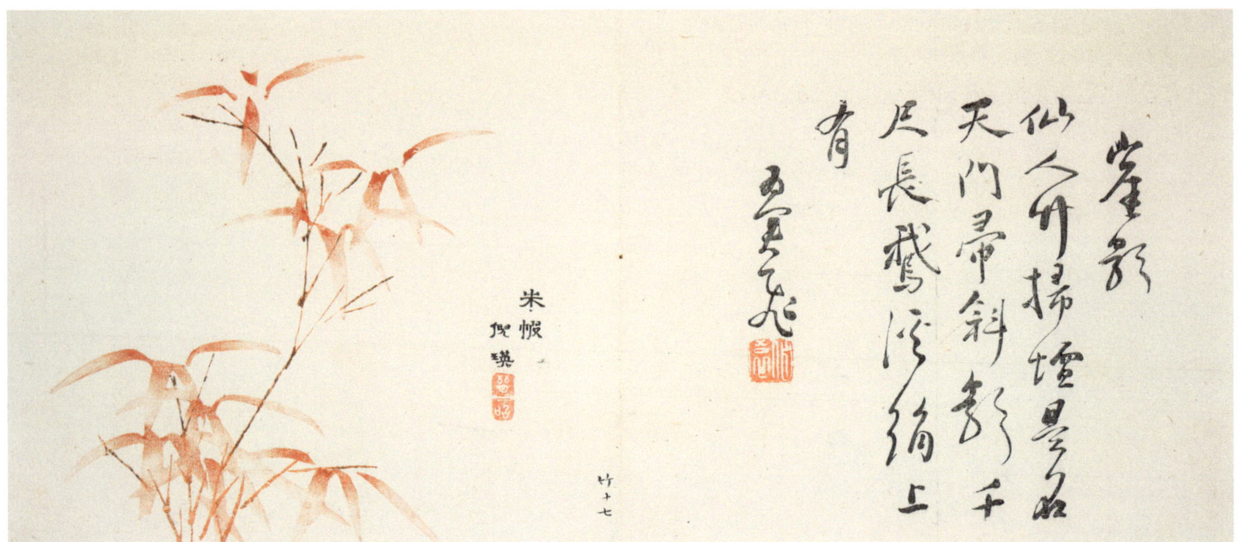

Hu Zhengyan, *Red Bamboo*, 1663, woodblock print, ink and color on paper

benchmark for art as well as for the nascent discipline of natural history.[17] It is no coincidence that the study of zoology emerged from that of botany; the optical coordinates, methodologies, and linguistic parameters of the former were predetermined by the properties of the plant kingdom.

Meanwhile, a predilection for ever more realistic representations of plants was also flourishing in India. During the 1620s, the artist Ustad Mansur visited Kashmir, in the northernmost reaches of the Indian subcontinent, where he documented more than a hundred indigenous flowering plants.[18] Mansur's work stood apart from that of his forebears and contemporaries in large part due to his observations from life. In collaboration with Emperor Jahangir, an enthusiastic supporter of natural studies, Mansur produced some of the most detailed representations of plants and animals in Indian history. And by incorporating precise depictions of the insects that frequented the flowers into his botanical studies, the artist also expanded the botanical register to include an ecological dimension that had hitherto been disregarded. This move foreshadowed the emergence of artistic approaches that would gain prominence in Europe during the eighteenth century.

While in the Middle East and Europe the study and representation of plants was entwined with medicinal, and to an extent agricultural, purposes, China and Japan nurtured an appreciation of plant life that transcended any kind of practical application. The art of flower painting as an independent school emerged in China during the Tang dynasty (618–907 CE). Artist Hsü Hsi, the school's founder, would keenly observe the plants in his garden and carefully outline each part of the leaves, flowers, and branches in ink before applying color. In doing so, he was able to improve on the precision of earlier plant representations.[19] By the eleventh century, careful observation of botanical subjects in preparation for painting had become standard practice. In an essay on landscape painting written during the eleventh century, artist and theorist Kuo Hsi instructed: "Those who study flower painting take a single stalk and put it into a deep hole, and then examine it from above, thus seeing it from all points of view."[20]

But not everyone agreed that art should provide accurate representations of reality. During the eleventh century, toward the end of the Song dynasty (960–1279), the poet, politician, writer, calligrapher, painter, and aesthetic theorist Su Shi landed in hot water for subverting the traditional representation of bamboo. Having run out of black ink, he decided to depict the plant in red ink left over from exam marking. His colleagues asked him, "Where have you ever seen red bamboo?" to which he replied, "Where have you ever seen one as black as ink?" Eager to make his point, Su Shi argued that anyone who regards painting as a realist pursuit has "the understanding of a child." This exchange got him banished from Emperor Huizong's court. But it didn't take long for this revolutionary, nonconformist gesture to inspire others. Su Shi is today remembered as a pioneer of the abstract Mandarin painting tradition.[21] His red bamboo radically altered the history of Chinese painting. From that point onward, the Northern School aimed to depict nature realistically, and the Southern School emphasized abstraction and primarily used black ink.

But new approaches to the portrayal of bamboo changed more than Chinese art history; they also played an important part in the gender revolution. In China, aristocratic women were only allowed to learn painting under the tutelage of an open-minded, literati husband. It was under these circumstances that Guan Daosheng found the path that led her to become one of the most prominent female Chinese artists in the country's history. Guan's father encouraged her talent from an early age, and Zhao Mengfu, her calligrapher, painter, and artist husband, helped her study traditional botanical works. In 1296 she began to paint orchids, regarded as a feminine subject for their incarnation of rarity, fragility, and purity. Her work was extremely detailed, based on careful observation from life. But it was her bamboo paintings that sealed her status as a true and legendary artist.[22] Historically, bamboo was considered a symbol of masculinity due to its tenacity in the face of inclement weather and its capacity to bend without breaking, which were read as signs of unwavering companionship and fortitude. Guan single-handedly broke with this long-standing patriarchal tradition. Her groundbreaking depiction of the plant's overall character conveyed an audacious wholesomeness that would later become a reference point for Chinese female painters.

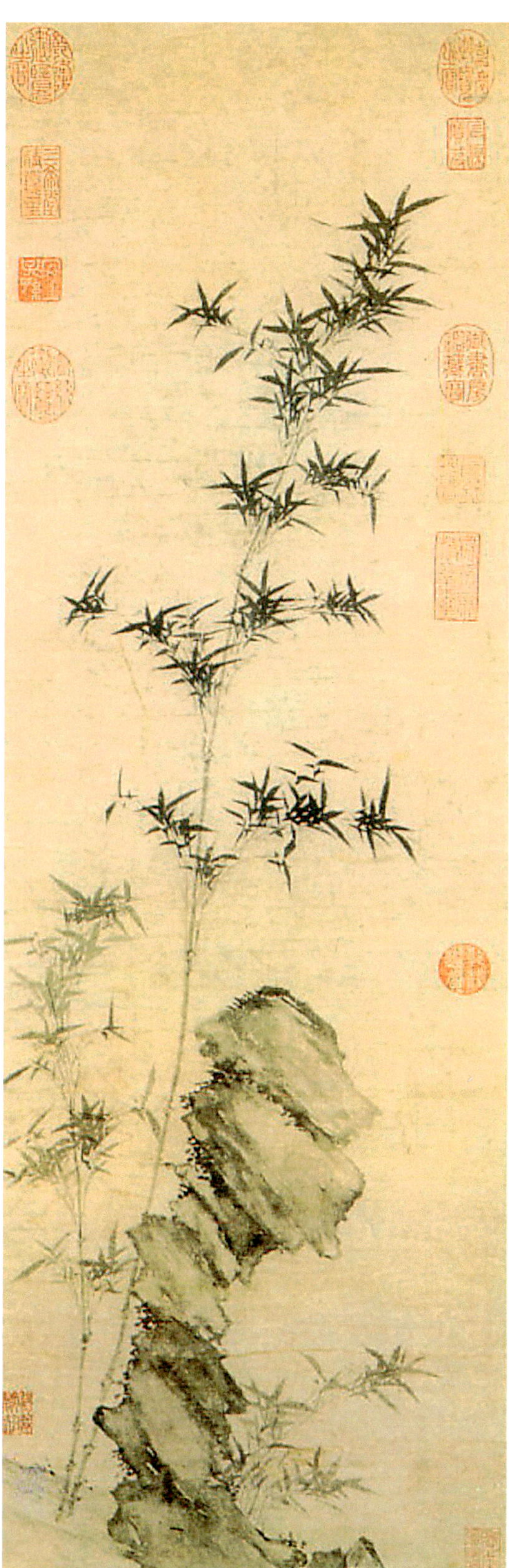

**Guan Daosheng, *Bamboo and Stone*, Yuan Dynasty, ca. 1262–1319, ink on paper**

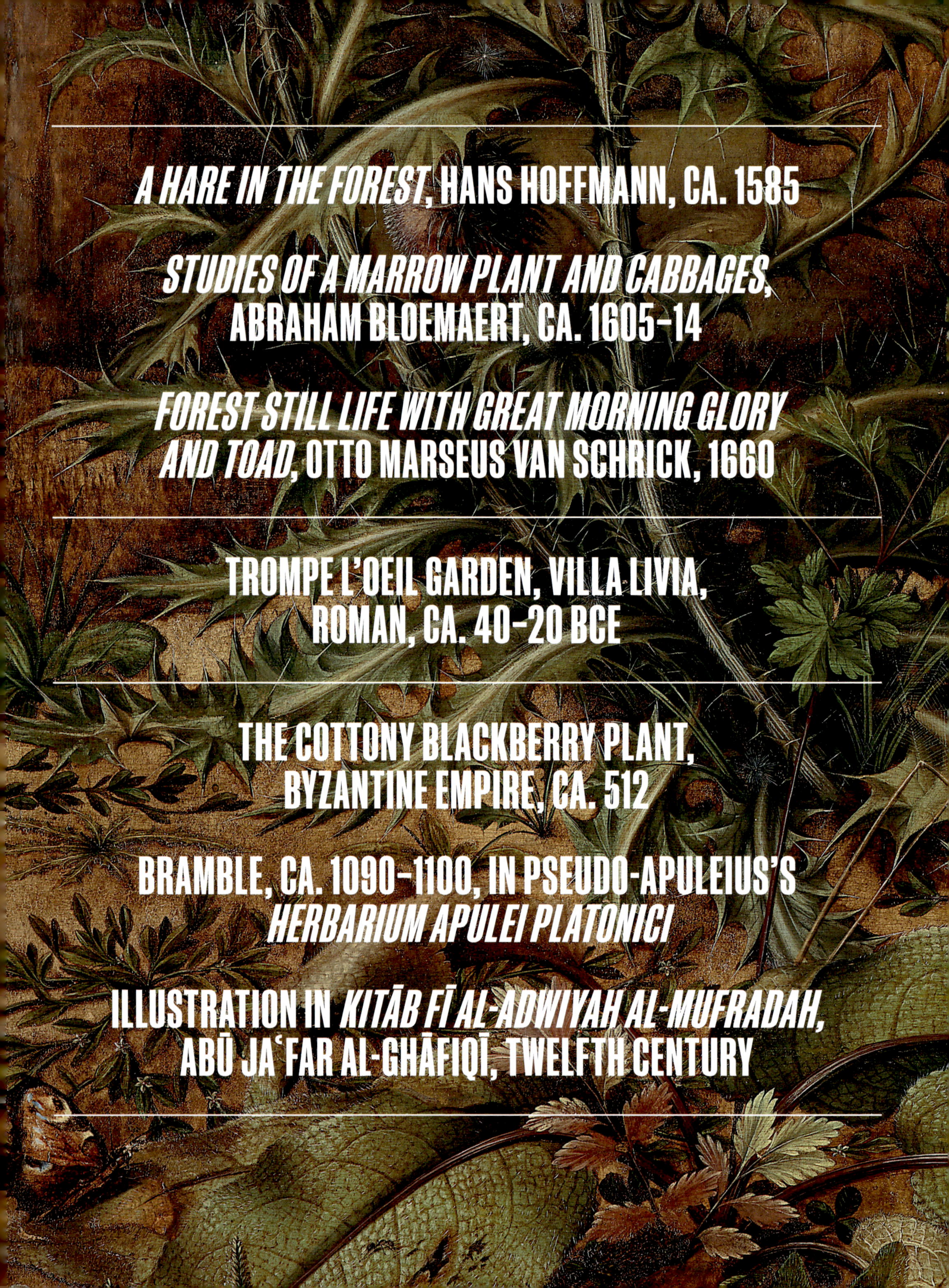

*A HARE IN THE FOREST*, HANS HOFFMANN, CA. 1585

*STUDIES OF A MARROW PLANT AND CABBAGES*, ABRAHAM BLOEMAERT, CA. 1605–14

*FOREST STILL LIFE WITH GREAT MORNING GLORY AND TOAD*, OTTO MARSEUS VAN SCHRICK, 1660

TROMPE L'OEIL GARDEN, VILLA LIVIA, ROMAN, CA. 40–20 BCE

THE COTTONY BLACKBERRY PLANT, BYZANTINE EMPIRE, CA. 512

BRAMBLE, CA. 1090–1100, IN PSEUDO-APULEIUS'S *HERBARIUM APULEI PLATONICI*

ILLUSTRATION IN *KITĀB FĪ AL-ADWIYAH AL-MUFRADAH*, ABŪ JAʿFAR AL-GHĀFIQĪ, TWELFTH CENTURY

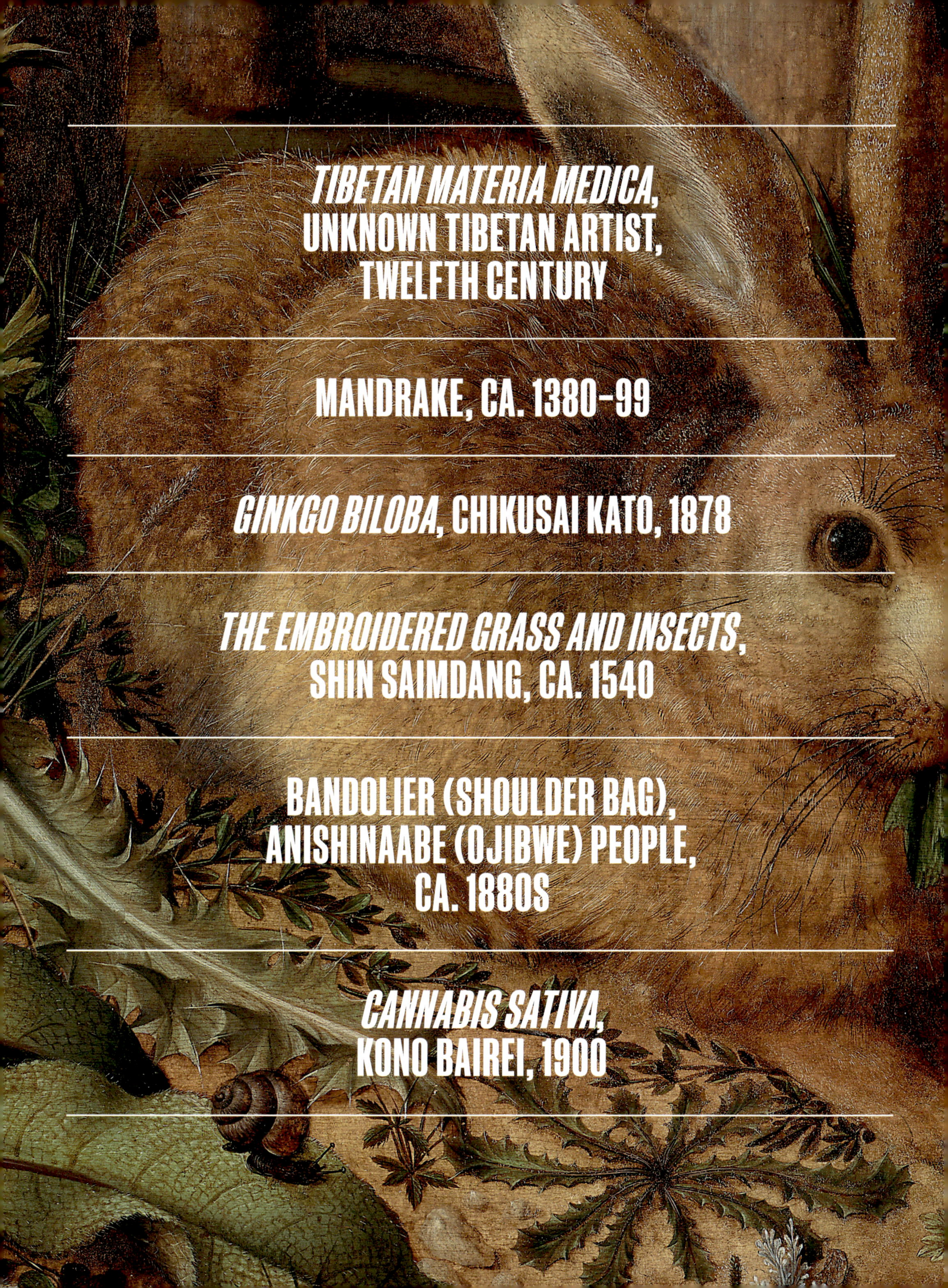

*TIBETAN MATERIA MEDICA*,
UNKNOWN TIBETAN ARTIST,
TWELFTH CENTURY

MANDRAKE, CA. 1380–99

*GINKGO BILOBA*, CHIKUSAI KATO, 1878

*THE EMBROIDERED GRASS AND INSECTS*,
SHIN SAIMDANG, CA. 1540

BANDOLIER (SHOULDER BAG),
ANISHINAABE (OJIBWE) PEOPLE,
CA. 1880S

*CANNABIS SATIVA*,
KONO BAIREI, 1900

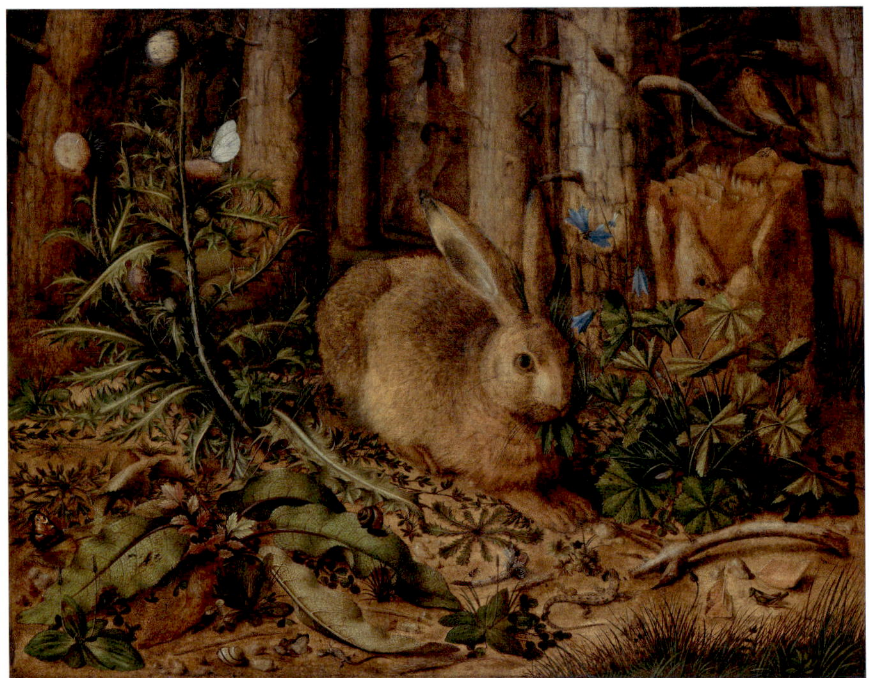

Hans Hoffmann, *A Hare in the Forest*, ca. 1585, oil on panel



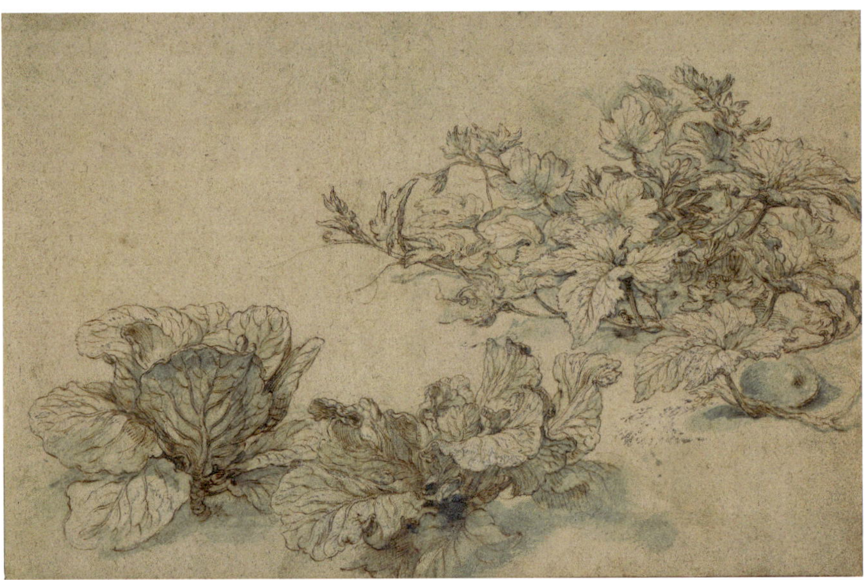

Abraham Bloemaert, *Studies of a Marrow Plant and Cabbages*, ca. 1605–14, ink, wash, and gouache

The resurgence of Greek and Roman classical culture in Italy at the end of the fourteenth century fostered a return to realistic representations of the natural world. More than ever before, artists endeavored to accurately reproduce the glorious complexity of creation as a way of parsing the meaning of God's master plan: the more naturalistic the representation, the higher the spiritual conquest. The Renaissance marked a return to the Aristotelian empirical model—the theory within philosophy that we can only acquire true knowledge from experience of the physical world, gained through the senses. And the emerging current of humanism—attaching prime importance to human life over all other forms—fostered a desire to produce more objective knowledge of nature. Yet religion continued to exert a significant influence on the depiction and portrayal of plants and animals.

Following the pioneering work of Leonardo da Vinci and Albrecht Dürer, several painters began to cultivate a profoundly symbolic yet realistic vocabulary, directing their attention to the intricate marvels found within the undergrowth. To these artists, the forest bed became a stage upon which to dramatize the perennial fight between good and evil. Toads, hares, snakes, lizards, butterflies, moths—the colorful cast

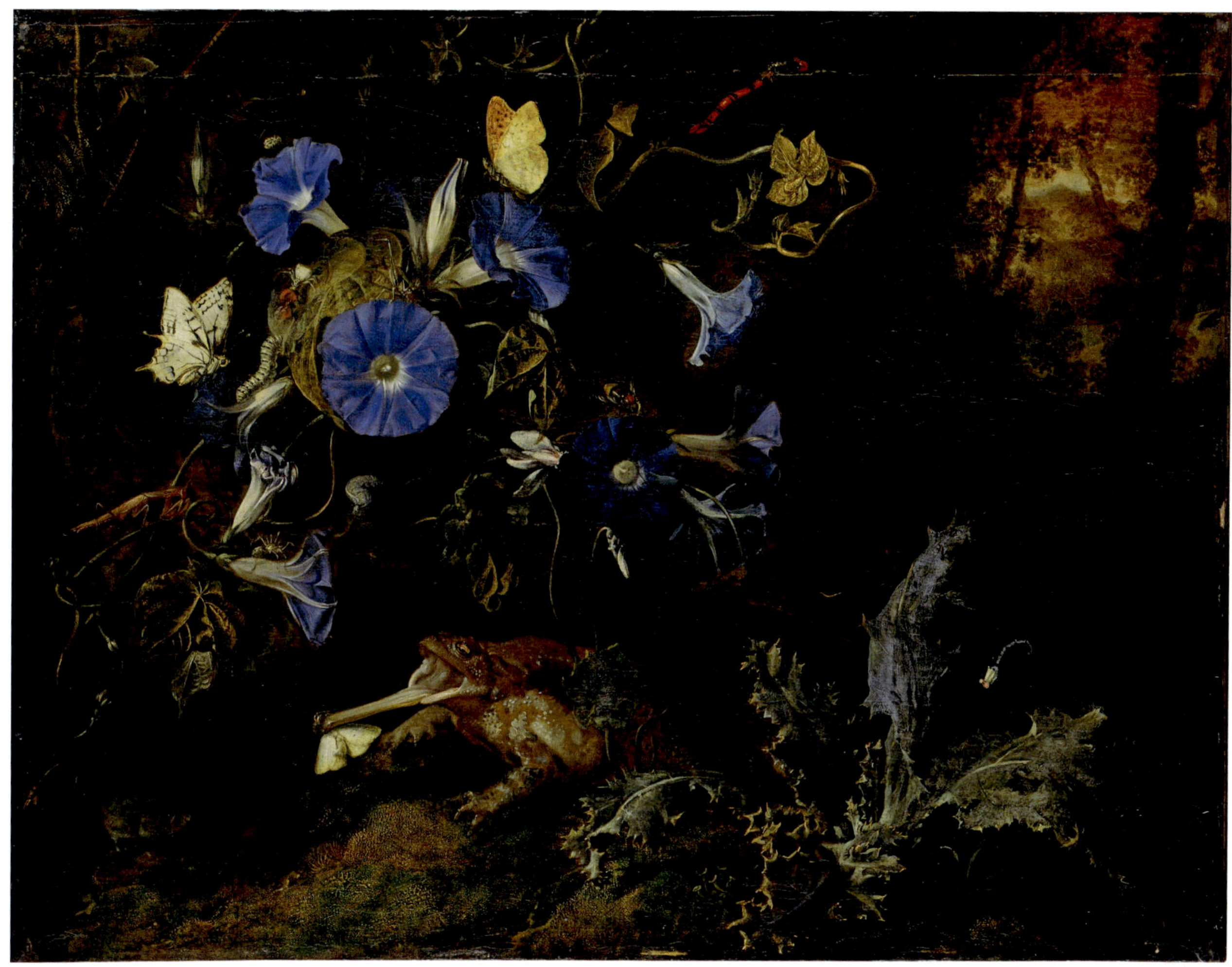

Otto Marseus van Schrick, *Forest Still Life with Great Morning Glory and Toad*, 1660, oil on canvas



of cold-blooded species battling to survive served as allegories for Christian morals. Butterflies symbolized the human soul, and snakes the devil. Hares were symbols of birth and resurrection, while bees represented the idea that collaborative hard work is rewarded in Heaven. Plants played critical roles in the construction of context in the emerging genre of *sottobusco* (undergrowth). It was no coincidence that natural-looking yet highly staged confrontations between good and evil often were portrayed as taking place at the foot of a tree, in a subtle allusion to the Tree of Life. To convey a sense of unmediated truth, artists favored wild flora over the groomed cultivars that thrived in gardens. The spiky anatomy of various species of thistle, for instance, referred to Christ's agony during his crucifixion. Through vivid realism, these paintings essentially inscribed Christian values directly into the natural order, implicitly affirming God's preeminence over everything.

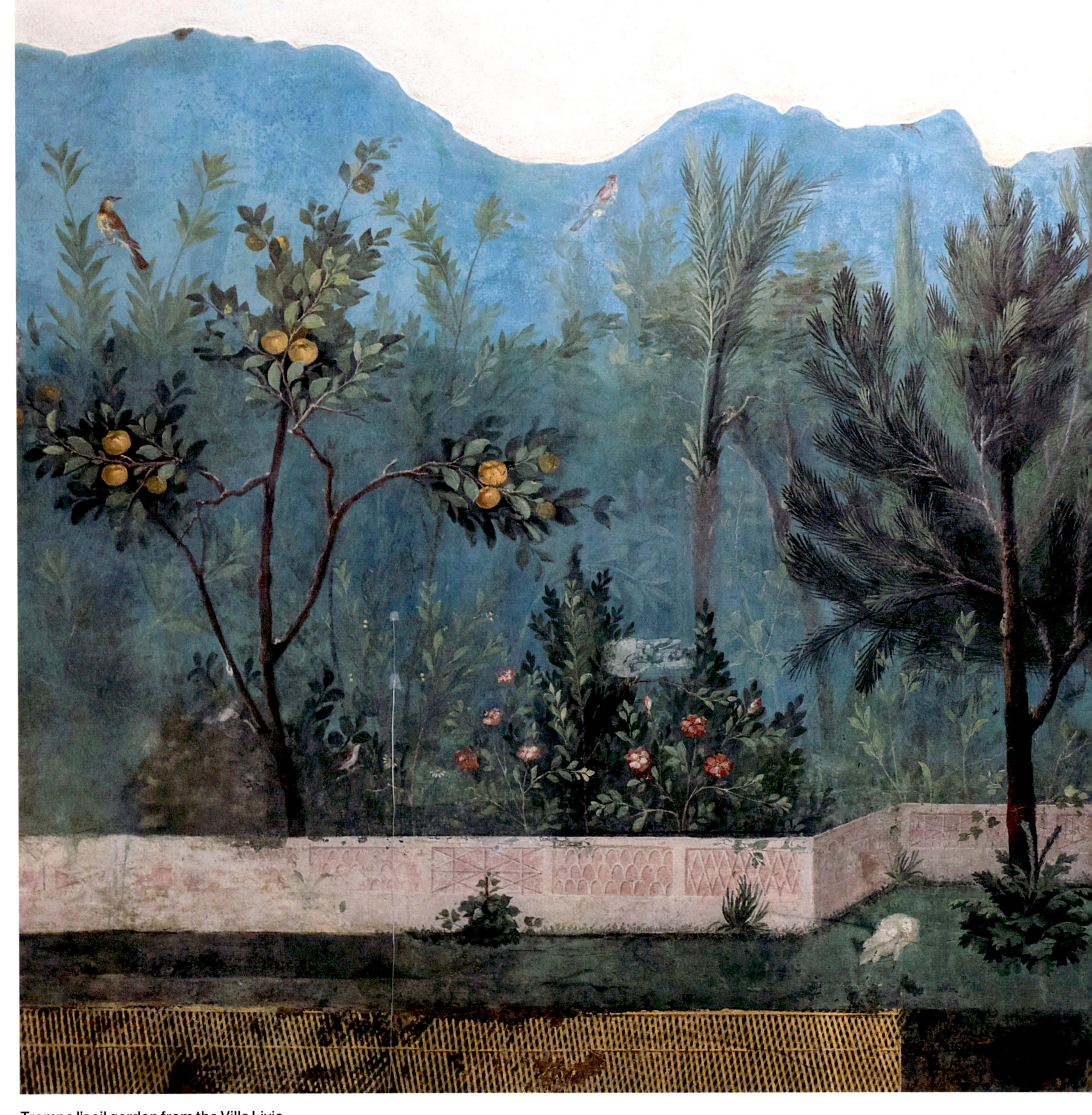

Trompe l'oeil garden from the Villa Livia, Roman, ca. 40–20 BCE, fresco

This image of a verdant garden is one portion of a rare and exquisitely executed fresco that covers an entire subterranean chamber at Villa Livia in Prima Porta, close to Rome. Painted by an anonymous artist around 40–20 BCE, this imaginative work was commissioned by Empress Livia Drusilla, wife of Emperor Augustus. In a remarkable example of early trompe l'oeil, a low wall enhances the compositional sense of depth and perspective. On either side of it, a multitude of plant and

# TROMPE L'OEIL GARDEN

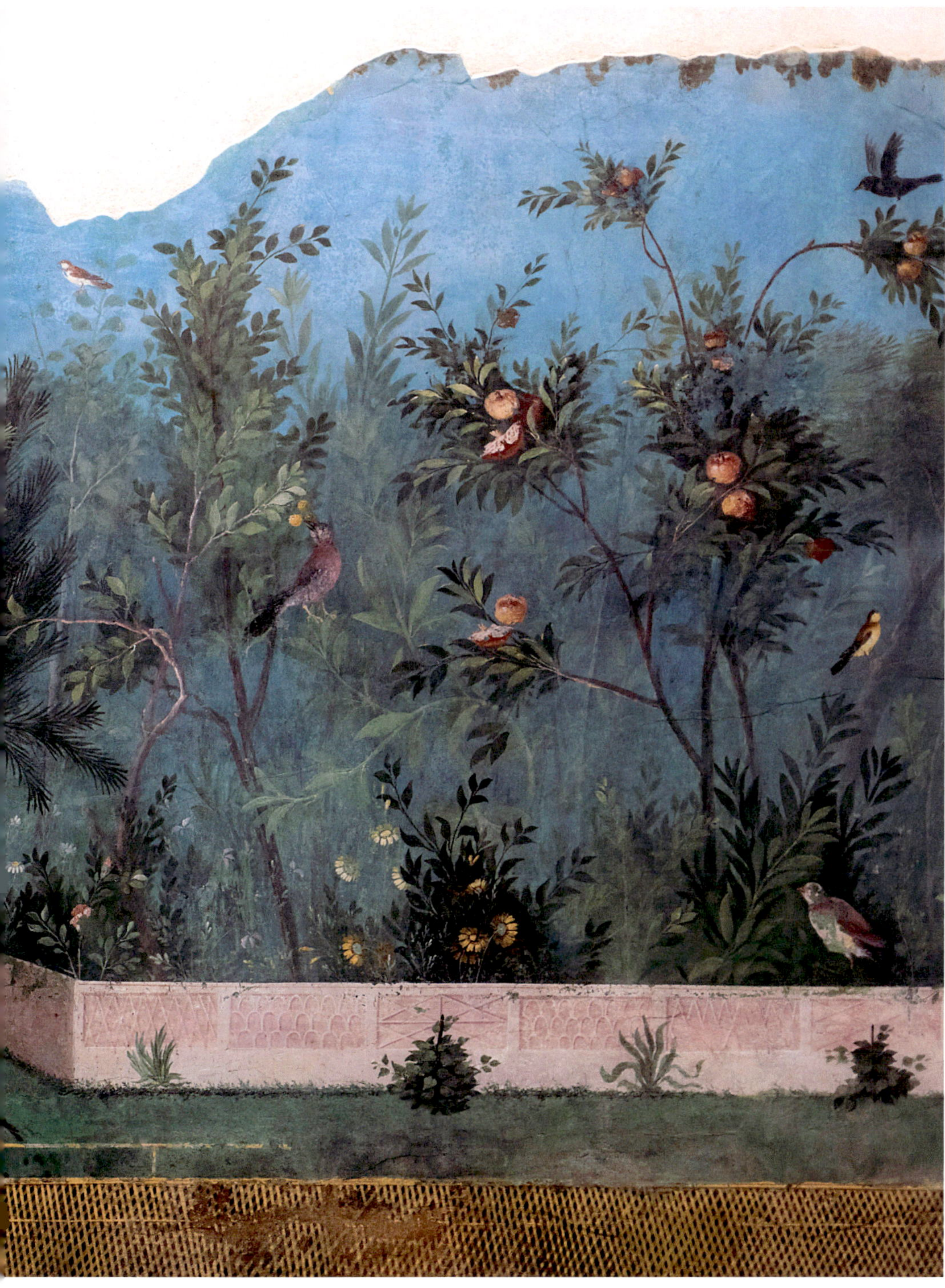



tree species are represented with impeccable realism and attention to detail. All of the depicted flora, which include pines, oaks, quinces, and a variety of wildflowers, are local to the area, making this far from a fantastical garden. While it remains unclear whether the theme and composition served a specific allegorical function, it is thought that this room was used in the winter to evoke serene memories of summer outdoor dining. The fresco's originality lies in its indeterminacy: it is neither a formal garden nor a forest, but a transitional zone where plants seem to embrace human activity in a comforting and benevolent way.

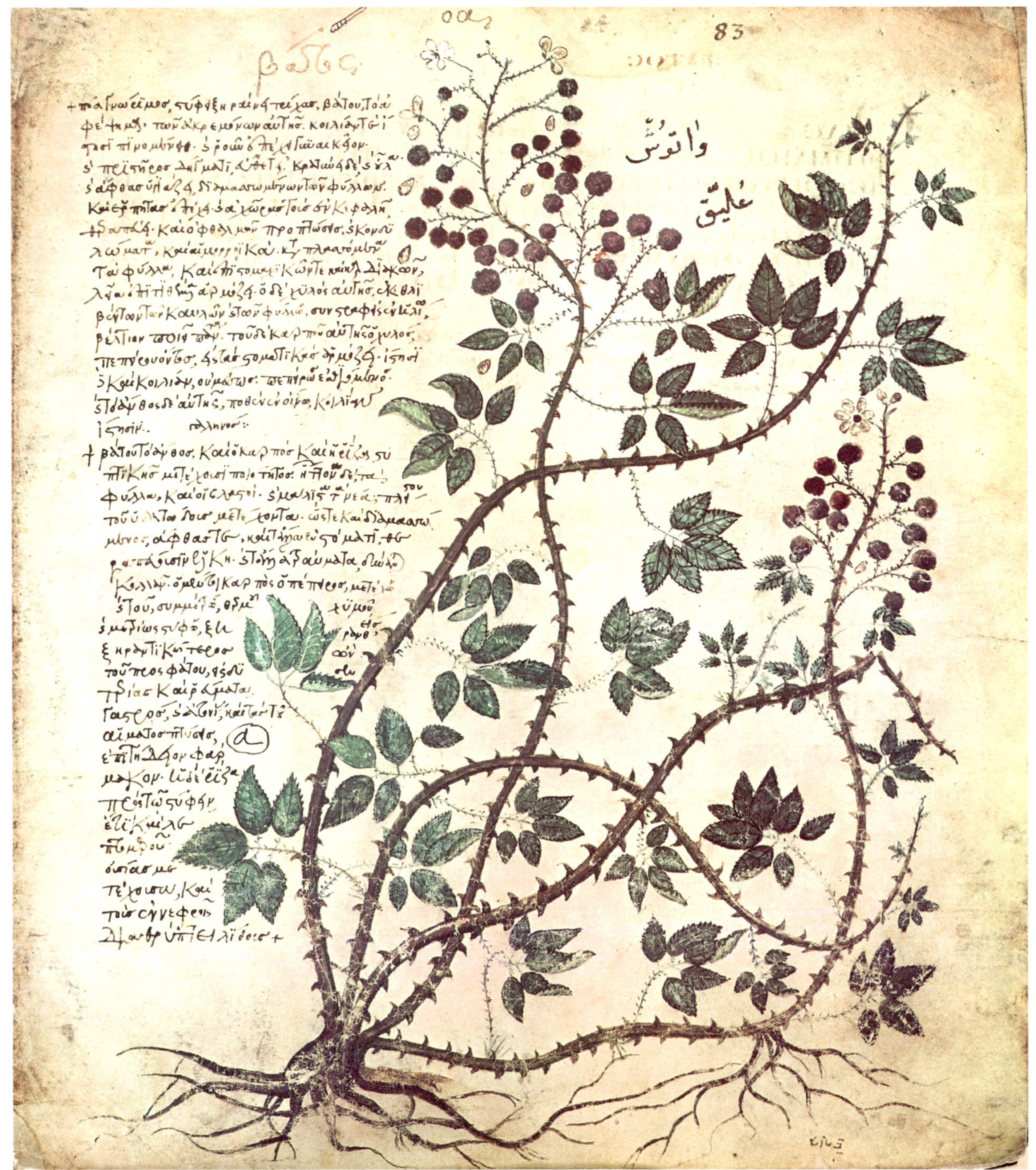

**Unknown Byzantine artist, Illustration of the cottony blackberry plant (*Rubus tomentosus*), with roots, leaves, and fruits, ca. 512, parchment**



Herbals are among some of the most important books ever written. Surviving examples are priceless repositories of wisdom and traditions. The most valuable are lavishly illustrated, often featuring hand-colored woodblock prints. The degree of realism differs considerably from one herbal to the next, but it generally improved with newer editions. One of the most famous and oldest existing illustrated herbals is the *Vienna Dioscorides*, created around 512 CE for the imperial princess Anicia Juliana in Constantinople, whose 491 folios feature four hundred images of plants and animals. Like other herbals, it is a compendium of several different scientific texts written by many authors. The vast majority derive from *De materia medica* by Dioscorides, a Greek medical practitioner who served as a physician in the Roman army during the first century CE.

A significant portion of the knowledge that eventually

# ILLUSTRATION OF THE COTTONY BLACKBERRY PLANT

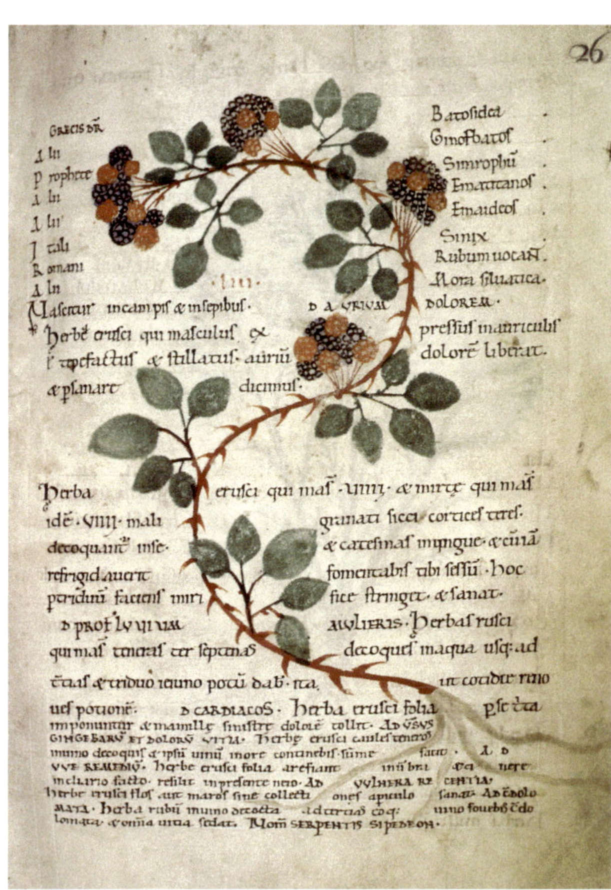

Bramble, in Pseudo-Apuleius's *Herbarium Apulei Platonici*, ca. 1090–1100, parchment

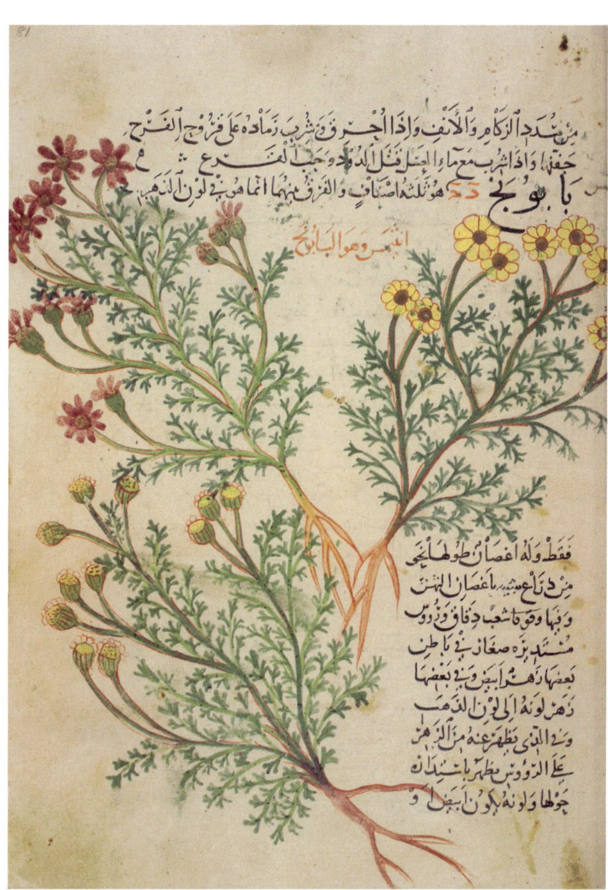

Abū Jaʿfar al-Ghāfiqī, Illustration in *Kitāb fī al-adwiyah al-mufradah*, twelfth century, Andalusia, thick, wove Oriental paper

formed the basis of Western herbals traces back to the Middle East, for instance *Kitāb al-Jāmiʿ li-mufradāt al-adwiya wa-l-aghdhiya* (The Book of Medicinal and Nutritional Terms), compiled in the early thirteenth century by Ibn al-Bayṭār and collecting more than fourteen hundred accounts of plants, foods, drugs, and their uses. Over time, unacknowledged information from other authors was frequently incorporated into new editions of old books, their translations, and entirely new titles. With each successive edition, artists reimagined the intricate connection between plant imagery and textual elements, often pioneering compositions that seamlessly integrated the two, aesthetically embodying a need for a naturally harmonious sense of fluidity between nature and knowledge.

## BRAMBLE

## ILLUSTRATION IN *KITĀB FI AL-ADWIYAH AL-MUFRADAH*

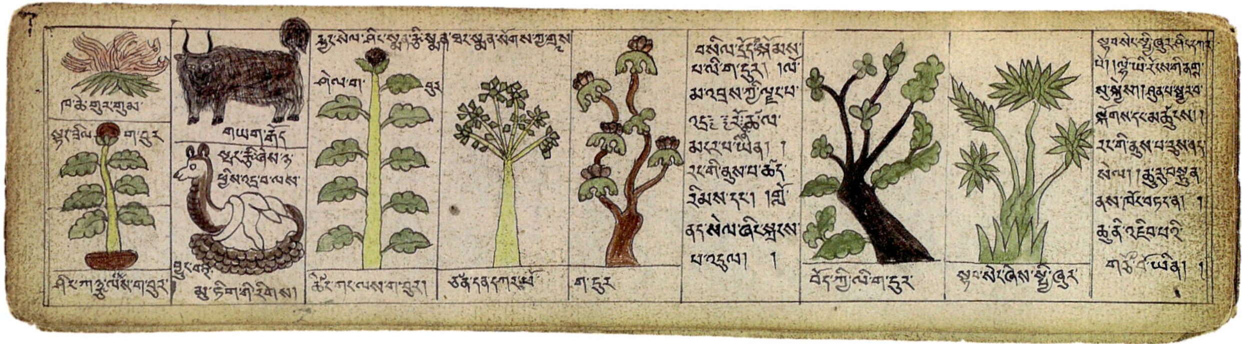

84 Unknown Tibetan artist, Illustration in *Tibetan materia medica: A Selection of Substances Used for the Production of Medicine Based on the Teaching of the Four (Medical) Tantras*, twelfth century

A seminal work of the Tibetan medical canon, the anonymous manuscript *Tibetan materia medica: A Selection of Substances Used for the Production of Medicine Based on the Teaching of the Four (Medical) Tantras* was written in the Trungpa style of medical literature. Produced in the twelfth century, its forty-four illustrated pages feature more than 250 descriptions of animals, minerals, and plants relevant to medicinal traditions. The illustrations are small in size and limited in their realism. Interestingly, the images of plants are separated from the words. Most pages include nine or ten cells, but occasionally one cell contains two plant species—still kept separate by a thin line—or a detailed view of a flower, fruit, or seed of a plant as well as a full representation of its anatomy. The title, *Tibetan materia medica*, might point to the influence of Dioscorides's aforementioned first-century CE text.

# TIBETAN MATERIA MEDICA

Fruct madragore.

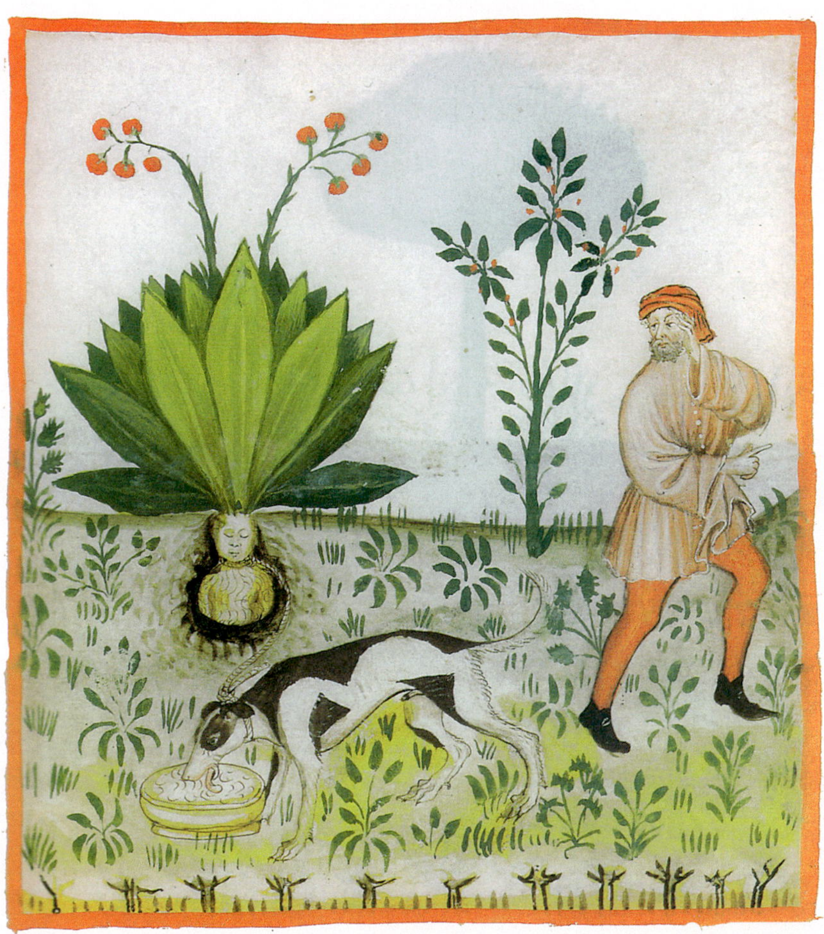

Mandrake, in *Tacuinum sanitatis in medicina,* ca. 1380–99, parchment

By the fourteenth century in Europe, women practicing medicine and leading unconventional lives became targets of the Christian church. An extensive botanical knowledge and ability to mix elixirs, potions, and poisons was associated with paganism and sorcery. In a culture that celebrated the presumed superiority of humans, associating oneself too closely with plants could prove fatal. In 1486, the publication of *Malleus Maleficarum*—a guide on how to identify and kill witches—fueled a series of executions that over 150 years took the lives of forty to sixty thousand people. Those found in possession of a mandrake root (*Mandragora officinarum*) would most likely end up on the scaffold or burned alive, since it was widely thought that this plant served as a crucial ingredient in the concoction of witches' flying ointments.

Mandrake is one of the most famous plants in world history. To the Egyptians, it was a potent medicine; to the Romans, an anesthetic; and to the Greeks, an aphrodisiac as well as the fundamental component of love potions. Much of its fame is attributable to the unusual shape of the root, which can vaguely resemble a human body. This uncanny quality became the stuff of legends. Some believed the plant screeched so loudly upon being pulled out of the ground that those within hearing distance would instantly die. Therefore, as seen in this illustration, it was advised to tie the plant's base to a dog, walk some distance, and then put down a bowl of food. As it rushed to the food, the dog would rip the root out while the owner watched safely from afar.

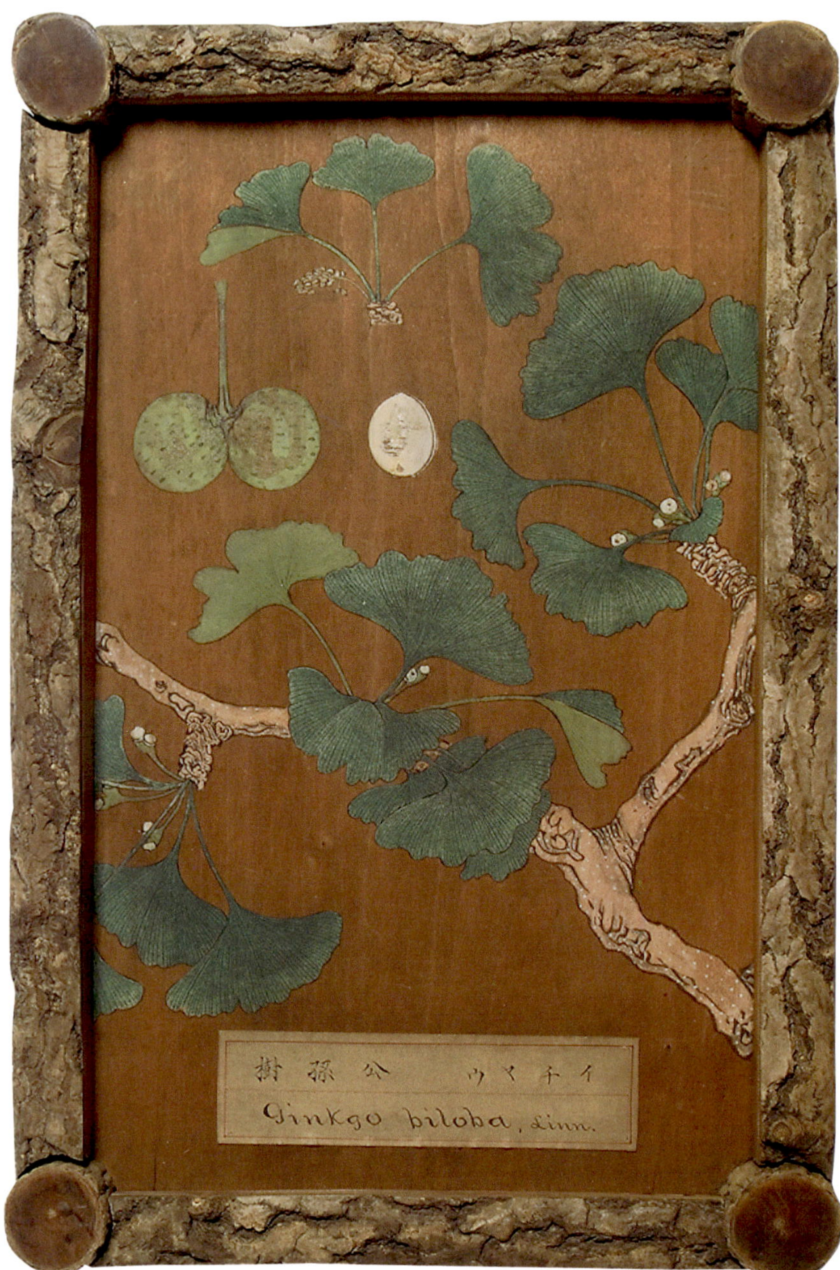


Chikusai Kato, Illustration of *Ginkgo biloba*, 1878, artwork on board made of gingko wood

This unusual botanical illustration of *Ginkgo biloba* is painted on a board made from the wood of the tree it represents. It is part of an unusual xylotheque—a special form of herbarium that consists of a collection of authenticated wood specimens—from early in the Meiji era of Japanese history (1868–1912). The panel is the work of Chikusai Kato, an innovative artist who worked at Tokyo University in collaboration with botanist Keisuke Ito during the late nineteenth century. Of particular interest is the fusion of Western and Japanese aesthetics with the realism of the botanical representation. Japanese as well as Latin names are used. These boards were probably created for the classroom rather than for a scientific archive, but very rapidly became something else—sought-after collectible artworks in their own right. They are now exceedingly rare.

# GINKGO BILOBA

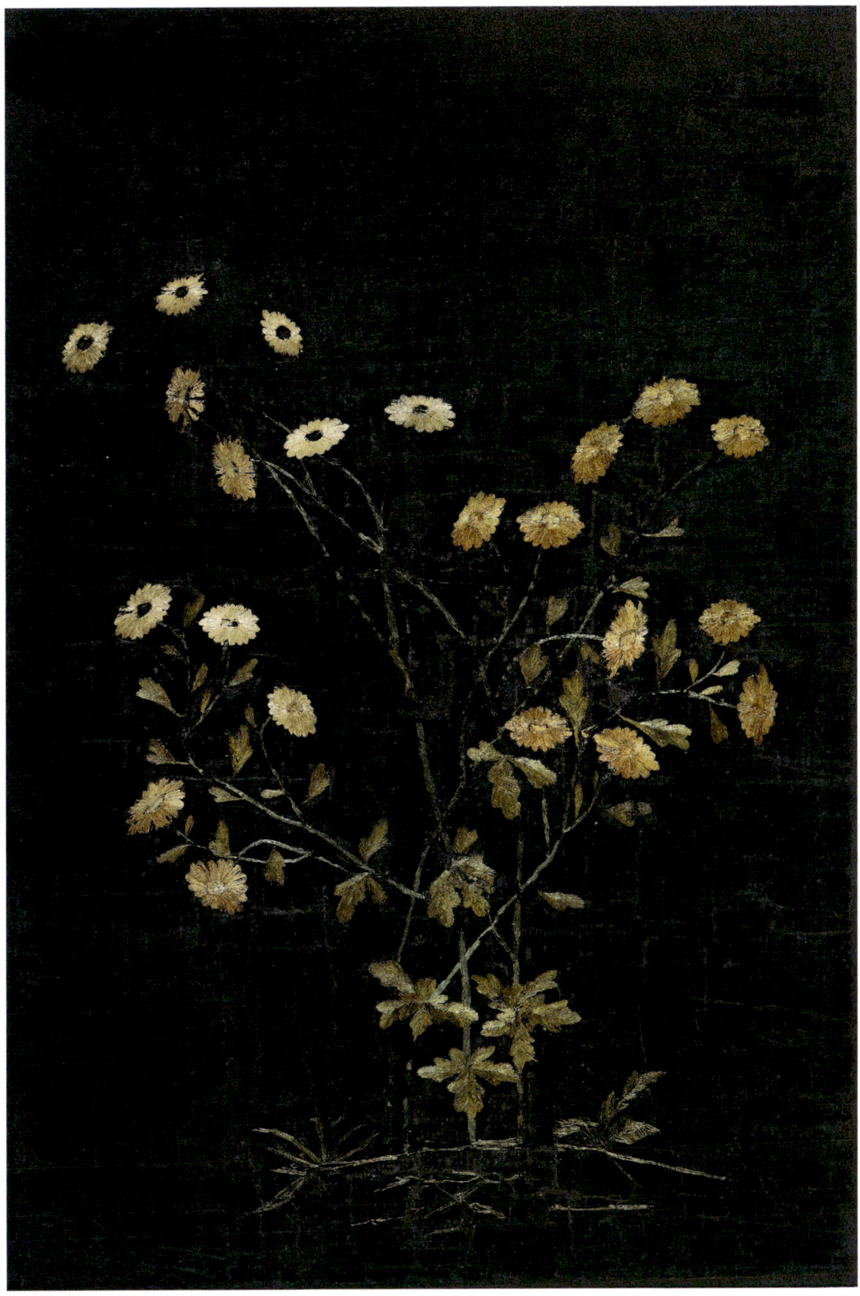

Shin Saimdang, *The Embroidered Grass and Insects*, ca. 1540, embroidery on black satin



Shin Saimdang was an exceptional Korean artist and poet active in the 1500s. In the absence of a male heir, her grandfather gave her, and her four sisters, a rigorous education normally designated for males only. Anticipating the ecological visions of Western pioneers like Maria Sibylla Merian by nearly two hundred years, Shin painted elegantly delicate scenes immortalizing the intricacies that bind insects and plant life. Her work, which can be seen as an advanced and unconventional example of Chochungdo—a genre of Korean folk painting—favored a highly realistic style. It is believed that Shin executed a significant number of her artistic creations inside the confines of her garden, employing a meticulous combination of sharp observation and precise documentation. She frequently painted on black paper, and some of her best works were transformed into intricate embroideries on black silk. In 2009, Shin became the first woman to appear on a Korean banknote.

## THE EMBROIDERED GRASS AND INSECTS

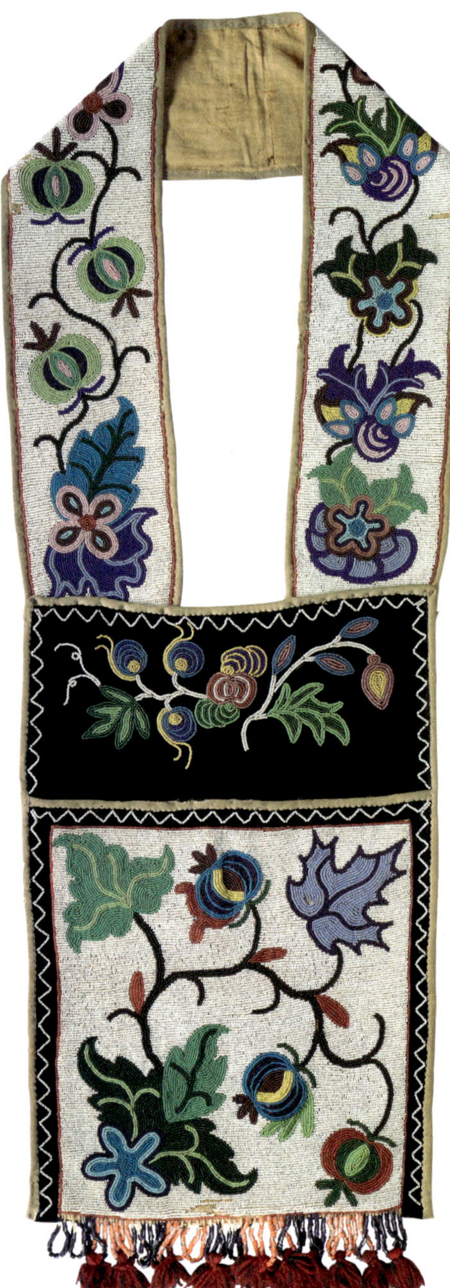

Bandolier (shoulder bag), Anishinaabe (Ojibwe) People, ca. 1880s, various media

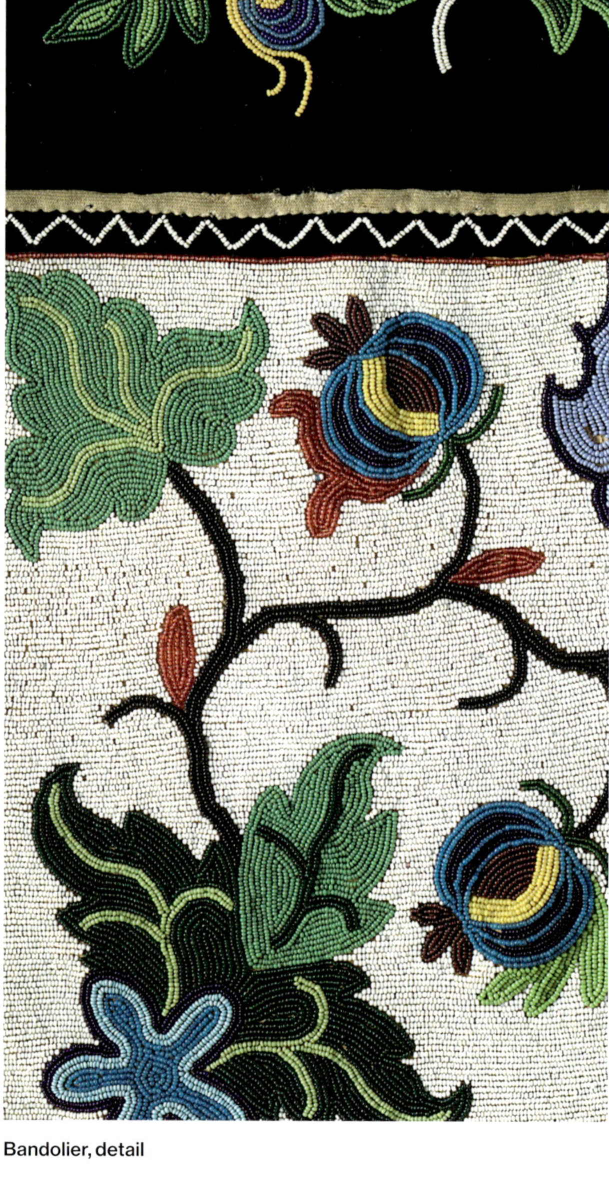

Bandolier, detail



Often worn at rituals and ceremonies, or for occasions such as treaty trips to Washington, DC, bandoliers like this are traditional shoulder bags made by the Ojibwe tribe of Native Americans. Some claim that they are an Indigenous iteration of the shoulder bags used by European soldiers to carry gunpowder and ammunition. Bandoliers are always embellished with floral themes accomplished through meticulous beading. The imagery tends to be more stylized than representational. Translucent glass beads enrich white backgrounds with a subtle glittery quality, while intensely colored opaque beads articulate the delicately rendered floral patterns. While bandoliers can certainly serve a practical function as bags, they are more culturally relevant as symbolic indicators of status and wealth among tribe members.

# BANDOLIER (SHOULDER BAG)

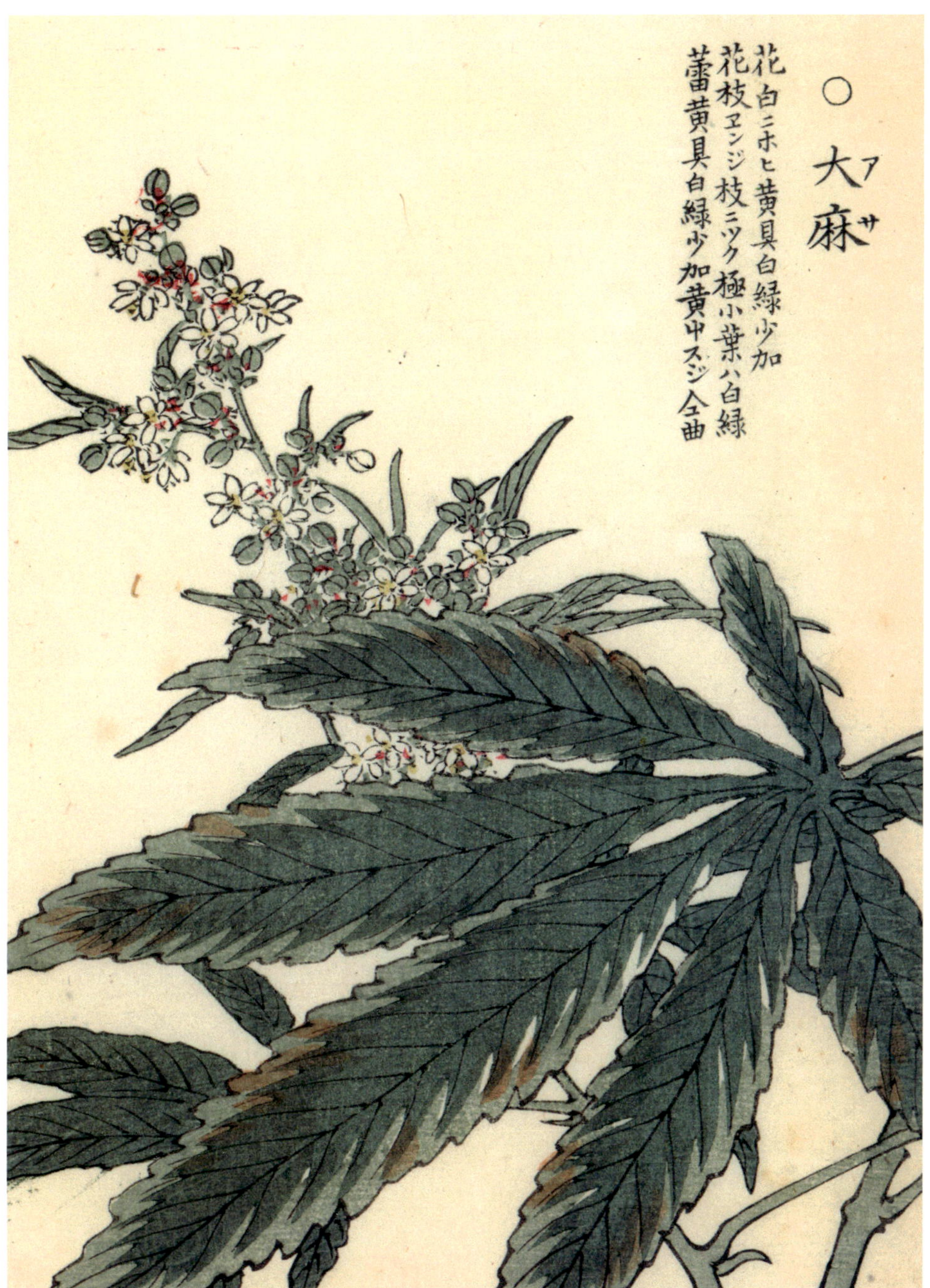


Kono Bairei, *Cannabis sativa*, 1900, woodblock print

Traditional Chinese medicine conceives of the body as a condensed incarnation of the universe ruled by the forces of yin and yang, and frequently turns to plants to address its vast complexity. Cannabis is thought to have evolved about twenty-eight million years ago on the eastern Tibetan Plateau and to have thrived in northwestern China before being introduced to other parts of Asia and India. Ritual burnings of cannabis at funerals and other social gatherings in central Asia, as well as in Japan, are known to have taken place for as long as five thousand years. The first known mention in writing is by Shennong in a treaty dating to 2737 BCE. The *Pen Ts'ao Ching*, the earliest Chinese *materia medica* book, dating from the first century CE, featured more than one hundred cannabis-based remedies. Some authors occasionally remarked on the potent side effects that overconsumption induced, such as visions, restlessness, or deep apathy.

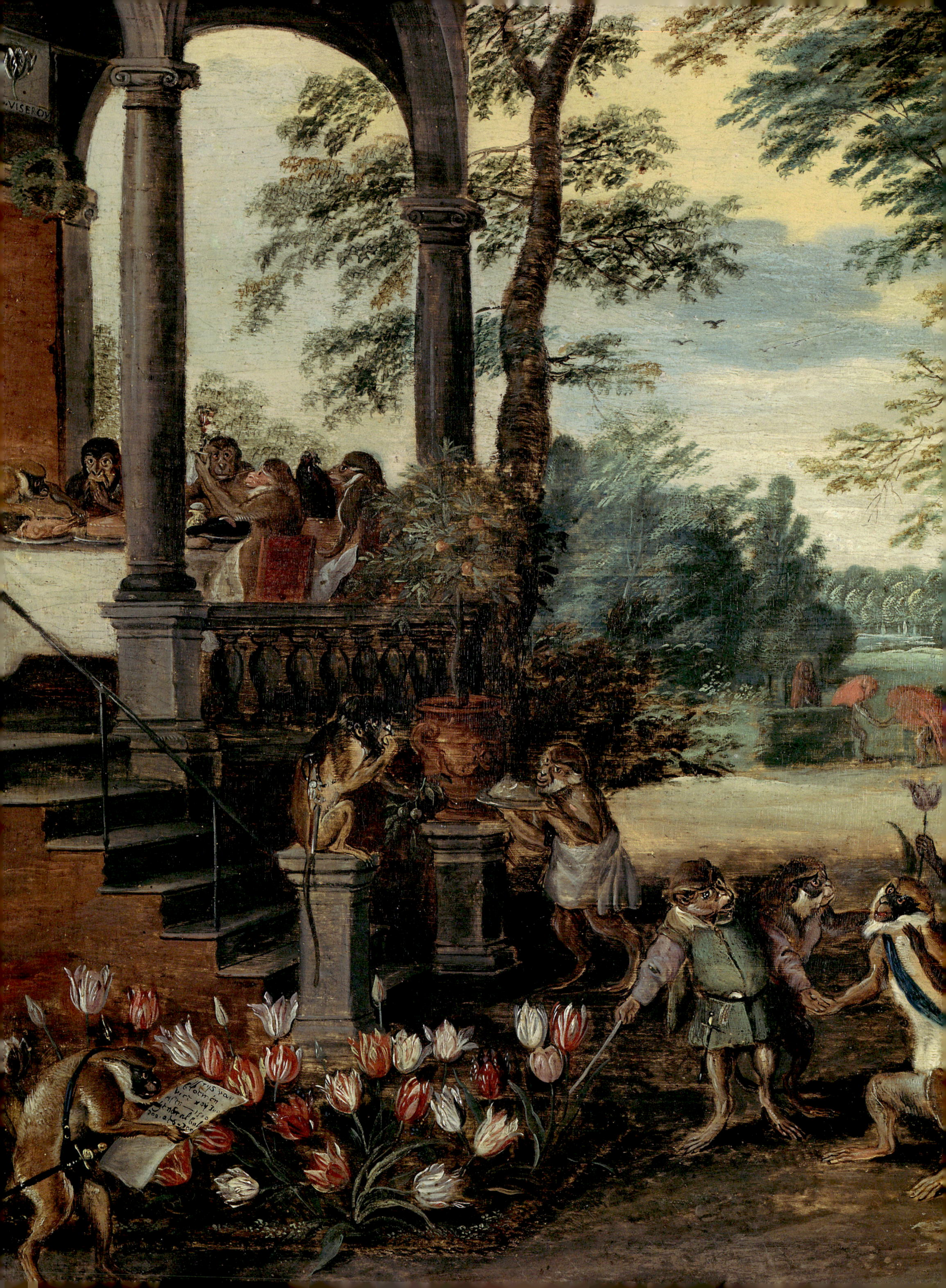

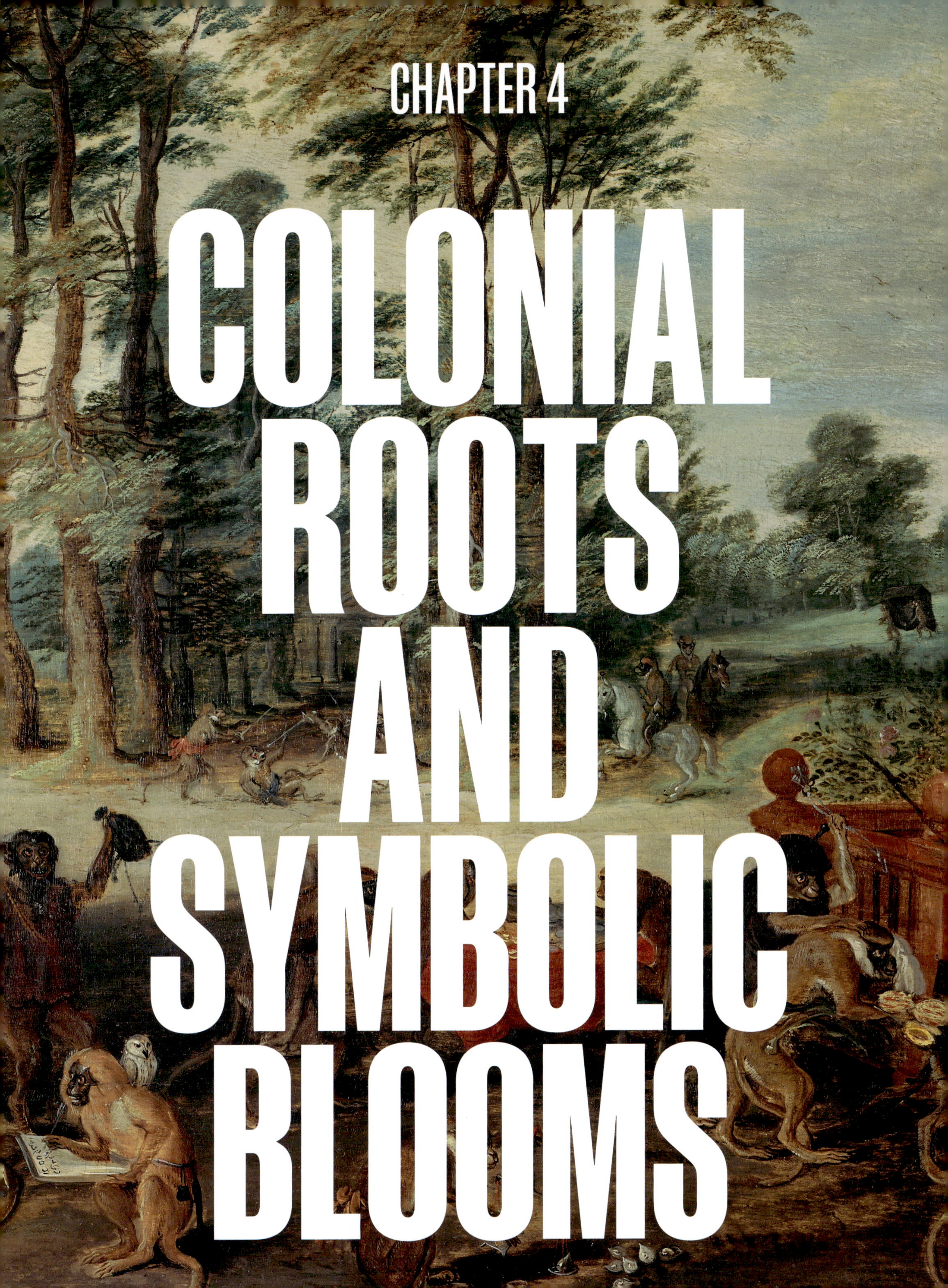

CHAPTER 4

# COLONIAL ROOTS AND SYMBOLIC BLOOMS

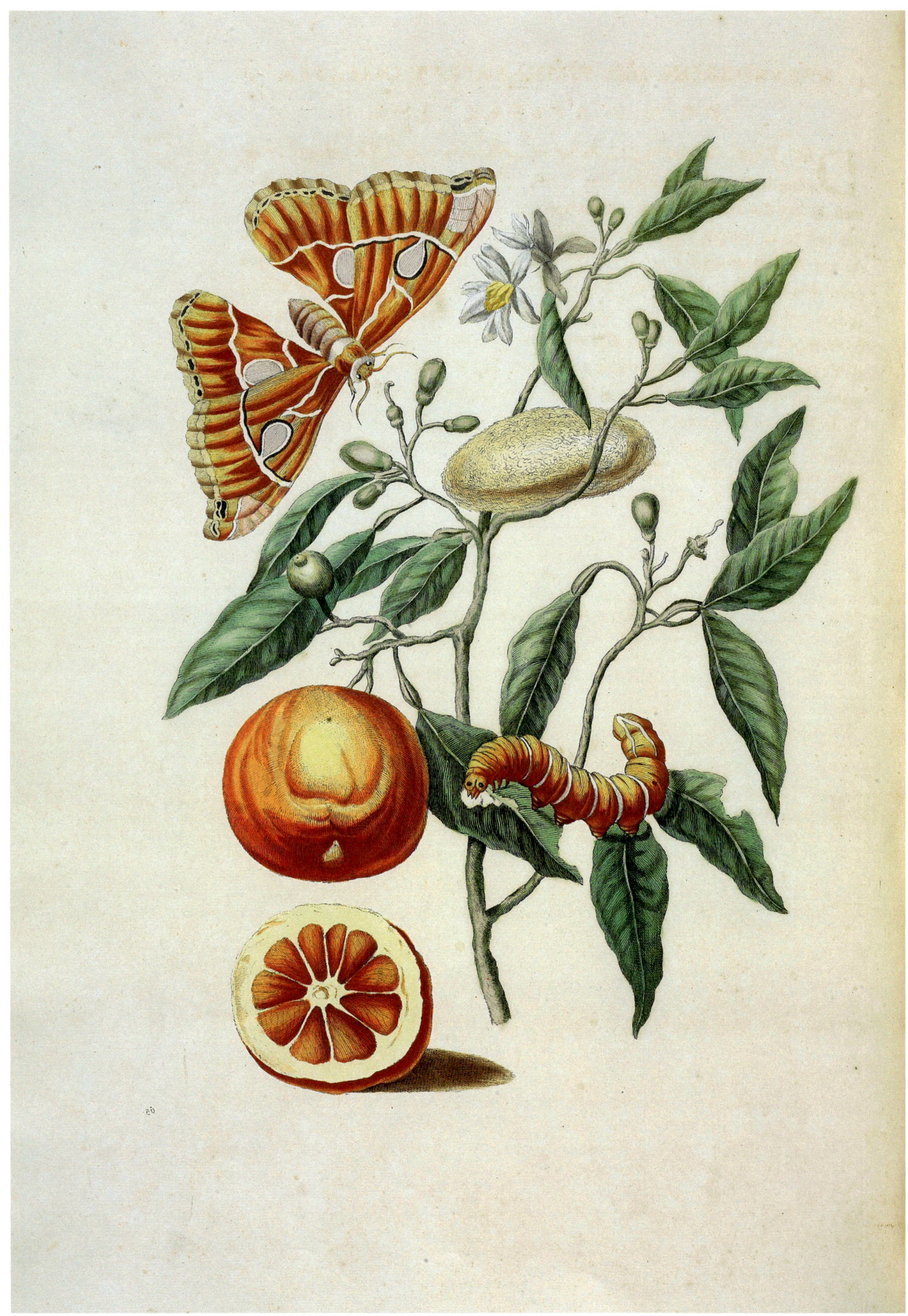

Maria Sibylla Merian, Branch of sweet orange tree (*Citrus sinensis*) with metamorphosis of *Rothschildia hesperus* moth, 1719, transfer engraving, hand colored

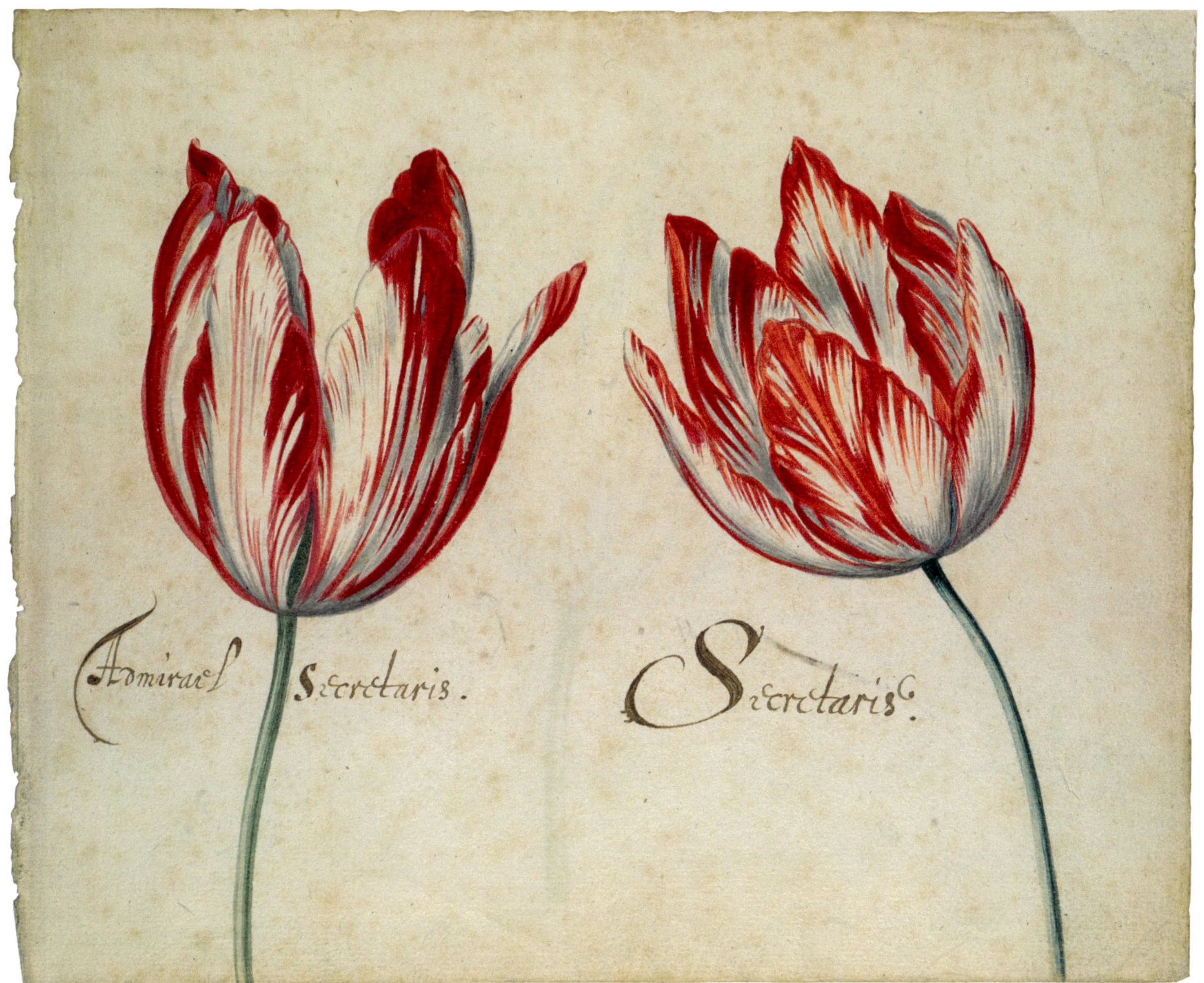


Unknown Dutch artist, *Two tulips* (recto), ca. 1633–37, watercolor and wash (drawing) and ink (inscriptions) on laid paper

What does drawing a plant mean? Answers to this question vary greatly based on historical era, geographical region, and cultural perceptions. Even the most realistic representations of plants, those that seem to do nothing more than faithfully transcribe every detail from reality to paper, are deeply shaped by ideologies. The point of view, the lighting, the framing, the cropping—every aesthetic decision is the manifestation of a philosophical framework, a distillation of the power relations that shape the reality from which the botanical representation emerges. Herbals, particularly those with vivid and detailed drawings, have been among the most important plant-related publications, possessing as they do the power to save lives or to kill. The sixteenth-century German physician and botanist Leonhart Fuchs revolutionized the field of botanical illustration by growing nearly five hundred plants in his own garden so that artist Albrecht Meyer could draw them with the utmost accuracy. It took Meyer thirty-five years to complete his *De historia stirpium commentarii insignes* (Notable Commentaries on the History of Plants, 1543), a book that for decades set the benchmark for excellence in the field.[1]

The most useful herbals were arguably those that included clear and comprehensive drawings of plants vividly delineated against a plain backdrop. Yet this isolating process, while necessary for careful study, is ideologically fraught. The heightened focus on vegetal anatomy foregrounds the plants as subjects. But removing plants from their habitat separates them from the ecological enmeshments that bind them to pollinators, parasites, and other vegetal companion species, therefore eradicating their actual composite identities at once.

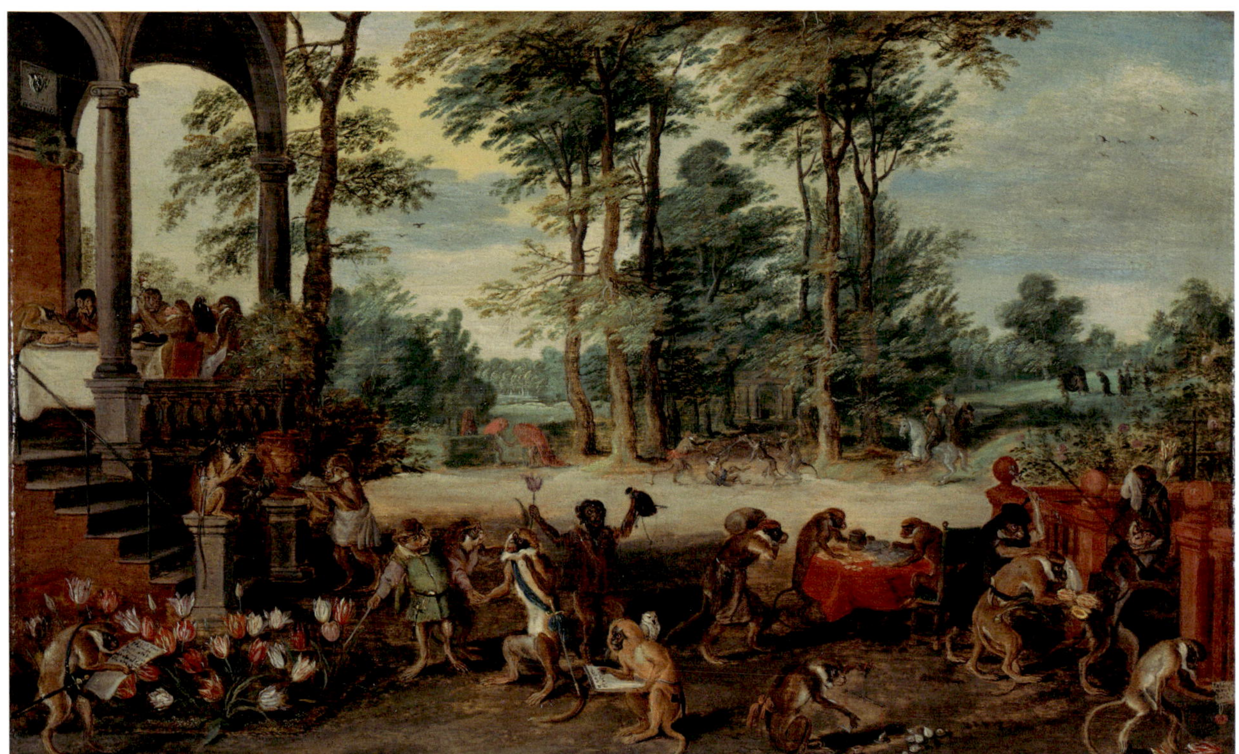

Jan Brueghel the Younger, *Satire of Tulipmania*, 1640, oil on panel



These shortcomings became apparent to pioneering naturalist and scientific illustrator Maria Sibylla Merian, who in 1699, accompanied only by her younger daughter, traveled to the Dutch colony of Suriname in South America. Published in 1705, her opulently illustrated *Metamorphosis insectorum Surinamensium* offered a remarkable chronicle of nascent ecological philosophy. Merian, an entomological collector with an unquenchable curiosity, was the first to illuminate the previously enigmatic existence of insects through her investigation of plants. For instance, owing to her careful observations, she dispelled the widely believed assumption that insects self-generate from mud. Merian noticed that different species of butterflies lay eggs on specific plants and documented their metamorphosis with unprecedented accuracy. She recognized interactions between different plants and insects where others only perceived individual species. Everything in her conception of nature appeared to be in flux, and each earthling represented in her plates brimmed with ecological agency.[2]

In time, gender biases and her lack of formal education led male academics to sideline Merian's scientific contributions. Indeed, in the West, for the past five hundred years, plants and women have shared a deeply entwined history of cultural marginalization, their perceived passivity relegating them to the lower ranks of existence as beautiful objects, resources to exploit, or both. Academies across Europe excluded female students, with very rare exceptions, until the end of the nineteenth century, justifying this on the basis of the subject matter's sexual content. Carl Linnaeus's gendered system of plant classification quickly gained popularity across Europe, and just as swiftly, it became one more opportunity to restrict women from botany.[3] As in art, where the study of the nude, at the time essential to training for history, religious, and mythological painting (the genres held in the highest regard), was forbidden to aspiring female artists, in England and northern Europe some feared that women's exposure to Linnean botany would trigger libertinism, radical Jacobinism, feminism, and anarchy.

By the mid-seventeenth century, depictions of landscapes, animals, and plants had officially been declassed to the status of inferior art genres, deemed decorative, even frivolous—lacking the conceptual depth, moral integrity, and ethical elevation of art portraying grandiose human narratives.[4] Or at

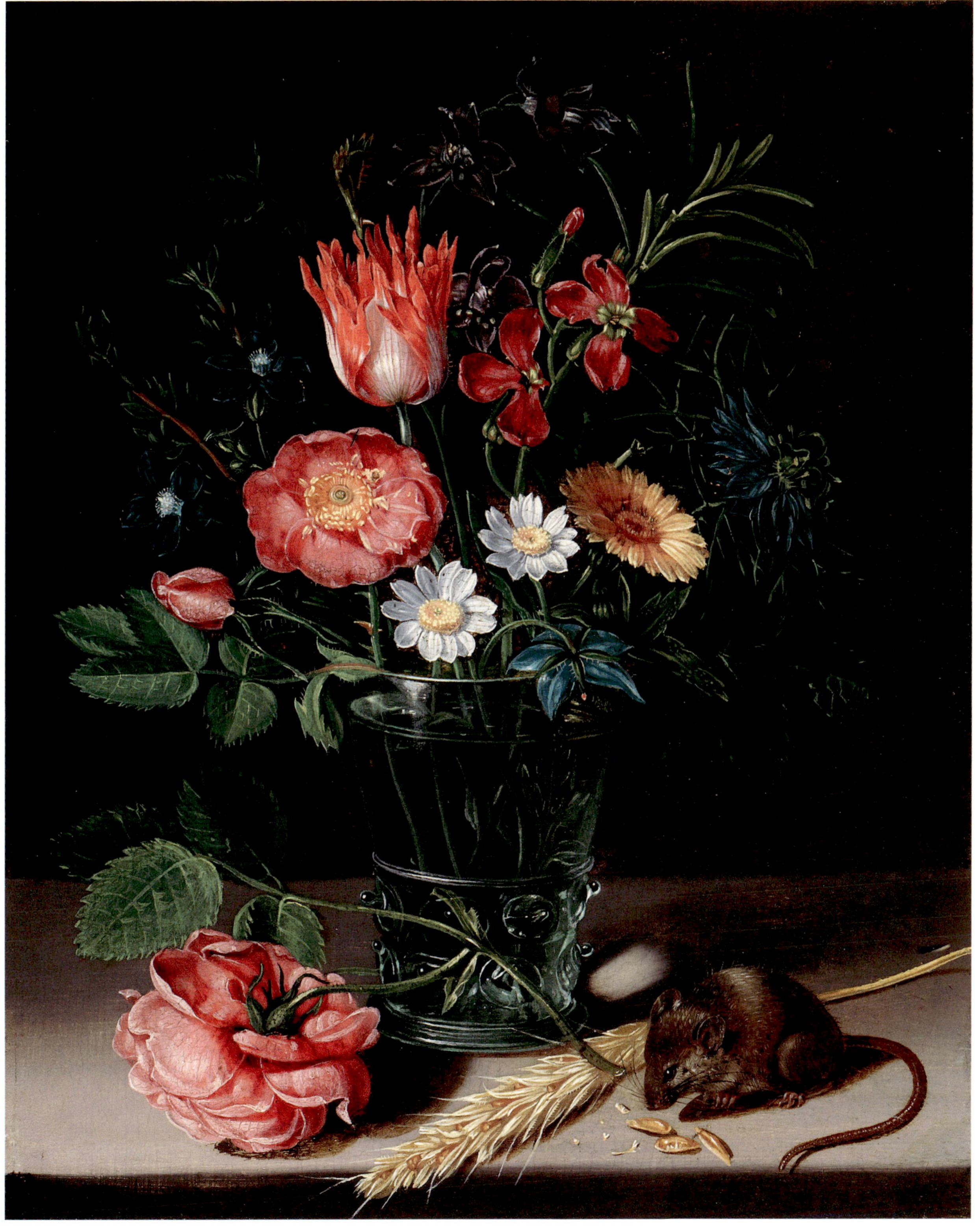

Clara Peeters, *Flowers in a Vase with a Nibbling Mouse*, seventeenth century, oil on wood

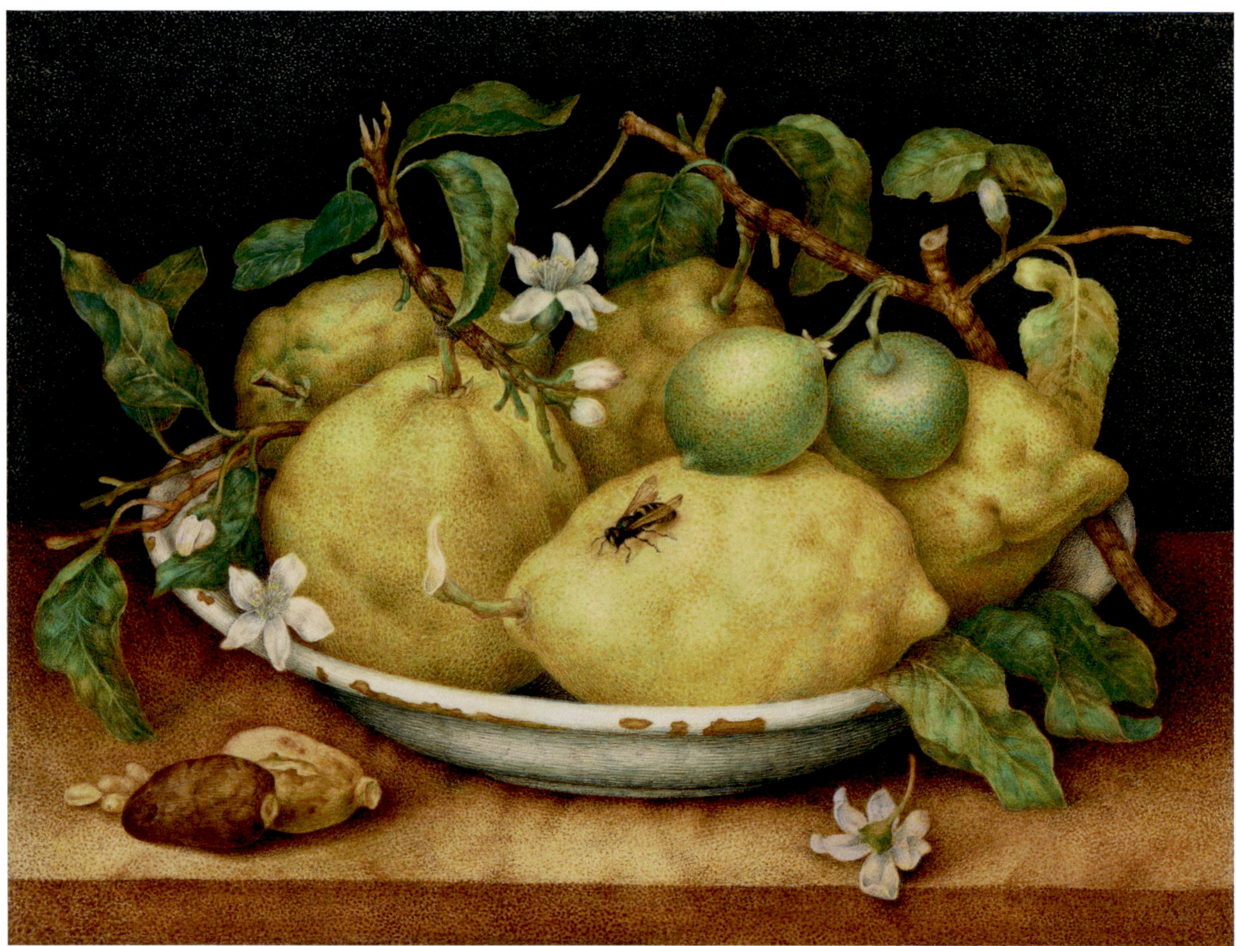

Giovanna Garzoni, *Still Life with Bowl of Citrons*, ca. late 1640s, tempera on vellum

least that was the case until aspiring female artists like Maria Moninckx, Johanna Helena Herolt, Helena Forde, Berthe Hoola van Nooten, Barbara Regina Dietzsch, Lise Cloquet, Rachel Ruysch, Maria van Oosterwijck, Frances Elizabeth Tripp, Augusta Innes Withers, and Lydia Byam, among others, turned to painting plants and flowers, spearheading an unparalleled botanical revolution in Western art. Initiating an unwavering, albeit gradual, ascent in the arts and in society, these women artists made the most of what was available to them to showcase their aptitudes, talent, and conceptual acumen.

But while it helped women artists gain a firmer stronghold, the symbolism of flowers in Western art proved to be a double-edged sword for plants. In time, floral still lifes had become extremely popular owing to the Protestant Reformation's prohibition on depictions of religious figures, which were thought idolatrous and associated with Catholicism. Especially in northern Europe, where Protestantism held the most sway, many artists swapped saints for flowers. In doing so, they tapped into and expanded a preexisting wealth of floral symbolism that covertly conveyed Christian morals. Daffodils, some of the earliest flowers to return every spring, spoke of rebirth and resurrection. Daisies told stories of innocence, beauty, and love. Strawberry flowers professed the value of chastity.[5] At times it was color that carried meaning: cherries, red carnations, and poppies evoked the blood of Christ's Passion. At others, a combination of scent and color would unlock a symbol: the whiteness and fragrance of lemon blossoms, lily of the valley, or jasmine incarnated the purity of the Virgin. Baroque in style but medieval in essence, such still-life paintings manifested the dogma that God's presence pervades every fiber of this world, and that everything, even plants, proclaims his might.

Notwithstanding the exponential increase in the quantity of paintings featuring plants exclusively

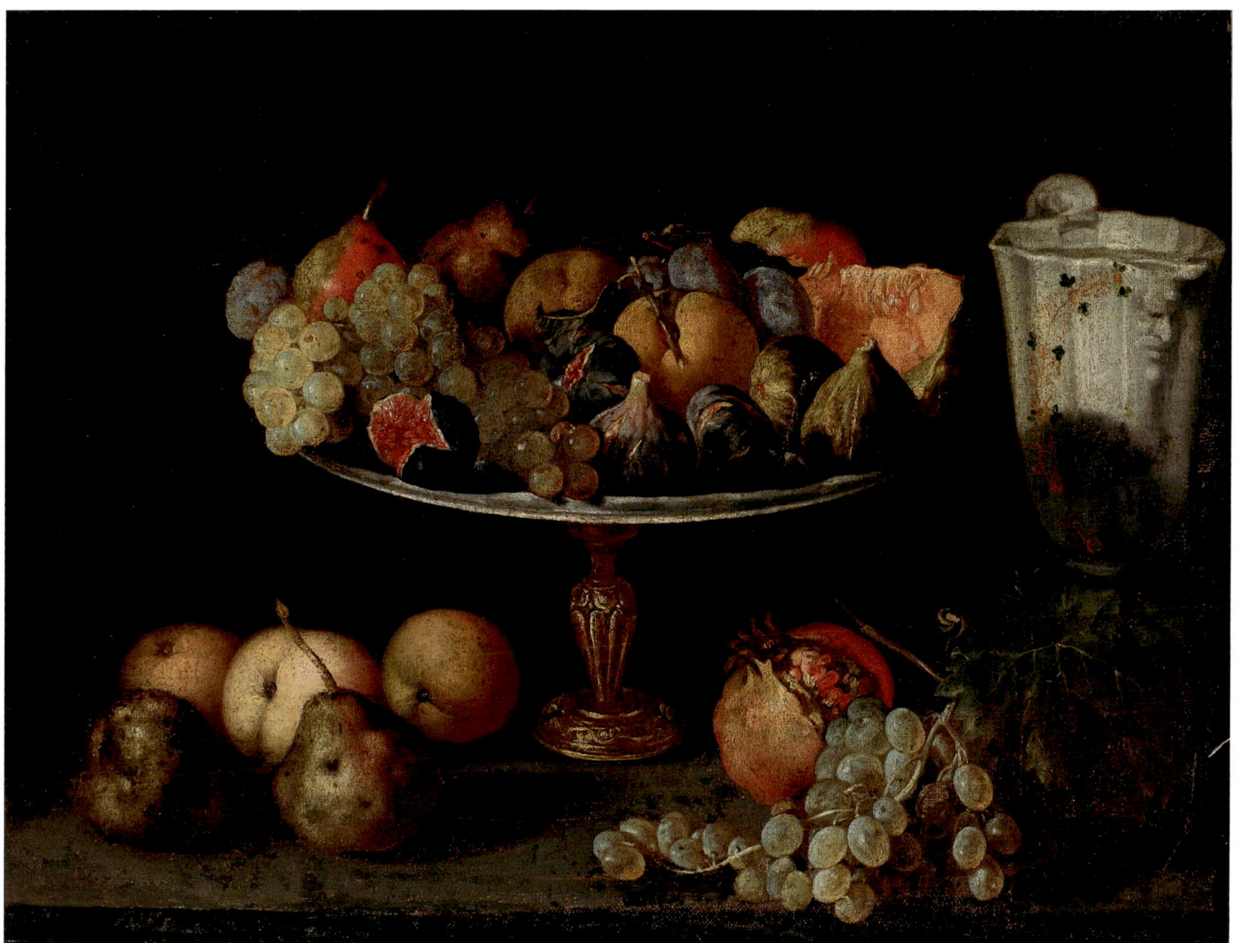



Fede Galizia, *Pedestal Plate with Southern Fruit*, ca. 1600–25, oil on canvas

as the focal point throughout the sixteenth, seventeenth, and eighteenth centuries, symbolism essentially filled the silence of plants with human voices. Still-life floral compositions constantly chattered about human fears, dreams, morals, and values. Once again, the subtlety of vegetal essence was smothered by an anthropocentric conviction that plants are not quite enough on their own. Their silence started to be seen as an unsettlingly forceful proclamation of difference that could not be ignored.

Floral still lifes initially garnered the interest of collectors from the burgeoning colonial merchant elite class, who desired to exhibit their affluence as a signifier of social status. In response to increasing demand, artists crafted novel trade structures by selling their creations directly from their studios or via dealers, as opposed to operating on a commission basis, and the modern art market was born. The surge in popularity of these works of art sparked a dramatic surge of interest in the mid-1630s in rare tulip varieties introduced to Holland from the Ottoman Empire. These much-sought-after blooms became an instant status symbol. Those with random speckles or plumed flares of different colors were particularly prized. The sophisticated variations mirrored the veining found in variegated marble and the fluidity of Mannerist draperies; these "broken tulips," as they were colloquially referred to, genuinely resembled works of art. Thus, it is unsurprising that art patrons who favored still-life paintings frequently spent substantial amounts of money on tulip bulbs, too.

"Tulipmania," as the phenomenon became known, spawned a new publishing model, as it presaged the commercial catalog that would propel many businesses to international success in modern times. To evidence each detail, variegated flowers were accurately painted against a white background. The tulip's and grower's names were listed together—sometimes even merged to generate pseudoscientific proper names of new cultivars—with bulb costs often indicated at the lower margin of the illustration. During the peak of the frenzy surrounding variegated tulips, which arose starting in 1634 and dramatically crashed in February 1637, the price of bulbs increased twelvefold, with some reaching a value of 5,000 guilders—a sum of money that at the time could buy a mansion. The flowers themselves were never really of interest to most of the speculators who flocked to the trade; rather, it was the seemingly easy money to be made. The first week of February 1637 ended with a price bubble brought on by reckless speculation, followed by a devastating nosedive that some attribute to a plague epidemic. Tulips sparked the first market meltdown in Western history.[6]

This unfortunate turn of events, however, did not discourage painters from continuing to depict gorgeous flower arrangements. Clara Peeters, Jan Brueghel the Elder, Giovanna Garzoni, Jan van Huysum, Fede Galizia, and more would go on to create some of the most exuberantly lush floral compositions yet seen. Although meticulous accuracy was required to convey the intended symbolism, painters often purposefully disregarded the reality of blooming seasons, depicting both spring and fall flowers in the same work of art.



In essence, floral still lifes were painterly collages: specimens studied in botanical gardens (one of the earliest was established in Leiden, the Netherlands, in 1590), sketched in fields, or copied from herbals and other artists' paintings. It is in the floral still lifes of the so-called Dutch Golden Age—an era in which Dutch trade, science, art, and military forces were among the most acclaimed and brutal in the world, roughly 1588 to 1672—that we can trace the blueprint for a nascent capitalist attitude that significantly aided in the objectification of plants, and the environment more broadly, in the decades that followed.

In a pre-photographic world, paintings and illustrations were indispensable tools for the study of plants, allowing naturalists to correctly identify species and draw genealogies among them, part of a desire to unlock the secrets of life. At a time in which European colonial powers were taking over much of the rest of the Earth, the visual cataloging of the vegetal kingdom grew exponentially. Botanical illustrations helped Charles Darwin formulate his theory of evolution. Darwin was able to understand the significance of interdependence among biological forms through the study of drawings by his mentor, the botanist and geologist John Stevens Henslow, and his close friend, the explorer and botanist Joseph Dalton Hooker. Henslow in particular was known for his complex teaching sheets, complete with magnified detailed and accurate notes illustrating so-called abnormal specimens—curiosities that put in motion Darwin's train of thought.[8] But this portentous production of knowledge came at a dire cost. As more and more factual knowledge of plants was produced, the Western thirst for knowledge stripped plants of their magical aura, thus, at least in part, impacting our relationship with the vegetal world in detrimental ways.

At their origins in the Renaissance, the disciplines of natural history and botany were characterized by a desire to recount as much information as possible. Early researchers gathered and collated as many disparate facts and fragments of evidence about each species as possible, embracing local knowledges, agricultural processes, myths and legends, culinary recipes, and songs and poems, as well as descriptive accounts. The knowledge was holistic and mostly nonhierarchical. But by the eighteenth century, Enlightenment natural history had become obsessed with organizing, categorizing, and hierarchizing. It devolved into an exclusionist discipline that sought to purge all "nonscientific" information.[9] This approach led to the development of extremely valuable knowledge of previously unstudied minutiae and inner vegetal workings. But it also rejected other kinds of cultural knowledge that regarded plants as more than resources or beautiful objects.

In the East, this was far less the case. Throughout history, Asian artworks portraying plants have conveyed a sense of tranquility, introspection, and intimate connection with the vegetal kingdom, rooted in its fundamental nature. A similarly parsimonious approach guided the practice of flower arrangements in which Taoist principles were expressed through the grace and balance of a single stem. Rather than dazzle with exotic compositional pyrotechnics, Japanese paintings of plants focused on the subject's subtle essence and demeanor. Of course, symbolism also played a role, but rather than representing fundamentally arbitrary links between

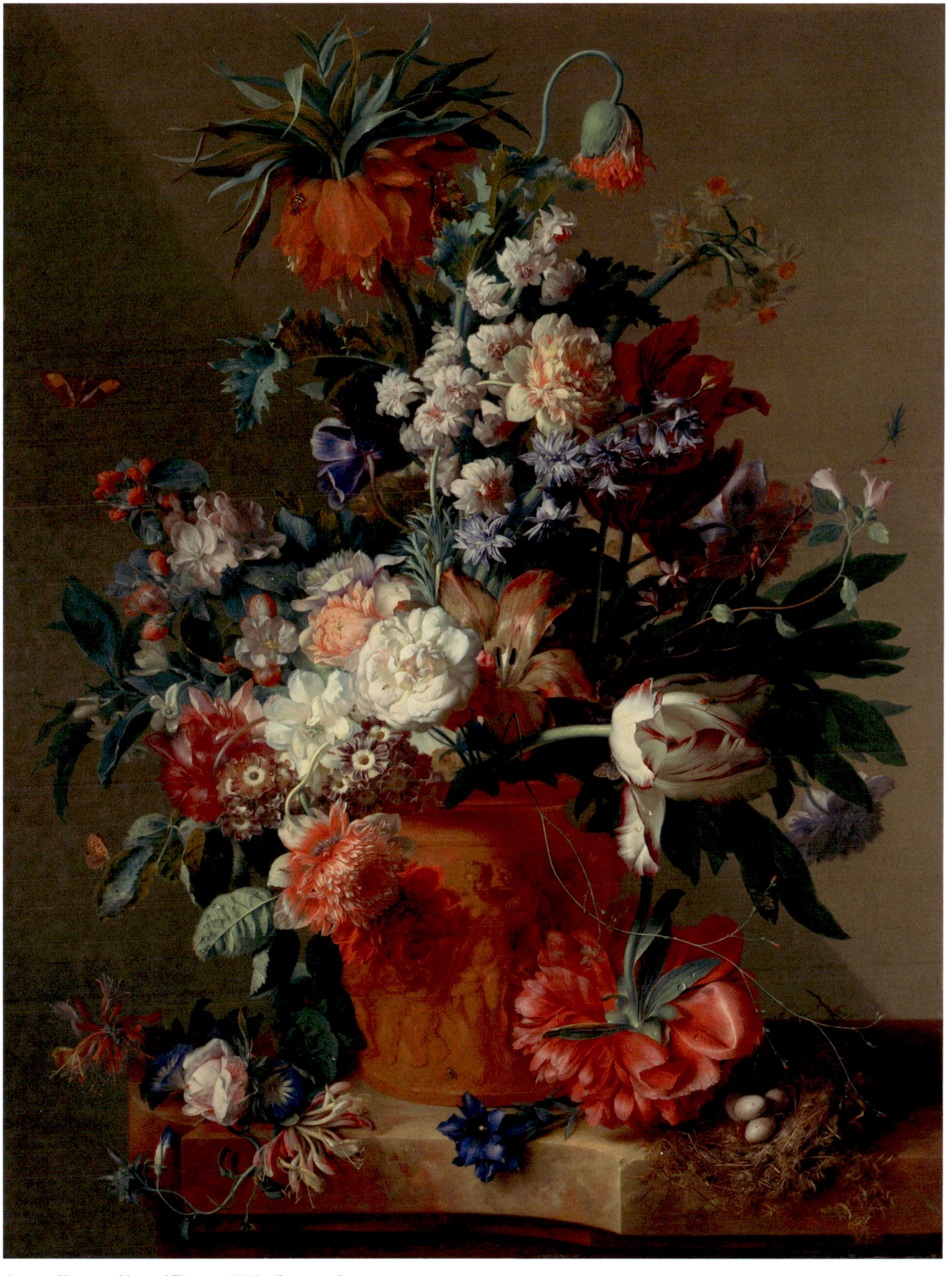

Jan van Huysum, *Vase of Flowers*, 1722, oil on panel

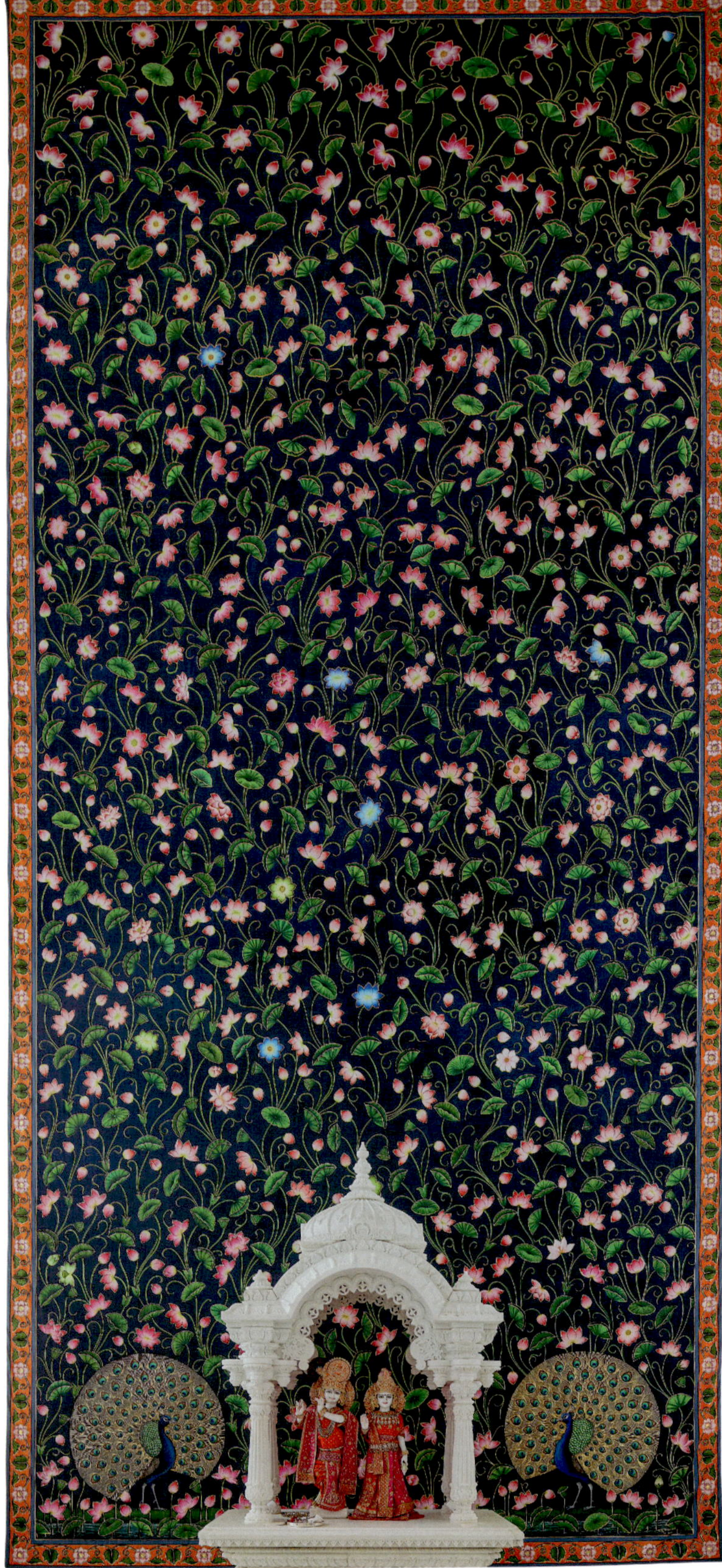

Raghunandan Sharma and Pichwai artists from Nathdwara, *Kamal Kunj*, 2019–20, Nathdwara pichwai painting on textile

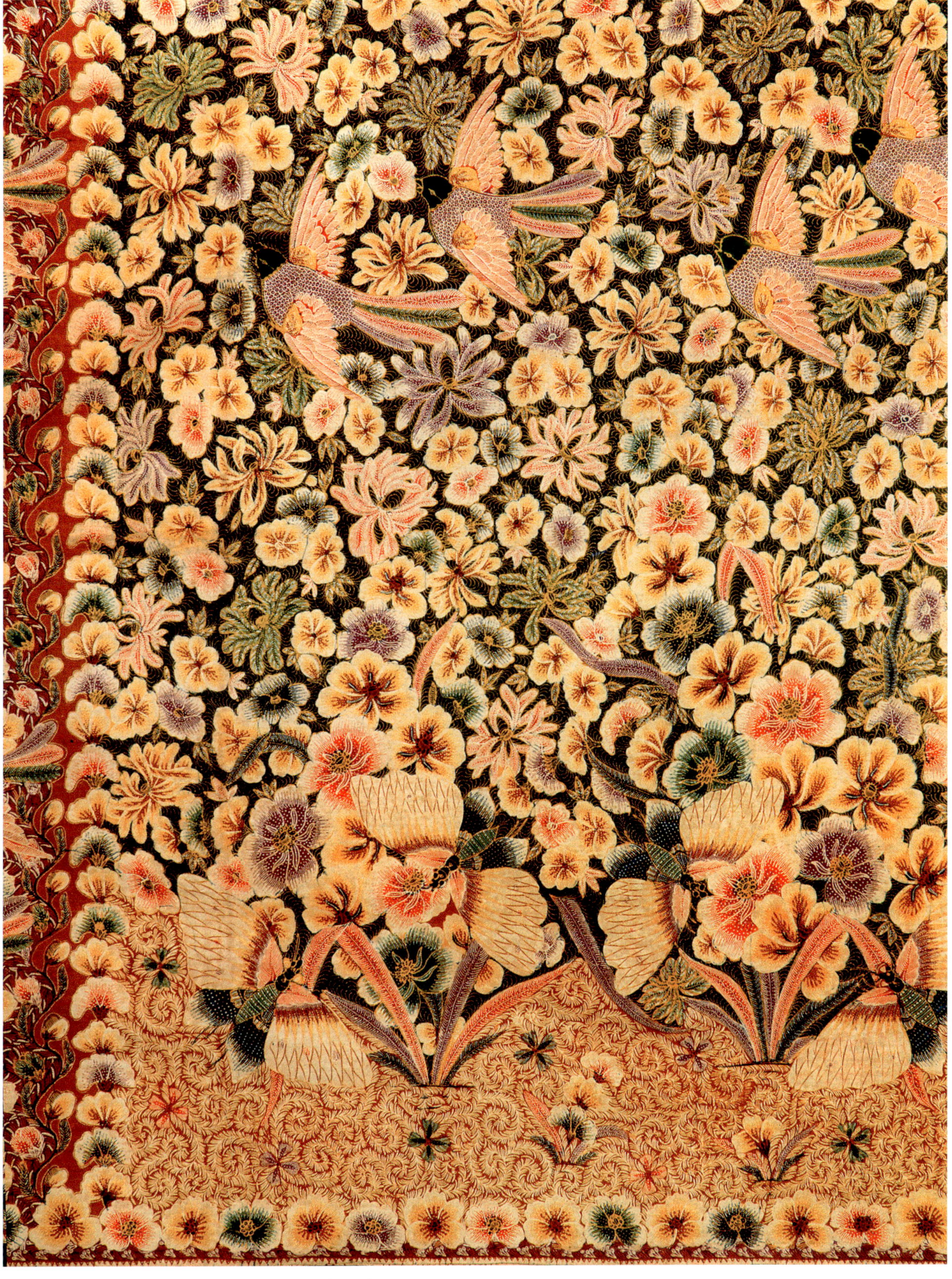

Panel, Pekalongan, Indonesia, ca. 1920s, cotton (detail)

plants and human virtues, Eastern floral symbolism frequently arose from close study of the plant's life.

The lotus flower, for example, which is depicted in innumerable works of art across India, became over time a symbol of purity, metamorphosis, and transcendence. These Hinduism-inspired symbolic ideals came about from observations that the lotus bud rises from murky water and lifts its head with dignity and power. As the flower blooms, its glowing petals unfurl untainted by the plant's lowly, muddy origin. Its entire life cycle is therefore seen as an incarnation of spiritual ideas—moral elevation, propagation, rebirth. Furthermore, the birth of the lotus is associated with the emergence of language as a shaping force in the genesis of the universe.[10] Therefore, in paintings and sculptures, Buddha, Lakshmi, and other deities are often shown sitting on lotus thrones.

The meaningfulness of the lotus flower has made it a popular symbol across many cultures. Vibrant batik designs developed in Indonesia and made and used in Singapore, Sri Lanka, Malaysia, and Nigeria (where the Yoruba people absorbed the patterns into their preexisting textile culture) also feature lotus flowers as symbols of plenty. Motifs are drawn with hot wax, often derived from plant resins, on a cotton cloth that is dipped multiple times in different dyes to obtain intricately layered patterns.[11] Although it is frequently thought of as uniquely African, batik gained popularity in Africa thanks to the Dutch, who in the eighteenth century appropriated Indonesian textile designs and used machines to create the cloth more quickly and cheaply, then sold it widely in West Africa. Following the colonialist expansions of the seventeenth and eighteenth centuries, Western influence radically altered the aesthetic and contextual approaches to batik as well as flower painting across the Middle East, China, and India.

At this time, as accuracy in botanical representation gained importance, publishers teamed together with regional artists who had access to living specimens. Up until then, dry specimens of rare species would be steeped or boiled for hours to restore some degree of vegetative naturalness, then painted rapidly before they dried and crumpled for good.[12]

Three-dimensionality, heightened realism, and image standardization were promoted by British botanists keen to document local flora for Western natural historians and collectors.[13] The British East India Company—a monopolistic trading body responsible for much imperial plunder in India and East and Southeast Asia—gave rise to a new hybrid style in floral representation that combined European approaches with the detailed linearity of local Mughal art. Most Indian artists trained to produce botanical drawings for the colonizers remained anonymous, but Vishnupersaud was highly esteemed and known by name; his illustrations were much sought after by collectors in Europe.[14]

The growing interest in botanical illustration that pervaded Europe and its colonies during the eighteenth century also led to the invention of new media. It is frequently forgotten that collage was originally devised in an effort to capture the color and texture of botanical specimens. The Western art historical narrative attributes the origin of collage to Pablo Picasso and Georges Braque, who began experimenting with combining scraps of newspaper, sandpaper, and cardboard on various substrates in 1912. But the process of piecing together fragments of paper to produce a lifelike image had been already invented in 1772, a hundred and forty years prior, by amateur botanist and artist Mary Delany. Rebuilding her life in the aftermath of a wrecked marriage that had left her penniless and homeless, Delany spent time with relatives, who introduced her to botanists Joseph Banks and Daniel Solander. One day, a seventy-two-year-old Delany glanced at a scarlet geranium petal fallen from a vase and initially mistook it for a tiny piece of paper. This misrecognition turned into her eureka moment. Armed with blades and scissors, she began to cut up myriad colored paper fragments and assemble them with impeccable precision to resemble the anatomies of particular plants.[15]

Delany worked hard on 985 plant collages over the span of eleven years, only ceasing when her eyesight deteriorated. Banks famously said that her collages were the only imitations of nature he had seen from which one could "describe botanically any plant without the least fear of committing an error."[16] Nevertheless, despite the high caliber and uniqueness of her work, Delany was forgotten by her fellow scientists due to gender and professional biases. Because of the craft-based character of her original contribution to art, art historians likewise tended not to laud her work as the pioneering effort it was. Today,

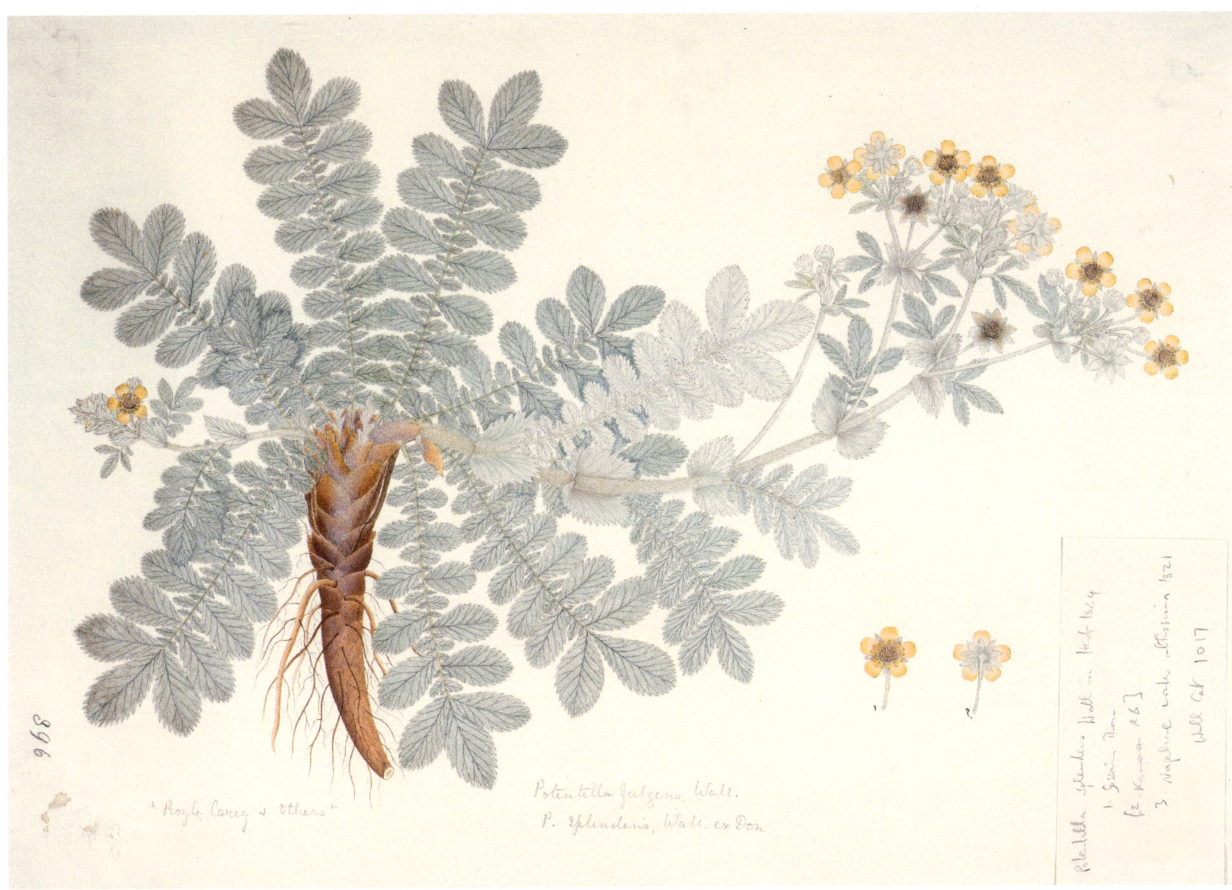


Vishnupersaud, *Potentilla fulgens*, ca. 1821, drawing

however, Delany has become a widely cited source of inspiration—a woman artist working in an unconventional manner at the intersection of art, craft, and science; an independent mind determined to demonstrate that creative maturity can be attained at any age; and a fierce individual committed to challenging norms and expectations through sheer talent and passion for the vegetal world.

While women's contributions to the field of botanical illustration have become more openly valued over time, being a woman botanical researcher has remained much harder. One exception is Mexican American pioneer Ynés Enriquetta Julietta Mexía, who began studying botany at the University of California at Berkeley in 1921, at the age of fifty-one, then proceeded to identify two new genera, collect more than 145,000 species, and discover about six hundred new ones before her death in 1938.[17] Sometimes, plants can be at the forefront of revolutions that take centuries to fully unfold into true societal change.

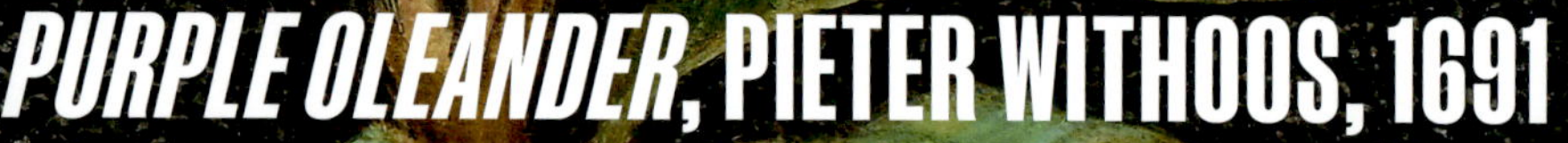

*PURPLE OLEANDER*, PIETER WITHOOS, 1691

*STILL LIFE WITH GRAPES AND OTHER FRUIT*, LUCA FORTE, 1630S

*FRUIT PIECE*, JAN VAN HUYSUM, 1722

*STILL LIFE WITH A BASKET OF FRUIT AND A BUNCH OF ASPARAGUS*, LOUISE MOILLON, 1630

*POPPY*, PHILIPP OTTO RUNGE, CA. 1800–1803

*DANDELION*, BARBARA REGINA DIETZSCH, CA. 1755

*PAEONIA TENUIFOLIA*, MARY DELANY, 1778

*NEPENTHES NORTHIANA, A PITCHER PLANT FROM THE LIMESTONE MOUNTAINS OF SARAWAK, BORNEO*, MARIANNE NORTH, 1876

*VASE OF FLOWERS*, GIUSEPPE CASTIGLIONE,

EIGHTEENTH CENTURY

BRAHMINY STARLING WITH TWO *ANTHERAEA* MOTHS, CATERPILLAR, AND COCOON ON INDIAN JUJUBE TREE, SHEIKH ZAIN AL-DIN, 1777

---

*FLOWERS OF THE FOUR SEASONS*, SAITŌ IPPO, CA. NINETEENTH CENTURY

*MORNING GLORY AND ORIENTAL GREENFINCH*, UTAGAWA HIROSHIGE, 1871–73

---

*FLOWERS OF DATURA AND HUMMING BIRDS, BRAZIL*, MARIANNE NORTH, CA. 1873

---

*MALTESE CROSS, MONKSHOOD, AND INSECTS*, JOHANNA HELENA HEROLT, DATE UNKNOWN

---

GARDEN BALSAM, F. SANSOM JR., 1810

---

*BIRDS AND FLOWERS*, ATTRIBUTED TO KANO SHÔEI, LATE SIXTEENTH CENTURY

---

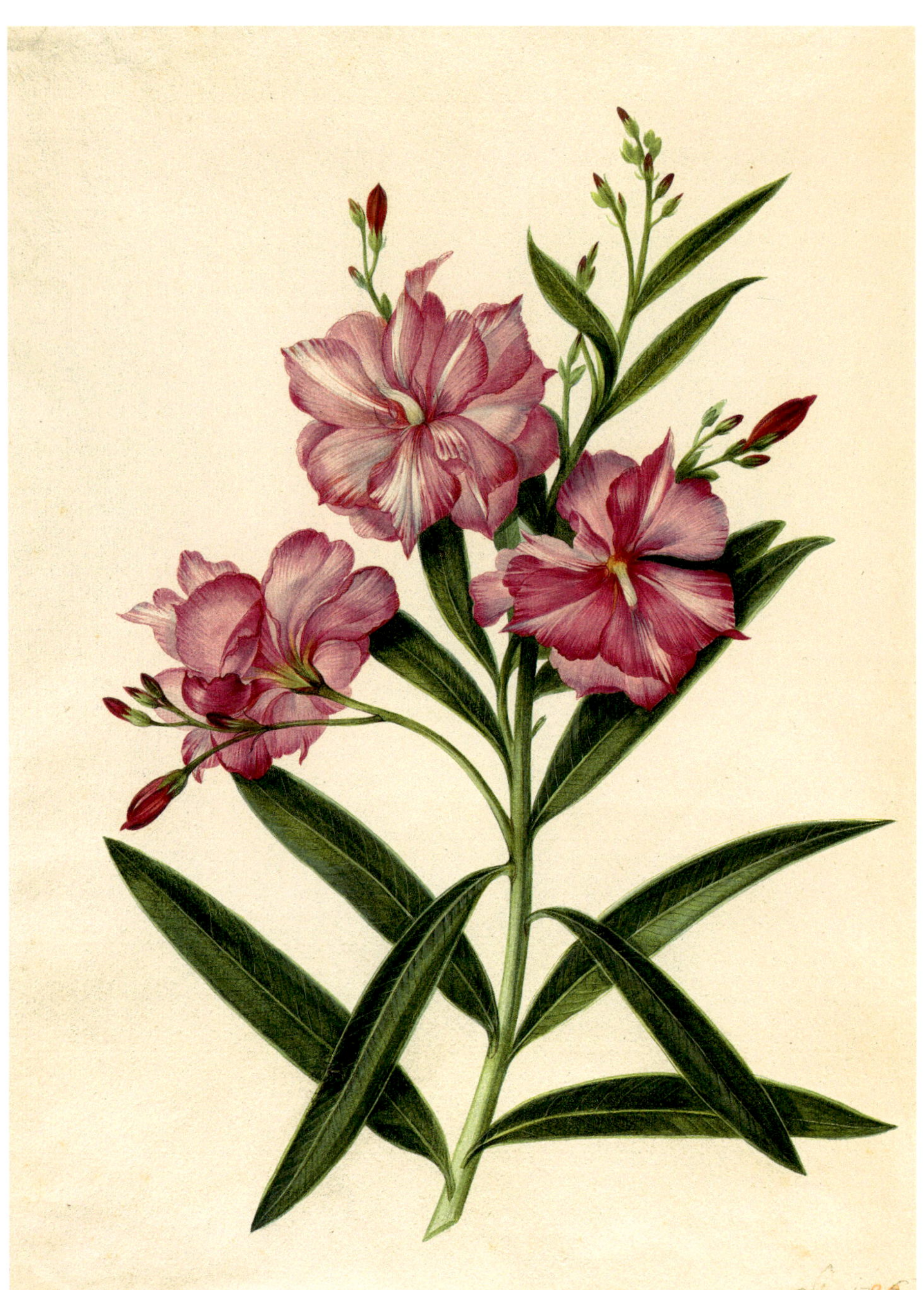

Pieter Withoos, *Purple Oleander*, 1691, watercolor with applied gum on laid paper

*Nerium oleander*, the name for a highly poisonous plant, might derive from a Latinized form of the Greek compound noun *ollyo* (ὄλλύω), or "I kill." According to some sources, the name may refer to the olive-like shape and color of the plant's foliage. Native to the Mediterranean region—especially southern Italy, Greece, and North Africa—oleander is today a garden staple in temperate to warm climates, where it generously blooms from May to October. In this detailed illustration, Pieter Withoos follows the botanical iconographic conventions that by the end of the seventeenth century were established among scientific professionals. The upper portion of the plant is favored over the lower sections, since it is where the blooms and seeds are found. The purpose of the illustration is to present various perspectives of flowers and leaves while maintaining a respectful representation of the plant's anatomical structure. The white background, a recurring element of Western botanical illustration, objectifies the plant in positive as well as negative ways. Visually and conceptually, this mode of representation removes the specimen from its natural environment, highlighting certain characteristics while concealing the plant's ecological connections with the soil, animals, and other plants.

# PURPLE OLEANDER

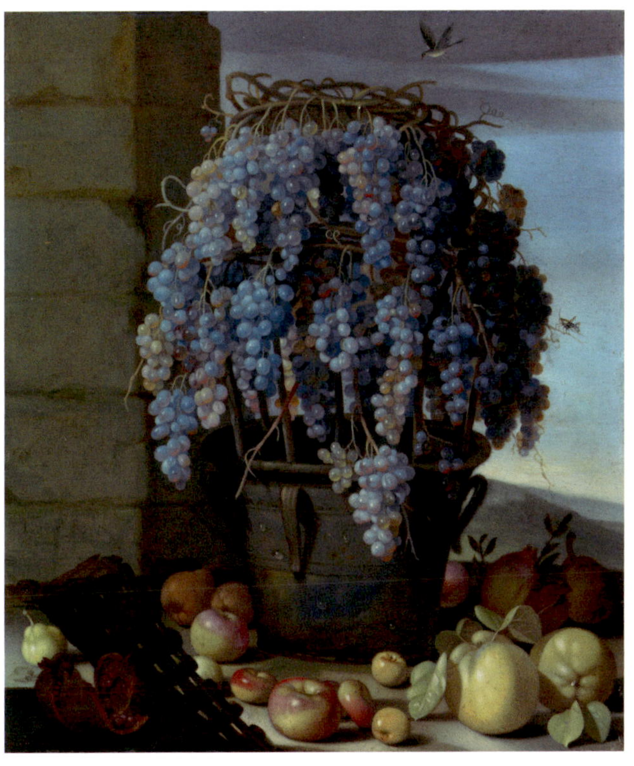

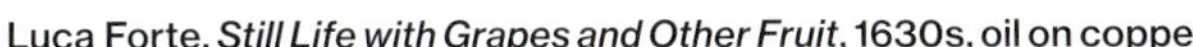

Luca Forte, *Still Life with Grapes and Other Fruit*, 1630s, oil on copper

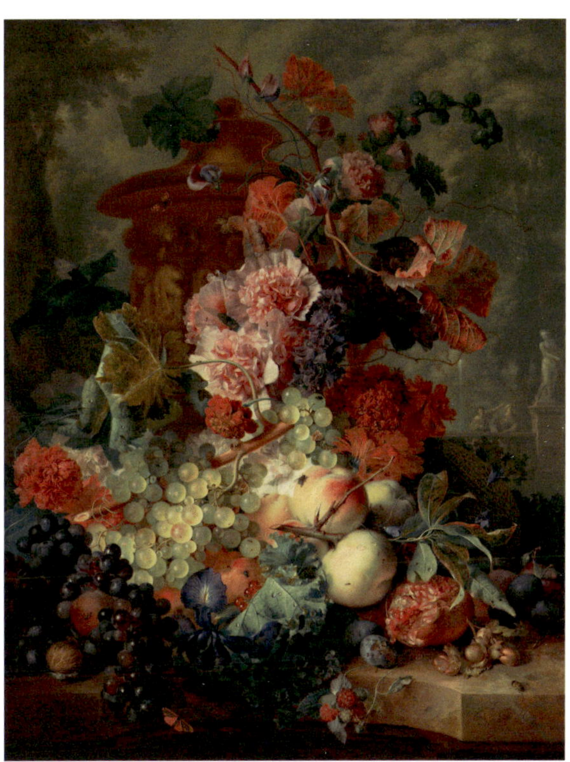

Jan van Huysum, *Fruit Piece*, 1722, oil on panel



It is not coincidental that the still-life genre flourished in the aftermath of the Protestant Reformation that swept Europe during the sixteenth century. Forbidden from painting icons representing saints and other sacred human figures, artists embedded divine messages in flowers, foliage, and fruits. And due to the intricate symbolism attached to each, it was necessary to depict the specimens with the utmost precision. Plants began to train artists in the art of realistic accuracy. Misidentification would jeopardize the complex web of encoded Christian teachings and moral associations.

Luca Forte, a still-life pioneer active in Naples, added context and atmospheric effects by painting landscapes in the backgrounds of his studies. This innovation deviated from the more canonical flat backgrounds of works like Caravaggio's *Canestra di Frutta* (Basket of Fruit, ca. 1599) and gained popularity especially in northern Europe. Still-life paintings depicting fall fruits and vegetables often allude to the inherent nobility of a morality guided by Christian principles: devotion, piety, and rectitude lead to a copiously rich spiritual life. Along with the fruits, the flowers depicted in this highly exuberant still life by Jan van Huysum would have carried individual meanings, but as a whole, they also emphasized the ephemeral nature of youth and beauty, thereby implying the importance of spiritual devotion given the inevitable decay that is the destiny of all earthly things.

## STILL LIFE WITH GRAPES AND OTHER FRUIT

## FRUIT PIECE

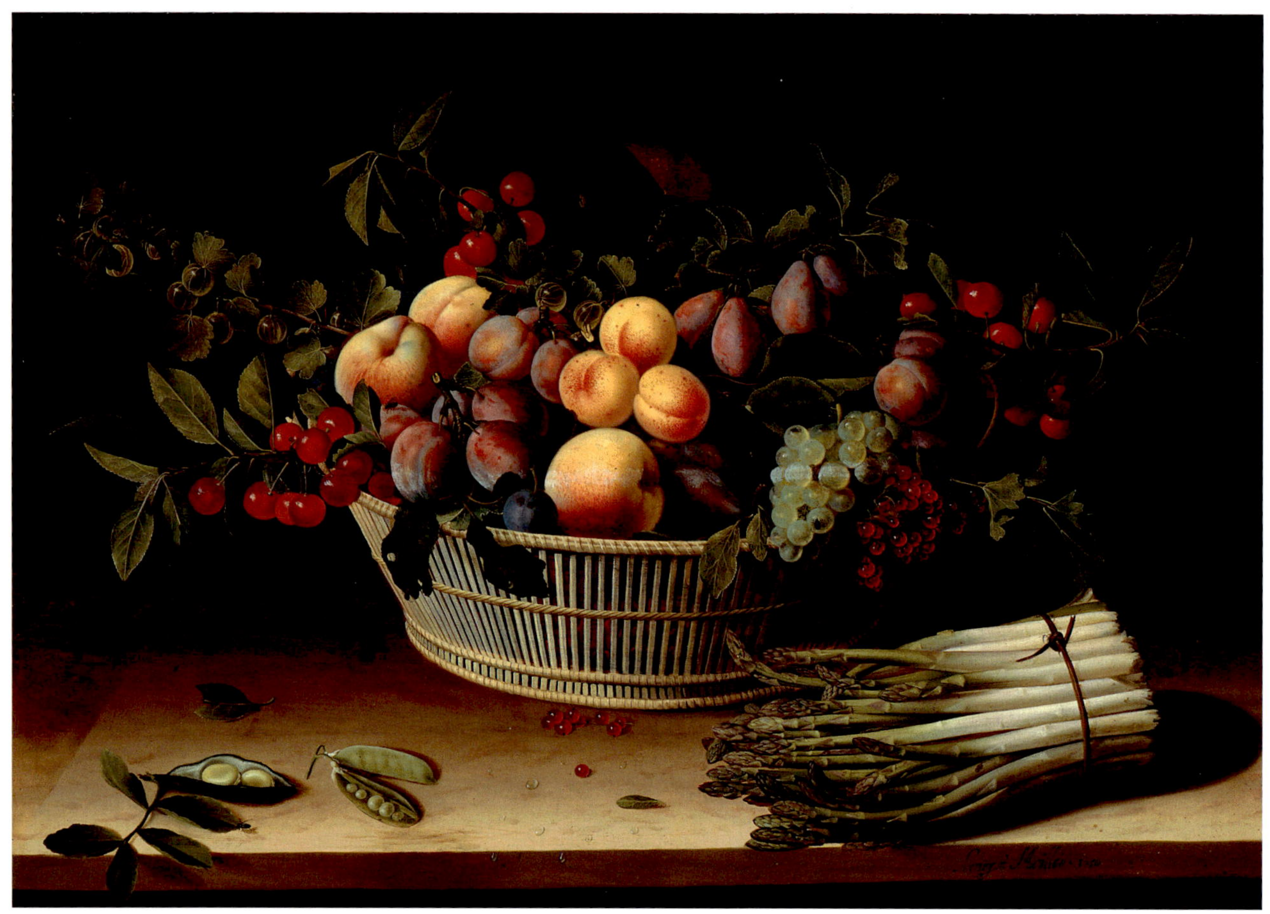

Louise Moillon, *Still Life with a Basket of Fruit and a Bunch of Asparagus*, 1630, oil on panel

Louise Moillon was an outstandingly talented artist whose ability to capture the minute details of plants made her famous across Europe. This painting was completed when she was just twenty years old. In Europe at this time, Christianity motivated the production of symbolic paintings. The concept of divine authority permeated all aspects of the natural world, in accordance with the perception that the natural realm was profoundly shaped by the omnipotence of God. As a form of memento mori, or reminder of mortality, still-life paintings served to admonish viewers that their material possessions, like life itself, were ultimately fleeting and subject to God's willful withdrawal. This artwork is filled with references to Christ's Passion—for instance cherries (blood) and grapes (the Eucharist)—as well as a substantial celebration of femininity, represented by peaches and apricots. The bunch of asparagus in the right-hand corner is an elegant and understated phallic reference, indicating fertility and abundance. Oftentimes, however, the meaning of certain fruits and plants is less clear. Art historians were long puzzled by the unusual open pods of broad beans and peas in the left-hand corner, but it is now assumed that they represent a family unit—parents and children, respectively.

## *STILL LIFE WITH A BASKET OF FRUIT AND A BUNCH OF ASPARAGUS*

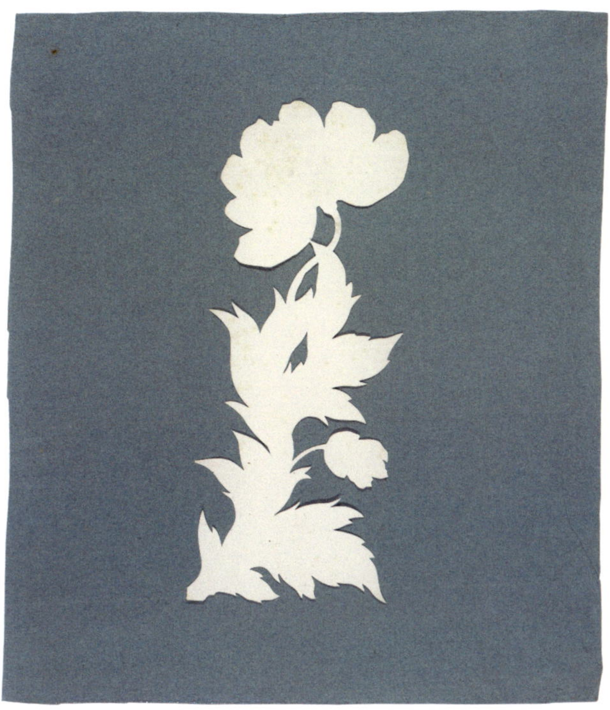

Philipp Otto Runge, *Poppy*, ca. 1800–1803, paper cutout affixed to paper

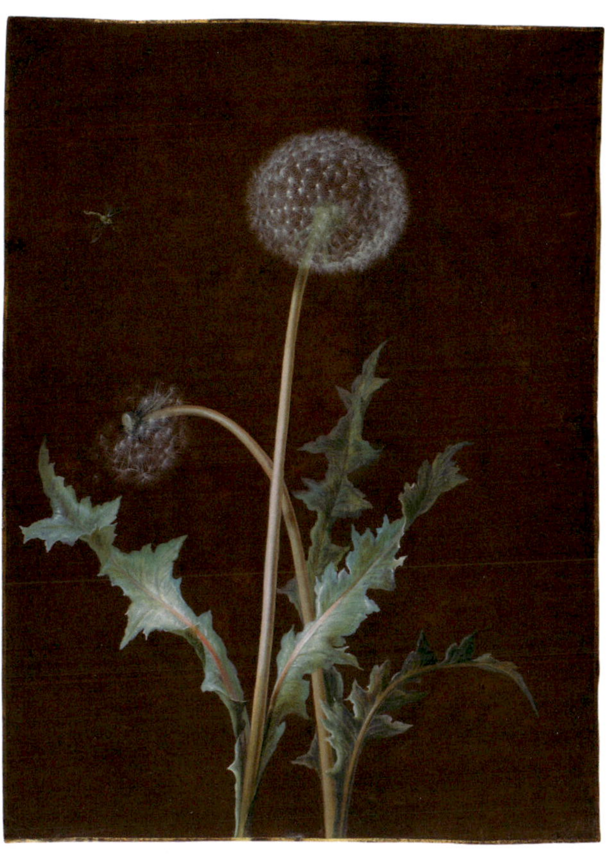



Barbara Regina Dietzsch, *Dandelion*, ca. 1755, watercolor and gouache on vellum bordered in gold

The complexity and the beauty of plants have frequently inspired artists to devise new ways to depict a particular vegetal quality or essence. Philipp Otto Runge, one of the leading color theorists and artists of German Romanticism, saw in nature a particularly intense form of mystical existentialism; in this he was inspired in great part by the work of his friend, the poet Ludwig Tieck. As a child, Runge suffered from poor health, and his mother taught him the art of scissor cuts as a means of keeping him entertained during the long hours he had to spend indoors. The numerous meticulous plant silhouettes he created throughout his short life (he died of tuberculosis at age thirty-three) seemingly sought to extract the essential characteristics of each subject. The works have an uncanny absent-presence that pertains to the species as well as to the individual specimen.

Barbara Regina Dietzsch worked in a similar vein, although her approach more closely aligned with the rhetoric of still-life painting and botanical illustration. Dietzsch saw plants as mystical harbingers of existentialist secrets—the masters of nature's cyclical rhythms. In this delicate gouache, the artist accurately represents a dandelion, capturing the last stages of its life cycle from full blowball to the seeds' final dispersal. While Runge's silhouettes seem to transcend the passing of time, Dietzsch's paintings emphasize it. But both artists resisted the temptation to include withering leaves, a motif that always alludes to the ineluctability of death.

## POPPY

## DANDELION

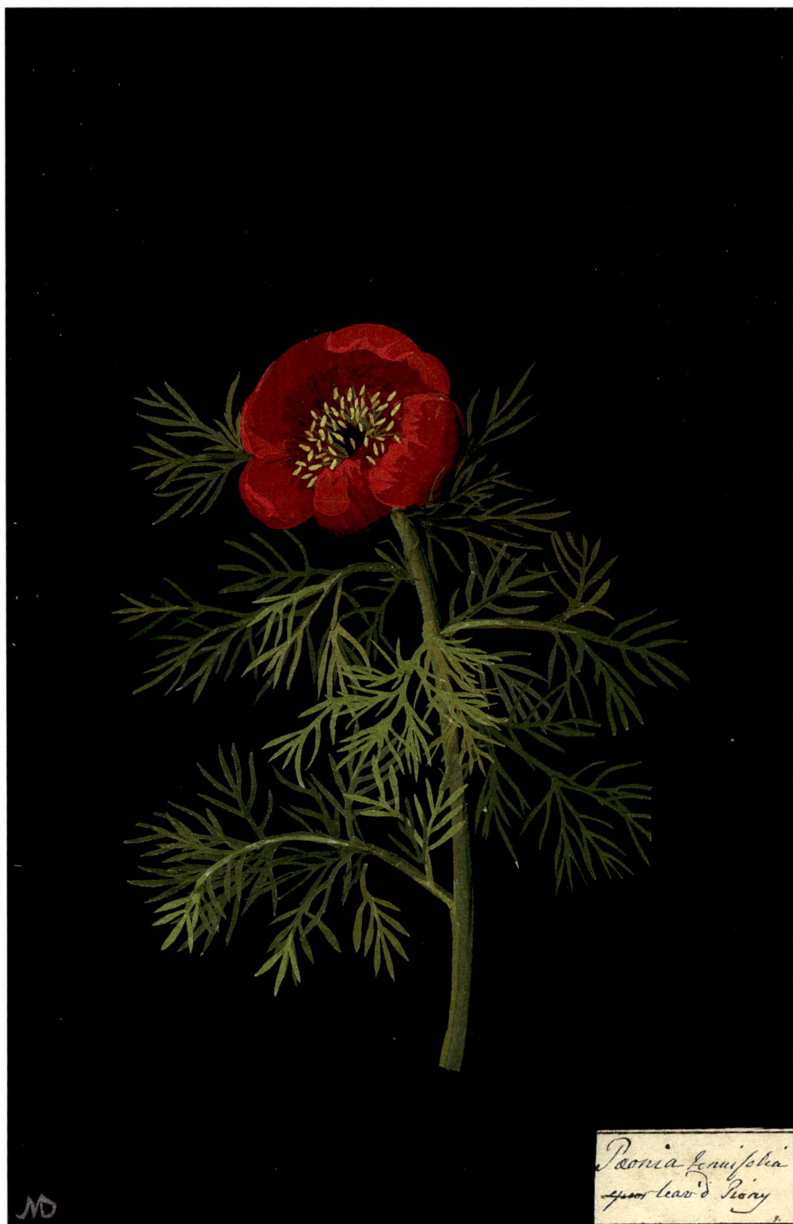


**Mary Delany, *Paeonia tenuifolia*, 1778, paper collage with bodycolor and watercolor on ink background**

Mary Delany was a British artist who at the age of seventy-two embarked on an ambitious and unprecedented botanical project. The artist recorded botanical specimens with exceptional accuracy—but not using paints or pencils. Her preferred medium was collage. Some of her works involve more than two hundred minute pieces of paper, meticulously assembled to create subtle textures, even elaborate shadows, attached to the substrate with egg yolk or flour glue. The narrow and filamentous leaves of *Paeonia tenuifolia* represented a particular challenge for the artist. This work, one of her most complex, demonstrates the artist's determination to push her newly invented medium to the limits of representability. Delany often favored black backing cards to the typical white of scientific illustration in order to emphasize the coloration of each specimen beyond the objective role of identification. Delany was prominently concerned with the importance beauty plays in the appreciation of art and plants alike, and produced work with the intention of doing justice to both.

# PAEONIA TENUIFOLIA

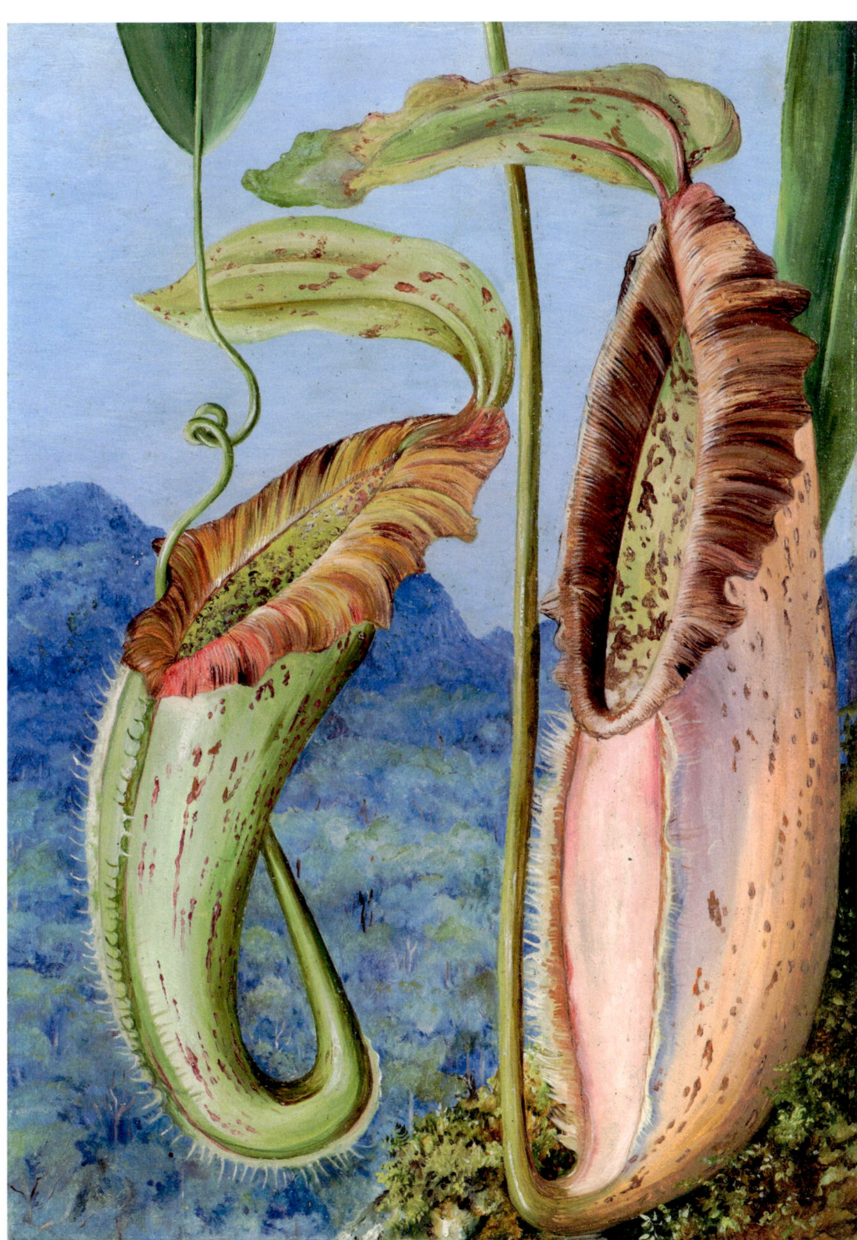

**Marianne North, *Nepenthes northiana, a Pitcher Plant from the Limestone Mountains of Sarawak, Borneo*, 1876, oil on board**

Marianne North's father first took her to Kew Gardens in London when she was twenty-six years old, sparking the beginning of a lifelong love of plants and what would eventually become an illustrious career as an accomplished and prolific botanical illustrator. Traveling almost always on her own and thus defying social restrictions that at the time greatly limited women in pursuit of scientific careers, between 1871 and 1885 North visited fifteen countries, including India, Brazil, Jamaica, and Japan; indeed, it was not common for even her male colleagues to travel so wide and far. A rebel in other respects as well, North questioned the fundamental principles of botanical illustration techniques when she shifted from watercolor, the traditional medium for depicting vegetal topics, to oil painting. The artist aimed to enhance the coherence of her representations and to accentuate the aesthetic appeal of flowers and leaves through a bolder approach. She also disregarded the classical botanical iconography according to which plants should be represented against plain backgrounds. To North, plants were unquestionably an integral part of intricate ecosystems; they belonged in the landscapes where they prospered, alongside the animals whose existence they depended on and whose lives they sustained. The pitcher plant species *Nepenthes northiana* was named after North, who was the first Westerner to discover and paint it during a journey to Borneo.



## NEPENTHES NORTHIANA

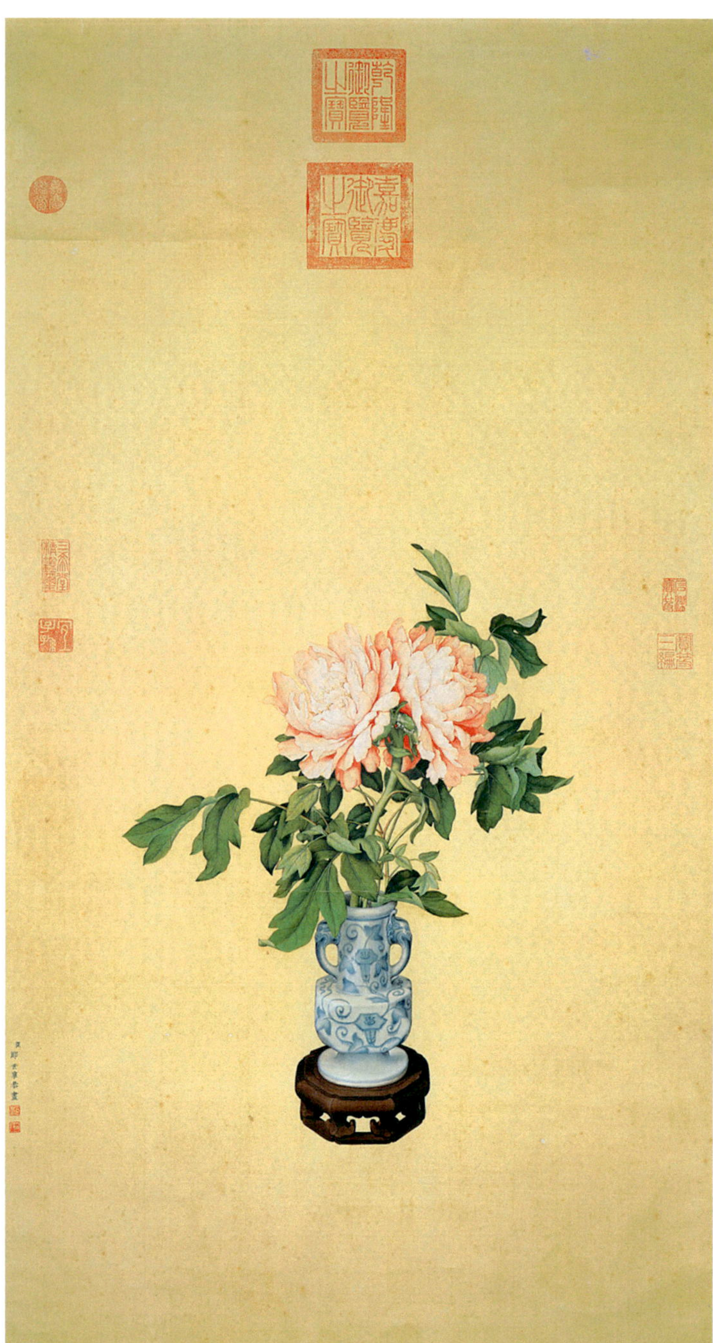

**Giuseppe Castiglione, *Vase of Flowers*, eighteenth century, ink on silk**

Western cultural impacts on Indian and Chinese art became evident throughout the seventeenth and eighteenth centuries in the emergence of optical realism, the incorporation of perspective, and a heightened focus on three-dimensionality. In botanical illustrations, the adoption of a white backdrop to clearly display the specimen became a frequent aesthetic solution. At other times, the process of cultural assimilation was more subtle, and resulted in novel and unexpected aesthetics.

Born in Milan, Giuseppe Castiglione was an Italian Jesuit missionary who, in 1715, traveled to Beijing on the order of Emperor Kangxi. Castiglione's work embodies the perfect fusion of Western realism and Eastern sensitivity. His floral still lifes exhibited the precision typical of Western art, but they were the polar opposite of the Dutch style of the time, in which impossibly sumptuous cascades of blossoms and foliage jostle for the viewer's attention. Castiglione's objective, in keeping with Chinese cultural traditions,

# *VASE OF FLOWERS*

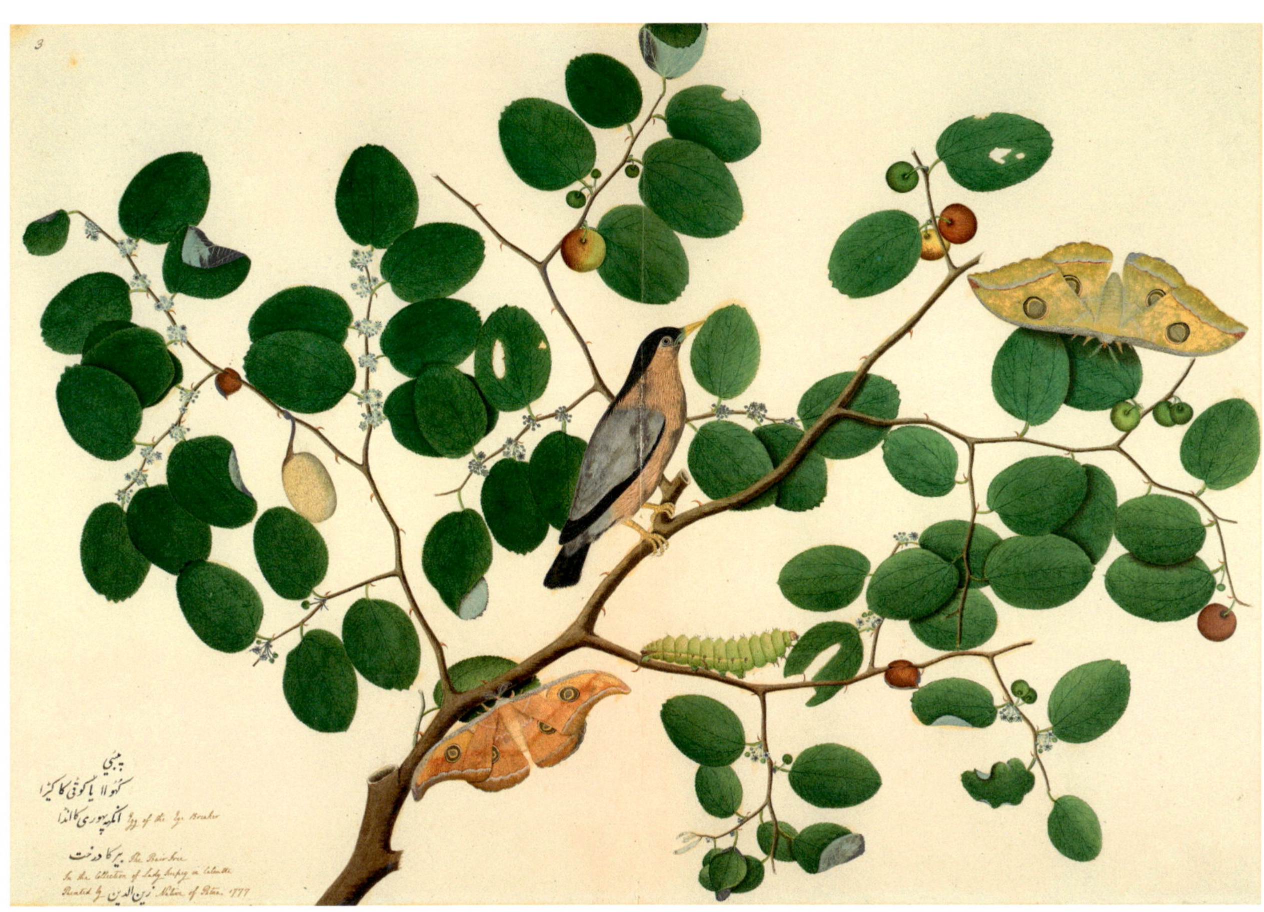

Sheikh Zain al-Din, Brahminy starling with two *Antheraea* moths, caterpillar, and cocoon on Indian jujube tree, 1777, opaque colors and ink on paper



was to concentrate on a limited number of flowers in order to better appreciate their delicate intricacy and fragile beauty.

Similarly, Sheikh Zain al-Din's illustration of a jujube tree is considered a masterpiece in which Western and Indian traditions meet. The elegantly balanced branching provides shelter for moths, a caterpillar, and a starling. The image is evenly and brightly lit, and the attention to detail is impeccable. It is a spectacular example of what became known as Company Painting: botanical and zoological illustrations produced after the 1760s, as the British East India Company began to dominate trade over the subcontinent, manifesting a distinct Anglo-Indian style combining the realism of Western art with the flatness and intricacy that distinguished Indian art.

## BRAHMINY STARLING WITH TWO *ANTHERAEA* MOTHS, CATERPILLAR, AND COCOON ON INDIAN JUJUBE TREE

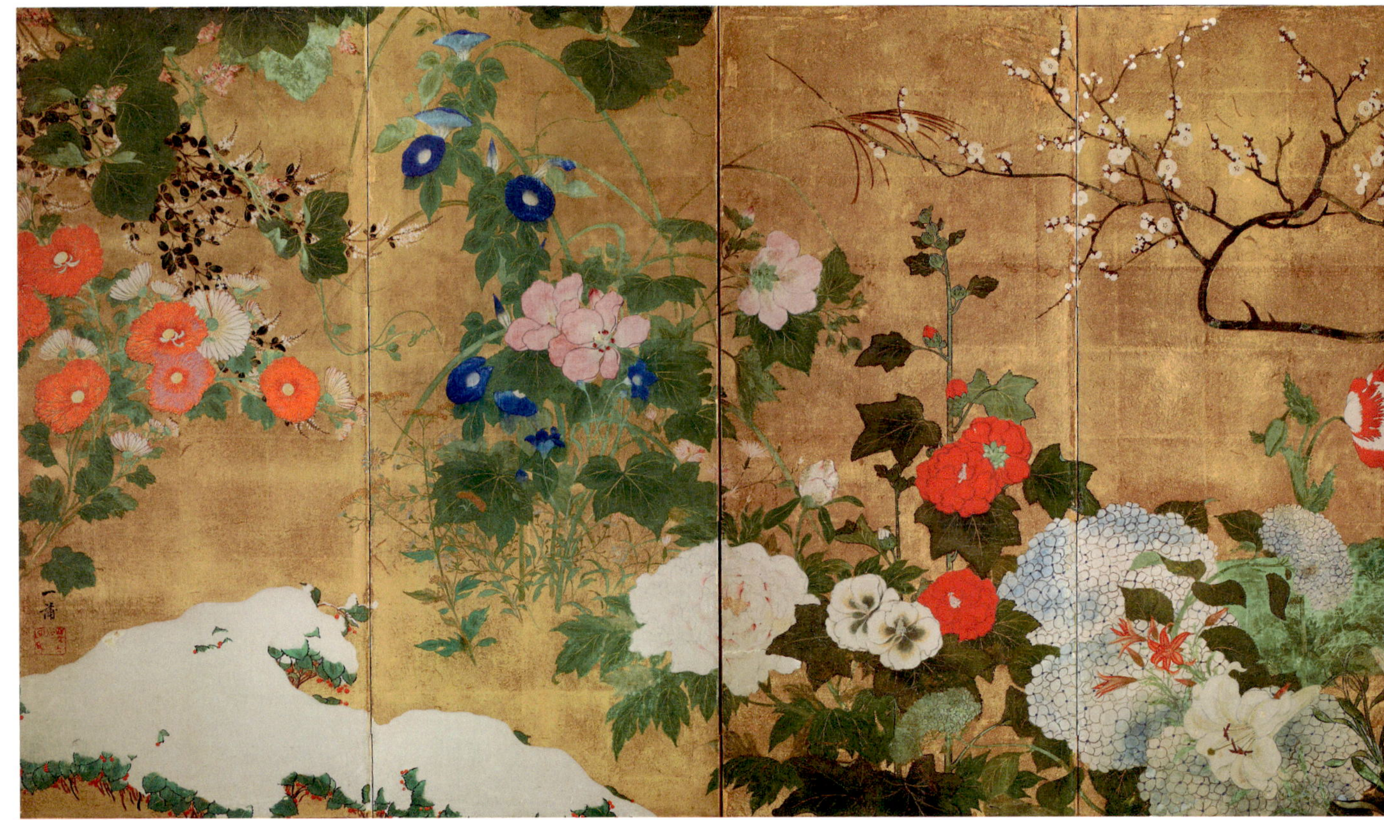

Saitō Ippo, *Flowers of the Four Seasons*, early nineteenth century, ink and colors on gold leaf, six-fold screen

Japanese artists have persistently sought to depict vegetation and blossoms. From right to left—spring to winter—Saitō Ippo, the painter of the six-panel screen, has enlisted the help of plants to evoke the passage of time and the different moods of the seasons. The composition evokes a sense of otherworldly serenity and harmony imprinted upon the golden radiance of spiritual transcendence. The plants here are not just the distant and perfected specimens of Western botanical illustration, but part of a shared existence governed by time.

Utagawa Hiroshige's *Morning Glory and Oriental Greenfinch* produces a sense of intimacy with the vegetal world by positioning the viewer close to the flowers and birds, most likely in the setting of a garden. The scene implicitly evokes the serenity of an early morning moment that, like the ipomoea flowers represented in the image, will quickly fade.

## *FLOWERS OF THE FOUR SEASONS*

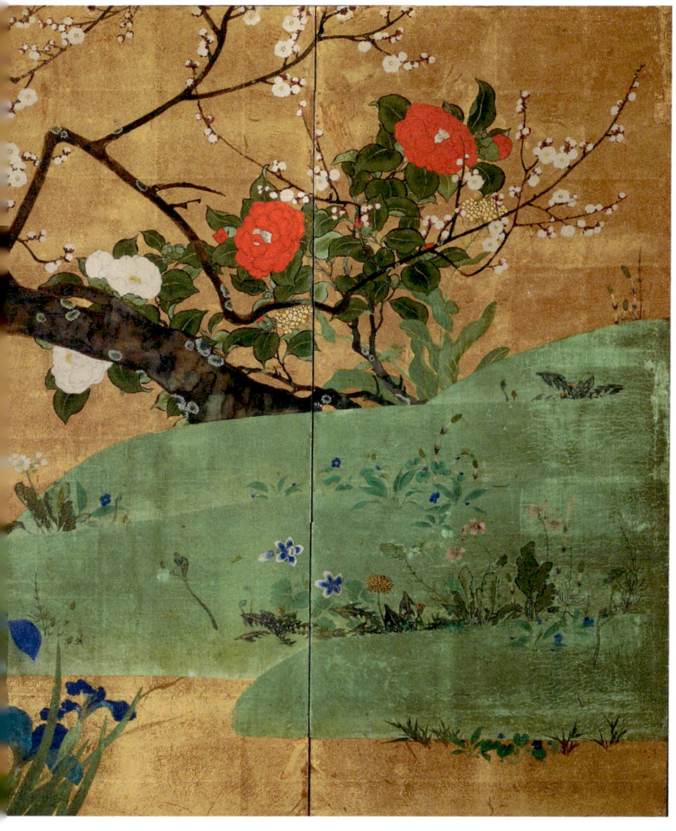

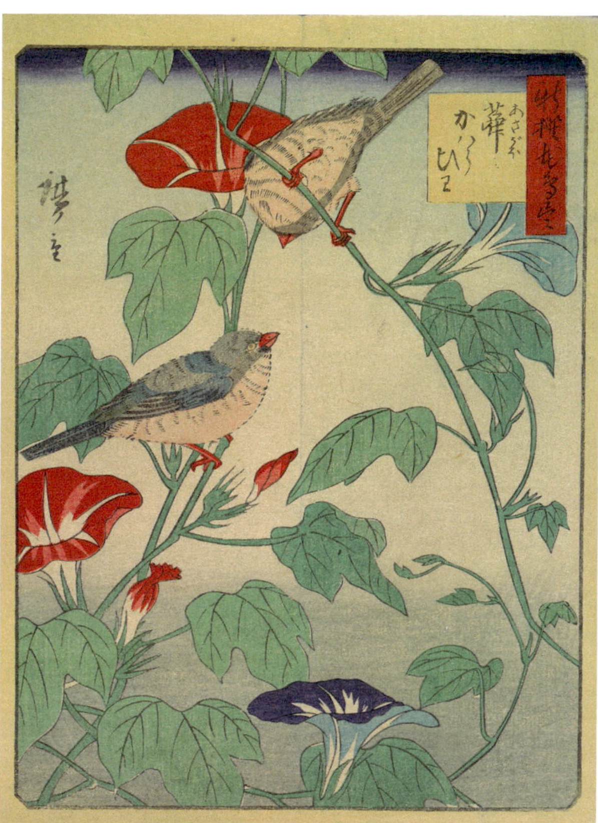

Utagawa Hiroshige, *Morning Glory and Oriental Greenfinch*, 1871–73, color woodcut on Japanese paper



# MORNING GLORY AND ORIENTAL GREENFINCH

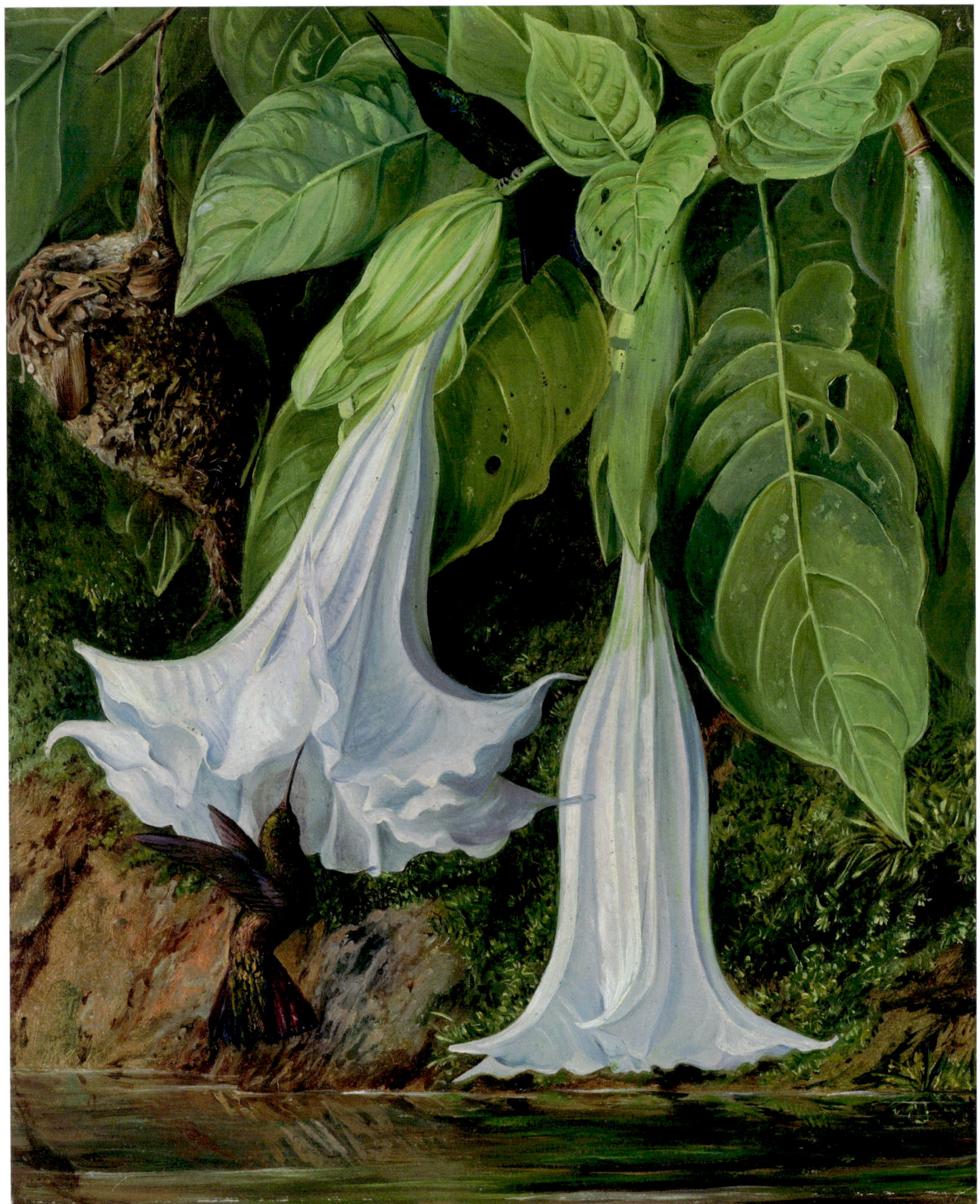

Marianne North, *Flowers of Datura and Humming Birds, Brazil*, ca. 1873, oil on board

No other woman botanical illustrator traveled as far and wide as Marianne North. The British artist's first expedition in 1871 took her to Jamaica, the United States, and Canada. A year later she spent eight months in Brazil, painting more than one hundred specimens from life. It was on this journey that North encountered a beautiful specimen of angel's trumpet (*Brugmansia*), one of the most seductively scented yet deadly poisonous plants in the Solanaceae (nightshade) family. A plant with a long history of medicinal and psychotropic applications, *Brugmansia* has been a key ingredient in rituals and ceremonies in different cultures, especially to connect with the spirits of bygone ancestors. In medicine, it has been used as an anti-inflammatory and to cure gastrointestinal disorders. Parts of the plant are used as a recreational drug, although this is strongly discouraged by medical authorities, since the amounts of psychoactive chemical compounds present in each specimen can vary dramatically and are thus difficult to safely standardize. Although the plant is native to South America, the wild ancestor of contemporary cultivars went extinct many centuries ago. All *Brugmansia* plants encountered in the wild today are accidentally rewilded cultivars.

## FLOWERS OF DATURA AND HUMMING BIRDS, BRAZIL

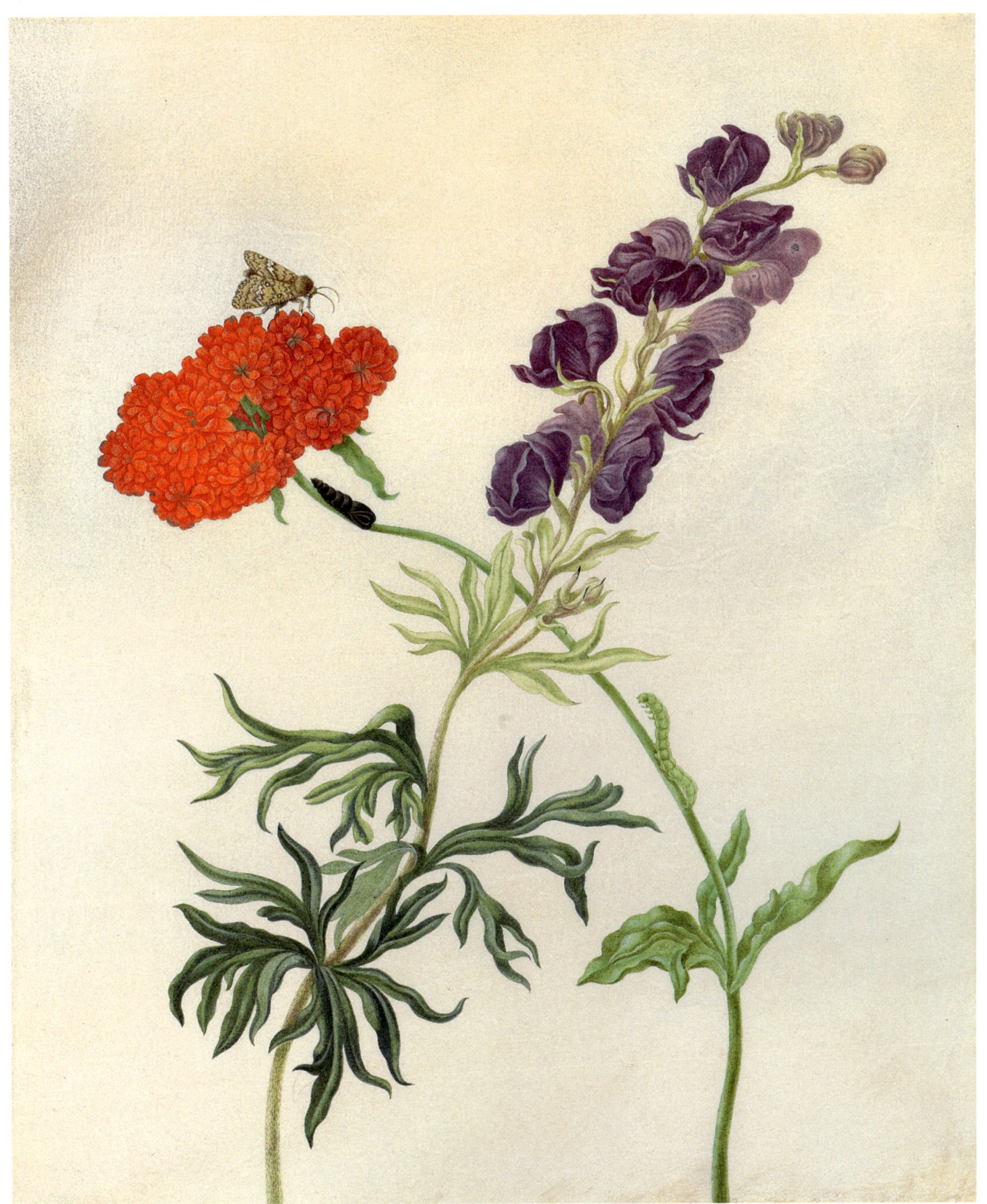

**Johanna Helena Herolt, *Maltese cross* (Lychnis chalcedonica), *Monkshood* (Aconitum napellus), *and insects*, date unknown, watercolor and bodycolor on vellum**

Johanna Helena Herolt learned how to draw plants and insects from one of the absolute masters in the field: her mother, Maria Sibylla Merian. In this illustration, Herolt pairs two poisonous plants, monkshood and Maltese cross. Monkshood was used as bait in traps for unwanted animals. It contains the alkaloid aconitine, and it has been used in China as well as in the West. Its fast-acting properties made it a favorite for poisoning arrows, and during the Middle Ages it became one of the key ingredients in witches' ointment, a strong hallucinogenic potion. Native to Russia, the Maltese cross is thought to have been introduced to Europe by either Louis IX after a visit to the Holy Land or by knights of the first Crusades. The plant had been grown in the Middle East as an ornamental variety for centuries. Although not feared as much as monkshood, it contains saponin, a substance that can induce the rupture of red blood cells.

# MALTESE CROSS, MONKSHOOD, AND INSECTS

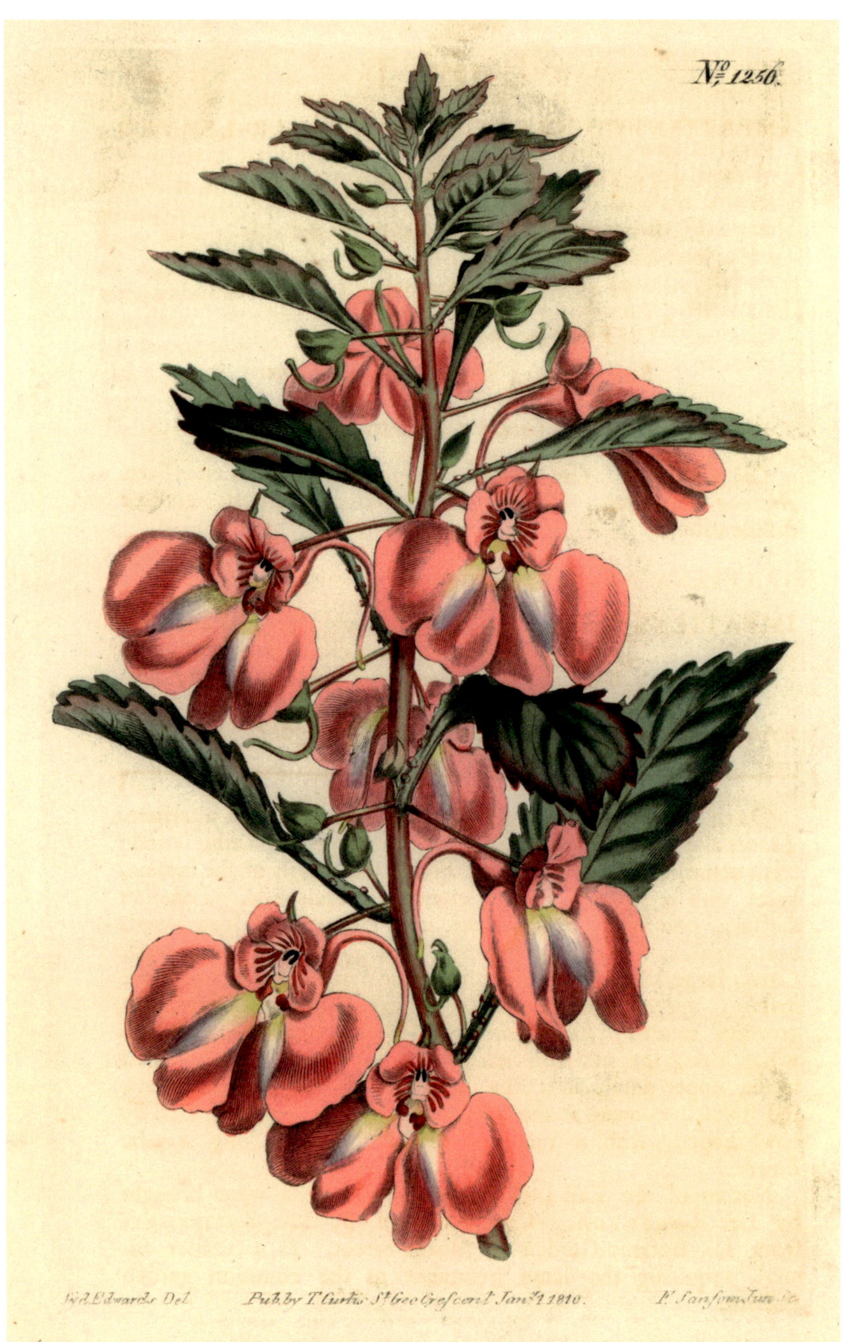


**F. Sansom Jr., Garden balsam (*Impatiens balsamina*), 1810, hand-colored copperplate engraving**

Impatiens have today become garden favorites. Available in many colors, from white to dark purple, this versatile, resilient, and generous plant is a preferred choice of many landscapers. Native to eastern Africa, impatiens was named after its seed dispersion mechanism: high-pressure pods burst open to shoot seeds up to three feet away from the mother plant, a strategy that prevents overcrowding and enhances the species' survival chances. This detailed illustration first appeared in *The New Herbal*, originally published in 1543 by German botanist Leonhart Fuchs, and was later reproduced in subsequent publications. More than five hundred species of plants were illustrated in this book using woodblock printing and hand coloring. In traditional medicine, *Impatiens balsamina* has been used to heal skin ailments: leaf extracts cure warts, while the flower soothes burns. In China, the plant is considered an antidote to snake and fish poison, while in Korea, it is used to dye fingernails red—a precaution warding off evil spirits.

# GARDEN BALSAM

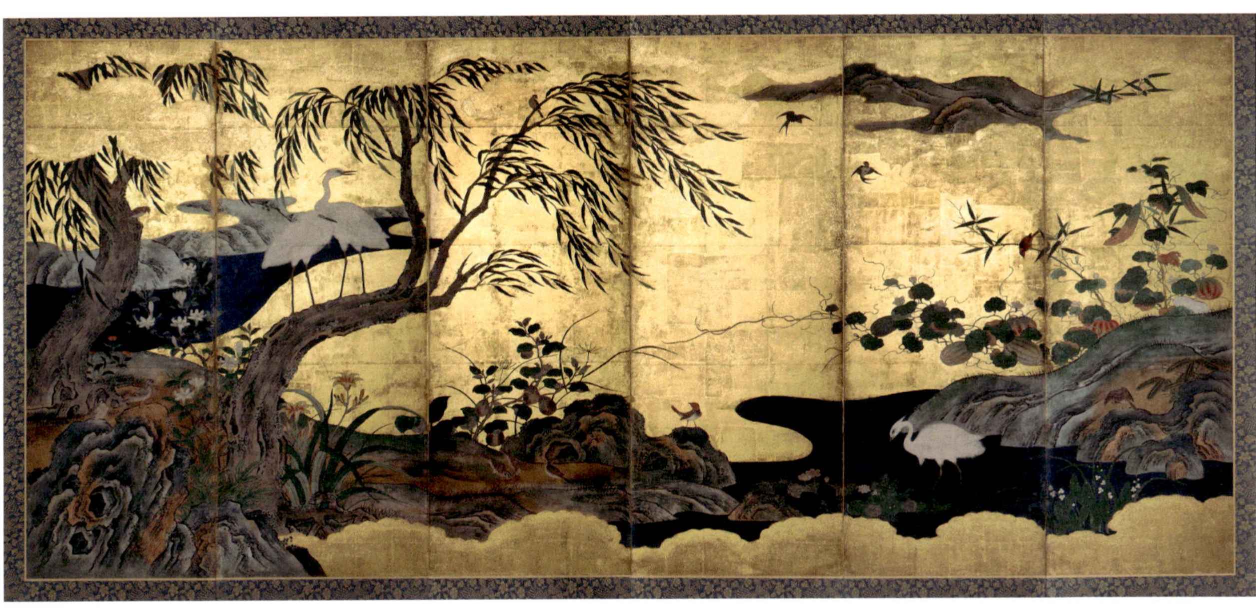



**Attributed to Kano Shôei, *Birds and Flowers*, late sixteenth century, ink, color, gold leaf, and gold fleck on paper**

This richly detailed Japanese screen features representatives of fifteen species of birds and at least twenty different plants. Arranged across six panels, the composition reflects ideals of balance and harmony central to Buddhist beliefs; the gold leaf portions, for instance, represent the timeless, divine dimension of creation. All plant species pictured here, including willow, bamboo, eggplant, and marigold, are associated with summer and early fall. As such, the theme of the panel points to the wisdom and fullness of maturity in human life as mirrored by the passing of the seasons in nature. Willow has for millennia been used in traditional medicine—chewing its bark reduces inflammation and fever. This part of the plant contains salicin, which would later become the basis of the invention of aspirin. In this screen, the willow also alludes to death, since in Japanese culture it is associated with ghosts. Nearby, a cluster of marigolds underscores the willow's message: these golden flowers symbolize the loss of a loved one.

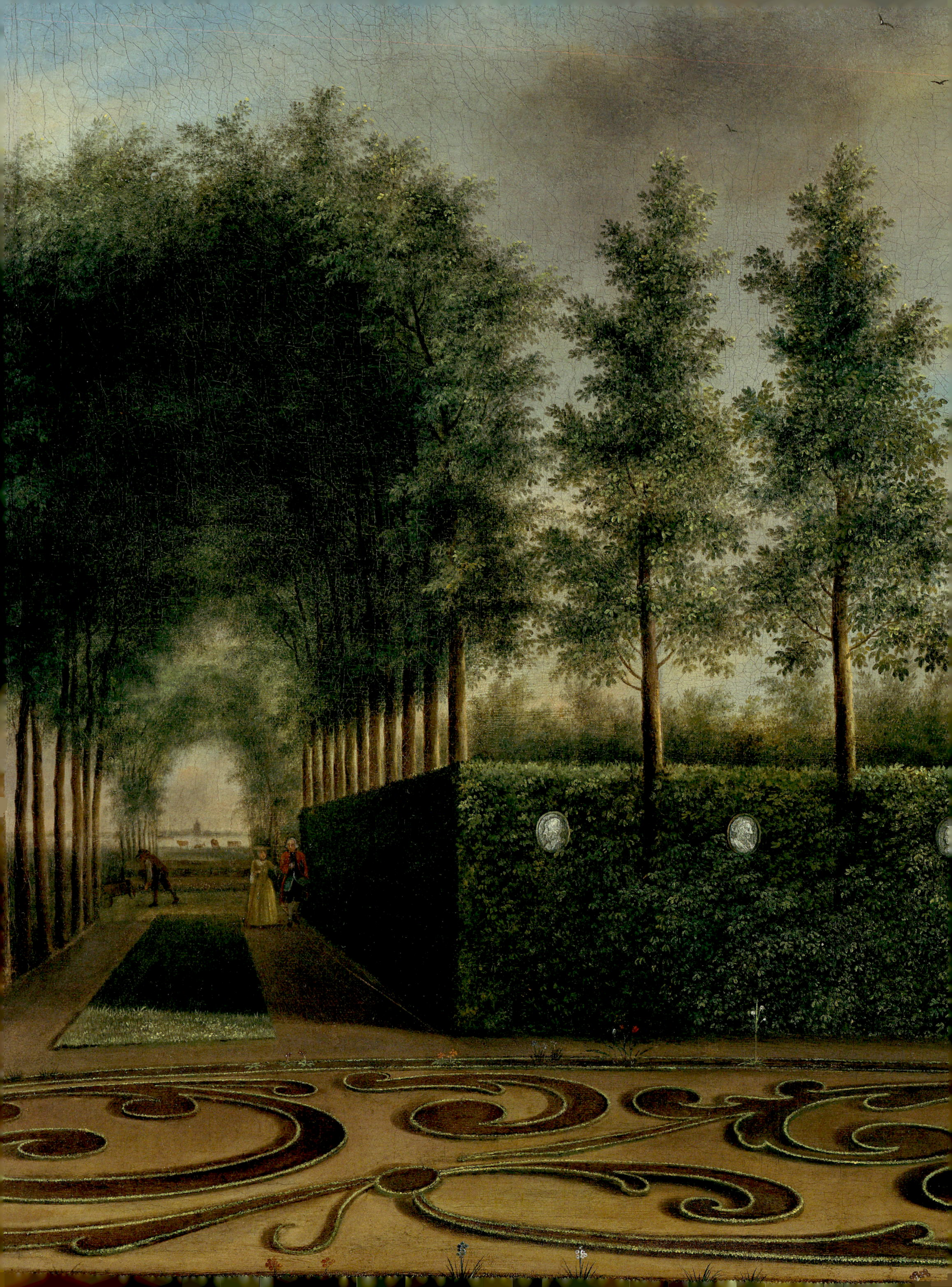

CHAPTER 5

# SHAPING OUR WORLD: BOTANICAL DESIGNS

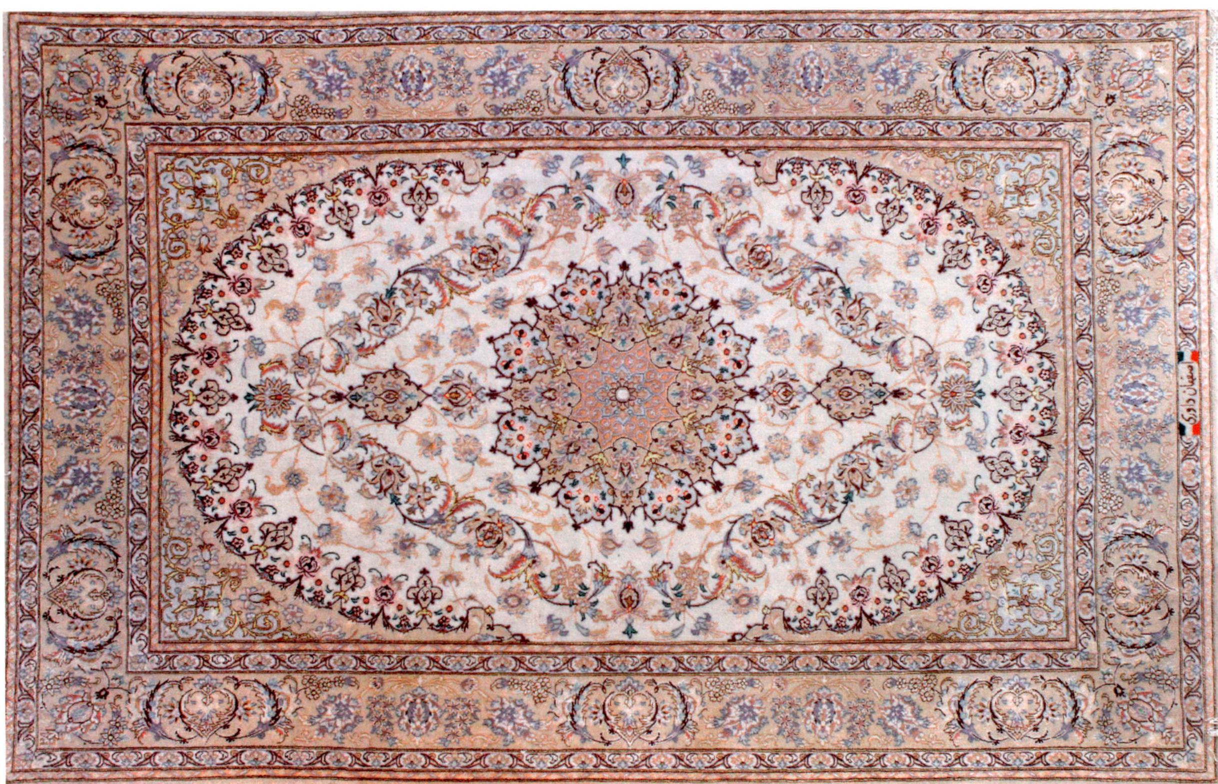

Isfahan carpet, 2013, hand-knotted carpet



The historic city of Isfahan is located in the middle of the Iranian Plateau, a vast area stretching from the Great Salt Desert in the east and north to the snowcapped Zagros Mountains in the west. Renowned for its intricate and elegant examples of Persian architecture, the city is also home to a community of rug weavers who keep old traditions alive. Isfahan rugs are among the finest in the world. Expertly woven by hand, on cotton foundations, they often count one million knots per square meter—a weaving density that enables the crafting of sophisticated and detailed designs.[1]

Rug weaving in this region blossomed during the sixteenth century under the rule of Shah Abbas the Great, a staunch supporter of the arts. The finest Isfahan rugs frequently include stylized vegetal patterns intricately arranged around a central medallion. Although the pattern's history is disputed, it is most likely related to the Islamic arabesque, a decorative motif that emerged in Baghdad in about the eleventh century, inspired by Hellenistic artisans in Asia Minor.[2] The aesthetic vegetal harmony that characterizes the arabesque—often representing local plant species—is a manifestation of the underlying unity that rules the cosmos. Only through the representation of plants could this archetypal characteristic be adequately depicted and expressed.

The portrayal of the Paradise Gardens in the Qur'an serves as the foundation for the significance of plant representation in Islamic culture. The intricate designs of Isfahan rugs, the assortment of arabesque motifs adorning the pointed domes of mosques (referred to as *qubba*), and carved marble panels spanning from Morocco to Malaysia feature linear motifs that unfurl from an unbroken vortex of a spiral, or fragment into fractals inspired by vegetation. This dynamism suggests expansion and growth and is directly informed by the life cycles of plants as they emerge from seed and reach toward the sun—an emblem of the creator. Therefore, the Isfahan rug's central medallion is a magnificent representation of the sun. Keen observation of plant anatomy and behavior also defines the prominent symmetry that rules the composition—reminders of the perfection and unity that maintain harmony on Earth. This is manifested in the mathematical rigor and modularity that pervades vegetal existence and underpins divine order.[3]

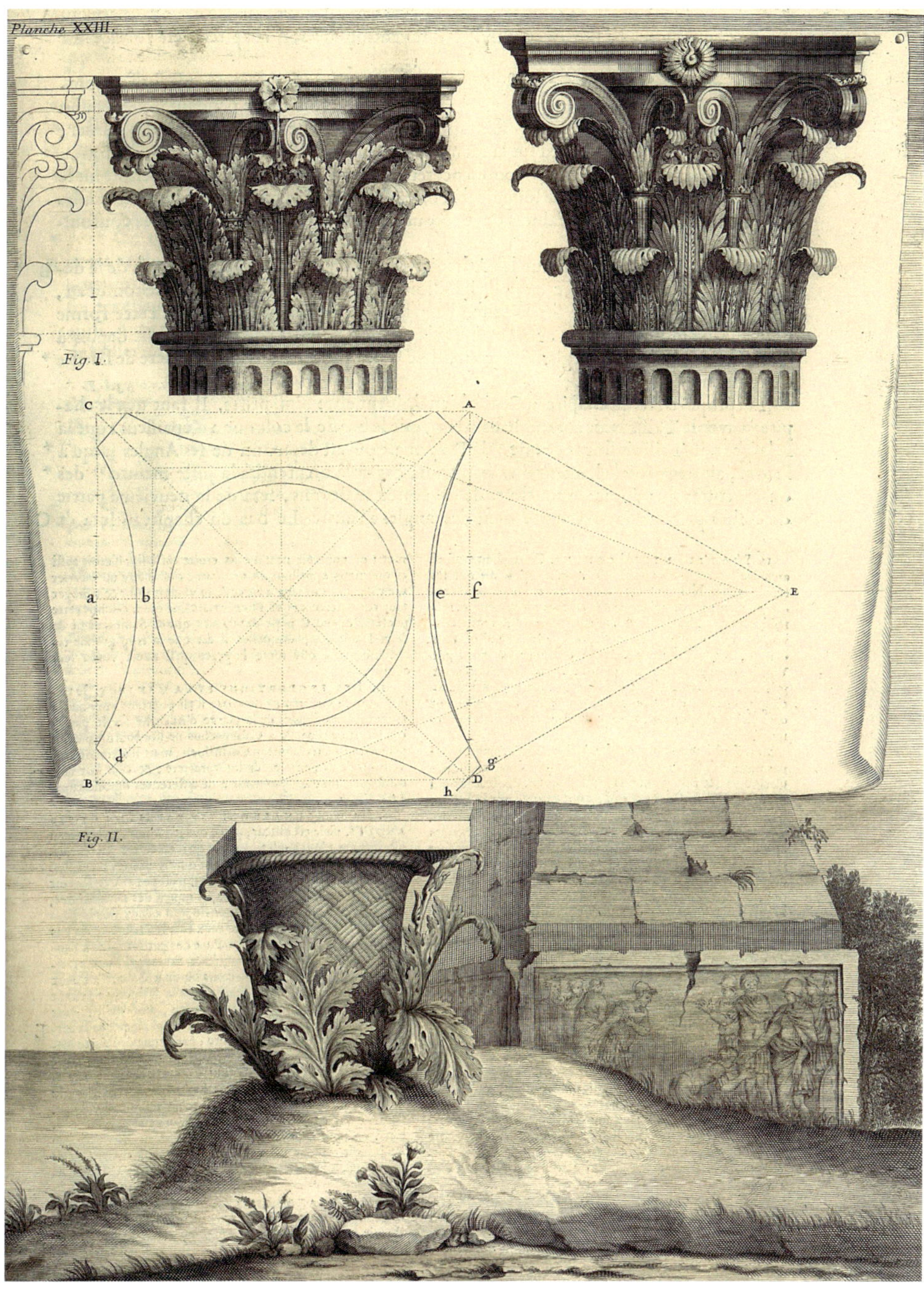


Various artists, *Acanthus mollis* in *Les dix livres d'Architecture de Vitruve, corrigez et traduits nouvellement en François, avec notes & de figures*, 1684, woodcut illustrations and engraved plates



One of the commonly depicted plants in Middle Eastern rugs and arabesques is *Acanthus mollis*. In time, its toothed leaves became the most influential vegetal motif in the history of global art and architecture. Vitruvius reports that the adoption of acanthus leaves as the quintessential element of Greek Corinthian capitals was first introduced by the architect and sculptor Callimachus during the second half of the fifth century BCE.[4] According to the story, a basket filled with toys was left on the grave of a young girl. A tile was placed on top of the toys to shield them from the elements. Callimachus returned to the tomb in the spring and saw that an acanthus plant had sprung from beneath the basket, its leaves curled down under the tile. Transfixed by the sight, he rushed to his studio to carve the vision into stone, thereby crafting the quintessential symbol of classicism. With its roots firmly planted

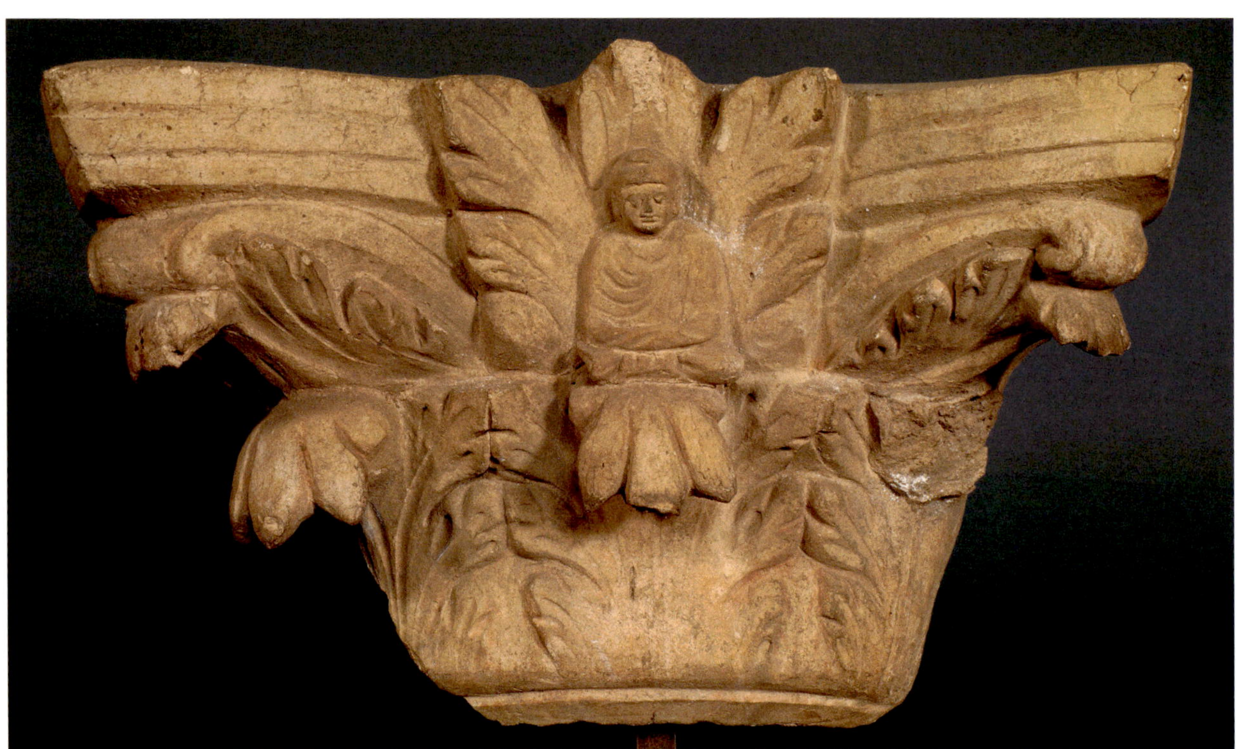

Buddha within acanthus-leaf capital, Gandhara, ca. third or fourth century CE, stucco



in this tender story, the plant quickly grew into a symbol of immortality and rebirth, reaching well beyond Greek shores.[5]

By the first century CE, acanthus had come to grace Indo-Corinthian capitals in Southern Asia as well as northern India, and appeared in Greco-Buddhist art. In the East, acanthus came to symbolize Buddha's protection and benevolence.[6] Its leaves adorned Malaysian and Chinese vases and funerary jars.[7] In the West, its most popular application remained the capital of the Corinthian column, owing to the Romans' high regard for traditional Greek art and architecture. Around the Mediterranean, acanthus leaves also prominently featured in Byzantine, Romanesque, Renaissance, and Gothic architecture. Thereafter, the revival of classical art and philosophy promoted by the Renaissance ensured that the legacy of the acanthus leaf would continue to bloom across the centuries. From Europe, traveling on colonialist routes, acanthus eventually spread to North America, South Africa, and Australia and became part of the emblems of many Western institutions.[8]

Nearly two thousand years after the emergence of acanthus as a vegetal icon, in 1875 textile design pioneer William Morris created plant-inspired wallpapers that changed the way the middle class saw and decorated their homes. Morris loathed how industrialization had led to what he perceived as the widespread uglification of architecture and design, as well as to a reckless and disastrous degradation of the environment.[9]

Since an early age, Morris had found inspiration in plants. As a boy he had discovered a copy of John Gerard's enormous and sumptuous 1597 tome *General History of Plants*, the most important herbal in English history, featuring 2,850 plant descriptions and 2,705 highly detailed illustrations. He regularly referred to this book as a plant identification guide throughout his life, both while visiting the nearby Epping Forest and when making his intricate wallpaper designs.[10] Morris's passion for plants ultimately led to the development of an ecosocialist agenda. He believed in social equality and was a feminist, an environmentalist, and an anti-imperialist who aspired to a deeper feeling of community fellowship. His acanthus wallpaper motif—one of the most complex and rich he ever attempted—revolutionized modern woodblock printing processes and is a vivid emblem of the

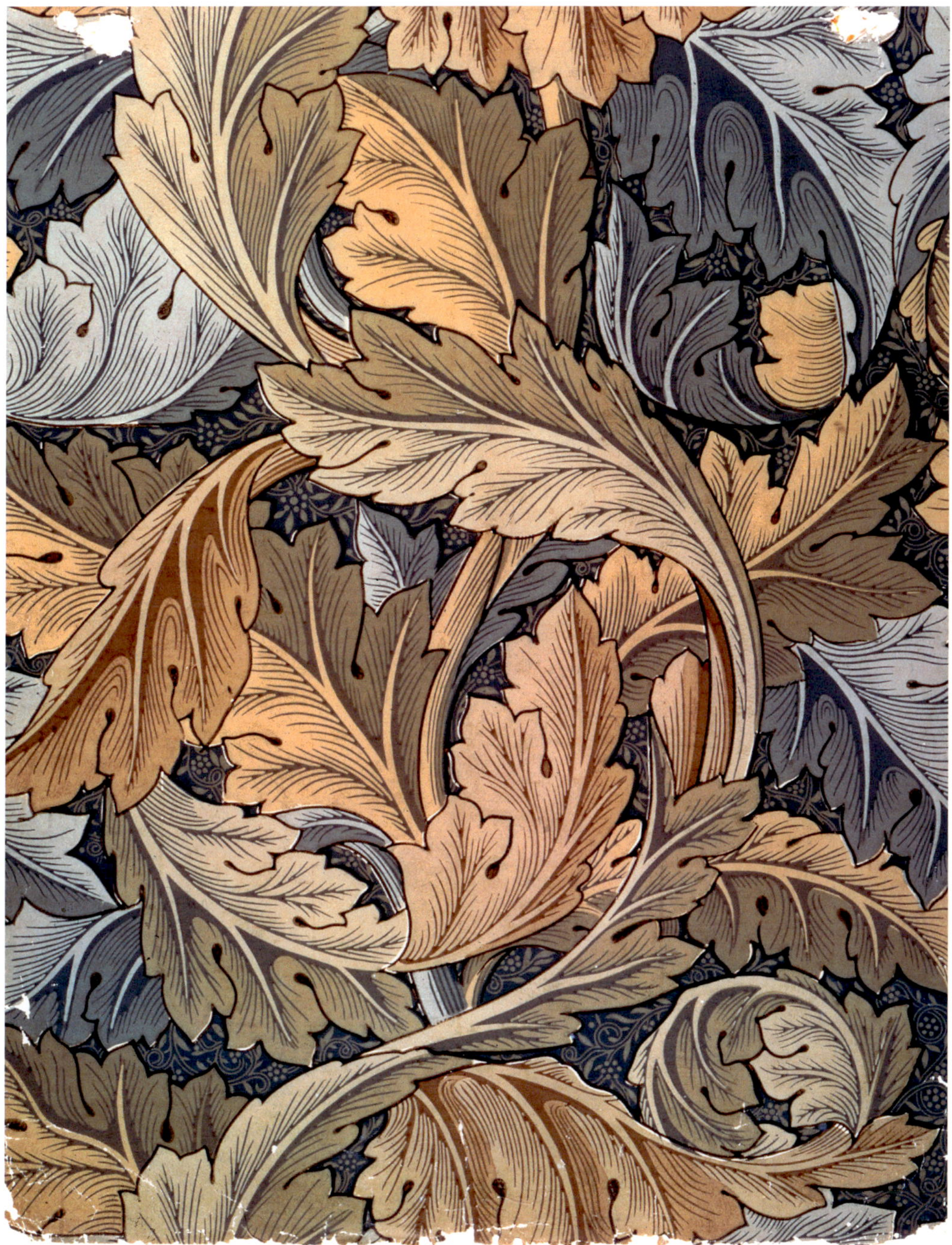

William Morris, *Acanthus*, 1875, block print in distemper colors on paper



values that pervaded the Arts and Crafts movement, with which he was deeply involved.

Equally blessed and cursed because of their beauty, plants have always straddled the thin line that, in the West, separates art and design. They have frequently strayed across creative categories and domains in ways that allowed for formal transfiguration, resulting in an unstable tension between conceptualism and sheer aesthetic ornamentation. In art and design, plants often emerge as transhistorical icons. It is therefore not a surprise that the formal medievalism Morris invented synthesized a range of vegetal influences from around the world. He looked into the past to envision a better future. Chromatic and compositional elements derived from Indian and Middle Eastern art played important roles in the sense of balance and harmony that his work embodied. Often inspired by Persian tapestries,

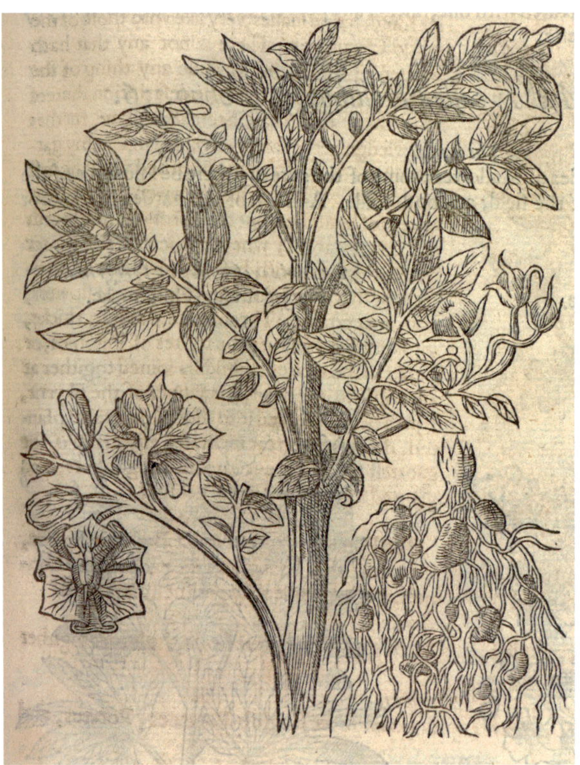

John Gerard, *Potato of Virginia*, in *The Herball or, Generall Historie of Plantes*, 1597, woodcut



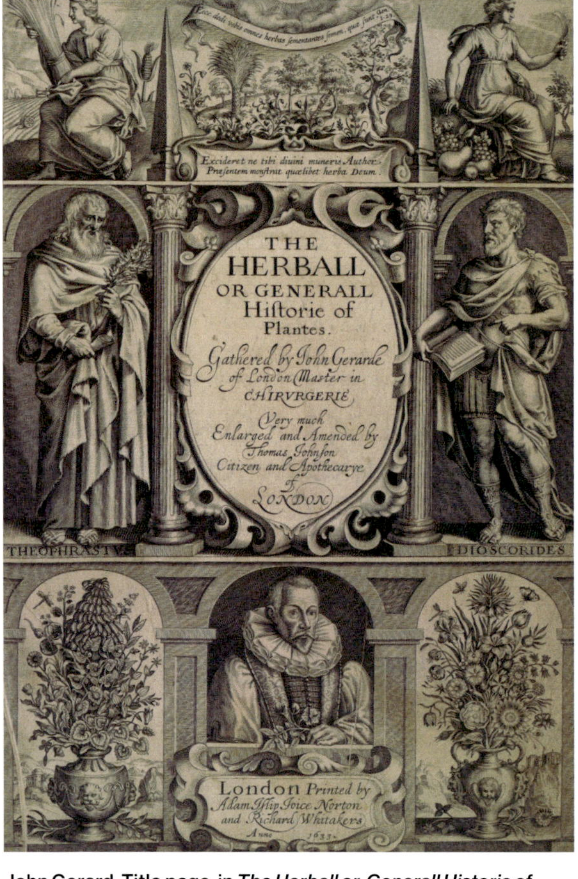


John Gerard, Title page, in *The Herball or, Generall Historie of Plantes*, engraving

conceptually as well as aesthetically, Morris's vegetal designs were not simply decorative but embodied the spiritual belief that nature holds the key to a healthier and more meaningfully lived life.

Morris's focus on non-mechanized methods and processes sparked renewed interest in vegetal dyes in the West, which at that time generally produced richer and brighter colors than their industrial, synthetic equivalents. In this case too, Gerard's book proved a treasure trove, as the many historic dye formulas that Morris resurrected for his weaving and printing procedures came from its pages. Dyes frequently used by Morris included red extracted from rose madder (*Rubia tinctorum*) and indigo blue from *Indigofera tinctoria*, a plant that played important roles in many botanical revolutions across the world.[11] Indigo blue, often described by the Greeks as "blue dye from India," was prized for its very rich, saturated color. In the fifth century CE, when commerce between sub-Saharan Africa and North Africa was at its height, Tuareg tribes began to dye their robes indigo blue. The intensely colored *daraa*—traditional clothing worn by men—sheltered them from the scorching sun and prevented dehydration. The blue color, obtained by fermenting indigo plants in lime or stale urine, was associated with a middle-class socioeconomic background; at the time, the higher classes wore white, and the working classes wore black.

The ancient Maya of Central America used indigo combined with white clay to decorate their vessels and temples.[12] The color played an important role in Persian and Indian manuscripts as well as in Greek frescoes, and for a long time indigo was the most popular choice for ink in China.[13] It was also highly prized by the Romans, but for centuries it was the weaker and more affordable blue dye extracted from woad (*Isatis tinctoria*) that dominated trade. A limited number of imported indigo-colored illuminations appeared in medieval manuscripts, but there as well indigo represented a cheaper alternative to the more expensive ultramarine mineral-based pigment that was imported from Iran.[14]

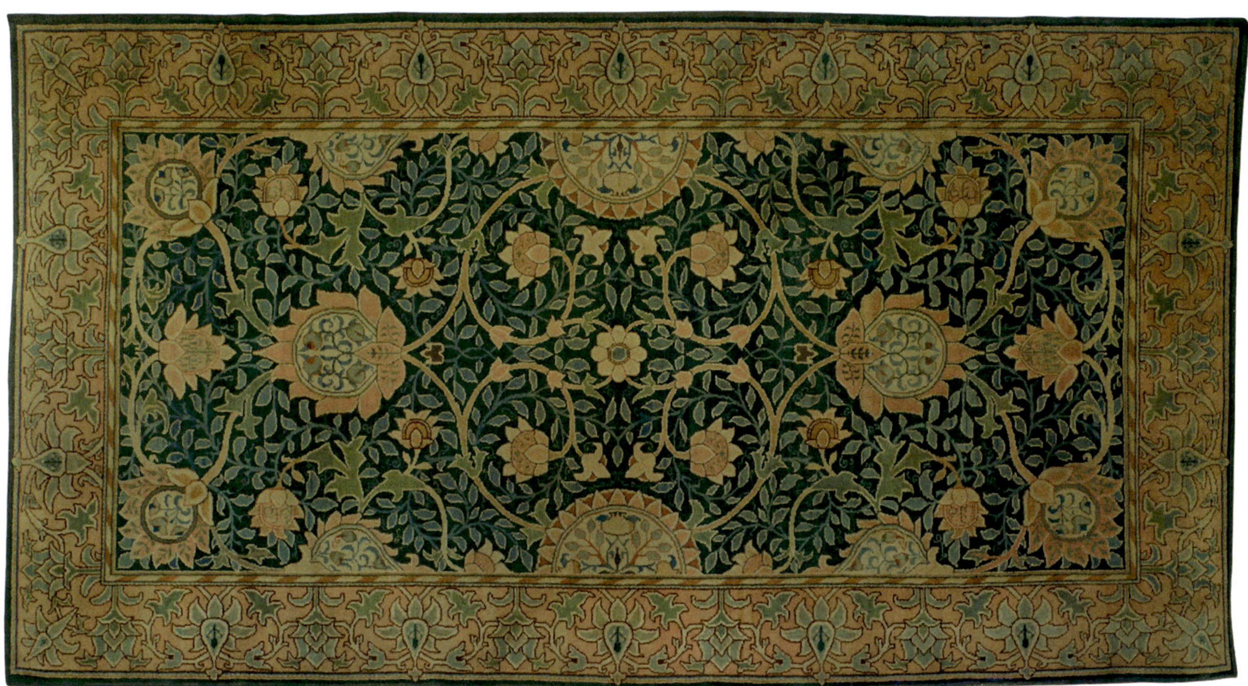

William Morris, Carpet, ca. 1881–83, hand-knotted wool on cotton warps with jute bindings

Between the twelfth and the eighteenth centuries in Western art, the color blue became emblematic of the Virgin Mary, whose cloak evoked the infinity of the sky and the depths of the sea. This pious, symbolic association heightened the desirability of the color across heraldry and fashion. Woad dye rapidly became a profitable business, and plantations maintained its consistent supply for various industries.[15] The new "blue gold" swiftly converted merchants into wealthy landowners, but mass production of this plant had a major negative effect on the land, since nitrogen- and phosphorus-rich woad depletes the soil. Concerned, Elizabeth I took swift action in 1585 to restrict woad plantations in England, prompting the establishment of an eight-year crop rotation system that alternated clover and oats to help the soil recover.[16] By the end of the first half of the seventeenth century, the steady demand for blue in art and fashion fueled the lucrative import of indigo into Europe, causing a war over the "blue market." Woad producers made a concerted effort to disparage indigo by spreading unfounded claims about its health threats, leading to bans in multiple countries.[17] Woad retained its market primacy for centuries, until eventually the continuous influx of indigo imports from the Dutch and English East India Companies progressively made the dye more affordable and eventually eliminated the stigma.

Large-scale indigo plantations were established throughout the Caribbean, West Africa, South America, and beyond, particularly in Jamaica, South Carolina, and the Virgin Islands. These farms were tended to and harvested by enslaved Africans. In 1791, the treacherous circumstances under which enslaved people were forced to process indigo in Saint-Domingue (now Haiti), a French colony at the time, ignited the first and only successful slave-led revolt in history. The event led to the abolition of slavery in Haiti and its establishment as an independent republic. Thus the symbolic significance of a plant-derived pigment set off a chain reaction of riches gained and lost, damaged ecosystems, imperialist exploitation, death, and freedom that radically changed the world.[18] By the end of the first part of the eighteenth century, the indigo monopoly had been broken owing to the accidental discovery of Prussian blue, which was produced by the oxidation of ferrous ferrocyanide salts and dried blood. The pigment was quickly adopted in Japan by Hokusai and Utagawa Hiroshige for their woodblock prints, and thereafter it became the favorite blue of Impressionist artists such as Claude Monet and Pierre-Auguste Renoir.[19]

In this pivotal moment of change, William Morris's desire to revert to natural colors sprang from his conviction that eco-friendly ways of living would be better for people and the Earth. And it is true that

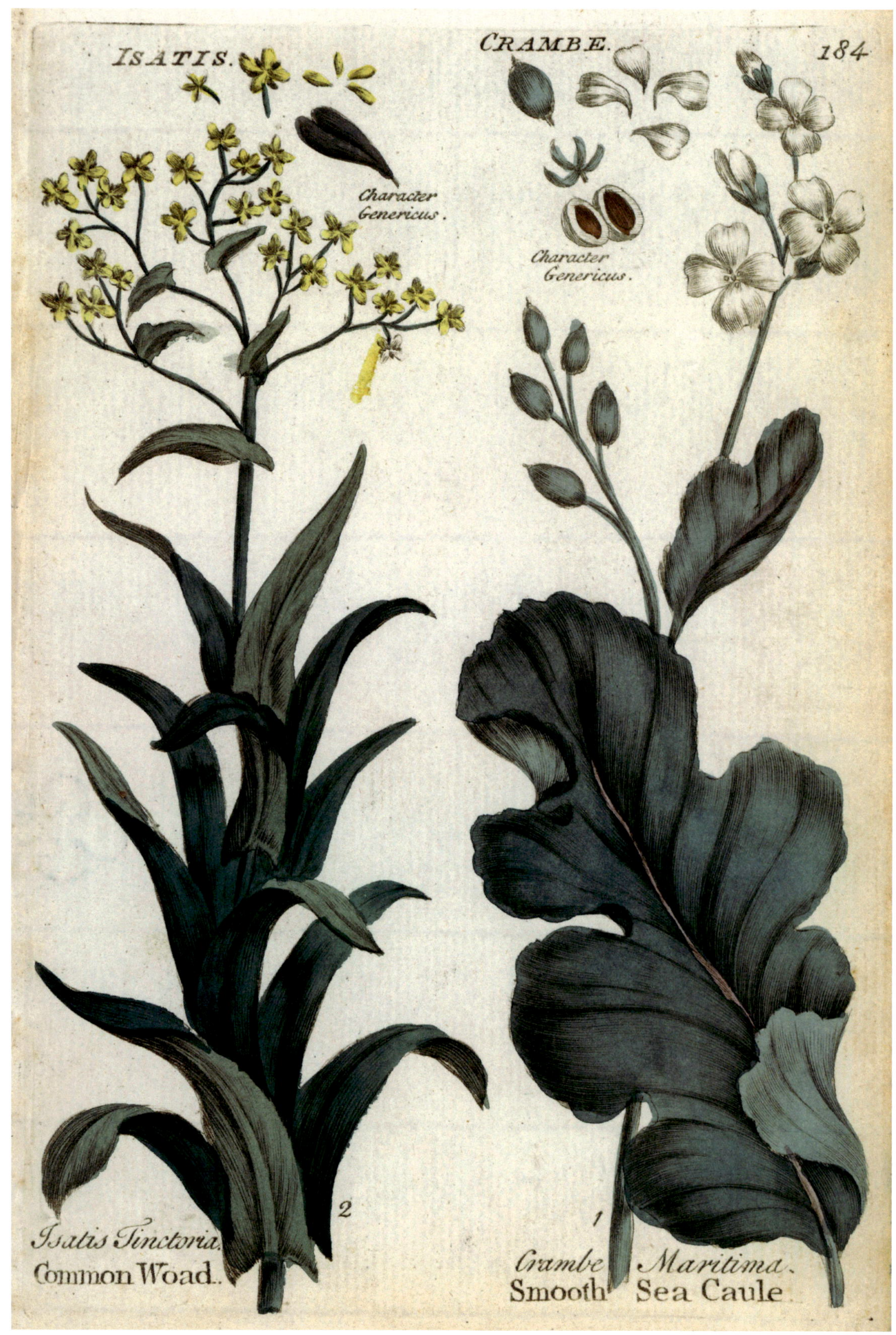


Unknown artist, *Isatis tinctoria* (common woad) and *Crambe maritima* (smooth sea caule), 1792, hand-colored copperplate engraving

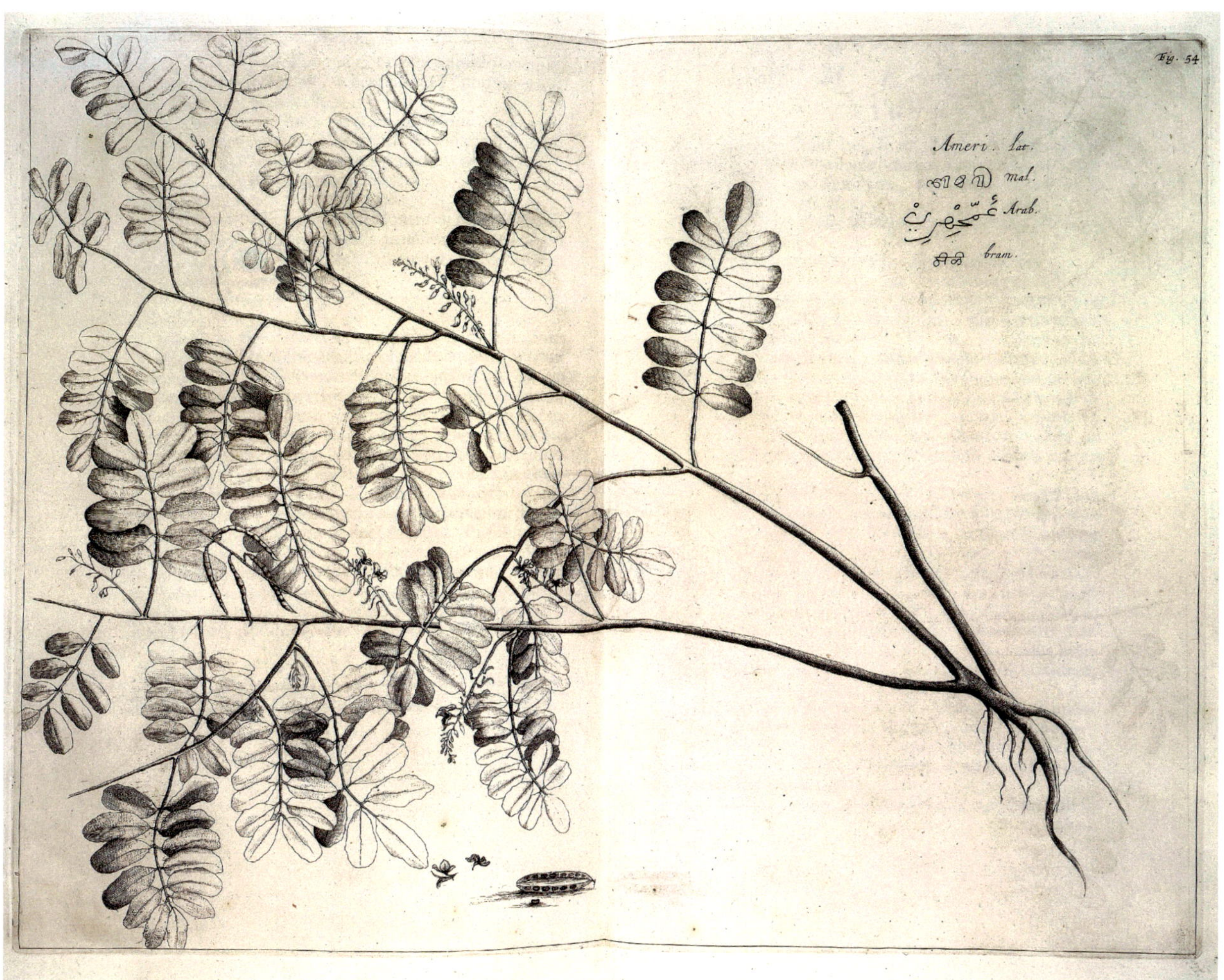


Hendrik van Rheede tot Draakenstein, *Indigofera tinctoria*, 1678–79, copperplate engraving

indigo dyes are far less toxic than the synthetic substitutes still used today in the fashion industry.[20] Morris opted for indigo dye in many of his tapestries and wallpapers—most notably in his famous acanthus design. However, his aspiration to circumvent the oppressive mechanisms and estrangement brought forth by the Industrial Revolution did not completely coincide with his socialist principles. The establishment of Morris & Co. was driven by the explicit objective of creating aesthetically pleasing items for the laboring class, but the decision to revert to natural dyeing techniques and hand equipment significantly escalated the expenses associated with Morris's creations, making them, ironically, financially inaccessible to most.[21]

Despite this, the vegetal-inspired influence of the Arts and Crafts movement reverberated far and wide, and directly contributed to the birth of Art Nouveau in France, which incorporated the sinuous roundedness of plant stems, leaves, and tendrils in architectural features as disparate as hand railings, lampposts, and cornices. In essence, this was a reaction to the increasing estrangement from nature that by the end of the century had become more palpable than ever throughout Europe. Abandoning the stern geometric linearity of classical architectural features in favor of the biomorphic curvilinearity of vegetal anatomy aspired to rekindle and reaffirm our structural dependency on the natural world. More than the simple decorative flourishes described in art history books, the transformation of pillars into trees, frames into entwined vines, and balcony railings into rosetum branches represented an existentialist quest to aesthetically reconnect with nature at a time when sprawling urbanization had reached a crisis point. From illustration to the applied arts, painting, sculpture, music, literature, performance, and architecture, Art Nouveau's determination to unify all arts into a

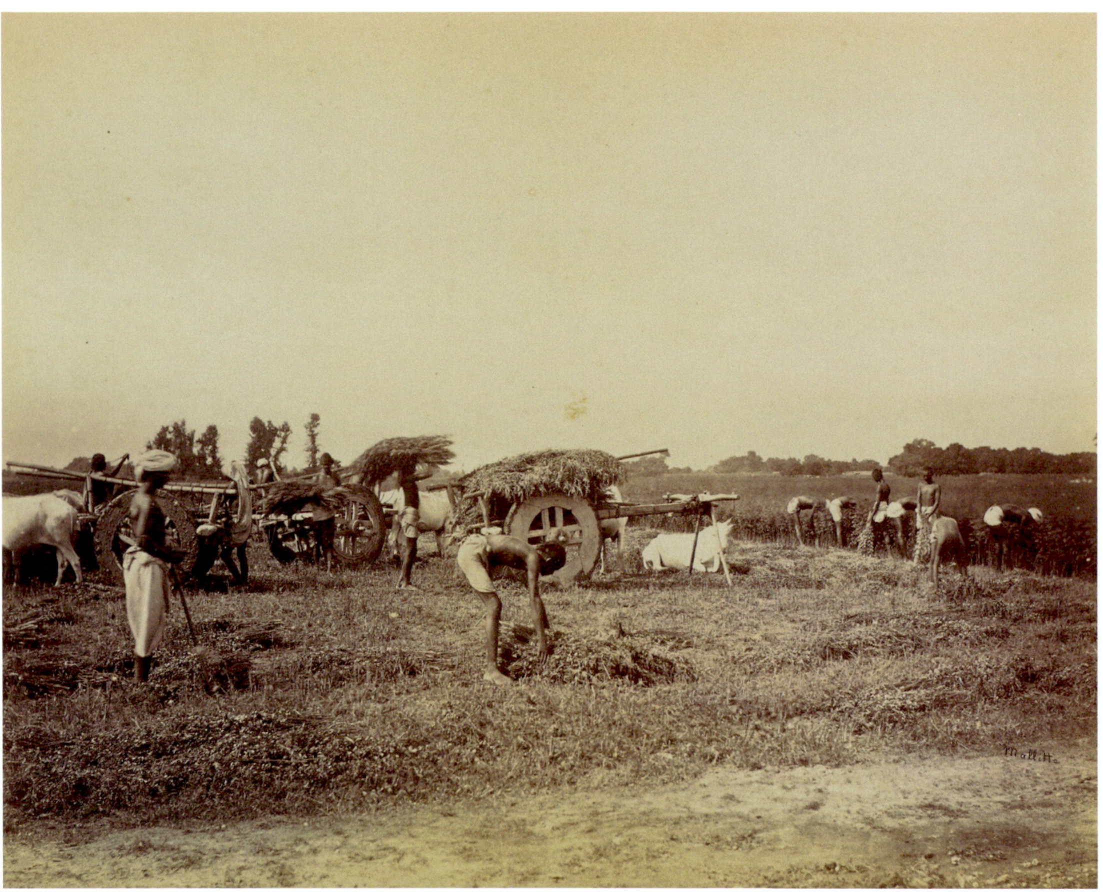

Oscar Mallitte, *Cutting Indigo Plant in the Field and Loading Carts*, 1877, albumen silver print

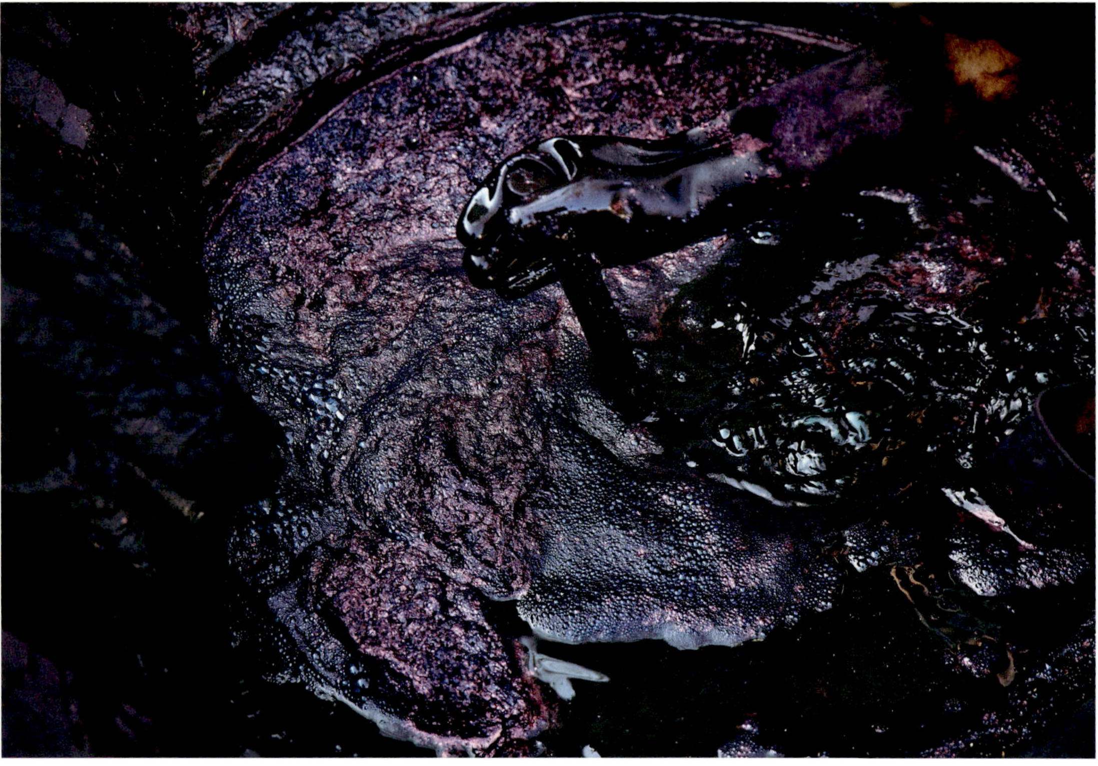

Barry Lewis, *Dye Making in the City of Jaipur, Rajasthan, India*, 2018, digital photograph

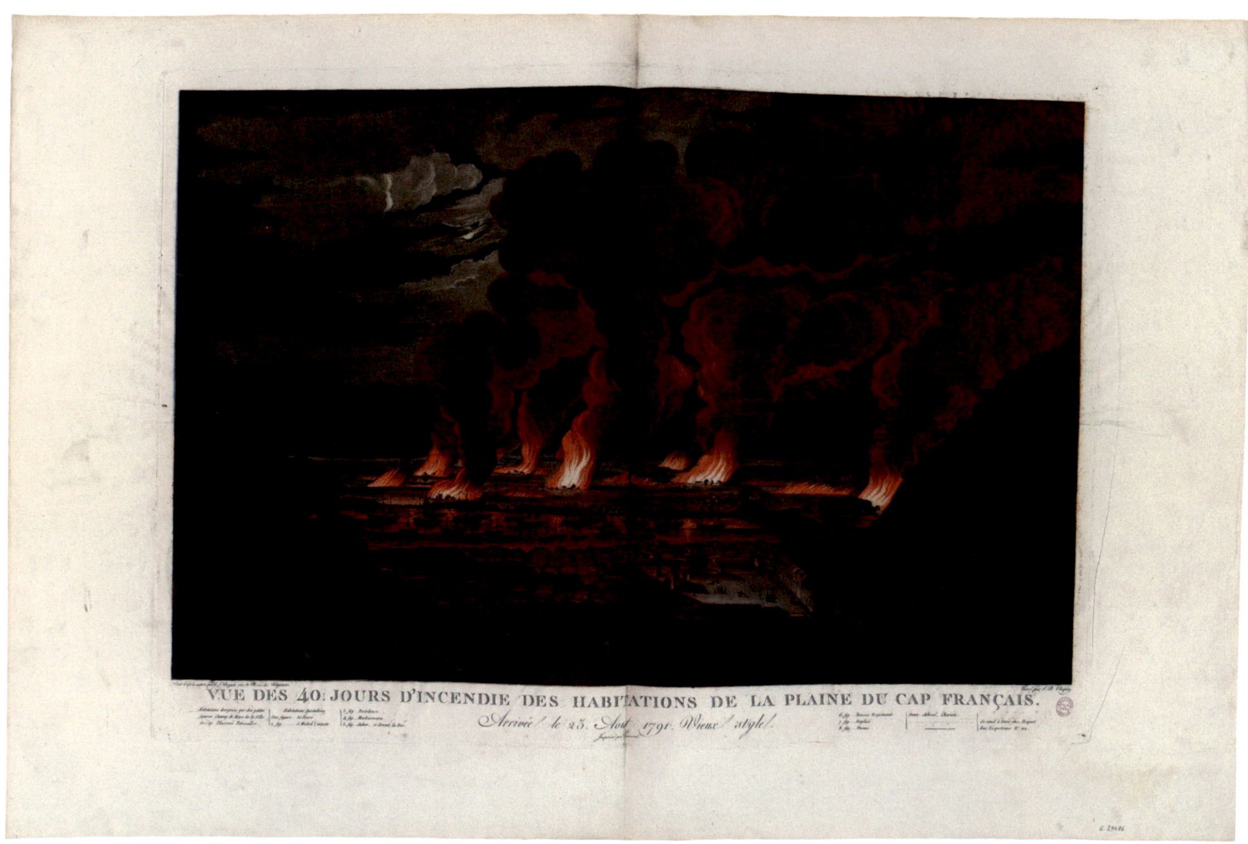


Jean-Baptiste Chapuy, *Vue des 40. jours d'incendie des habitations de la plaine du Cap Français*, ca. 1791, etching, color print



"total work of art" reflected a fervent sense of longing for the continuity and harmony typical of the natural ecosystems that modernity had shattered.[22]

Guided by vegetal principles, these ideas traveled across the Atlantic Ocean and emerged in Chicago through the Prairie style, as exemplified by Frank Lloyd Wright's Robie House (1909). The midwestern prairies—vast swaths of flat territory covered uniformly in tall grasses—served as the style's visual and contextual backbone. Big bluestem and switchgrass carpeted the land into expanses of fertile and rich biodiversity, and Wright's Prairie style treated the horizontality and linearity of the prairie grasslands as the architectural blueprint and vernacular of his creations. Prairie style houses, with shallow-hipped rooflines that echoed the land's horizontal flatness, spoke a natural language of aesthetic and material analogies. Materials were sourced locally in an attempt to establish an intimate dialogue between buildings and their natural surroundings. At times, a single plant motif would define architectural features, carvings, furniture, and fixtures in the same building.

Unlike European cities, Chicago was born out of the Industrial Revolution, and the political and economic models that ruled it favored production over life quality. When the Prairie style emerged, Chicago had been rapidly expanding into a global capital, but stockyard waste from the meatpacking district, soot, and thick smoke made the city insalubrious. Like Art Nouveau in France, in the United States the Prairie style was a response to the deeply ingrained sense of alienation caused by indiscriminate industrialization and a substantive deterioration of the environment. By developing plant aesthetics at a time of rapid and drastic change, architects and designers aspired to tap into more profound and ancient natural reference points. Deep down, these movements and their ambition to produce total works of art were a prescient call for action—manifestations of an awareness that a reconciliation between humanity and the natural world was urgently needed. This is a critical message that many of us in the Western world continue to disregard.

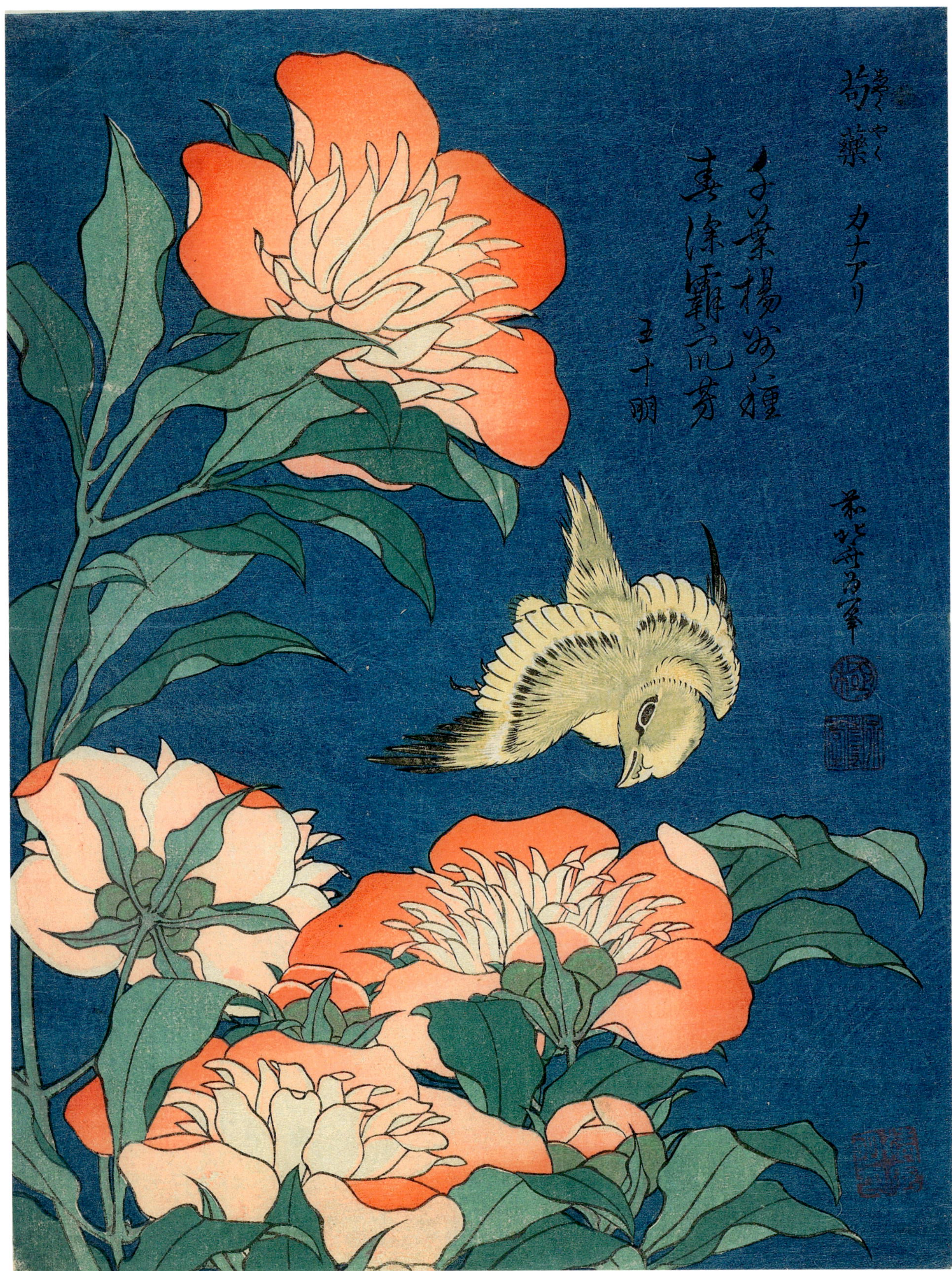


Katsushika Hokusai, *Peonies and Canary*, ca. 1834, woodblock print (*nishiki-e*), ink and color on paper

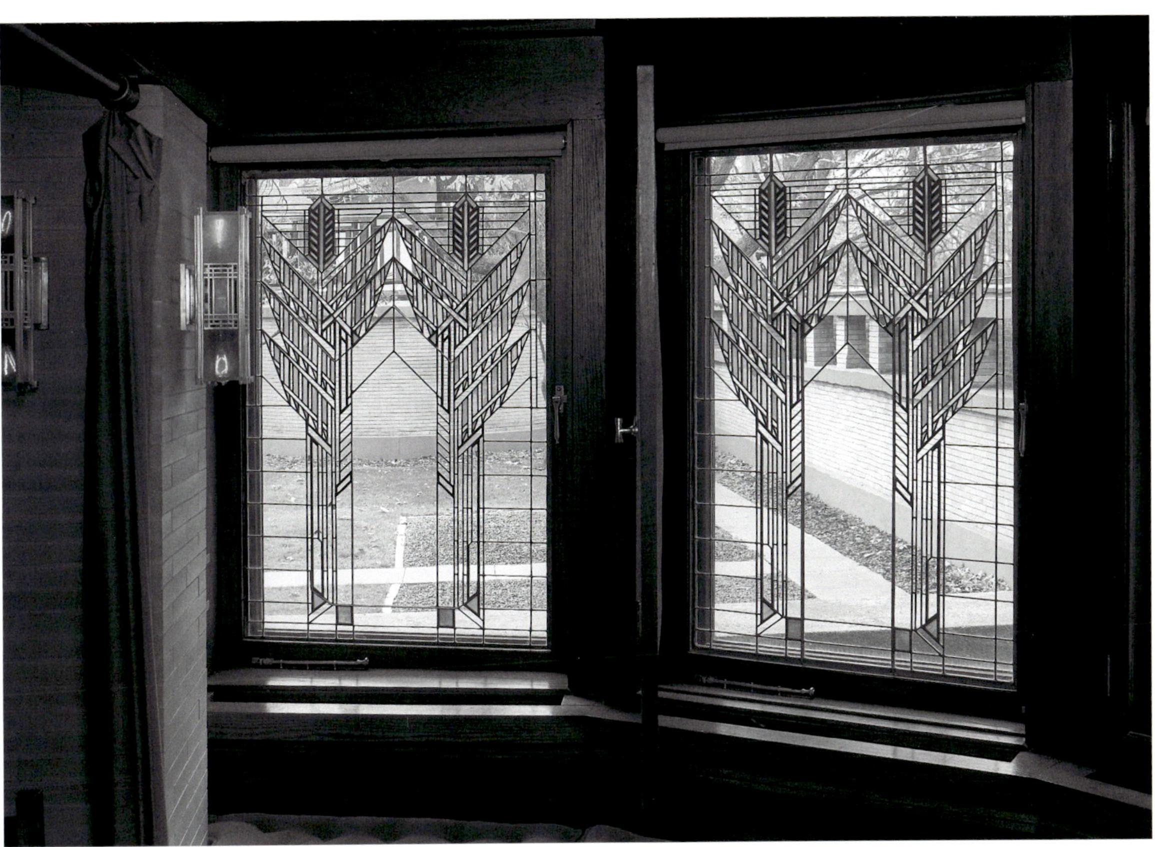

Frank Lloyd Wright, Dana-Thomas House, Springfield, Illinois, 1902



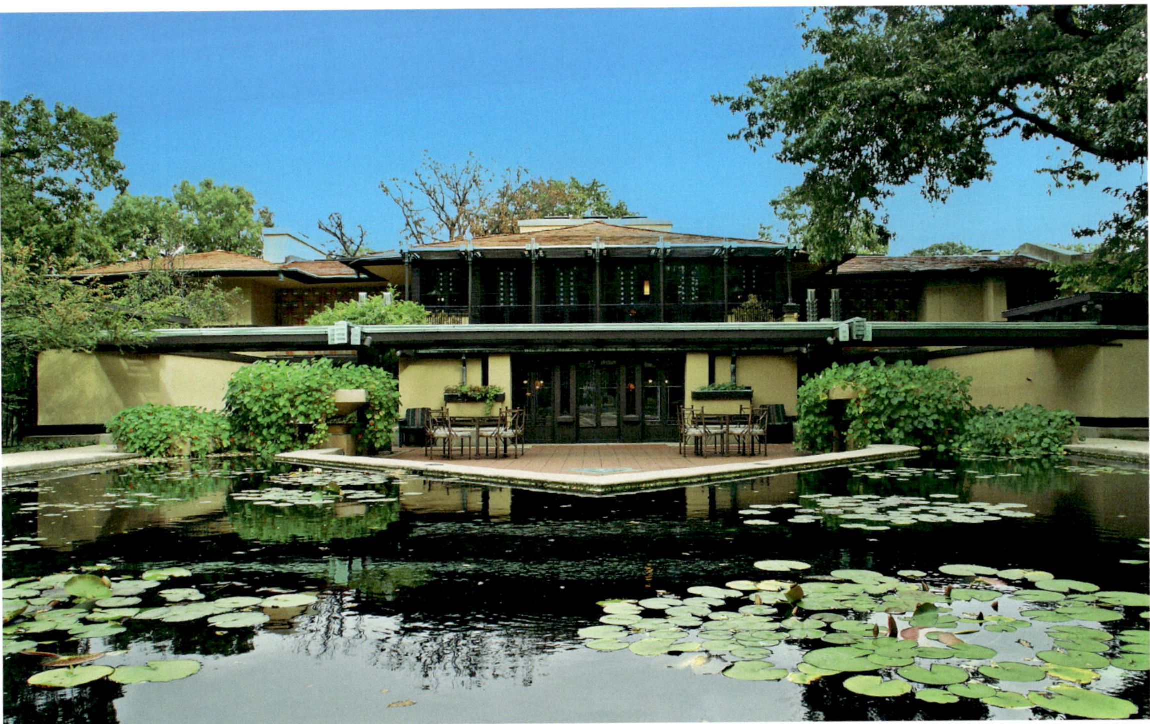

Frank Lloyd Wright, Avery Coonley House, Riverside, Illinois, 1908–12

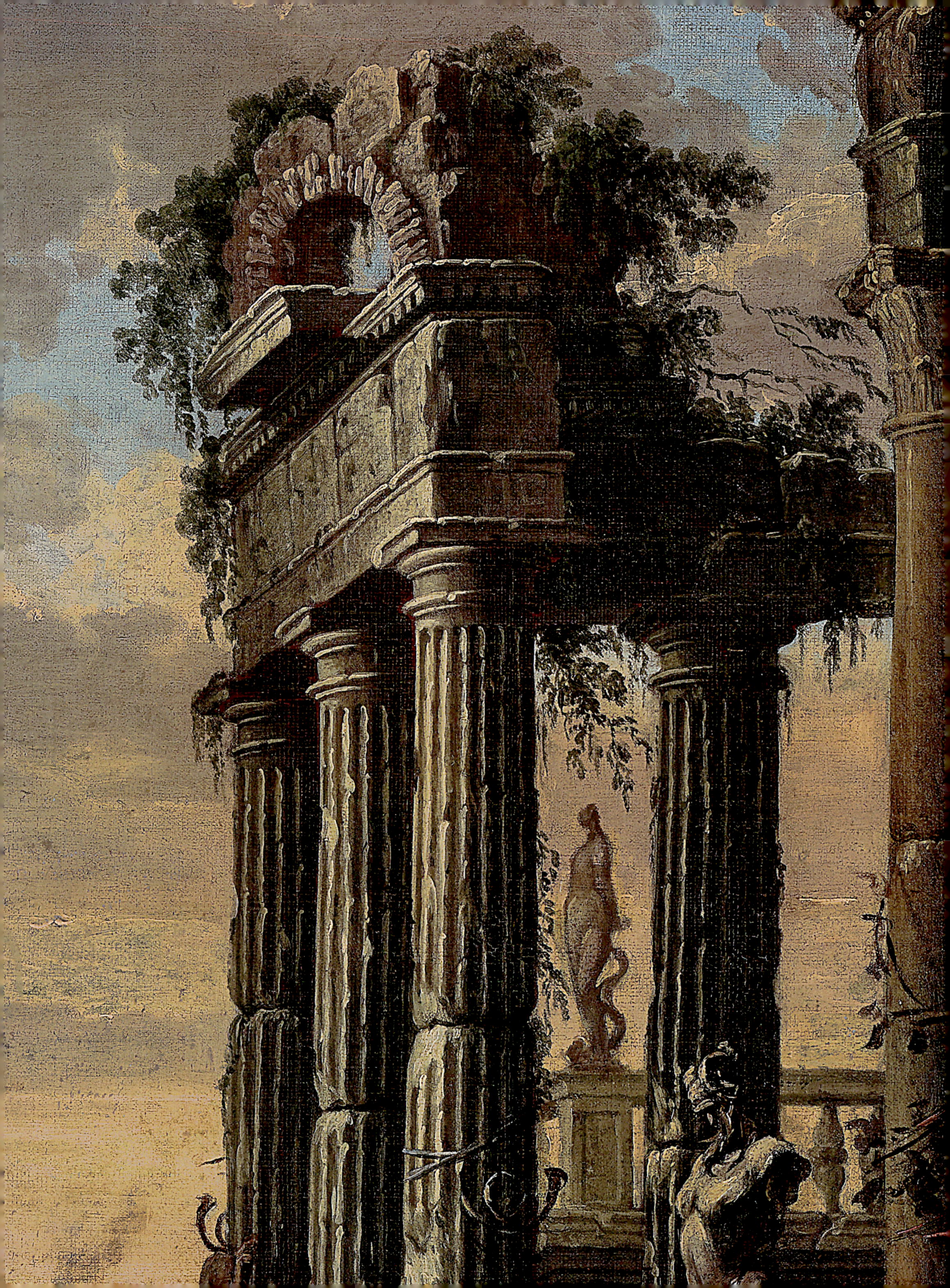

*THE TRIUMPH OF VENUS*, ALESSANDRO MAGNASCO, CA. 1720–30

*A FORMAL GARDEN*, JOHANNES JANSON, 1766

SALA DELLE ASSE, LEONARDO DA VINCI, CA. 1498

PARADISE GARDEN MURAL IN THE AUGUSTINE CONVENT AT MALINALCO, MEXICO, SIXTEENTH CENTURY

WAT ARUN TEMPLE, BANGKOK, LIKELY BEFORE 1656

RAYONNANT GOTHIC ROSE WINDOW, NOTRE-DAME DE PARIS CATHEDRAL, PARIS, CA. 1250

GATE OF CASTEL BÉRANGER, PARIS, HECTOR GUIMARD, 1895/1898

THREE AND FOUR-PANEL SCREENS, SAVONNERIE MANUFACTORY, FRANCE, EIGHTEENTH CENTURY

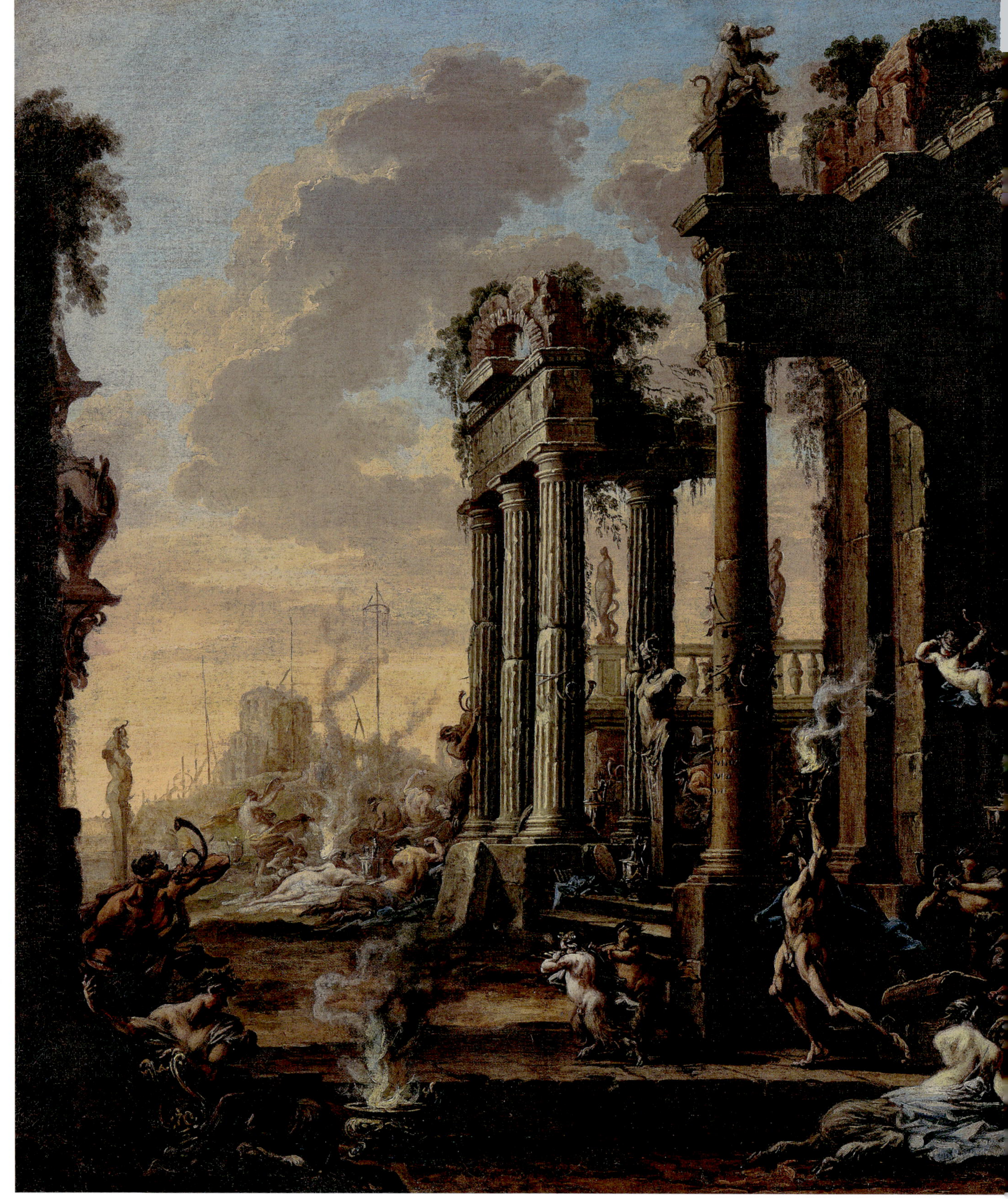

Alessandro Magnasco, *The Triumph of Venus*, ca. 1720–30, oil on canvas

## *THE TRIUMPH OF VENUS*

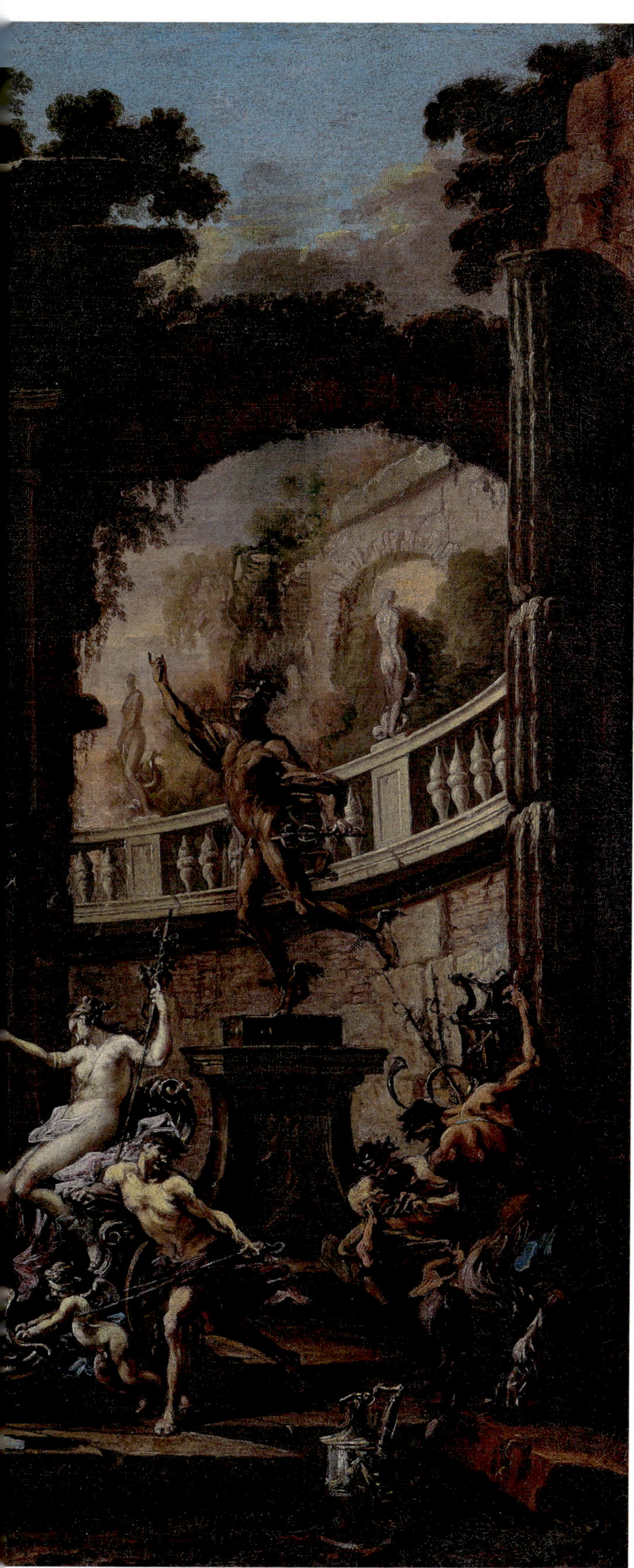



By the end of the seventeenth century, plants once again revolutionized Western art. Shrubs and weeds, rather than the manicured varieties grown in gardens, gained prominence in the minds of many artists. Crawling, tumbling, and climbing wild plants broke apart stone blocks and bricks, crowned arches, and flourished at the bases of columns. Indeed, the plants that fascinated these artists weren't growing just anywhere; they were specifically emerging from canonical classical architecture. With their unruly branching and lush exuberance, wild plants embodied the passage of time and the relentlessness of entropy. Guiding this new interest in weeds was a sense of loss and nostalgia. Unmaintained because irrelevant to modern life, once-prominent landmarks like the Colosseum, the solemn villas of the Roman Forum, and temples in Sicily had fallen into disrepair and were now monuments to loss of past greatness. In the paintings that immortalized them, plants represented nature taking over culture—seemingly illogical vegetative growth clouding the linear purity of the classical intellect. Symbols of cultural amnesia, agents of slow and irreversible corruption, the plant's roots reached deep into the classical canon so as to slowly but relentlessly crumble it. The representational barbarization of classical rectitude also served as a subtle reminder that, according to Western thought at least, nature and culture are mutually exclusive.

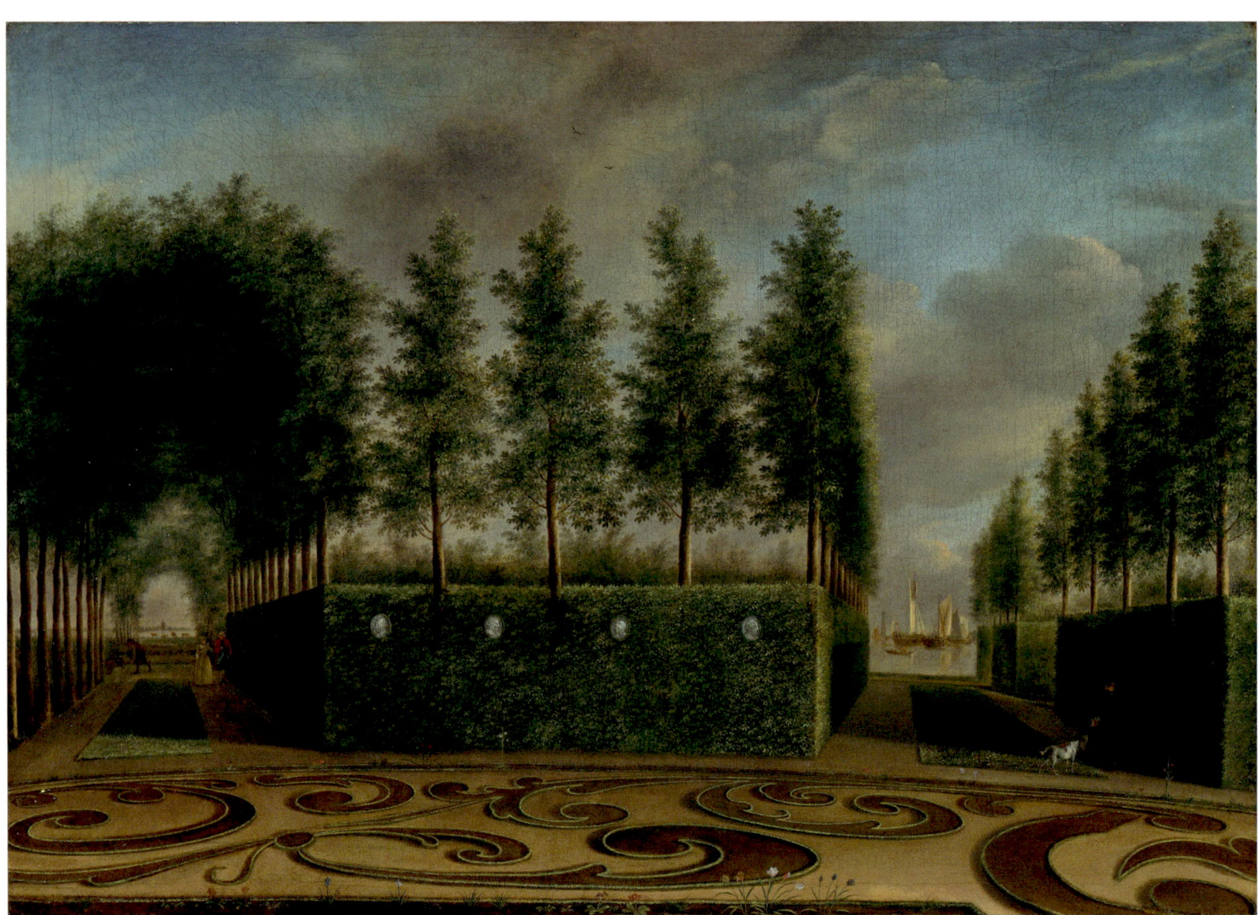

Johannes Janson, *A Formal Garden*, 1766, oil on canvas

Gardens are sites of privilege in some ways, representing as they do the attempt to create a miniature Eden, to carve out space separate from the hustle and bustle of the outside world, to rigorously arrange plants—which may have been acquired at some expense—in neat compositions that disregard natural ecosystemic flows. Prior to the invention of photography, people with the financial means to maintain a garden also felt compelled to capture its splendor on canvas. Artists have, consequently, tried to represent gardens in their most opulent and lush fullness. This painting by Johannes Janson elegantly captures all of this: the neat edging of the green walls, the perfectly arched trees, and the arabesque-inspired *broderie parterre* (literally "embroidery flower bed") speak of cultural refinement and aristocratic wealth. The intricacy of this garden would have immediately communicated to the observer the enormous expenses required for upkeep. And it is therefore no coincidence that the artwork also contains representations of the economic foundations that sustained the opulence depicted. In the background we see two paths: one leads to farmland, and the other to ships in a harbor.

# A FORMAL GARDEN

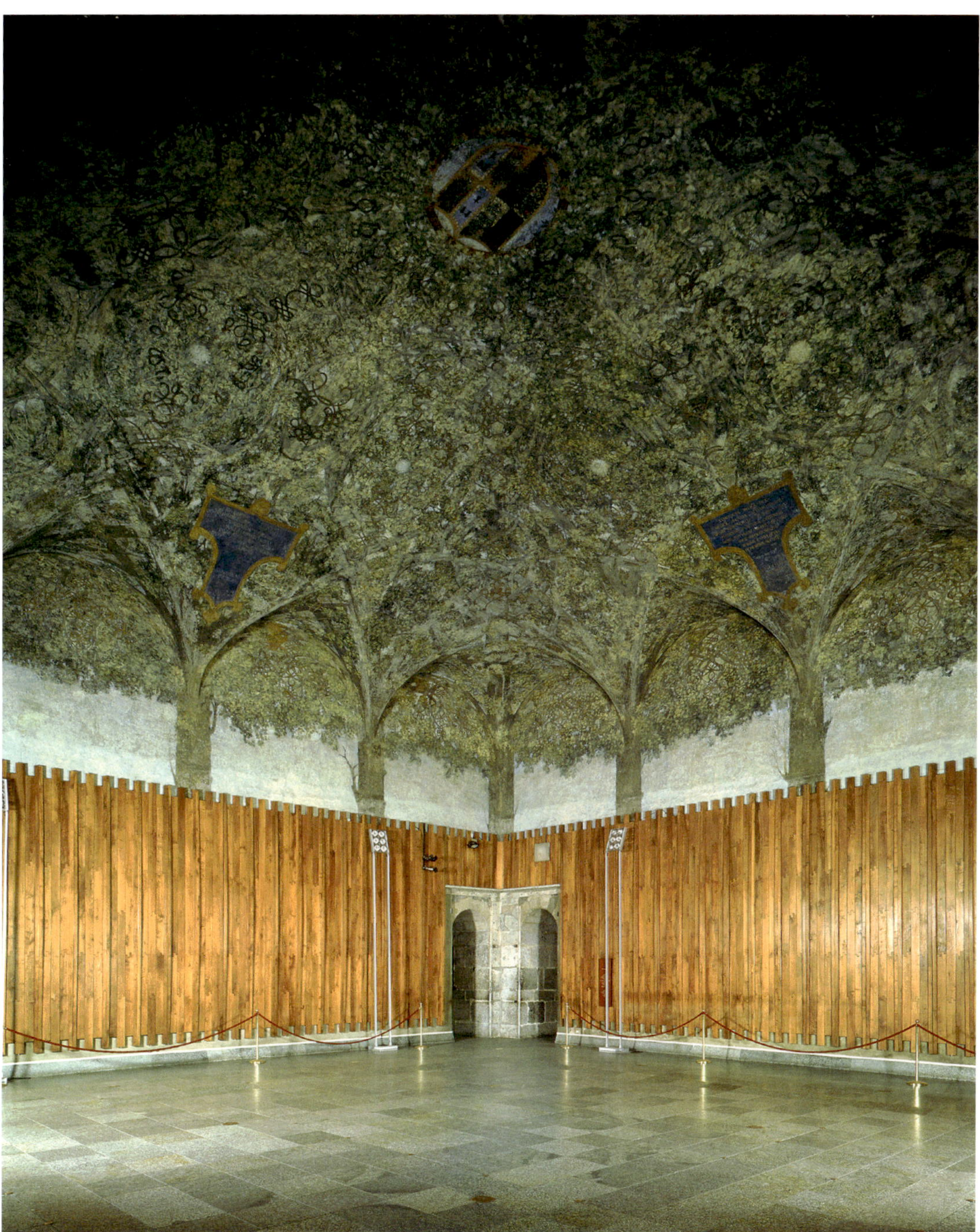

**Leonardo da Vinci, Sala delle Asse, ca. 1498, fresco**

For almost four hundred years, one of Leonardo da Vinci's botanical masterpieces languished, invisible behind a layer of white paint. Today it can be enjoyed in all its emerald splendor at Milan's Castello Sforzesco, where it was originally painted for Ludovico il Moro, one of the most powerful noblemen of the Renaissance. The square room, measuring roughly fifty by fifty feet, was reinvented by Leonardo into a lush grove of mulberry trees. The mural, a work in tempera, elegantly integrates the existing architectural structure of the room, transforming pillars into tree trunks and arches into branches. As a result, the linear volumetric rhythm of the vault dematerializes bricks and mortar for a stunning three-dimensional trompe l'oeil effect. While the original use of the room remains shrouded in mystery, it might have served some kind of entertainment purpose, particularly during the chilly, gloomy winter months typical of northern Italy.

# SALA DELLE ASSE

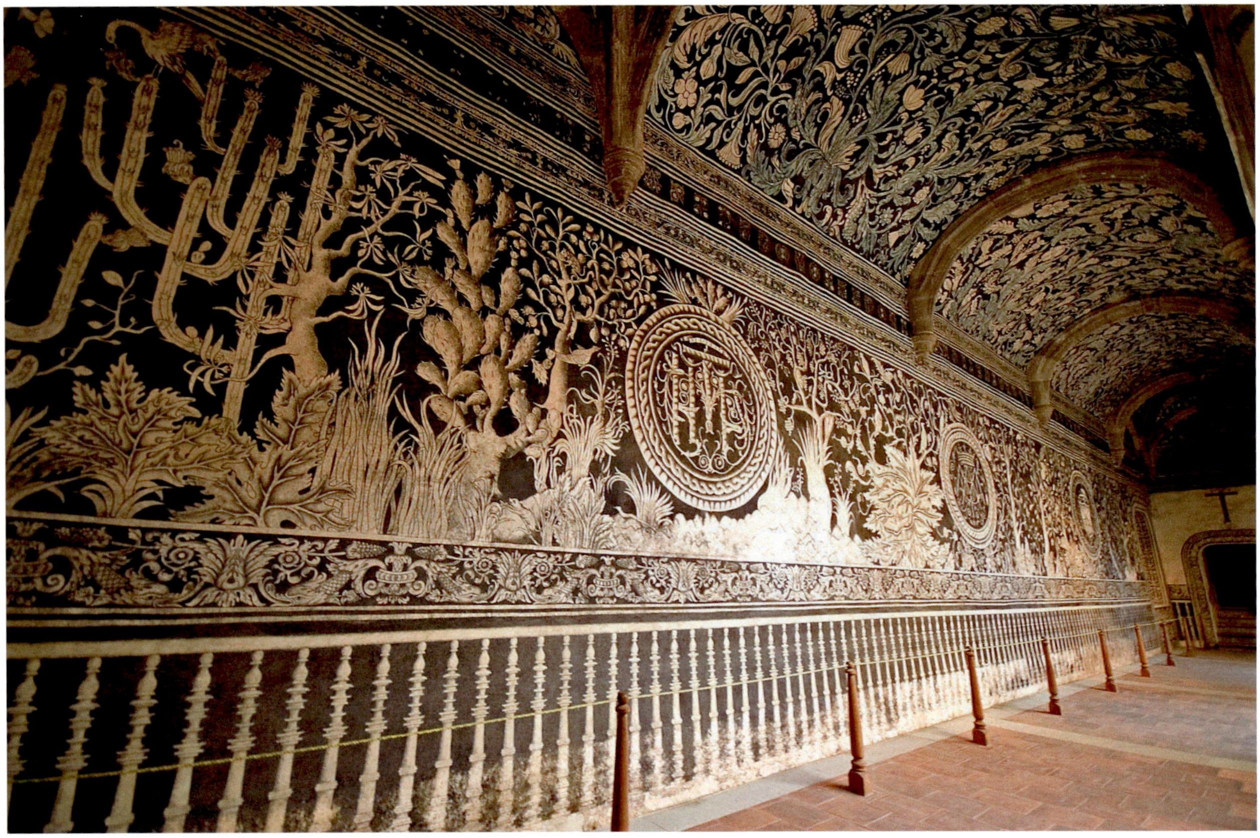

140 **Unknown artist, Paradise garden mural in the Augustine convent at Malinalco, Mexico, sixteenth century**

Also concealed under a thin layer of white paint for roughly four hundred years was an exceptionally detailed and intricate fresco of plants adorning the walls of the lower cloister at an Augustinian convent in Malinalco, Mexico. Painted in a monochrome style typical of Spanish sixteenth- and seventeenth-century aesthetics, the fresco depicts a sprawling garden filled with many species of local plants and animals. Cacti, trees, grasses, and bushes frame large armorial medallions emblazoned with Christian symbolism. Plant motifs, albeit rendered in blue and orange, also cover the entirety of the cloister's vaulted ceiling. Adam and Eve are the only human presence in an otherwise entirely vegetal world of harmony and peace. The frescoes were painted by *tlacuilos*—Indigenous artist-scribes—under the close scrutiny and guidance of European Augustinian monks. Interestingly, they feature a substantial number of Indigenous symbols—a sign of the initially tolerant approach of the Augustinians, who believed in integration rather than suppression. A subsequent historical turn in a less accepting direction might have motivated the later concealment of the works.

# PARADISE GARDEN MURAL

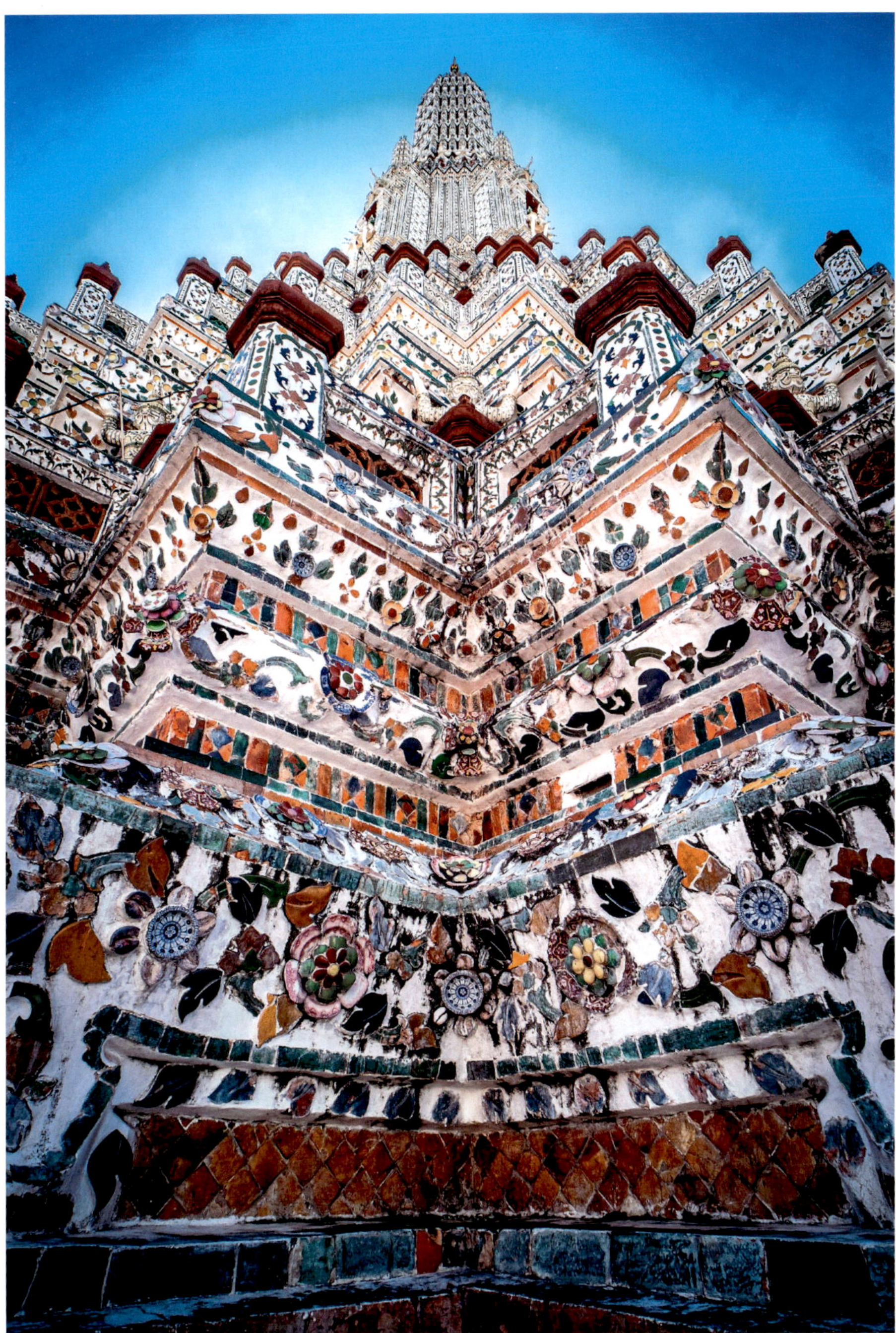

**Wat Arun temple, Bangkok, likely before 1656 (main prang completed in 1851), porcelain tile**



According to Buddhist belief, “flowers bloom to see the Buddha,” reflecting the transcendental tranquility that seamlessly connects the human mind and nature upon an encounter with floral beauty. In accordance with this, the entire exterior of the Wat Arun temple in Bangkok—one of the largest and most beautiful temple complexes in the city—is covered in vibrant mosaic tiles depicting floral and other foliage-related motifs. Close inspection reveals extraordinary details. The flower petals are not painted or sculpted, but made of broken plates, while leaves are composed from pieces of green celadon pots. This pioneering recycling idea came from King Rama III, who in the first half of the nineteenth century invited the local population to gift their broken or otherwise unusable pottery to ornament the temple. The majority of the materials originated from Chinese trading vessels; porcelain broken while in transit was frequently used as ballast, then unloaded upon arrival in port and repurposed in different ways.

## WAT ARUN TEMPLE

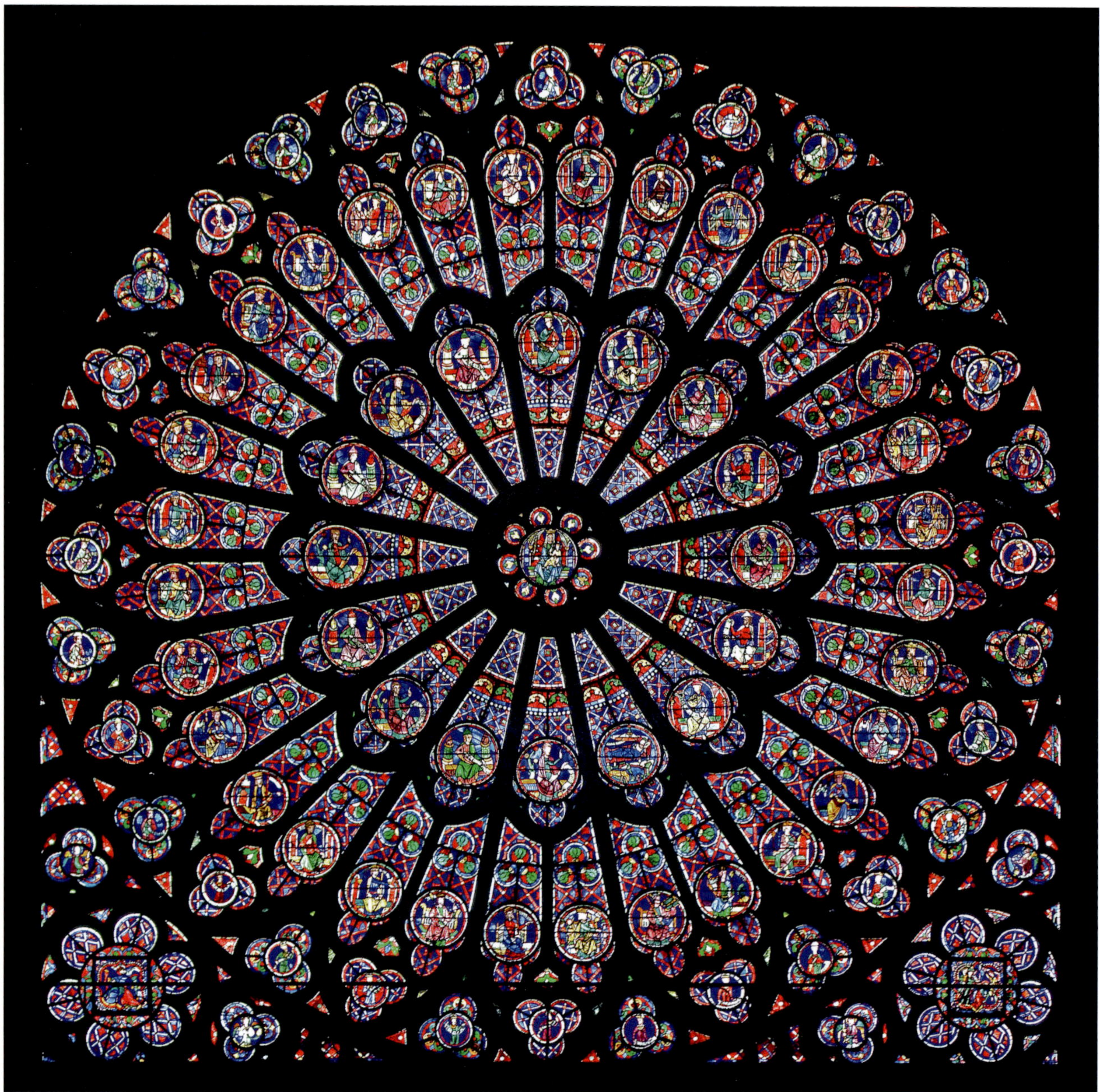

**Rayonnant Gothic rose window (north transept), Notre-Dame de Paris Cathedral, Paris, ca. 1250, stained glass**



A quintessential architectural feature of French Gothic cathedrals, the rose window developed during the twelfth century, inspired by the ancient oculus: a round opening featured in Roman and Greek architecture representing the eye and the enlightening power of vision. Throughout history and across cultures, the oculus has served as a symbolic connection between Earth and the heavens. Eventually adopted by Christianity, this mystical portal gave rise to the rose window's dazzling colored-glass geometric patterning, which in turn is said to also derive from the mandala—another powerful floral-inspired symbol. Mandalas summon the harmony of the universe and are a recurring motif in Hindu and Buddhist Tantrism. The rose window, as the culmination of these aesthetic and spiritual traditions, also connects the striking beauty of flowers to their reliance on sunlight. Its form is inspired by the simple floral structure of wild roses, with their five broad petals and centers crowned by a bright yellow cluster of stamens. The rose window at Notre Dame in Paris, one of the largest and most intricate in the world, luckily survived the 2019 fire that caused extensive damage to much of the cathedral.

# RAYONNANT GOTHIC ROSE WINDOW

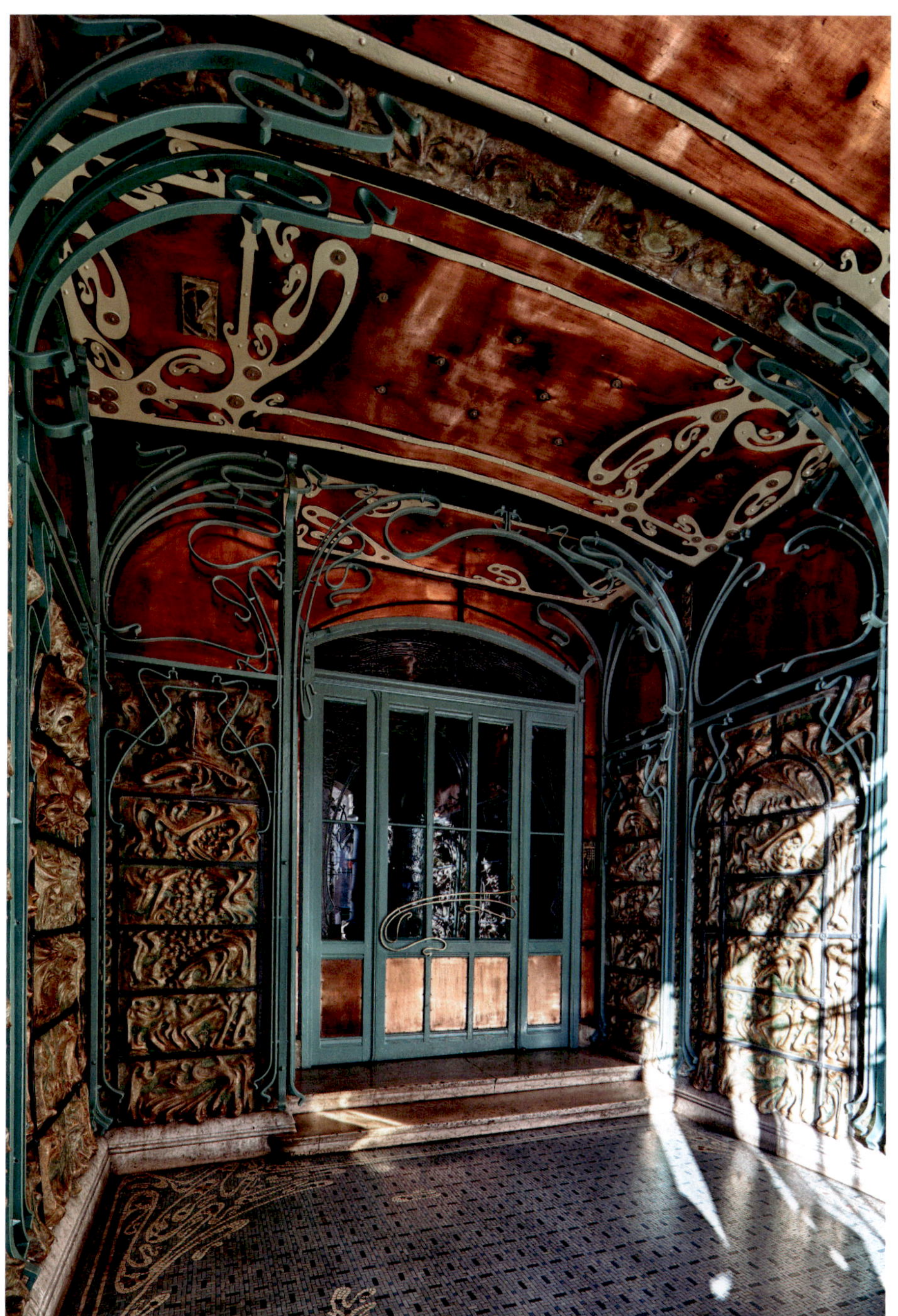

**Hector Guimard, Gate of Castel Béranger, Paris, 1895/1898, various media**



Designed between 1895 and 1898 by architect Hector Guimard, Castel Béranger is a Parisian architectural gem in the Art Nouveau style. The residential building in the 16th arrondissement was commissioned by Anne-Elisabeth Fournier. The curving lines of plant stems and leaves, especially the elegant shapes of nasturtiums, dominate the main entrance and other areas. The front gate, which is unusual for its asymmetry, comprises an elegantly arranged array of vegetal-inspired motifs. Other overt structural references to plant forms are visible on the building's facade, in the balcony railings' cast iron and copper moldings, and in the highly ornamental downspouts and gutters. While Art Nouveau emphasized plant biomorphism to create a sense of naturalness, Guimard's use of cast iron was also influenced by the utilitarian architecture of train stations and other industrial structures. This seeming contradiction was central to the architect's aesthetics and perhaps indicates that at that place and time, in the cultural realm at least, a conception of pure nature dissociated from technology could no longer be upheld.

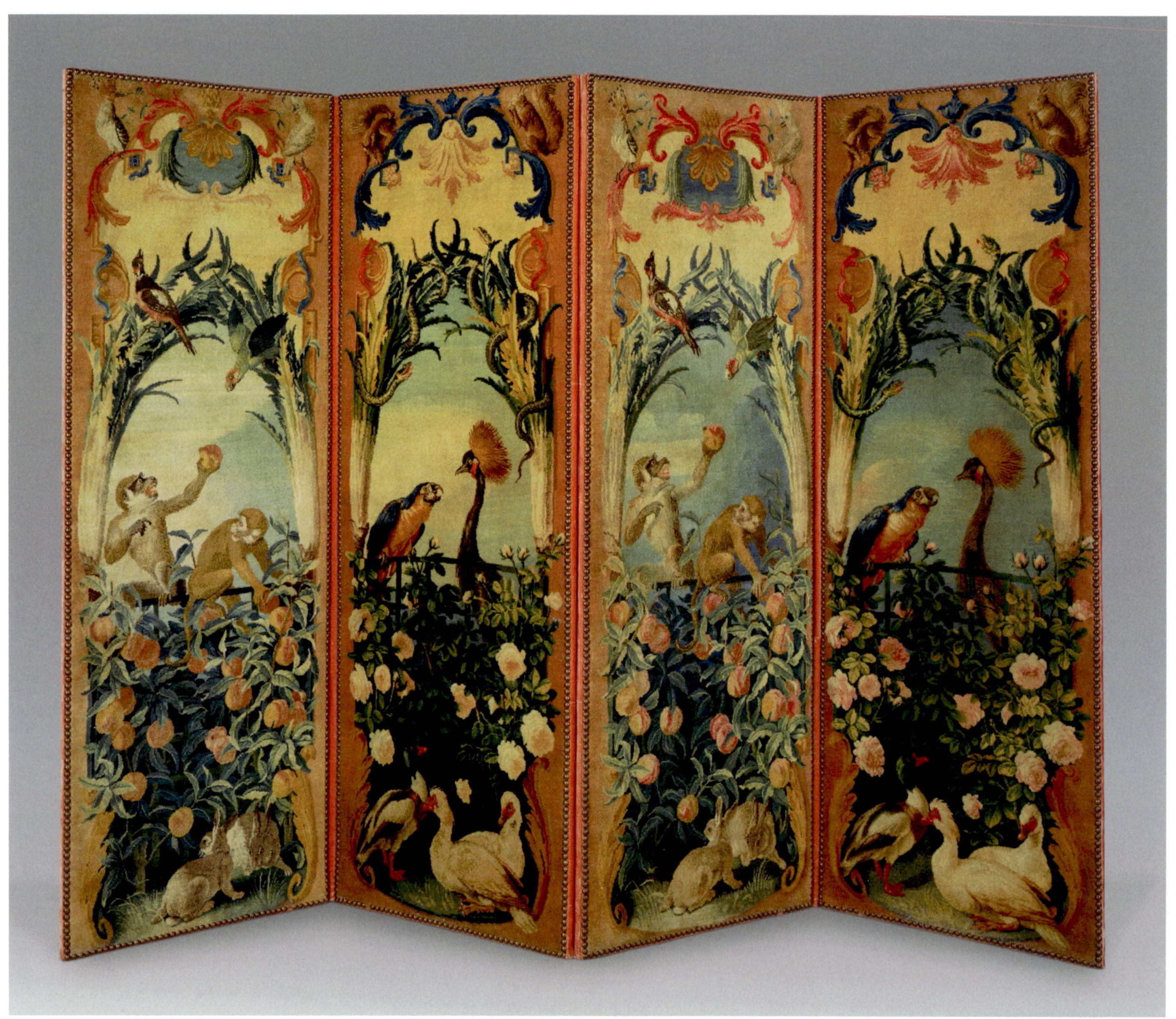

**After designs by Alexandre-François Desportes, Savonnerie Manufactory, Four-Panel Screen (Paravent), knotted between 1719–84, various media**

Throughout the eighteenth century, affluent European families adorned the interiors of their homes with floral-patterned furniture and carpets. The lower sections of the opulent three-panel paravent (pictured opposite) feature overflowing flower vases in the style of the Dutch still life. While the flowers are realistically represented, their respective blooming seasons are ignored, thus granting a fantastical aura to the compositions. Grapes and harvest symbols positioned in the upper sections are emblems of the wealth and abundance that plants provide, and also serve as understated reminders of Christian values as well as references to the Passion of Christ. The birds framed in the central medallions, mostly exotic species, are a nod to the fascination with faraway lands that colonialist trades perpetuated. As seen in the (four-panel) paravent here, designs often incorporated floral garlands as symbols of victory. Attention to detail in the representation of plant species was respected in all instances.

# FOUR-PANEL SCREEN

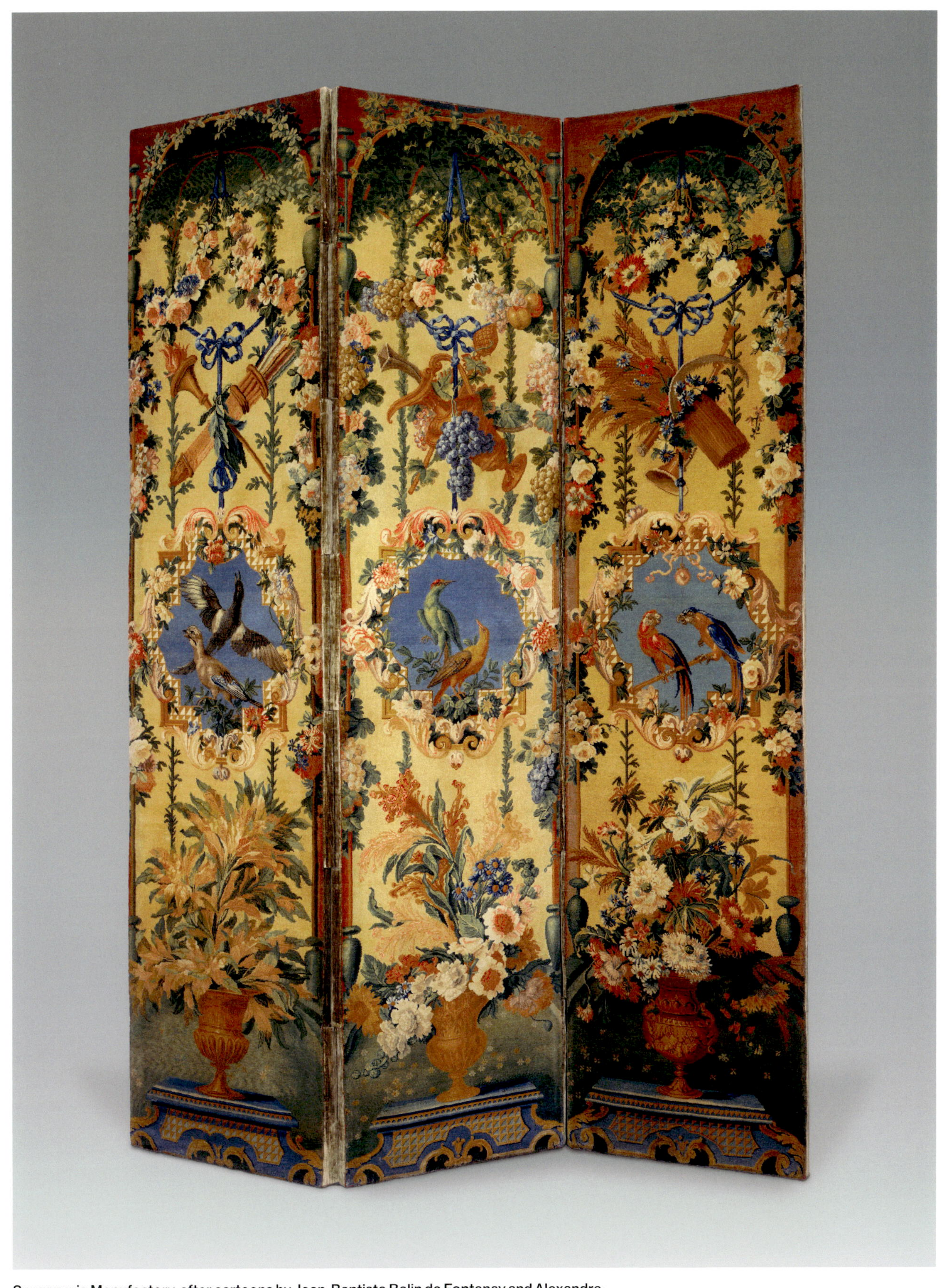



Savonnerie Manufactory, after cartoons by Jean-Baptiste Belin de Fontenay and Alexandre-François Desportes, Three-Panel Screen (Paravent), ca. 1714–40, various media

# THREE-PANEL SCREEN

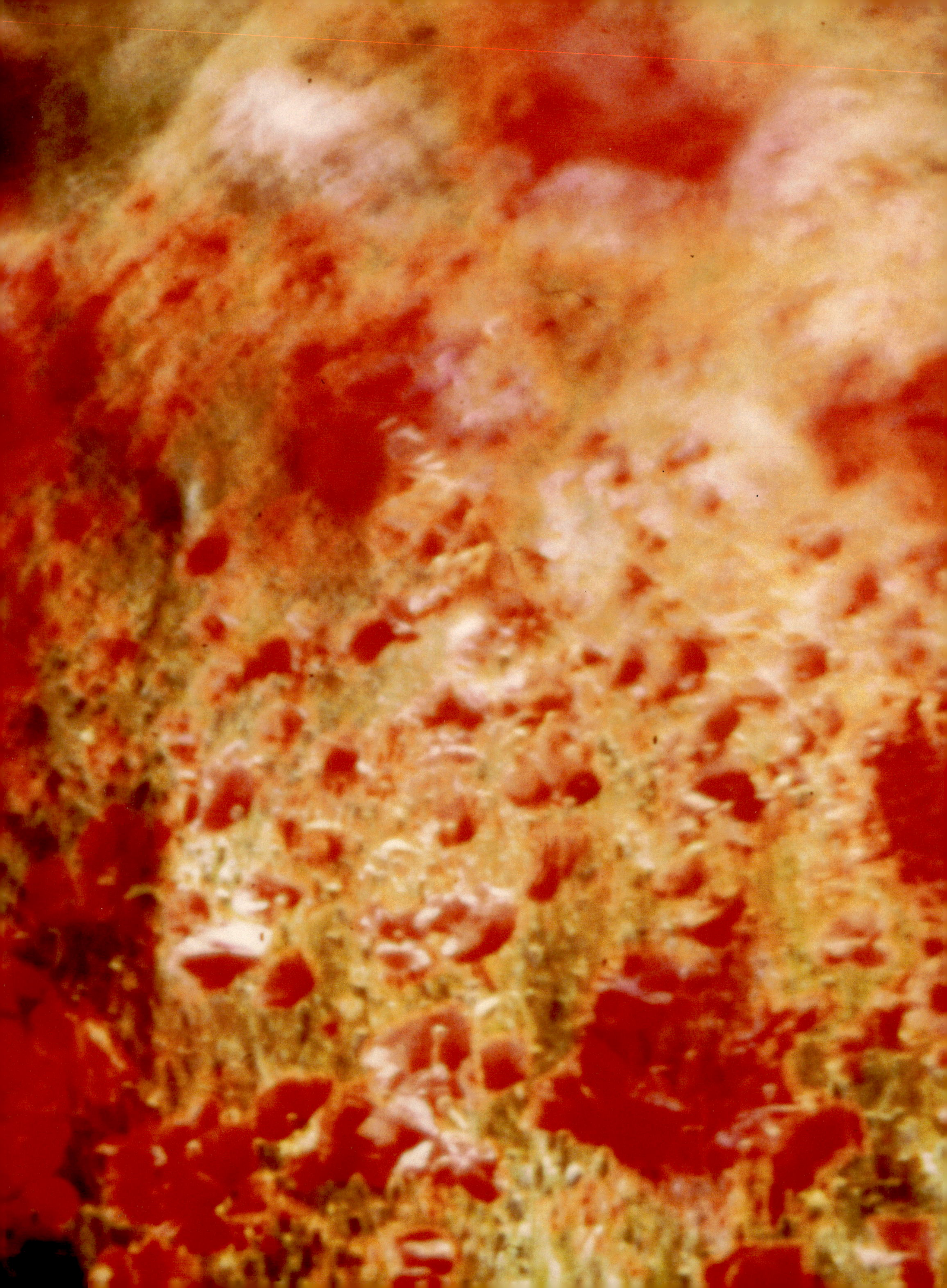

# CHAPTER 6

# EXPOSING VEGETALITY: FORM, MOVEMENT, ESSENCE

Scrolls, vellum, paper sheets, and book pages have tangibly determined the evolution of human thinking and knowledge for thousands of years. The flatness of the page echoes that of the planetary orbits; it is a potentially endless dimension where multiplicities are traced, recorded, aligned, stratified, and rearranged. It is at once microscopic and infinite, timeless and yet unmistakably present, thin and shallow while relentlessly withdrawing into abyssal conceptual depths. On that flatness, the same line that writes a word may also delineate the form, shape, and texture of plants, crystallizing the ephemeral materiality of the living into the permanence of knowledge. The material affinity that binds the flatness of the page to that of leaves has given birth throughout time to a diverse spectrum of vegetal representational techniques, each bringing forth a different, sometimes elusive feature of plant life.

The accurate description of plants has for centuries been central to medicine. In Africa, healers such as *ifas* and *juju* men held positions of religious importance in their communities. As in other cultures, they often relied on the doctrine of signatures—the belief that the creator hid in plants clues toward remedies for injuries and diseases, and that the correct identification of medicinal plants required keen observation of the resemblance between vegetal form and the afflicted parts of the human body.[1] The ancient Greek fathers of medicine Pliny the Elder (first century CE), Dioscorides (first century CE), and Galen (second century CE) were also fervent proponents of the doctrine of signatures, holding that walnuts, for example, could treat head problems since they resembled a human brain. Likewise, the leathery texture of St. John's wort leaves (*Hypericum perforatum*) indicated the plant's efficacy in the treatment of skin ailments.[2] The bean-shaped leaves of hazelwort (*Asarum europaeum*) were thought to alleviate liver complaints, while the heart-shaped petals of violets held the signature of cardiac diseases. Pulmonary emphysema, bronchial coughs, and asthma were thought to be cured with lungwort (*Pulmonaria officinalis*) because its speckled leaves resembled the look of diseased lungs.

As opposed to the bestiaries discussed in chapter 3, where words and images were loosely juxtaposed on the surface of pages to arouse the soul, on those of herbals, words and images wove irrevocable partnerships based on mutual affirmation. The close scrutiny of form invited by the doctrine of signatures tightened the relationship between images and words, giving rise to a kind of unprecedented complicity grounded in the intimacy between the two—something we call *truth.* The pursuit of evidential truth rose to prominence in the West during the Renaissance, as classical Greek and Arabic knowledges were reincorporated into cultural discourses. However, there is a lengthy history of very accurate representations of complex botanical anatomies that have greatly altered the creation and transmission of knowledge.

The parallels between the flatness of leaves and sheets of paper had already been widely explored in Polynesia, China, and Japan long before paper made its way to Europe. Since the tenth century BCE, Tahitian tribespeople impressed ferns and other leaves onto tapa cloth with tree sap.[3] Around the second century CE, artists began adopting dried leaves as printing blocks and tracing extremely fine vegetal impressions with soot and ink. The practice, known as nature printing, reached the West at least by the thirteenth century, as plant prints of fine quality appear in an illustrated Syrian copy of Dioscorides's *De materia medica.*[4] Hairy stems, veined leaves, and knotted roots, richly detailed with anatomical minutiae, facilitated identification and established the actual existence of plants even as fantastical creatures still populated the imagination. Their linear crispness far surpassed the optical remit of botanical illustration. The process in question was elucidated by Leonardo da Vinci around 1500, specifically on folio 197 of the *Codex Atlanticus.* This particular folio showcases a meticulously rendered depiction of a sage leaf, capturing its details in a visually striking manner in the uppermost section of the page.[5]

Nature printing was in every sense an almost exclusively botanical revolution—only the bodies of a few animals, for instance bats, snakes, and fish (as seen in the Japanese art of *gyotaku*), lent themselves to a process that required full and perfect adherence to the paper surface. The proliferation of the printing press at the end of the seventeenth century facilitated the development of more sophisticated techniques for nature printing. Motivated by a profound desire to communicate a heightened perception of authenticity, artists and botanists often opted for inks that closely resembled the colors of the live botanical specimen. The one-to-one

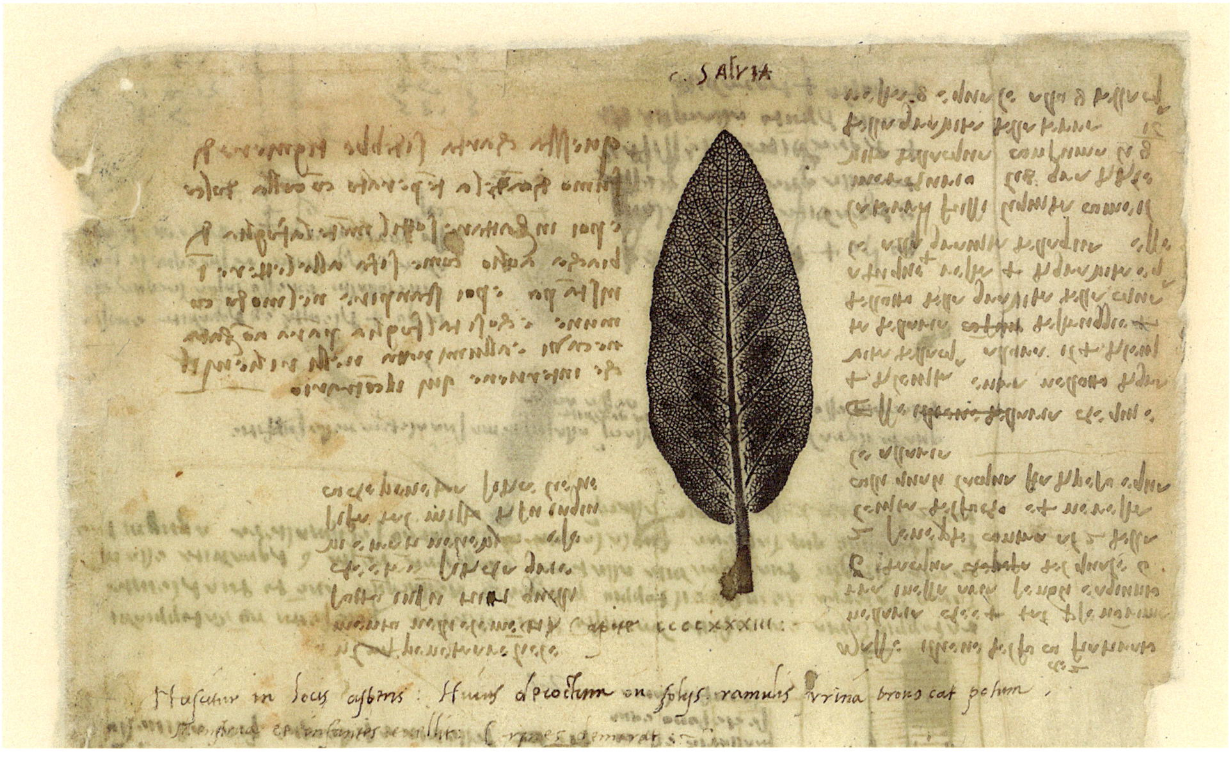

Leonardo da Vinci, Nature printing of a leaf of *Salvia*, ca. 1500, in *Codex Atlanticus*, paper



reproduction size typical of this process aided identification. For centuries, plant printing was a valued technique in botanical studies and the decorative arts, although it never fully replaced either illustration or dried specimens. That said, in the United States, a sage leaf print became fundamental to a botanical revolution that would alter the course of history well beyond the study of nature and art.[6]

In 1746, Benjamin Franklin, editor of the *Pennsylvania Gazette*, designed some of the first paper bills to serve as colonial currency. It didn't take long for forgers to produce fakes, since motifs on paper could be easily copied and printed. According to some historical accounts, the British government deliberately brought counterfeiting to the United States in order to raise inflation and maintain their monetary control over the colonies. Franklin's response to the matter came from his botanist and engraver friend Joseph Breintnall, who had long been actively engaged in experimental nature printing. Franklin understood that due to the unique characteristics of individual leaves, a printed leaf pattern could never be replicated with absolute precision. He then developed a sophisticated casting technique to retain the intricacy of a leaf's vegetal structure and produce lead-cast molds for mass printing. The uniqueness of plant forms turned out to be instrumental in history's first known successful anti-counterfeiting strategy. Franklin's solution strained ties with the British government, which, in reaction, outlawed paper money in 1764.[7]

It wasn't long before another world-altering event resulted from the placement of plant specimens on a flat surface. In 1802, British inventor Thomas Wedgwood discovered that nature printing could be perfected further by using silver nitrate on a prepared leather surface. Unfortunately, none of his experiments survive, although it is believed that some might have been seen by other inventors who perfected his experiments.[8] To realize Wedgwood's vision, in the early 1830s, British scientist and amateur botanist William Henry Fox Talbot started coating paper with salt and a silver nitrate emulsion. Once dried, he would lay a plant specimen on the paper, cover it with a sheet of glass, and expose it to sunlight. The end result was a new kind of inkless nature print that almost miraculously translated the plant's body onto paper. Today we call this image type a photogram.[9]

Although other sorts of objects were utilized in early photographic studies, vegetable forms retained a unique position, since the enchantment

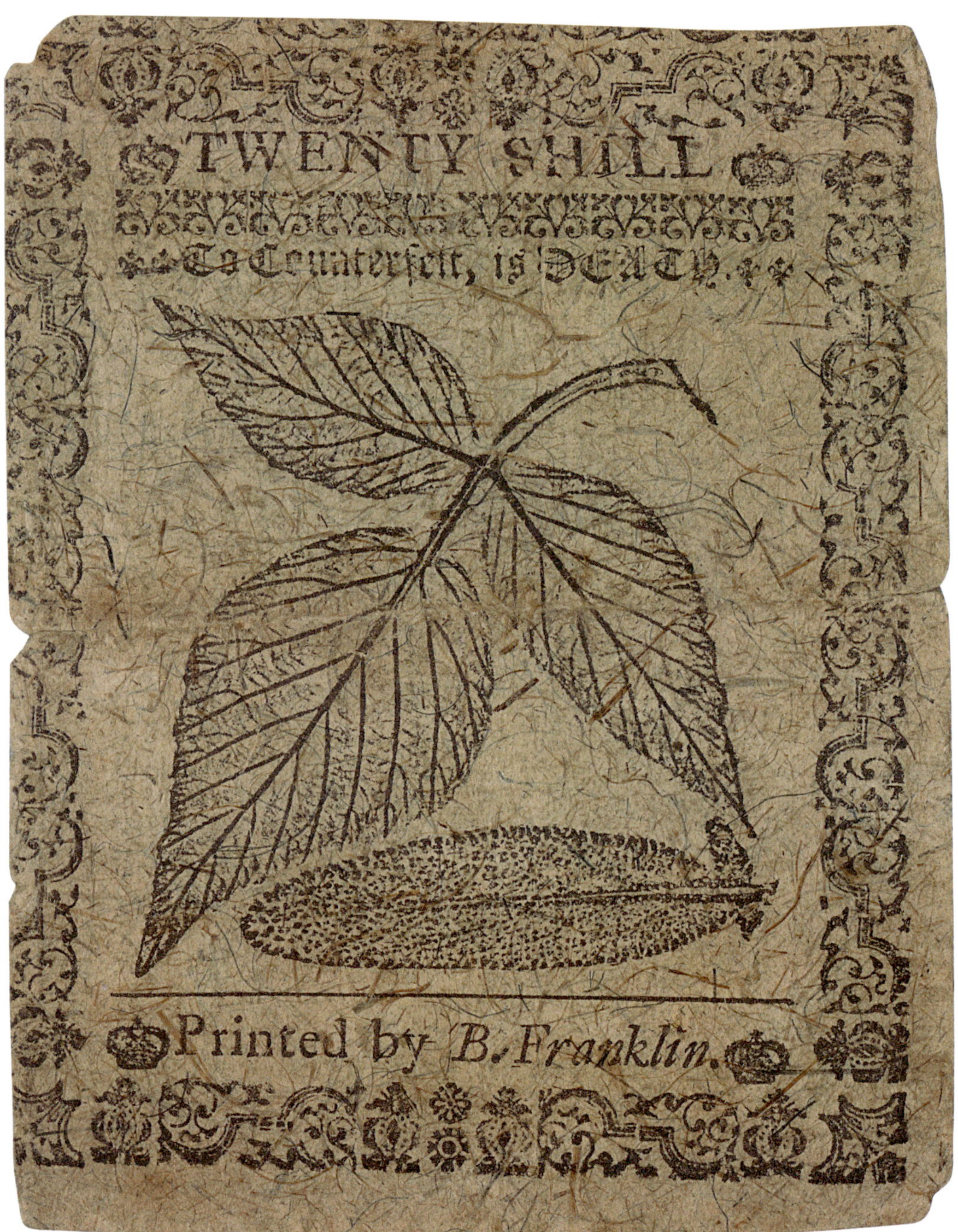


Benjamin Franklin, Nature-printed American currency, 1779, uncut Continental currency

of replicating nature's perfect imprint on paper was infused with the desire to reproduce the secret of vegetative life as closely as was then feasible. It was during the first half of the nineteenth century that the documentation, classification, and preservation of the natural world became a noble pursuit for the affluent and the middle classes. Amid this growing enthusiasm, Anna Atkins, a botanist with formal training, embarked in 1842 on the endeavor of refining the first tests undertaken by Talbot. She began to experiment with a then-novel medium known as the cyanotype, a monochromatic process in which iron salts oxidize to a rich hue of Prussian blue. With the help of plants, Atkins set out to reinvent the old nature-printing process once more. The result was the first photographic book in history—an outstanding collection of 382 prints, bound in two volumes and published in 1843, with

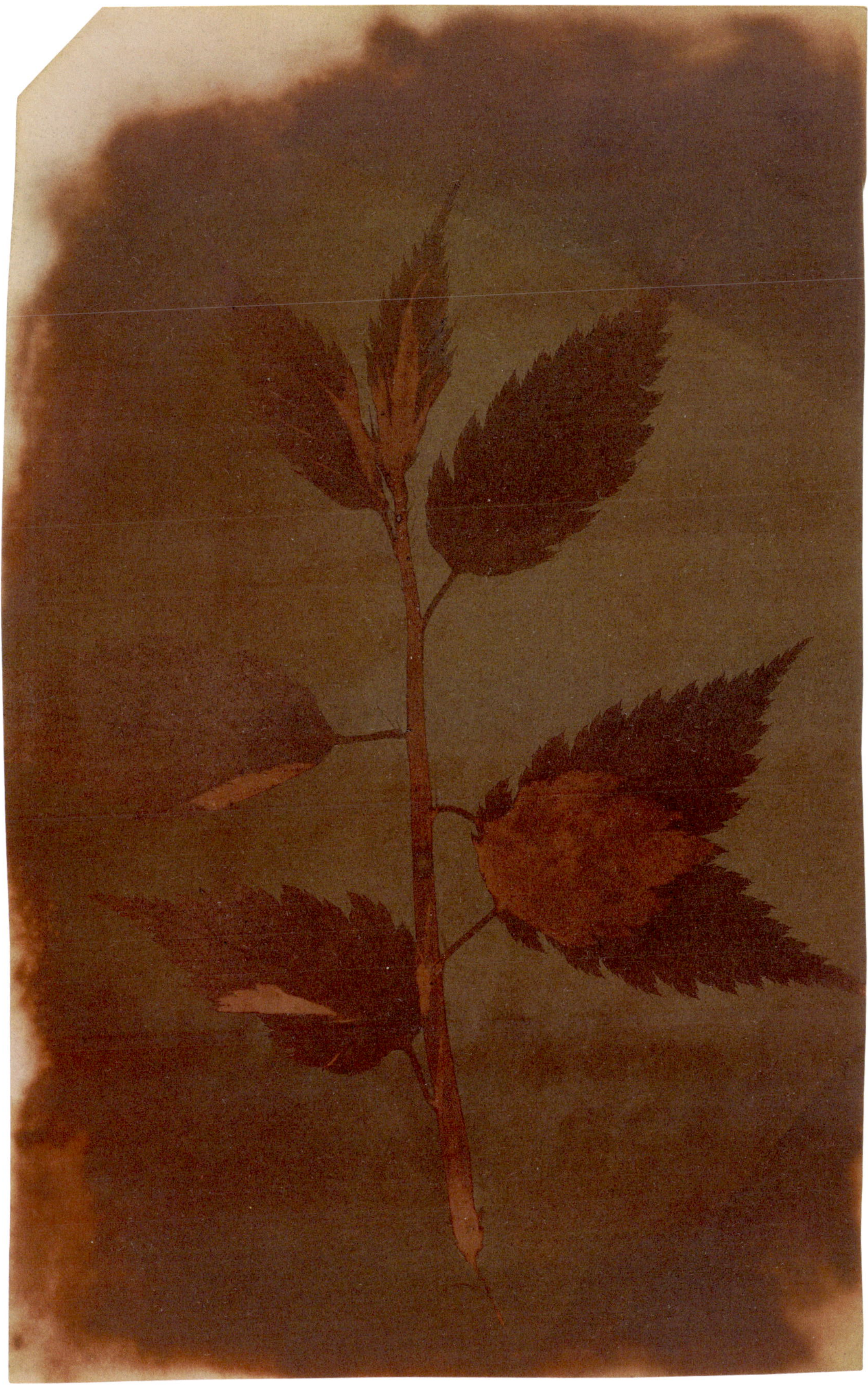

William Henry Fox Talbot, Botanical Specimen, 1840, direct positive photogenic drawing

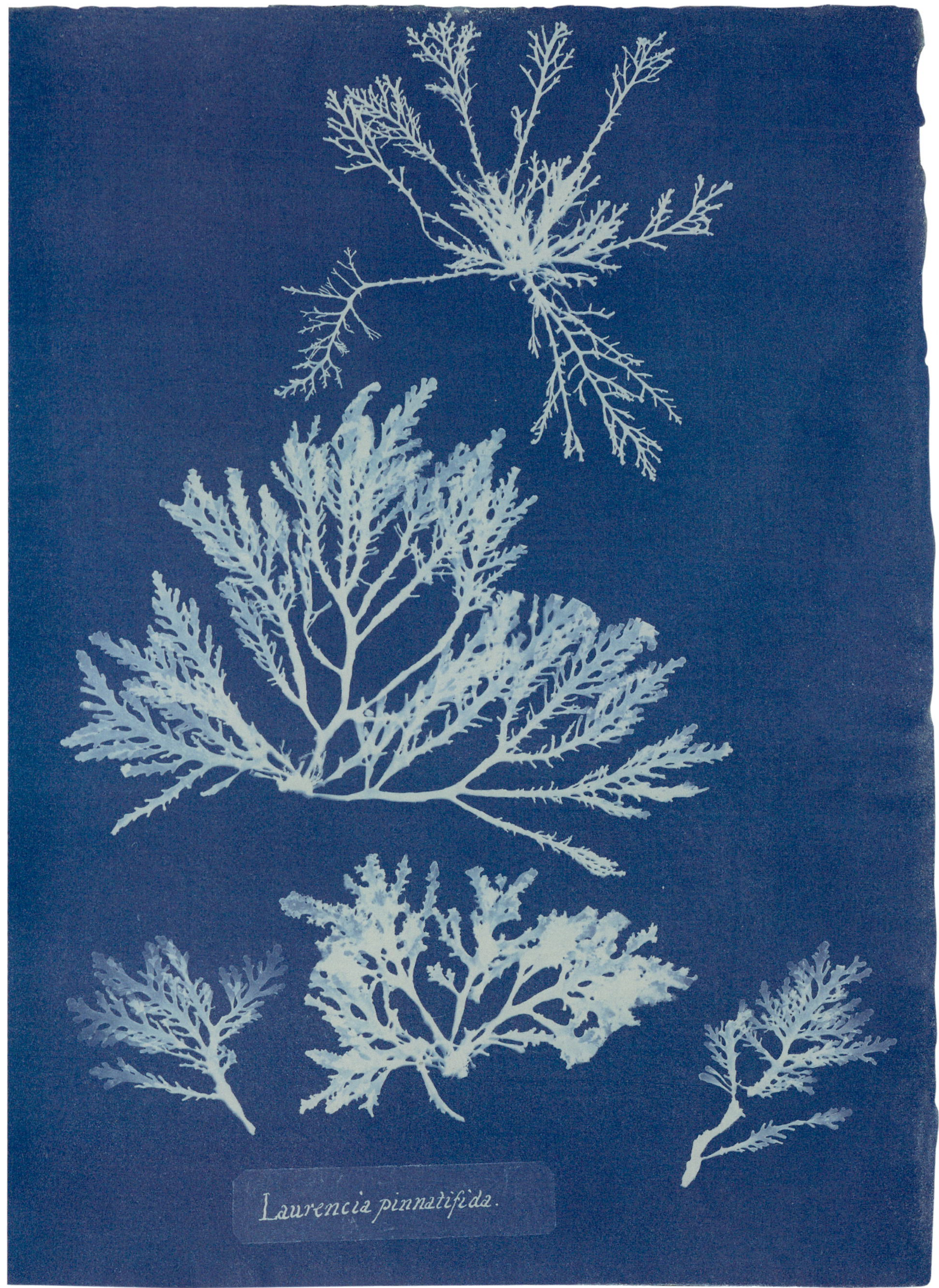


Anna Atkins, *Laurencia pinnatifida*, 1846–47, cyanotype

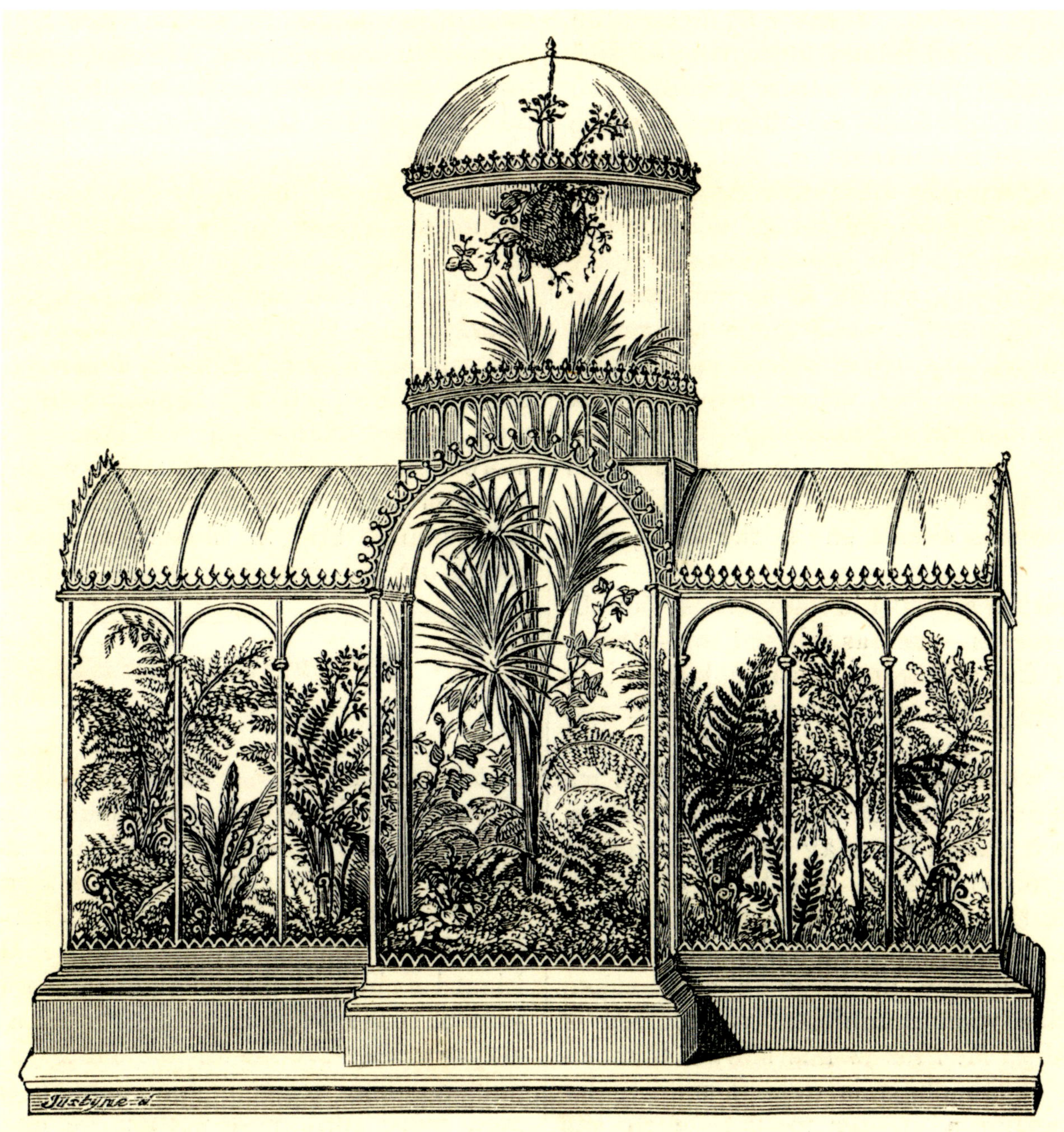


Artist unknown, Wardian case with plants, 1856, engraving

the title *Photographs of British Algae: Cyanotype Impressions.*

The following year, Talbot began publishing many of his own photograms in his book *The Pencil of Nature* (1844–46), while Atkins pursued the creation of a new volume titled *Cyanotypes of British and Foreign Ferns* (1853), which became the emblem of the Victorian "fern frenzy," or pteridomania, that swept the UK well into the 1890s. The flatness of fern fronds made them ideal for use in a variety of creative applications such as stenciling, decoupage, and the printing and etching of patterns on ceramics and glassware.[10] Collecting and growing ferns indoors became a favorite Victorian pastime. The invention of the ubiquitous Wardian case, a miniature domestic greenhouse, helped enthusiasts keep plants moist and adequately warm in drafty Victorian homes. The "nature appreciation" industry was born, complete with must-have books, tools, and merchandise. In it lay the blueprint for the capitalist

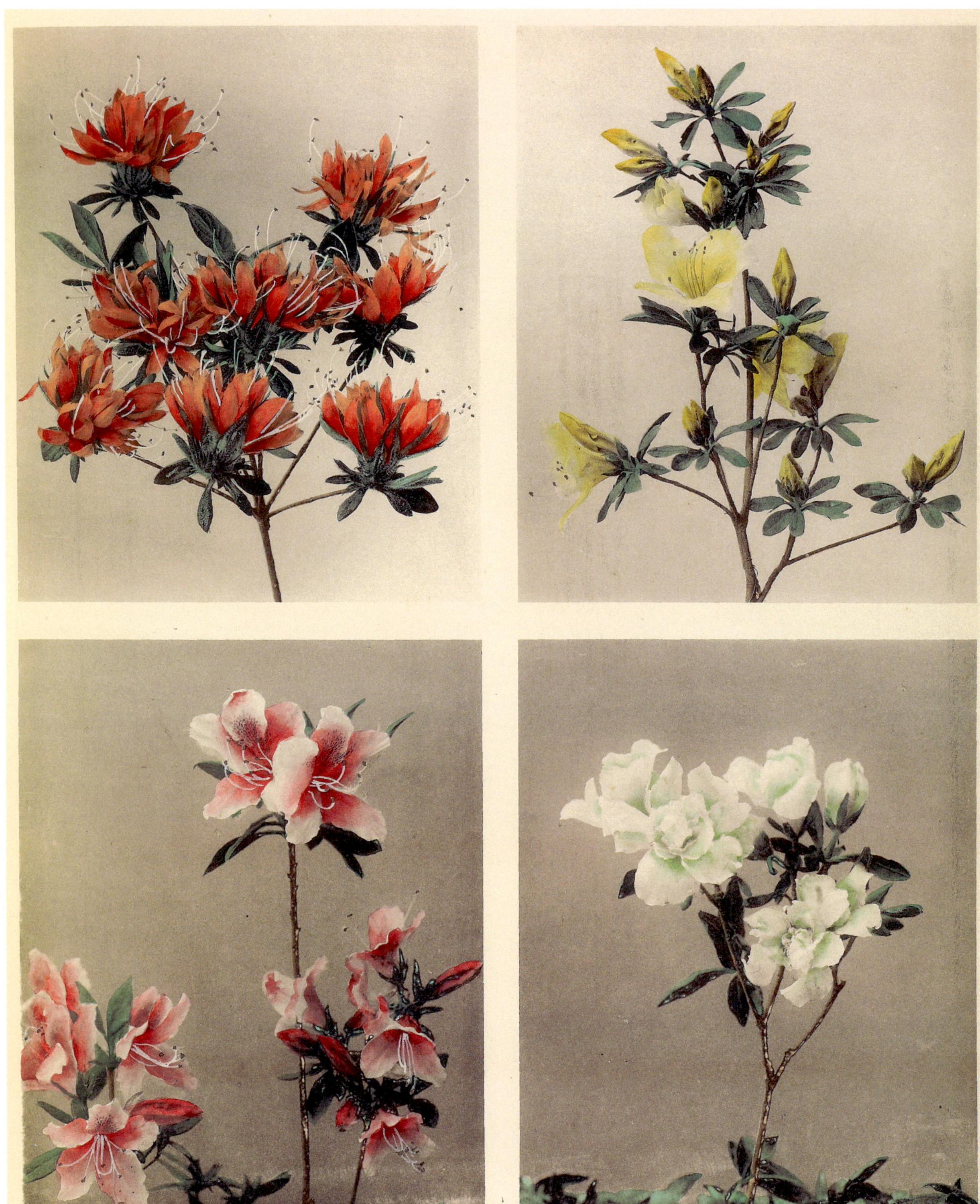

Kazumasa Ogawa, *Group of Azaleas*, 1896, colored collotypes

models that today shape gardening and hobby markets. Regrettably, as the collection and commerce of ferns lacked regulation, indiscriminate harvesting pushed some species perilously close to extinction.

Pteridomania was among the first fads fueled by the new illustrated publications. The proliferation of new photographic imagery capturing the beauty of exotic plants was also in part responsible for the mania that followed: orchidelirium, a distinctly more upper-class collecting pursuit. Individual orchids could fetch at auction more than £200—the equivalent of $30,000 today.[11]

Given the fervor that pervaded the botanical world, it's no surprise that plants also became some of the earliest and most commonly portrayed subjects in photography. Capturing a world in constant motion remained difficult until later in the nineteenth century, when technical advances significantly reduced film exposure times. Plants and flowers presented in the opulent manner of Baroque still-life paintings played an important role in the development and refinement of the new medium. The introduction of color in 1861 capitalized further on this underlying mediatic affinity between plants and photography. However, since early color prints lacked tonal richness, hand-colored black-and-white prints continued to dominate the market for decades. Great examples of this are the exquisite thirty-eight full-color pictures of an herbarium created by Kazumasa Ogawa, part of the book *Some Japanese Flowers* (1896).[12]

And it wasn't long before another botanical revolution loomed on the horizon. Patented in 1903 and marketed starting in 1907, the Lumière brothers' "autochrome" process proved able to capture a more stable and accurate color range.[13] Miniature granules of potato starch that had been dyed orange, green, and blue-violet were the source of color in this new and revolutionary plant-based medium. To the chagrin of professional photographers, it became very popular among amateurs—many of whom of course used it to capture flowers, plants, and gardens—and stayed in use until the 1930s.[14] A series of stereoscopic autochrome cards featuring lush still lifes of flowers and fern leaves became an instant hit, as did images of gardens in bloom. The *British Journal of Photography* noted: "Color is the very essence of the delight of the garden.... The garden lover wants photographs as records of what he has accomplished, and which will last long after the glory of the original has departed."[15]

By the end of the nineteenth century, the popularization of photography had fundamentally altered how humans see reality and interact with the natural world. Photography allowed us to see more, and more closely. In the year 1900, F. Percy Smith successfully developed a refined system of extension tubes that allowed him to capture intricate and remarkably sharp macrophotographs of insects and plants, surpassing any previous achievements in this field. Smith's contribution to the historical narrative of microscopic vision can be situated within a broader context that originated in the mid-seventeenth century, namely with the publication of biologist Robert Hooke's seminal work *Micrographia* (1665). The groundbreaking book featured thirty-eight plates of insects and plants magnified up to fifty times, including a macro view of a piece of cork that enabled Hooke to first theorize the existence of cells.[16]

Building on the success of his own macrophotography, Smith was quick to recognize the creative opportunity laid forth by the Lumière brothers' first moving-image captures in 1895. His 1910 *The Birth of a Flower* time-lapse film footage sped up plant life, revealing hitherto-unseen unfurlings of petals and movements of leaves. In Smith's short film, crocuses, daffodils, anemones, hyacinths, lilies, narcissi, Neapolitan onions, roses, snowdrops, and tulips look exceedingly alive, brimming with an intense desire to reach upward and outward, burst and unleash, filled with a previously unwitnessed, seemingly sensual desire.[17] Smith's time-lapse bridged the temporal abyss that separates us from the vegetal kingdom, greatly expanding our understanding of plant life. It is no surprise that this pioneering work would lead a reviewer to remark: "You find it difficult to believe ... that the life of a plant is not as sentient as your own."[18]

*BRANCHES AND VINES*, ERNESTINE EBERHARDT ZAUMSEIL, CA. 1875

---

*ERICA MUTABILIS*, WILLIAM HENRY FOX TALBOT, 1839

*RAVINE IN THE SIMPLON OPPOSITE ISELLA*, SIR JOHN FREDERICK WILLIAM HERSCHEL, 1821

---

*STILL LIFE WITH FLOWERS AND FRUIT*, CLAUDE MONET, 1869

*BOUQUET OF FLOWERS IN A VASE*, GUSTAVE COURBET, 1862

---

*IRISES*, VINCENT VAN GOGH, 1889

---

*STILL LIFE WITH APPLES*, PAUL CÉZANNE, 1893–94

---

HENRI MATISSE IN HIS STUDIO, HOTEL REGINA, NICE, 1948

*LA GERBE*, HENRI MATISSE, 1953

*SANDRINGHAM*, POSSIBLY FRANCES ELIZABETH JOCELYN, CA. 1850–60

THREE MEN STAND IN A GREENHOUSE, ARNOLD EAGLE, CA. 1940–42

---

*THISTLE*, KARL BLOSSFELDT, 1928

---

DIATOM ARRANGEMENT, J. D. MÖLLER, CA. 1870–90

---

*OAK TREE, SNOWSTORM, YOSEMITE NATIONAL PARK, CALIFORNIA*, ANSEL ADAMS, NEGATIVE 1948

*REDWOODS, BULL CREEK FLAT, NORTHERN CALIFORNIA*, ANSEL ADAMS, NEGATIVE CA. 1960

---

*SAHUARO*, GRACIELA ITURBIDE, NEGATIVE 1979

---

*FIELD OF POPPIES*, JACQUES-HENRI LARTIGUE, CA. 1960–78

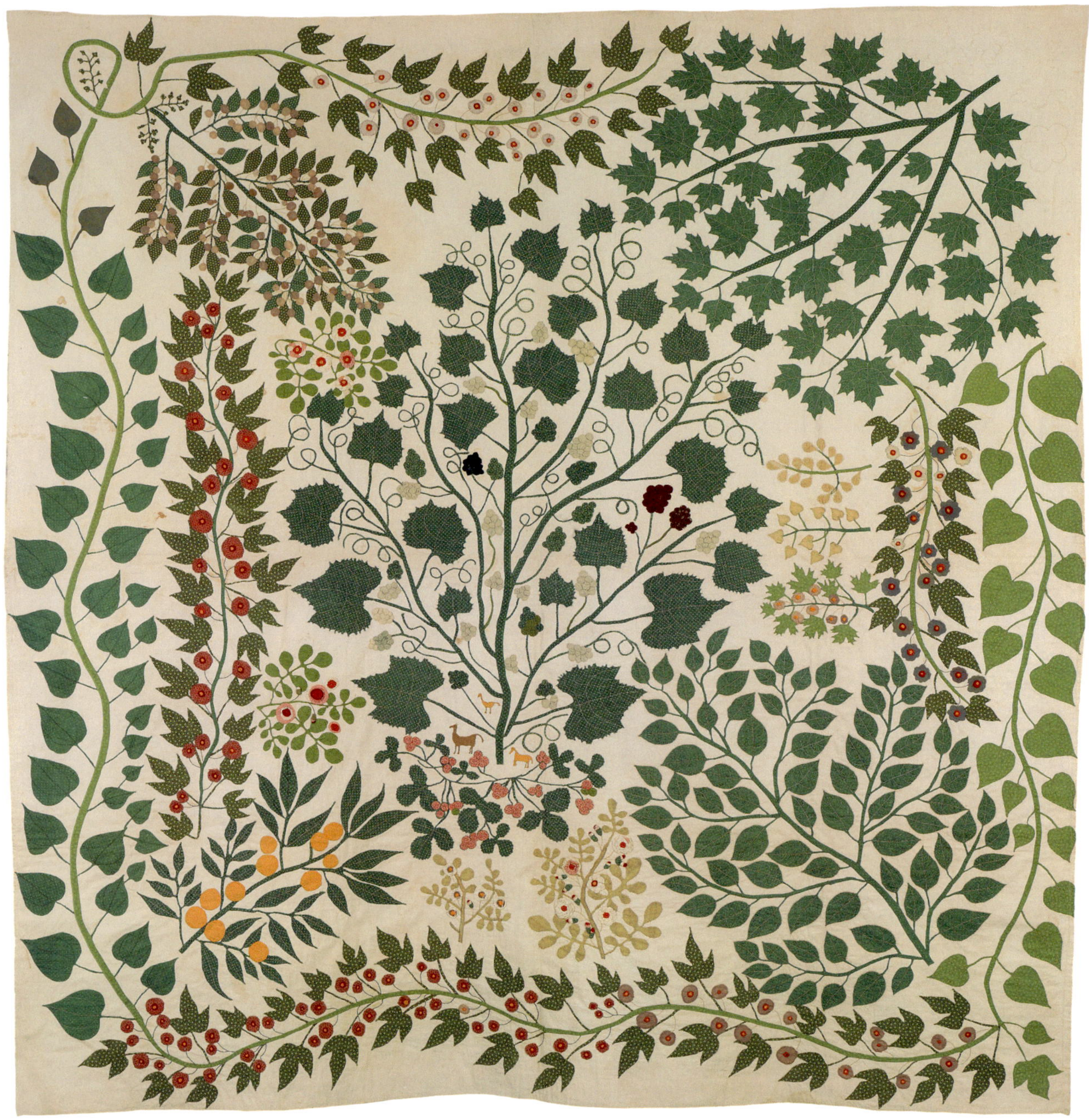

**Ernestine Eberhardt Zaumseil, *Branches and Vines*, ca. 1875, cotton, silk, and wool quilt**

This exquisitely detailed, botanically inspired quilt is the work of Ernestine Eberhardt Zaumseil. Titled *Branches and Vines*, it was completed in 1875, after many months of painstaking work. The intricate design marries traditional Indigenous American aesthetics with a Western attention to botanical accuracy. Zaumseil traced real plant leaves upon the fabric to produce a highly naturalistic effect. At the center of the quilt is a grapevine just beginning to bear fruit, in an unconventional but gentle reference to the classical Tree of Life motif that repeats in different cultures across the globe. The elegant way leaves and branches govern the harmony of the representational plane; how they sometimes merge, gracefully disrespecting the categories of species; and how a sense of symmetry is retained but in a non-rigorous way, all gesture toward a delicate balance between the unruliness of nature and the human desire to perceive and understand it. Originally intended to be used as a bedspread, the quilt was inspired by Indian fabrics called *palampore*. During the nineteenth century, these quilts were mainly produced for the export market. Zaumseil was a German immigrant to the United States, and this work therefore also captures complex colonialist and cultural entwinements in a way that only art can.

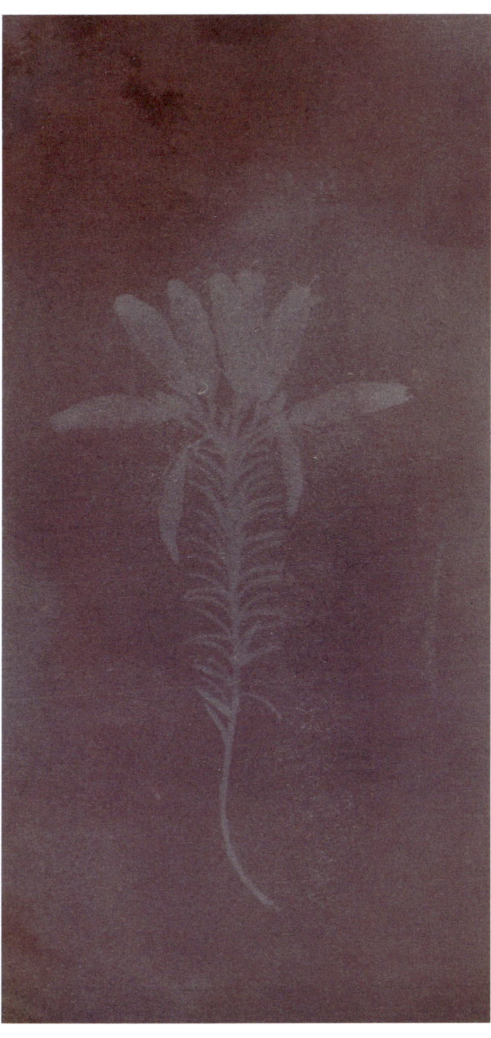

**William Henry Fox Talbot, *Erica mutabilis*, March 1839, photogenic drawing negative, salt fixed**

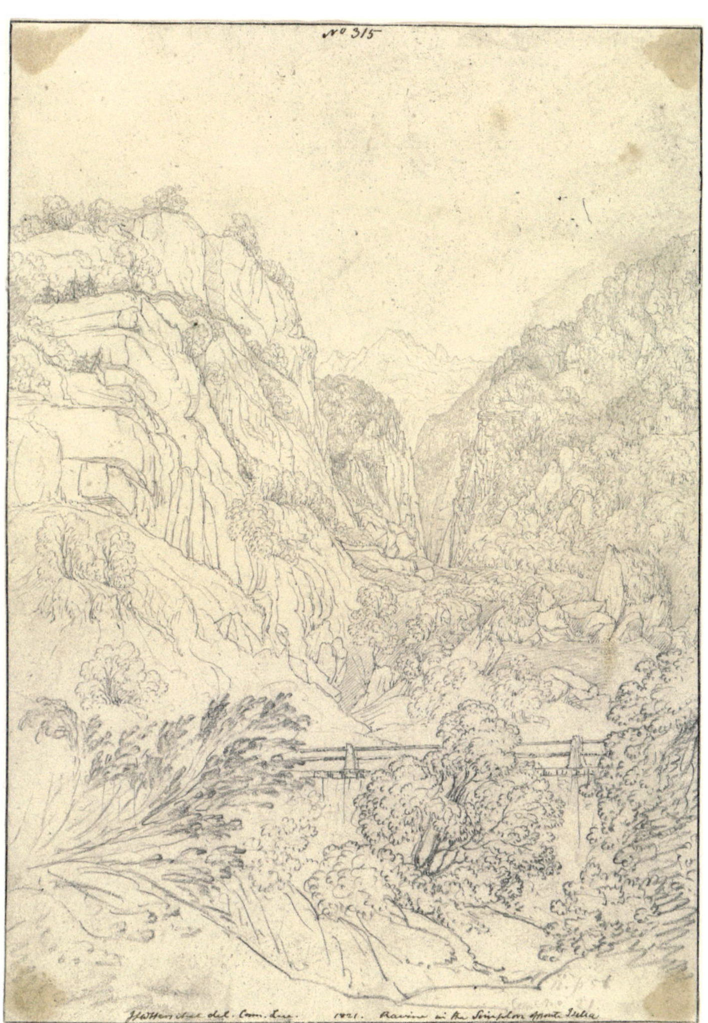

**Sir John Frederick William Herschel, *Ravine in the Simplon Opposite Isella*, September 1, 1821, graphite drawing made with the aid of a camera lucida**



William Henry Fox Talbot experimented with plants as he refined the image-making process that would eventually change the history of the world: photography. His image here is technically a photogram, a cameraless work made by laying the specimen on a sheet of paper coated with salt and silver nitrate and exposing it to light, so the silhouette of the plant imprints on the treated surface. Its spectral appearance is due to the inversion of highlights and shadows resulting from the process. This particular plate is of an Ericaceae plant, and it is of particular significance to the history of early photography, since it evidences an important collaboration between Talbot and his friend, the polymath and experimental photographer Sir John Frederick William Herschel. Talbot made two copies of this image (the one shown here is in the Getty collection, while the other is at the History of Science Museum in Oxford) and mailed one to Herschel with the note: "I send you a flower of health." Herschel, whose health had been broken in service as master of the mint, had become very fond of Ericaceae while spending time in South Africa, where more than six hundred species of the plant thrive. A few years later, Herschel's interest in plants led him to invent the printing technique known as anthotype, in which plant pigmentation is extracted and used as a light-sensitive emulsion to capture early photographic images.

## *ERICA MUTABILIS*

## *RAVINE IN THE SIMPLON OPPOSITE ISELLA*

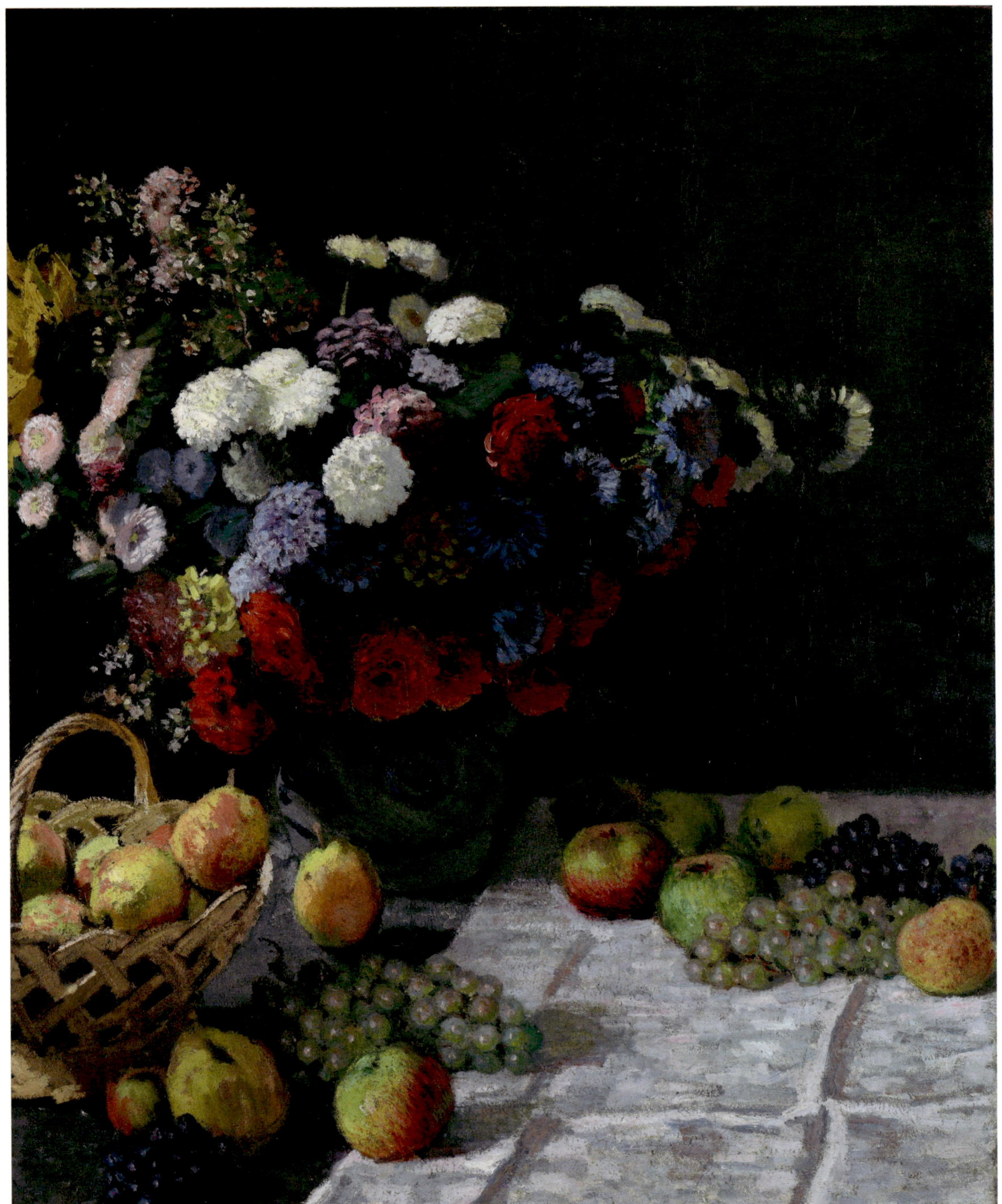

Claude Monet, *Still Life with Flowers and Fruit*, 1869, oil on canvas

By the second half of the nineteenth century, the traditional art market model based on commissions from the state, the church, and the aristocracy had crumbled, and the very definition of "artist" had undergone a radical transformation. Rebellion against institutional control and an insatiable desire for creative independence now drove painters and sculptors to focus on subjects for which a strong market did not yet exist. But when in need of money, artists knew that they could count on plants to tide them over.

Gustave Courbet and Claude Monet were two of the most revolutionary artists of their time; Courbet became a leader of the Realist movement and Monet of Impressionism. But for both, lush floral compositions in the Dutch Golden Age style always brought in money—the beauty of flowers spoke to all, and it transcended art trends and political views. Courbet enthusiastically embraced flower painting in 1862 while visiting his friend

## *STILL LIFE WITH FLOWERS AND FRUIT*

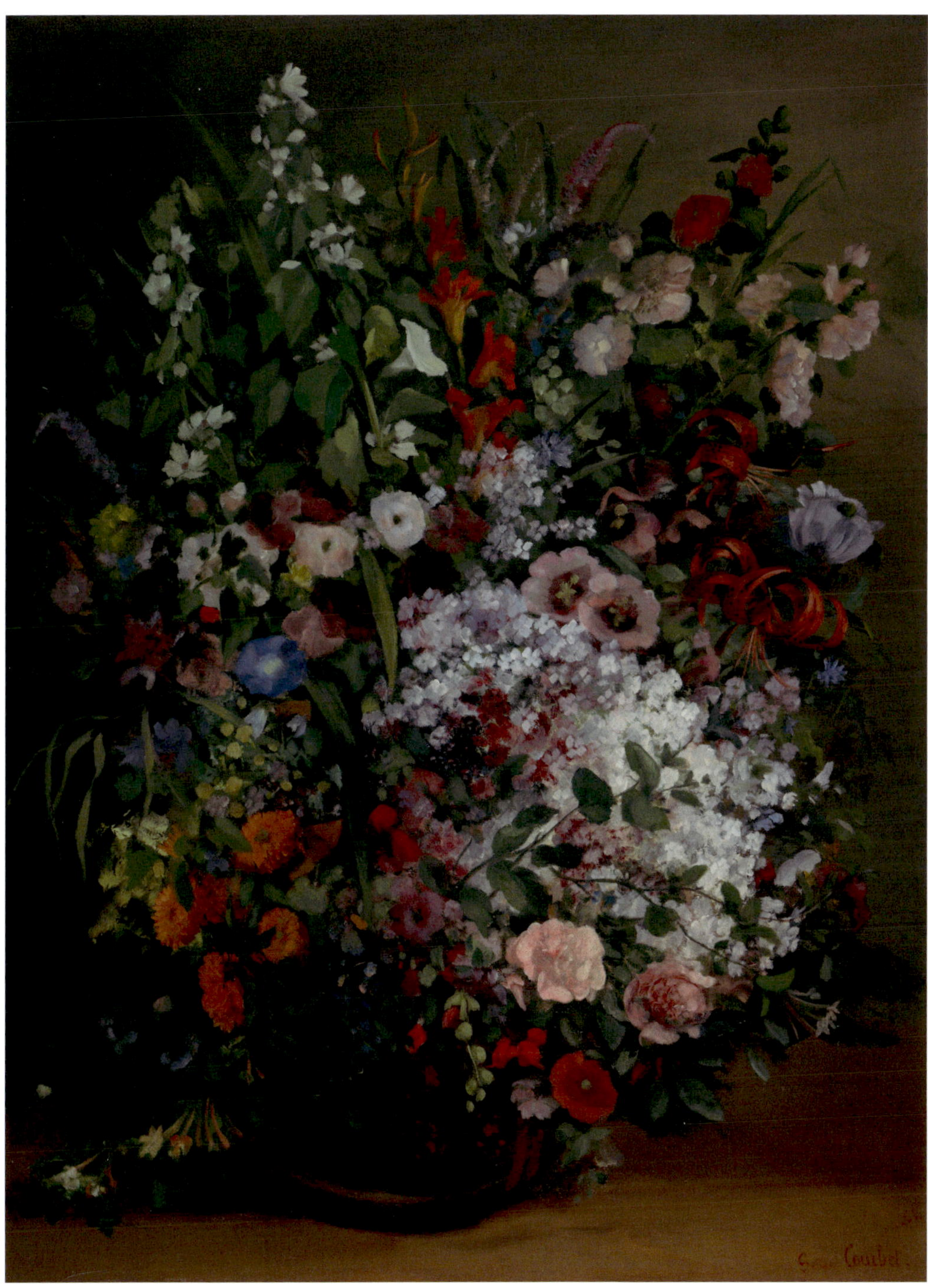

**Gustave Courbet, *Bouquet of Flowers in a Vase*, 1862, oil on canvas**



Etienne Baudry, a keen gardener. Finding inspiration in Baudry's greenhouses and botanical books, the artist painted roughly twenty pictures of cut flowers. He was confident about the monetary return, remarking to a friend: "I am coining money out of flowers." Monet's take on the subject was much closer to the ethics of the Realist movement, which was devoted to the representation of humble, everyday subjects. Whereas Courbet's composition was clearly inspired by the Dutch tradition according to which flowers are represented together regardless of their blooming season, Monet's chrysanthemums, single sunflower, apples, and grapes are coherently arranged around autumnal harvest themes.

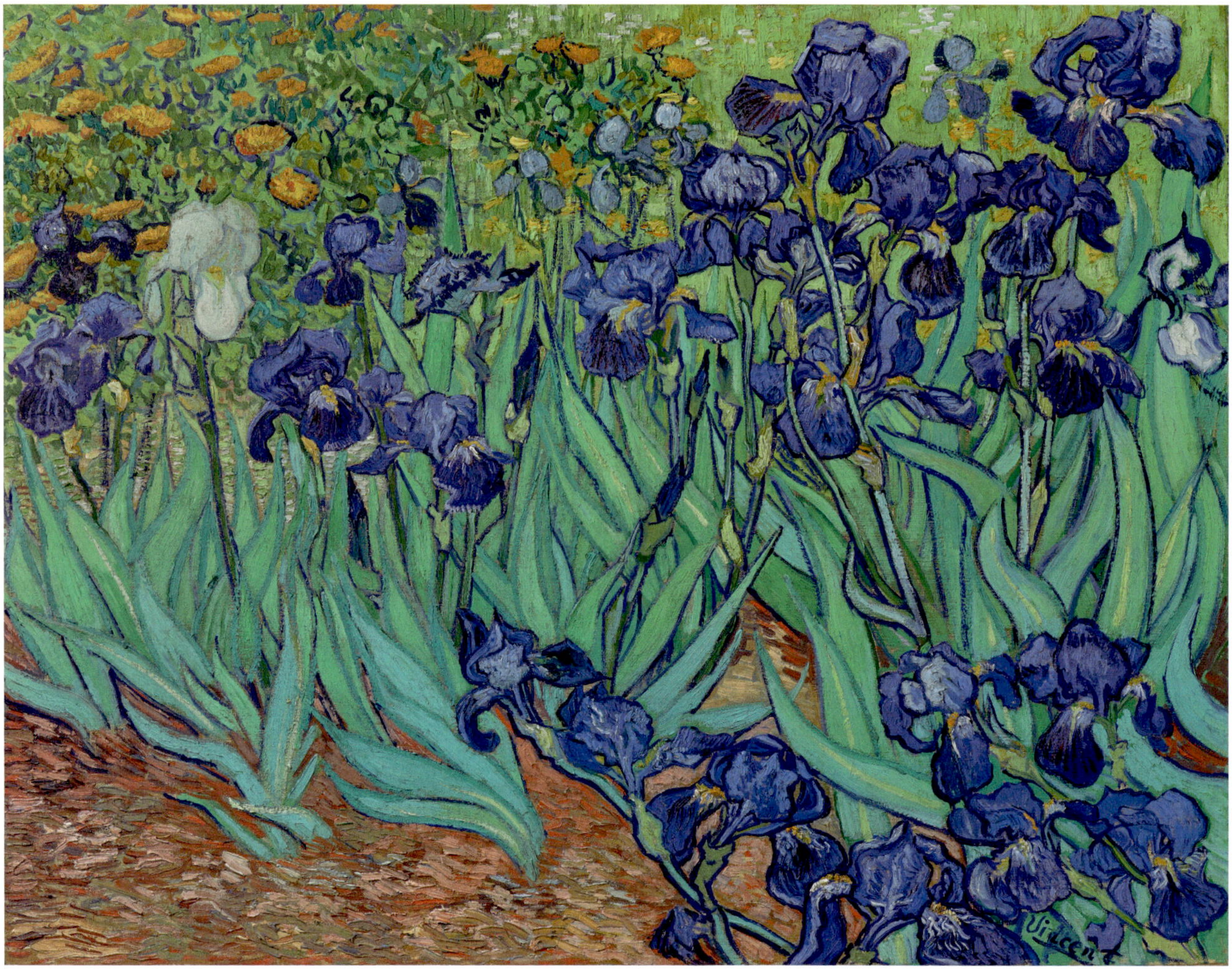

Vincent van Gogh, *Irises*, 1889, oil on canvas

This bold and original painting of *Iris germanica* was made during Vincent van Gogh's first week at the asylum in Saint-Rémy, France, where he voluntarily interned himself to seek help for his afflictions. Throughout his brief but productive career—Van Gogh only painted for ten years but made more than two thousand paintings and drawings—the artist portrayed a variety of cut flowers, olive trees, cypresses, wheat, and other plant species. His approach was strongly influenced by both Realism and Impressionism. From the former, he borrowed a predilection for humble and everyday plant subjects, and from the latter, a sensitivity for the clash of warm and cold colors. This iris painting defies Dutch tradition by stripping the subject of any Christian connotation. These irises don't belong in a fancy vase, juxtaposed with other expensive varieties. They are of the ground, humbly rising from the dirt but remaining anchored, gently bending in the wind while reaching for the sun. Despite the temptation to read the lone white iris as an allegorical self-portrait, no textual evidence supporting this interpretation has been identified.

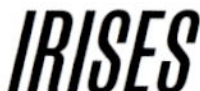

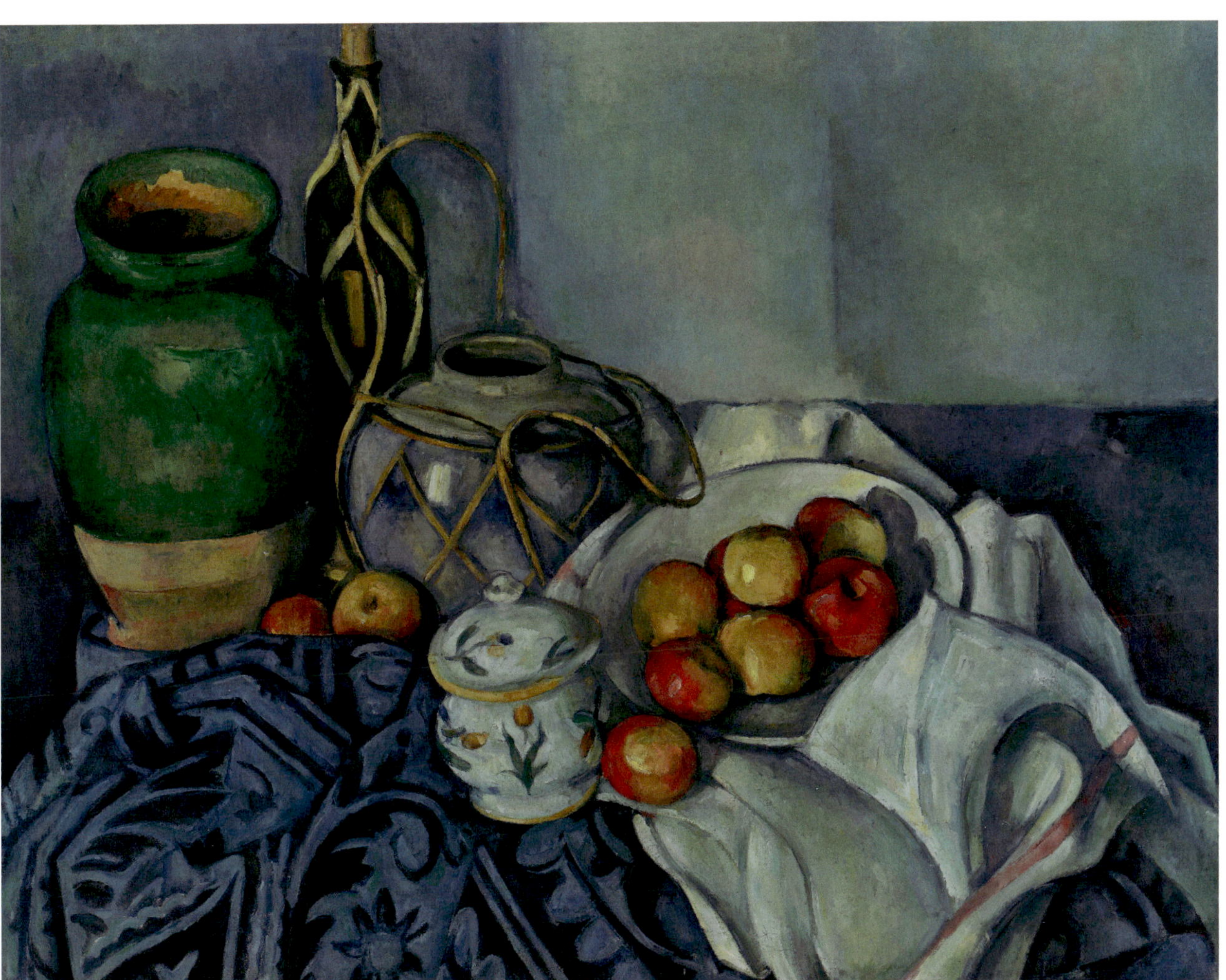

Paul Cézanne, *Still Life with Apples*, 1893–94, oil on canvas



A pivotal moment in the history of early modern art could not have taken place without the intervention of apples, oranges, and pears. Paul Cézanne collaborated with the Impressionists during the early stages of that movement. It was at the first exhibition of Impressionism in 1874 that harsh reviews spurred him to embark on a personal journey of discovery that forever changed the direction of modern art. Cézanne began to mistrust the airiness and flatness of Impressionism and sought to reinvent painting for modern times. The first step of his quest started with a departure from the perspectival construction of space typical of classical art; those canonical impositions, he was certain, limited the expressive potential of painting. His relentless experimentation with space and form resulted in more than two hundred still lifes featuring commonplace objects like baskets, drapes, and plates as well as apples, pears, and oranges. The rounder, the better—to Cézanne, round fruits represented the spherical perfection of elemental natural forms. Following this experimental path, the artist laid the groundwork for a new conception of relativity in art that Pablo Picasso and Georges Braque would later develop into Cubism, one of the most revolutionary movements in Western art and one of the creative paths that eventually led to abstract painting.

## STILL LIFE WITH APPLES

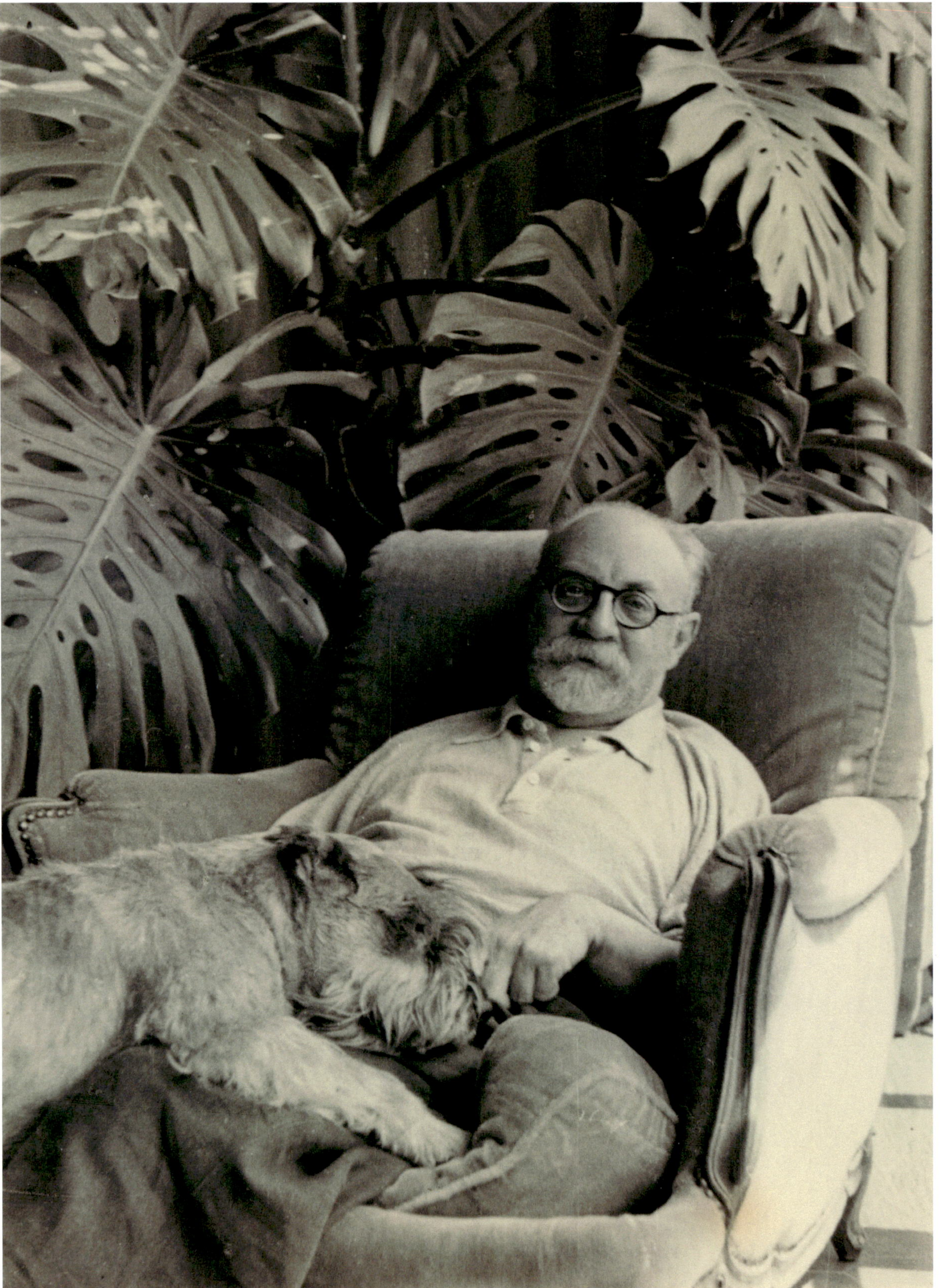

Unknown photographer, Henri Matisse in his studio, Hotel Regina, Nice, 1948, photograph

# HENRI MATISSE IN HIS STUDIO

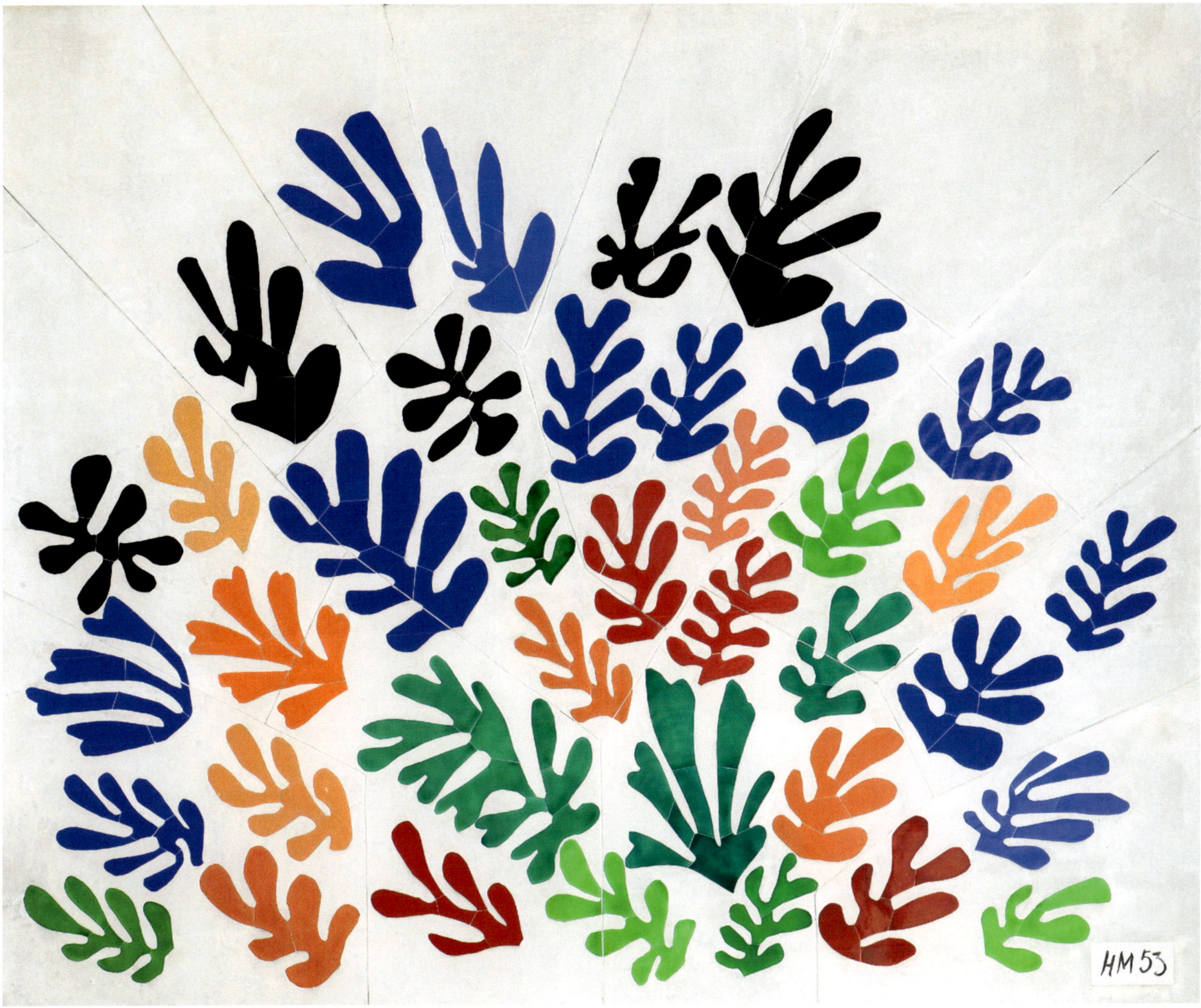

Henri Matisse, *La Gerbe*, 1953, ceramic tile embedded in plaster



Henri Matisse's cutouts are popular among art lovers, but not equally well known is that the inspiration behind these iconic works was a cluster of potted monstera plants the artist kept in his studio. Also known as split-leaf philodendron or Swiss cheese plant, monstera is highly adaptable to a wide range of conditions, including low light. The cutouts, a form of collage, became the artist's main artistic output from the 1940s onward. While collage had been popularized in art by Pablo Picasso and Georges Braque more than thirty years prior, Matisse made it his own, calling it "drawing with scissors" and employing bold colors and biomorphic motifs. Many of his 1950s cutouts were directly inspired by the massive monstera that thrived in his studio. In the artist's hand, the cut leaves became a portal through which to think about space and color in new ways. As Matisse's mobility deteriorated, the cutouts allowed him to work from bed and envisage oceanic worlds as well as dense woods. In his mind, plants were a universal, cosmological master key to the imagination.

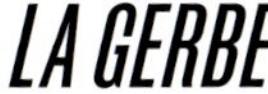

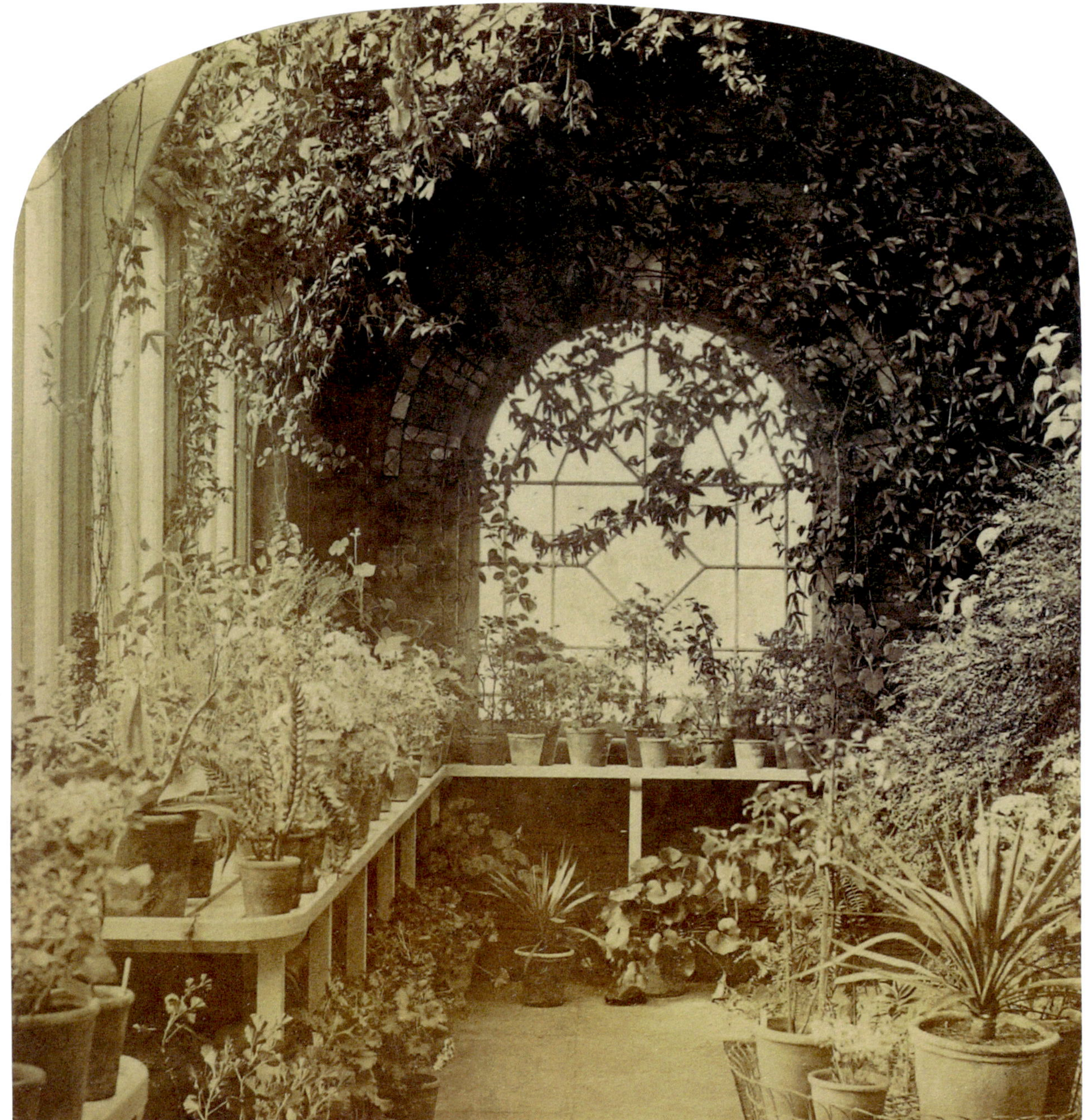

**Possibly Frances Elizabeth Jocelyn, Viscountess Jocelyn, *Sandringham*, ca. 1850–60, albumen silver print**

Conservatories and greenhouses gained in popularity among the higher classes in England and northern Europe as the second half of the nineteenth century progressed. These enclosed structures allowed gardening enthusiasts to re-create at home the wonders experienced at Kew Gardens or seen in early illustrated magazines. Greenhouses also promoted trade in exotic plants, which were often taken from colonial territories with little concern for the ecological spoilage caused. They enabled early photographers and amateur botanical illustrators to study plants from the comfort of home instead of traveling to faraway and possibly dangerous lands—a costly undertaking often entirely barred to women. A lively periodical publishing market arose to satiate the popular thirst for new and ever more precise illustrations of hard-to-find plants.

## SANDRINGHAM

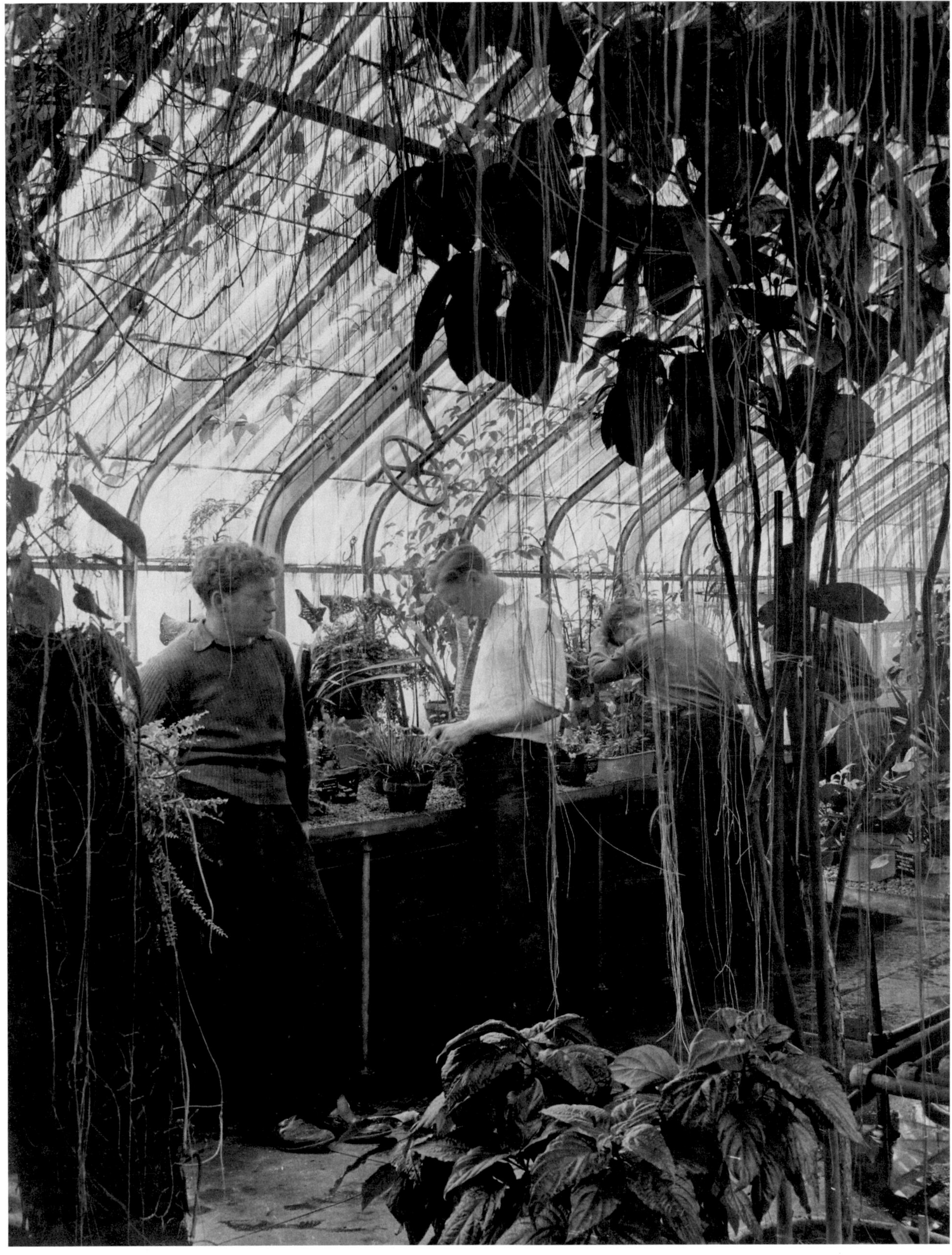

Arnold Eagle, *Three men stand in a greenhouse*, ca. 1940–42, gelatin silver print



*THREE MEN STAND IN A GREENHOUSE*

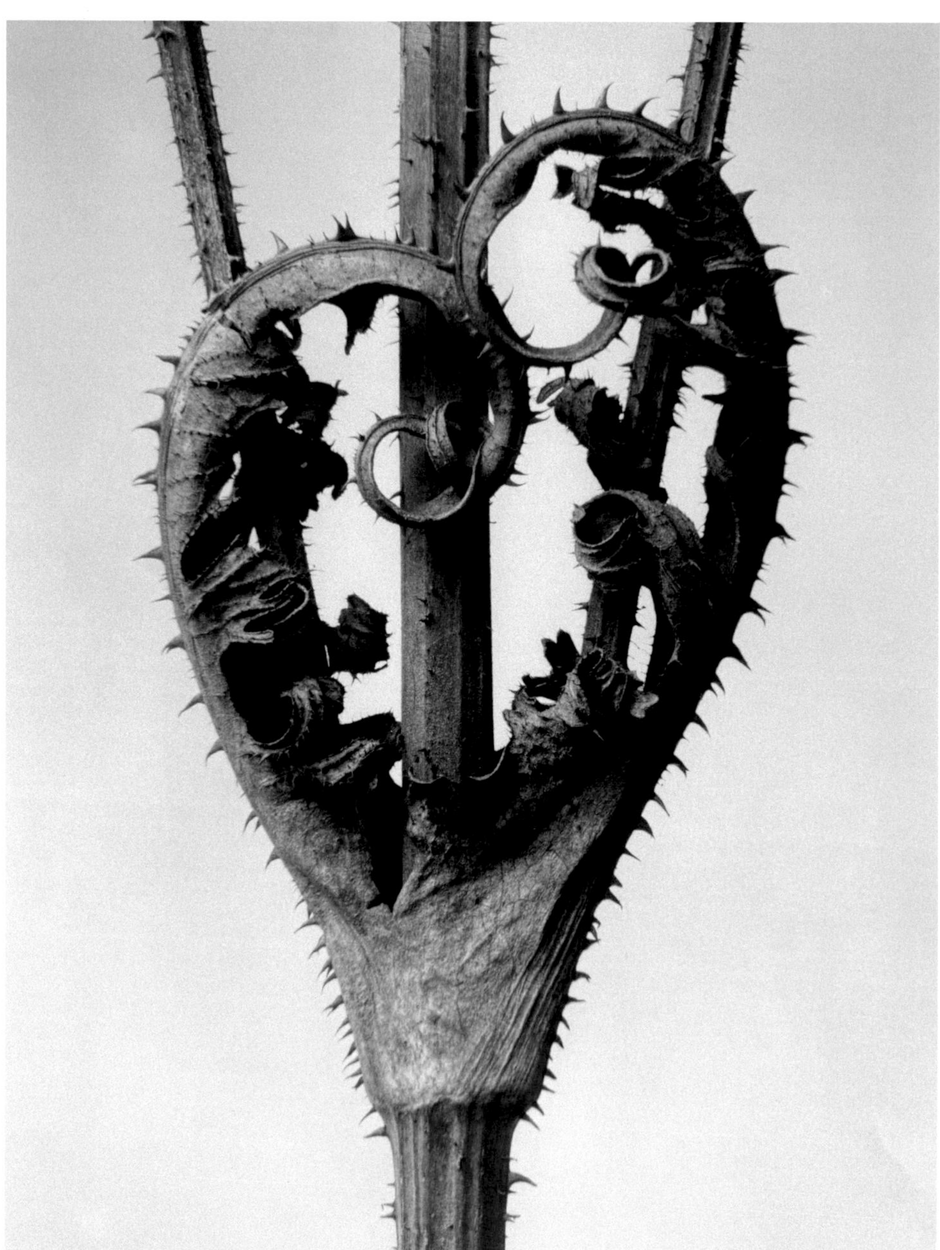

Karl Blossfeldt, *Thistle* (*Dipsacus laciniatus*), plate from *Urformen der Kunst I*, 1928, pigment print

Botanist and sculptor Karl Blossfeldt recognized the inherent beauty and design found in plants, which led him to capture their essence through photography. Inspired by the Arts and Crafts movement, which emphasized the importance of craftsmanship and the beauty of natural forms, Blossfeldt explored plant anatomy through macrophotography to present plants as works of art in their own right. His background as a teacher influenced his interest in the educational component of his plant imagery. He believed that by closely observing and studying plants, one could gain a deeper understanding of the natural world, and he was driven to explore macrophotography as a means of sharing his botanical discoveries with others. Blossfeldt's photographs were widely used in classrooms and textbooks to teach students about botany and plant morphology. By presenting plants in a visually captivating way, they made the subject more accessible and engaging, and enabled the study and appreciation of the intricate details of plants without the need for expensive equipment. These pioneering images thus played a great role in democratizing the study of botany.

## THISTLE

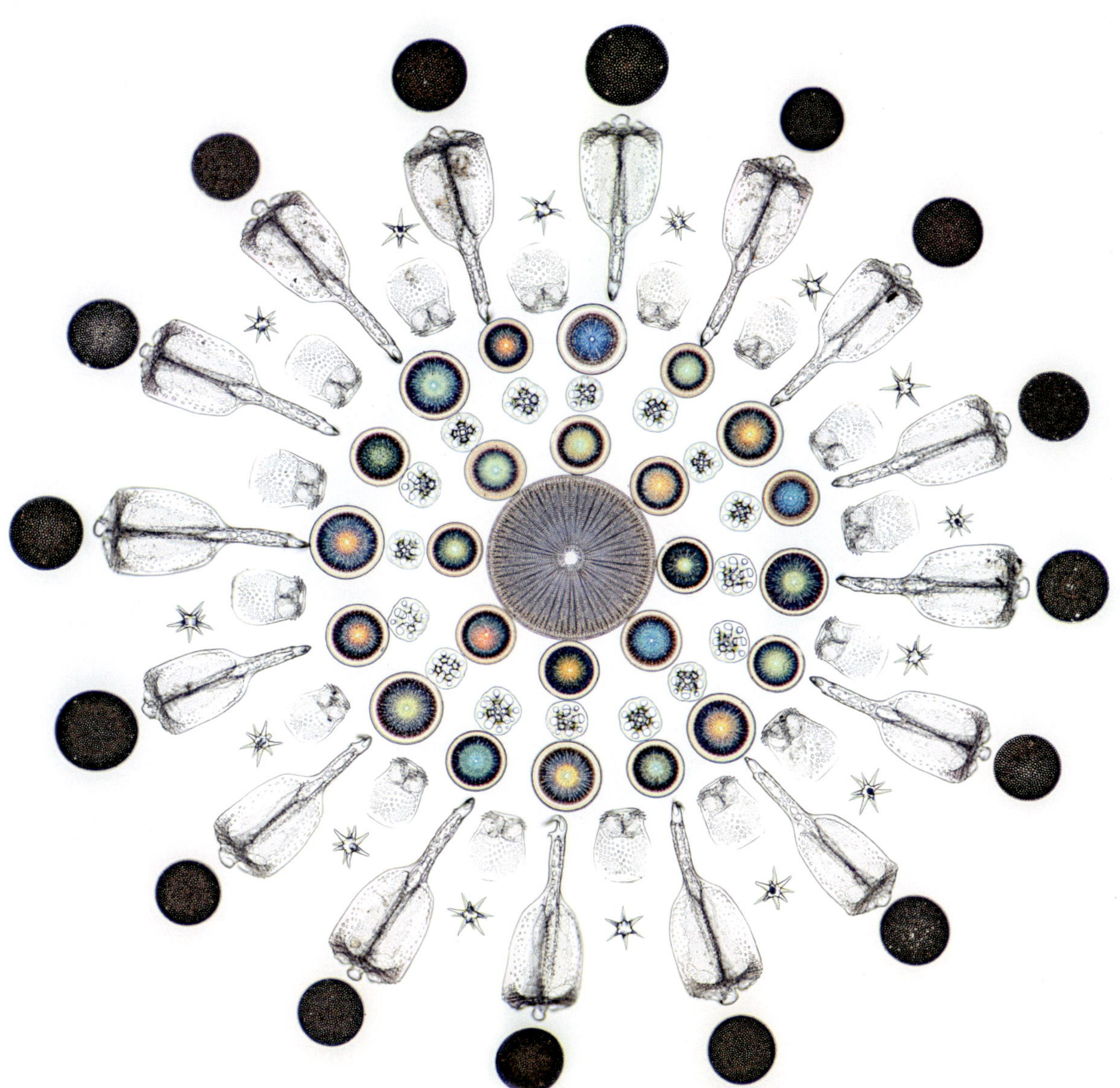



**J. D. Möller, Diatom arrangement, ca. 1870–90, glass slide**

J. D. Möller specialized in selecting and arranging diatoms on microscope slides. Through a combination of meticulous techniques and a deep understanding of diatom morphology, he created compositions that were both visually stunning and scientifically informative. Diatoms are single-celled plankton organisms that possess intricate silica cell walls called frustules that have unique patterns and structures. Möller likely employed various methods and tools, for instance a fine needle or brush, to manipulate individual diatoms into desired positions. This requires a steady hand, patience, and a keen eye for detail, and Möller proved himself a master, capable of meticulously arranging thousands of diatoms on a single slide according to complementary shapes and patterns so as to showcase their fascinating diversity and beauty. His precision set a standard for the field of scientific microscopy, and his emphasis on the aesthetic qualities of diatoms inspired subsequent artists as well. Diatoms play a crucial role in the Earth's ecosystems, contributing through photosynthesis approximately 20 to 40 percent of the total oxygen produced on the planet, helping to regulate the global carbon cycle and mitigate climate change. Additionally, diatoms form the base of many aquatic food chains, providing sustenance for a wide range of organisms, from microscopic zooplankton to larger marine animals.

# DIATOM ARRANGEMENT

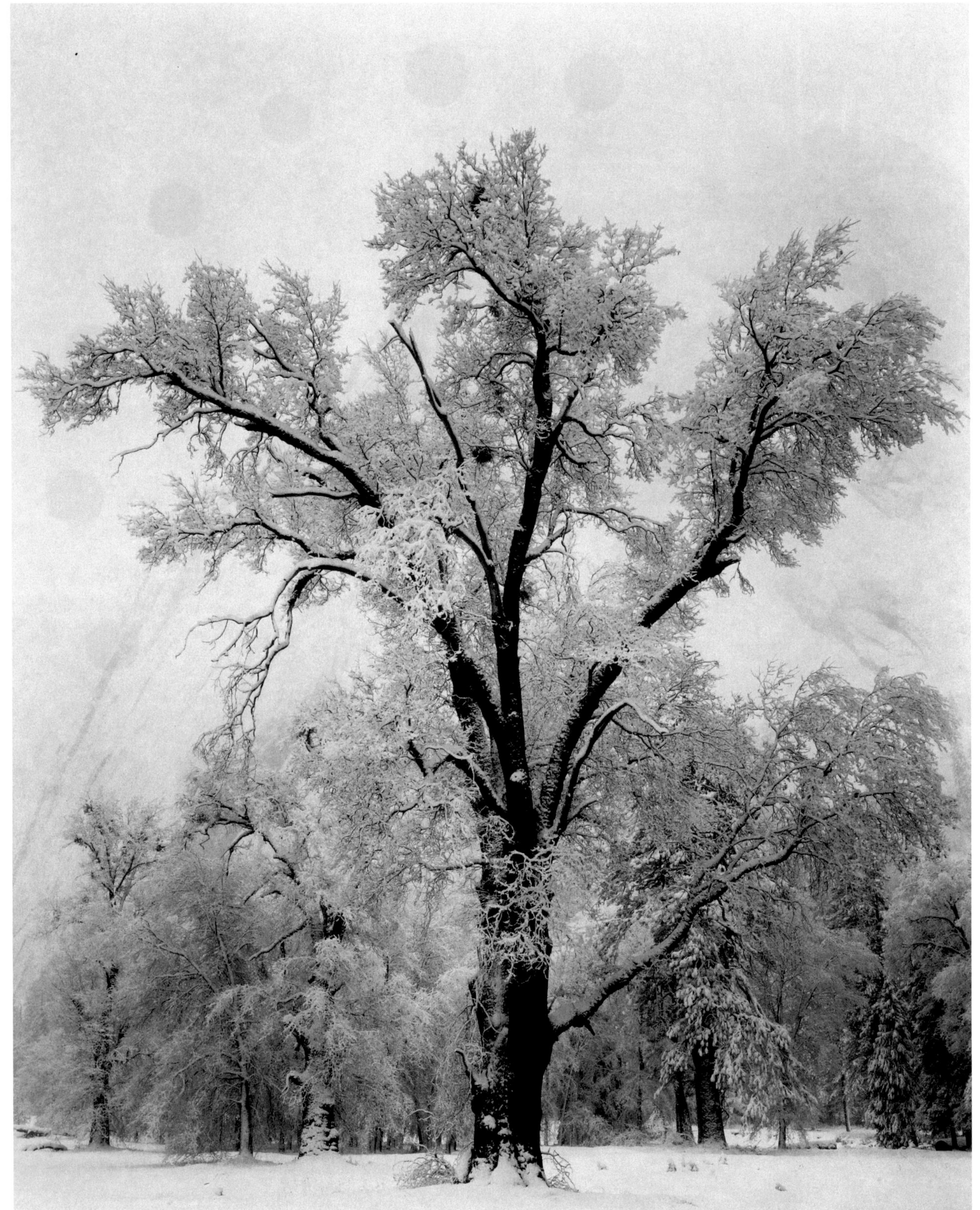

Ansel Adams, *Oak Tree, Snowstorm, Yosemite National Park, California*, negative 1948, print 1981, gelatin silver print

## *OAK TREE, SNOWSTORM, YOSEMITE NATIONAL PARK, CALIFORNIA*

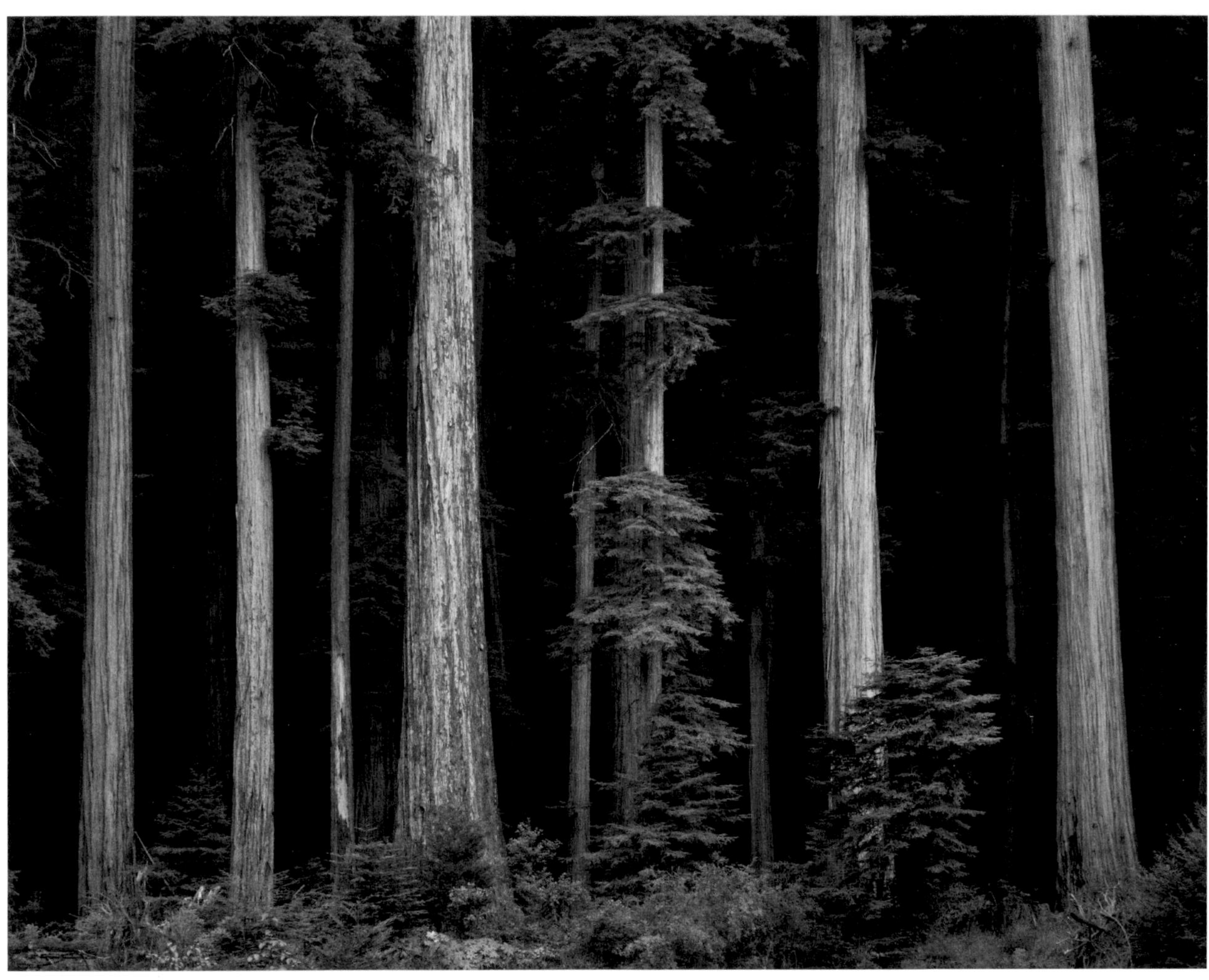

Ansel Adams, *Redwoods, Bull Creek Flat, Northern California*, negative ca. 1960, print 1980, gelatin silver print



Photography was central to the development of a nascent, cohesive idea of US national identity. Today, photographic imagery of any country is readily available online and technological advancements allow us to photographically record nearly every inch of the planet. But the construction of national identity is a much more nuanced matter—the result of a carefully calculated aesthetic approach that seeks to select and portray distinctive features of landscapes or people in ways that highlight a sense of singularity capable of instilling pride. Throughout the first half of the twentieth century, US photographers collectively amassed a range of iconic images showcasing the country's immense natural splendor. And among many, Ansel Adams was one of the most influential voices. His ability to choose just the right tree or the perfect angle from which to immortalize the majesty of a forest made him famous across the globe. His images of redwoods and other iconic tree species frequently emphasized scale, evoking the notion of an immutable and profound nature that predated the widespread degradation caused by humans. Adams's depictions of trees frequently summoned a sense of tranquility and introspection. They are sublime, solemn, and imperturbable, yet not dramatic—bearers of the land's secrets, and silent witnesses to its fraught history.

## *REDWOODS, BULL CREEK FLAT, NORTHERN CALIFORNIA*

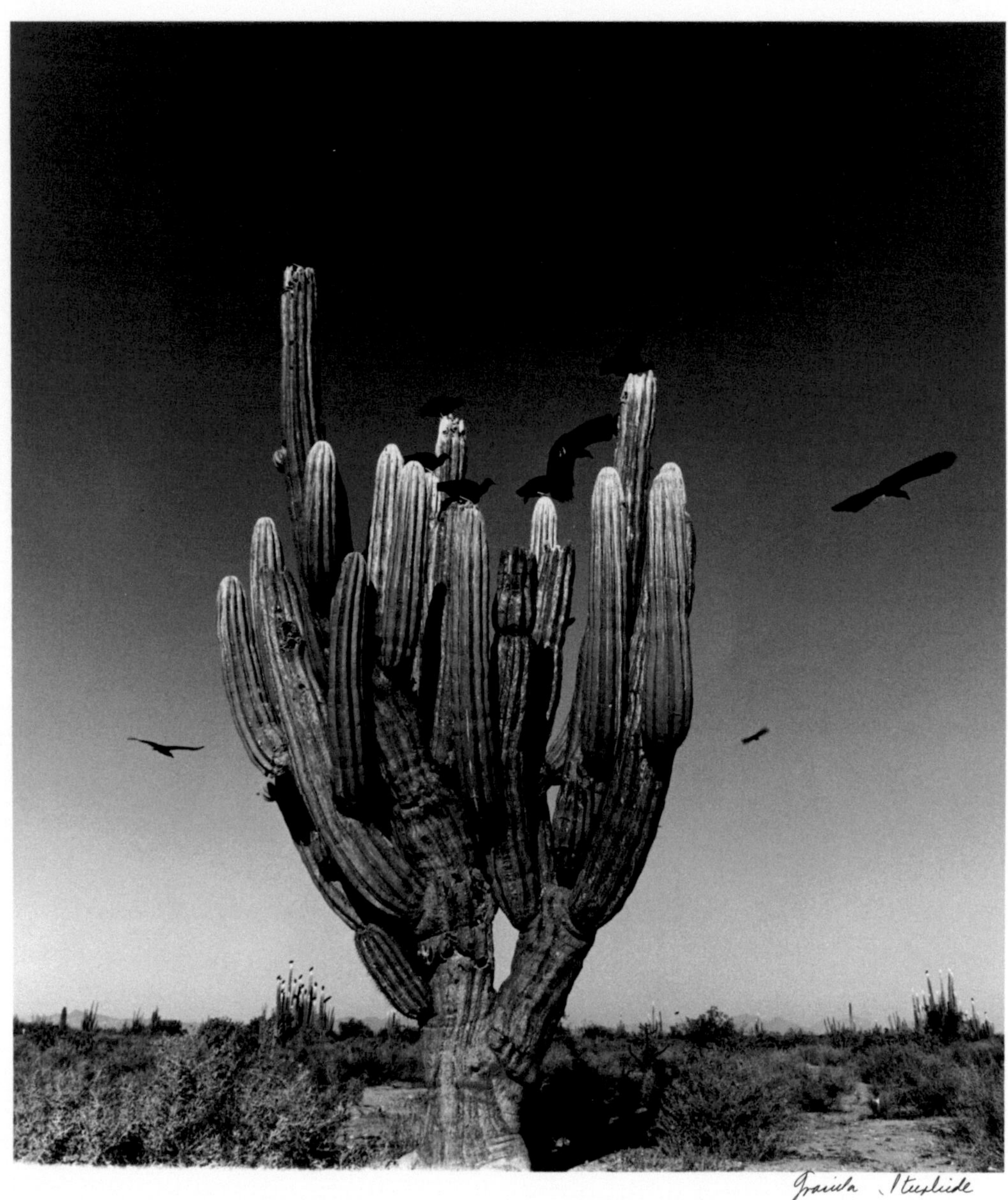

Graciela Iturbide, *Sahuaro* [Saguaro], *Los Seris, Desierto y Mar, Estado de Sonora, México*, negative 1979, print later, gelatin silver print

Informed by the stylistic incisiveness pioneered by predecessors Henri Cartier-Bresson, Tina Modotti, and Manuel Álvarez Bravo, Graciela Iturbide has captured some of the most interesting and original images of native Mexican plants. The saguaro is an iconic symbol of the American West, but in addition to the Sonoran Desert in Arizona and the Whipple Mountains and Imperial County areas of California, this species of columnar cactus is also native to the Mexican state of Sonora. A saguaro can live up to 150 years, and it does not produce its first side arm until the age of seventy-five or one hundred. Thus, the number of arms can, at a glance, provide a good indication of its age. This cactus has traditionally been central to the lives of Tohono O'odham, Pima, and Seri Indigenous peoples. Its fruits are harvested in June and July, and wine, syrups, and jam are made out of the sweet pulp.

## SAHUARO

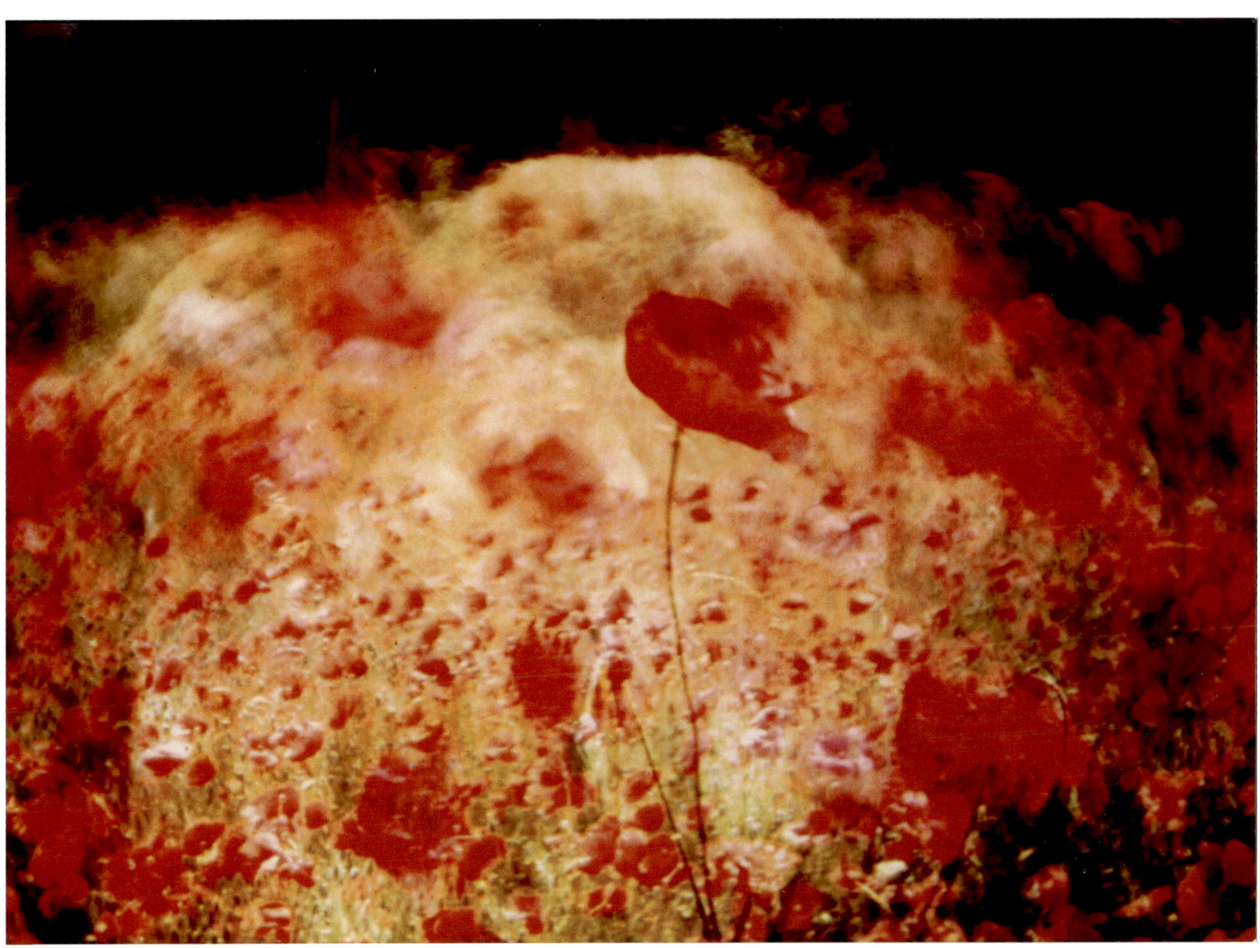



**Jacques-Henri Lartigue, *Field of Poppies*, ca. 1960–78, chromogenic print**

Jacques-Henri Lartigue was a painter who considered photography a hobby, but it was his photographic flair that eventually made him famous. And while he is most often remembered for his carefully composed black-and-white scenes of upper-class everyday life—fancy sports cars, airplanes, Parisian fashion models—after World War II he switched to Ektachrome color film and achieved decidedly more experimental and expressive results. This image of poppies captures the buoyancy of an early summer breeze. Precariously balancing on their thin and slender stems, the flowers sway in the air—part memory, part vision. Here Lartigue experiments with the involuntary movement of plants as an opportunity to transcend the limitation of their stillness and the descriptiveness of the documentary genre. Their vegetal trembling enlivens them with a non-religious mystical aura that loosely alludes to their narcotic and hallucinatory properties.

# FIELD OF POPPIES

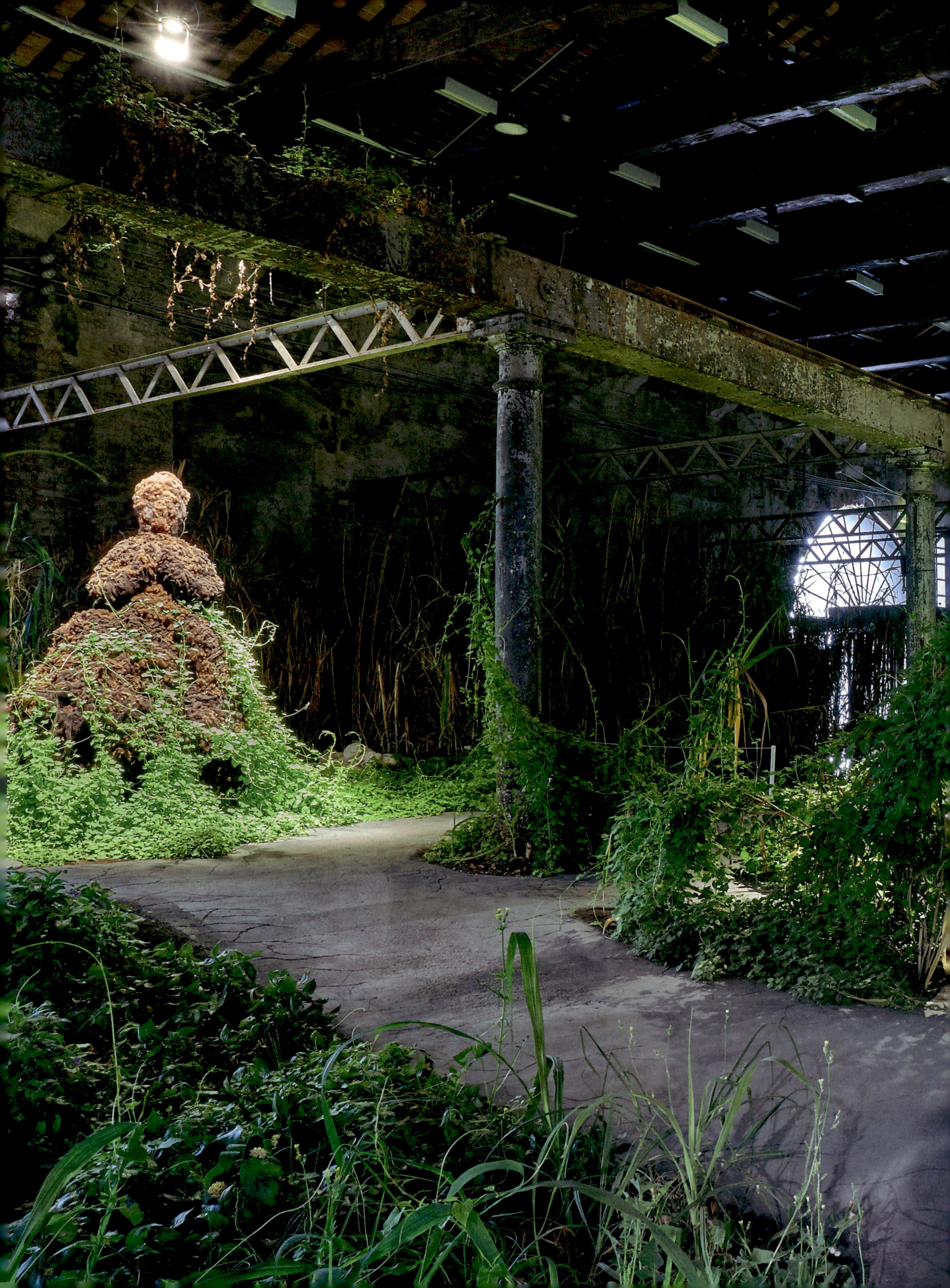

CHAPTER 7

# MODERN PLANTS: FROM OBJECT TO SUBJECT AND BEYOND

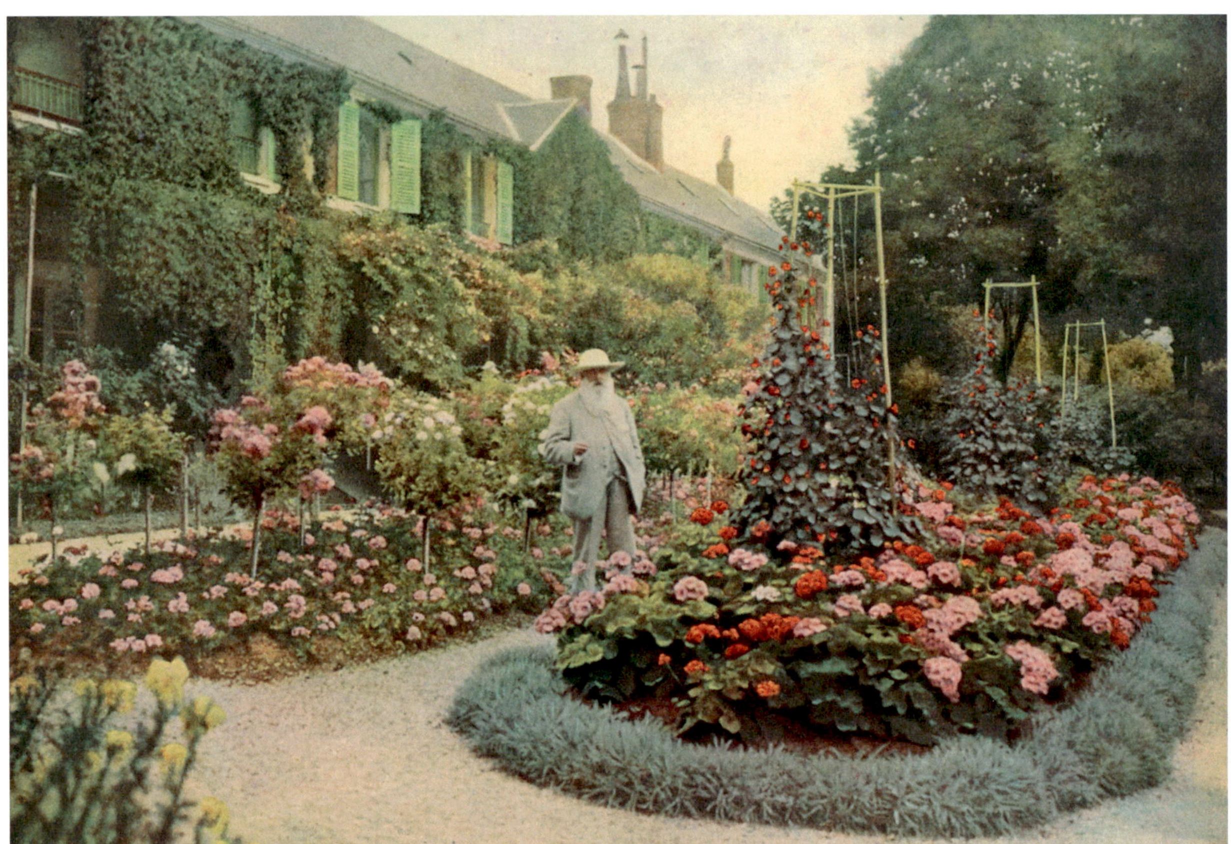



Photographer unknown, Claude Monet in the garden of his home at Giverny, France, April 10, 1905, photograph

During the summer of 1897, Claude Monet set his easel outdoors, by the pond in his garden at Giverny, France. There, under dappled lighting filtered by his beloved bamboo, he painted his first water lilies. Over the next twenty years, he would return to that subject more than 250 times, painting some of the most revolutionary masterpieces of early modern art.[1] Yet art historians don't tend to talk about Monet's love for actual plants, as opposed to representations of them. Few art books even mention that this preeminent Impressionist artist was also a keen botanist with a passion for gardening. Monet moved to Giverny in 1883, three years before the Impressionists disbanded, and purchased the house and grounds in 1890. In his spare time, he hybridized and crossed new varieties of flowers. Eventually, with a small army of helpers, he landscaped and planted roughly two and a half acres into what he called his "greatest masterpiece": the garden.[2] So determined was Monet to realize his vision that he illegally diverted the nearby Epte river to create what would become possibly the most famous pond in the world.

Monet's love affair with water lilies began in 1889 at the Exposition Universelle in Paris, where local horticultural pioneer Joseph Bory Latour-Marliac exhibited his new collection of *Nymphaea* hybrids. To the amazement of many, these new varieties flowered not in white (*Nymphaea alba*), as was common in Europe, but in yellow, pink, and crimson. Latour-Marliac spent years crossbreeding white varieties with others from South America and Asia to perfect and fix the desired coloration.[3] Monet placed his first order in 1894. Subsequent orders from 1900 and 1904 reveal the artist's growing fondness for crimson and carmine varieties.[4]

Deeply devoted to Zen philosophy and all things Japanese, Monet would spend time in the garden meditating as well as painting. By 1914, he had become acutely aware that his water lilies were more than flowers—that through painting, they could open up a portal to a spiritual dimension: "I painted them the way monks illuminated their manuscripts in times gone by; they needed nothing but the confluence of solitude and silence, nothing but the fervent and exclusive concentration which comes close to a hypnotic state."[5] By 1907, Monet's brushwork had become freer, blending the water lilies into a unified, multicolored whole with the surrounding water, reflections, sky, shrubs, and grasses. The monumental canvases on display at the Musée de l'Orangerie in Paris are an important embodiment of a new way of viewing the natural world, in which plants serve as the primary catalyst for a vast network of interconnection that binds living beings across geographical regions, historical periods, and cultural contexts.

Concurrent with Monet's monumental water lilies, the Swedish mystic and artist Hilma af Klint channeled the teachings of Christianity, Rosicrucianism, and Theosophy into paintings and sketches fusing human and vegetal forms in an attempt to explore the spiritual potential of plants. In her works, stems, branches, petals, and tendrils wrap and connect life forms across the astral planes ("soul worlds"), with an unprecedented sense of indissoluble communion. Af Klint, who had studied botanical illustration before becoming a fine artist, progressively incorporated abstracted vegetal motifs into her paintings during the 1920s. This turn was largely inspired by the teachings of occultist and architect Rudolf Steiner.[6] In a lecture from 1923, Steiner championed plants as supreme elemental spirits. Plant life, Steiner said,

> as it sprouts and springs forth from the earth, immediately arouses our delight, but it also provides access to something that we must feel as full of mystery.... The plant comes, as I shall presently show you, into connection with the extra-terrestrial universe; and, particularly at certain seasons of the year, spirit-currents flow from above, from the blossom and the fruit of the plant down into the roots below, streaming into the earth. And just as we turn our eyes towards the light and see, so do the root-spirits turn their faculty of perception towards what seeps downwards from above, through the plant into the earth.[7]

Across multiple sketchbooks between 1896 and 1906, the artist proceeded to create her own mystical herbal replete with diagrammatic languages as she grappled with supernatural vegetative forces. In her work, petals, leaves, and tendrils bridge the divide between the human and the divine, in a poetic aesthetic of connectivity and harmony.

Monet and Af Klint both collaborated with plants to herald the two major strands of aesthetic abstraction that would come to characterize modern art: painterly and geometric. Plants were thus the protagonists of the most radical aesthetic revolution Western art had witnessed since the emergence of naturalism in classical Greek art more than two thousand years prior. The descriptivism of realism, the moralization it relentlessly enacted, and the hierarchical structures it perpetuated, vanished into a vegetal whirl of existential rapture.

Little did these artists know that a decade later, plants would finally lead us to reconsider the very roots of Western art. Starting with the Romantic movement and proceeding with the invention of photography, the unstoppable multiplication of mechanically produced images, and the popularization of cinema, artists craving creative freedom sought to map new expressive territories—the cultural stronghold of classical art had begun to crumble. By the second decade of the twentieth century, the irreverent experimentations of the Dada movement, the readymade, found objects, collage, and unscripted performances had shaken the art system to its core. The first thirty years of the twentieth century, dramatically shattered by the horrors of World War I, then the Great Depression, led artists to repudiate the predictable certainties of a bourgeois system that had proved ethically and morally bankrupt. Black artists of the Harlem Renaissance in New York reinvented the artist as a poet, musician, editor, and social activist, while the Surrealists in Europe and South America summoned imagery from the depths of the unconscious.

Within the framework of these groundbreaking reimaginings of ideas and artistic methods, photographer Edward Steichen, with more than a little help from the plant kingdom, forever changed the course of art. At the end of the 1920s, the artist became involved in the hybridization of delphinium plants, which he mutated by dousing the seeds in a chemical bath of colchicine, causing a chromosomal deviation that in this case resulted in gigantic flowers. A substantial harvest of fully bloomed stalks up to five feet tall was exhibited at the Museum of Modern Art in New York for a week in June 1936. It was the first work of Bio Art (living art) ever staged

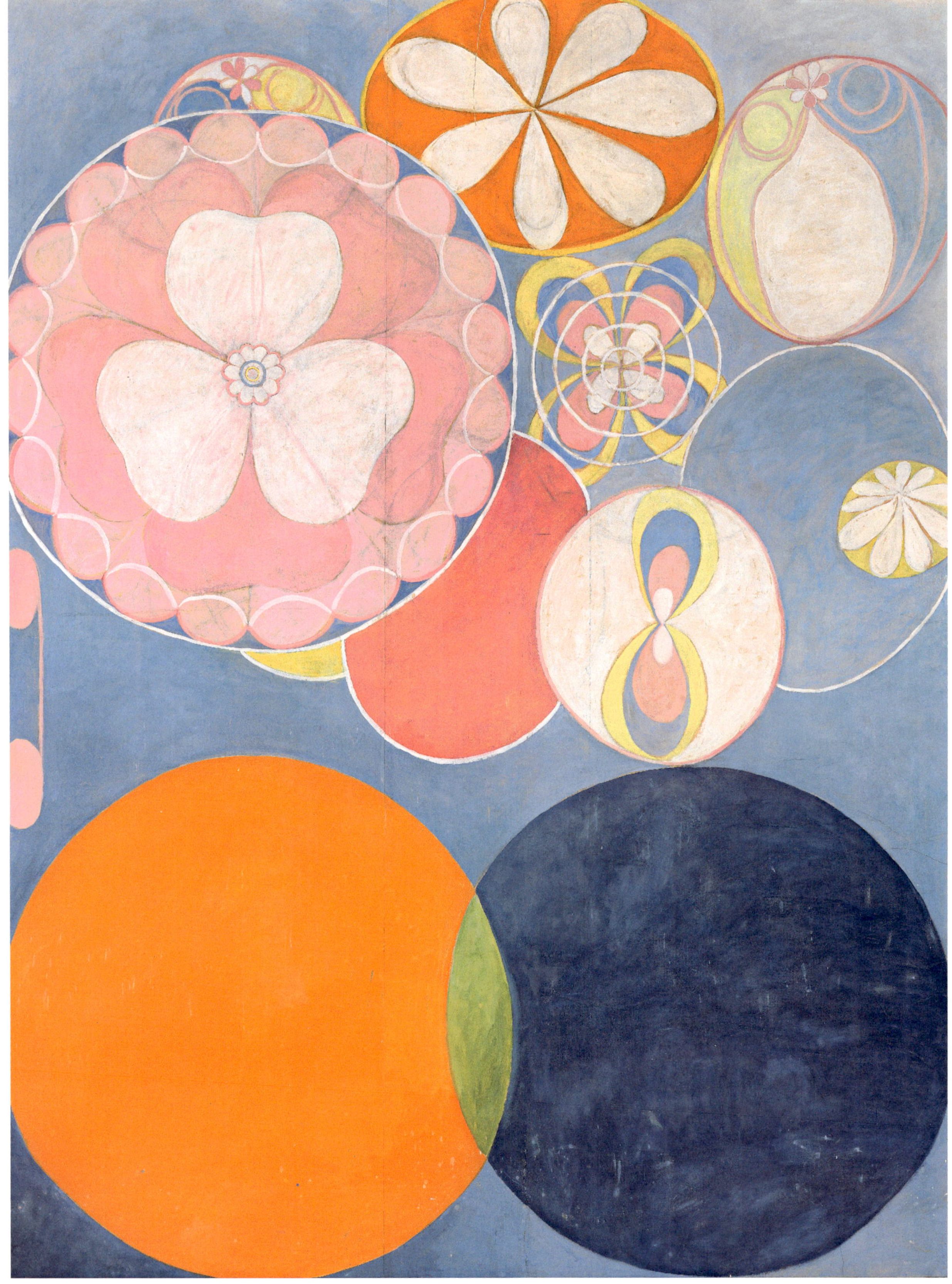

Hilma af Klint, *Group IV, The Ten Largest, No. 2, Childhood*, 1907, tempera on paper mounted on canvas

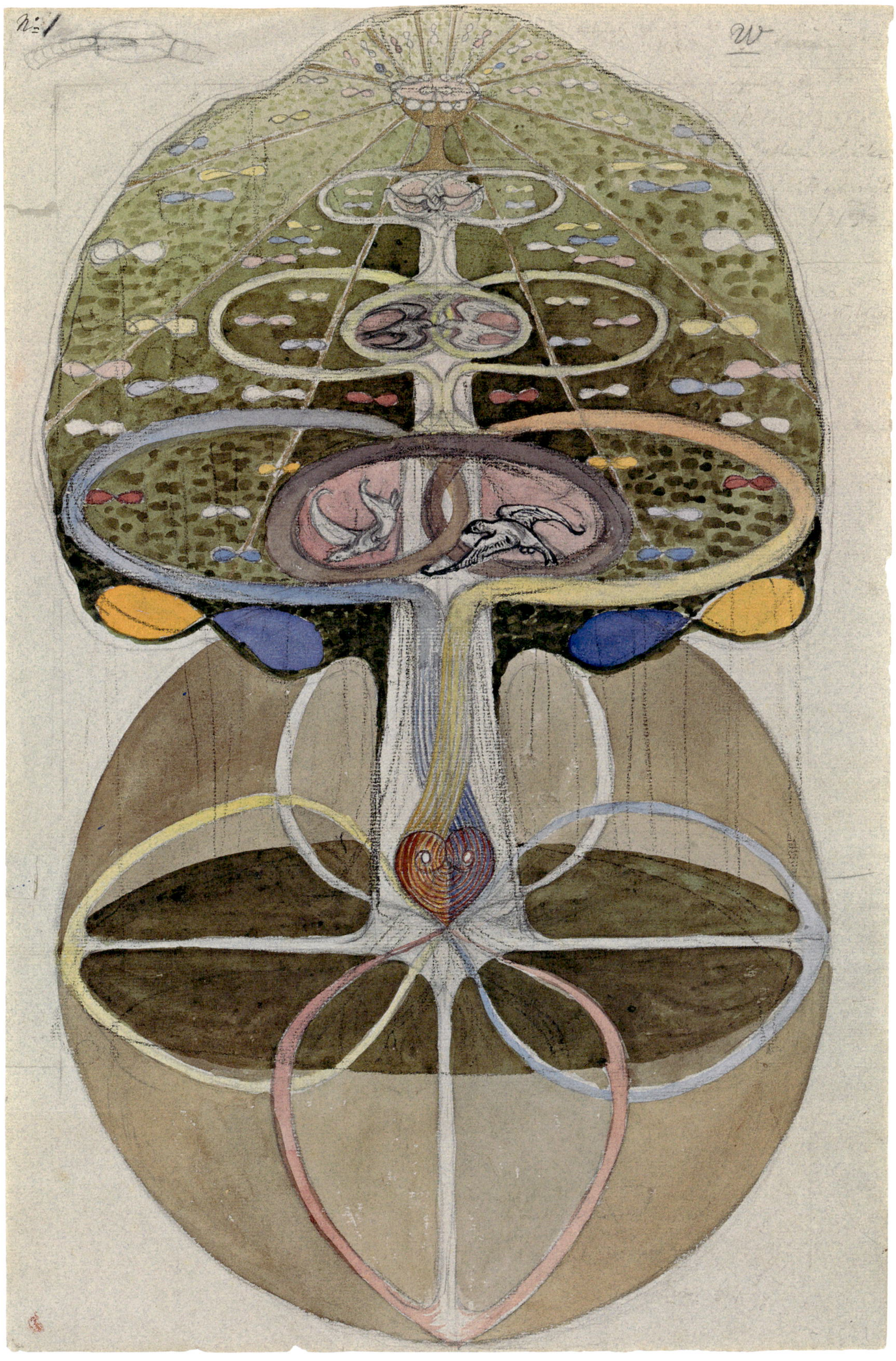


Hilma af Klint, *The W Series, Tree of Knowledge, No. 1*, 1913, mixed media

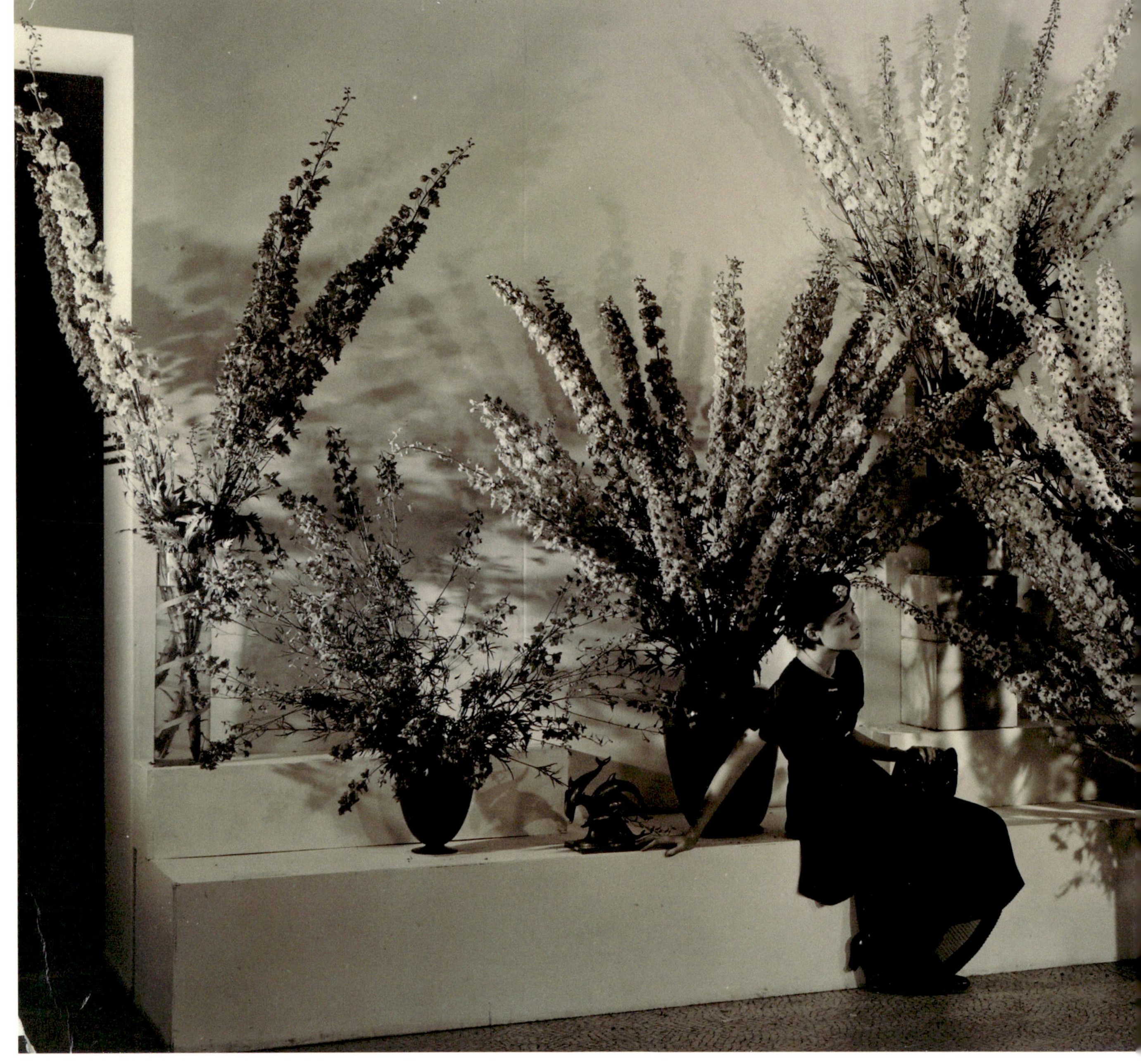

Installation view of the exhibition *Edward Steichen's Delphiniums*, Museum of Modern Art, New York, June 1936, gelatin silver print

in a museum. Steichen's delphiniums challenged the Aristotelian view that art perfects nature, by replacing the mimetic essence of art with the essential truthfulness of living plants.[8] If nature *is* the work of art, then the manipulation of the artist is no longer a lopsided, representational confrontation with the passivity of matter; it is an active co-creation with the nonhuman, albeit enlisting the help of new technologies. Steichen's delphiniums challenged preconceived notions of originality, authorship, market value, and permanence in art. Once again, it was the radical alterity of plants, their enigmatic quasi-object yet fully living essence, that allowed artists to expand notions of what art could be. Steichen's delphiniums are largely responsible for the now-common practice of including live plants in art installations.

Between the 1960s and 1990s, Conceptual artists enlisted plants to question the purity and rationalism that had come to define the modernist

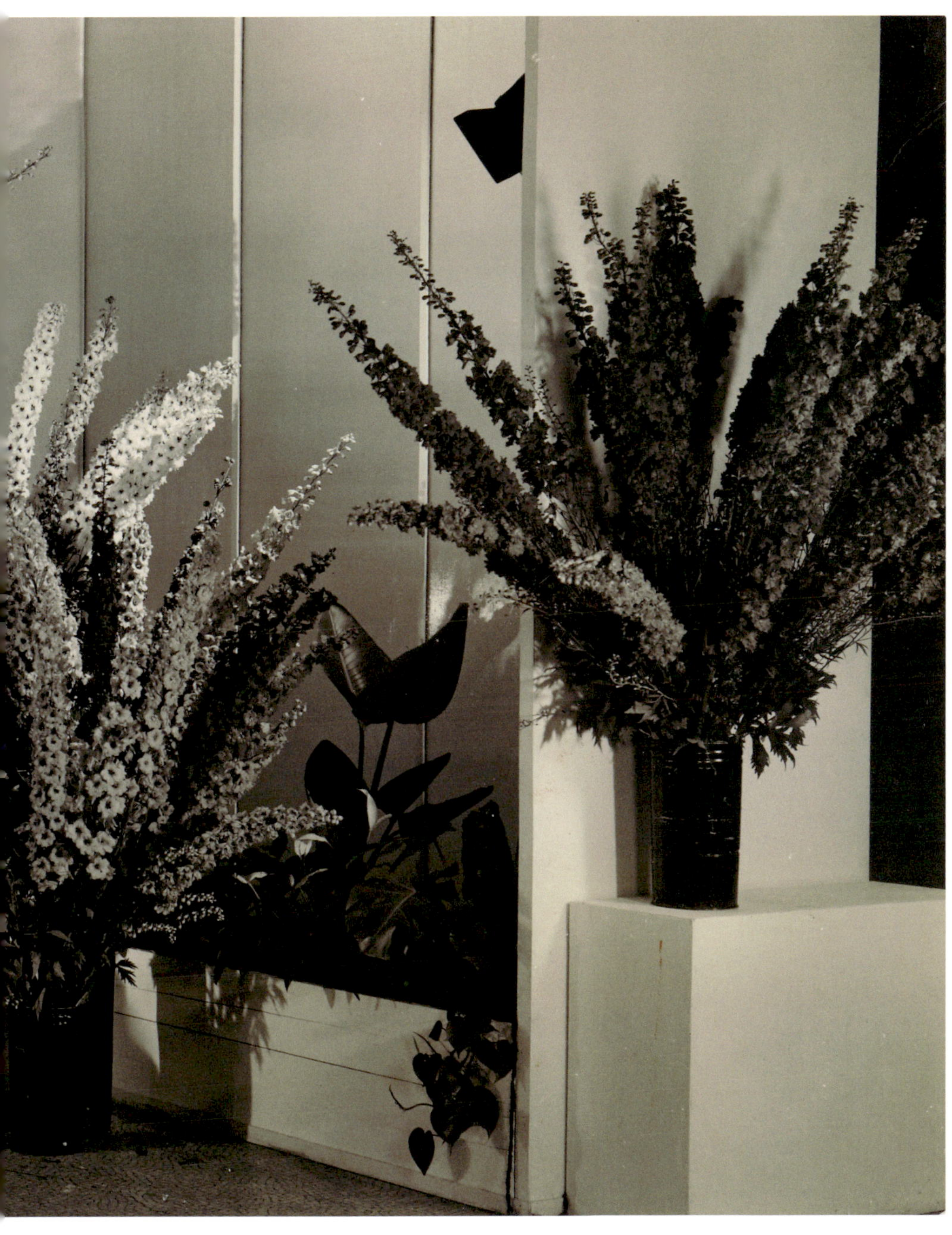



gallery space. Introducing living plants into the gallery challenges the nature-versus-culture dichotomy and disrupts the enduring fetishization of the artwork as a collectible commodity. In 1967, queer Brazilian artist Hélio Oiticica filled a gallery with potted exotic plants such as bromeliads, yuccas, and palm trees for his now-iconic *Tropicália* installation—a quasi-humorous-cum-tragic representation of Brazil as conceived by the colonizing gaze as an unproblematic, exotic tourist paradise.[9] Featuring a couple of live parrots, sand dunes, many potted plants, and makeshift structures, *Tropicália* pressured the museum administration due to technical complications and risks of biohazard contamination—soil often carries pests that might endanger other works of art. But for Oiticica's sharp cultural critique to land, the inclusion of live plants was essential: it underpinned the truthfulness of the message. The clay pots referenced the constructed cultural narratives

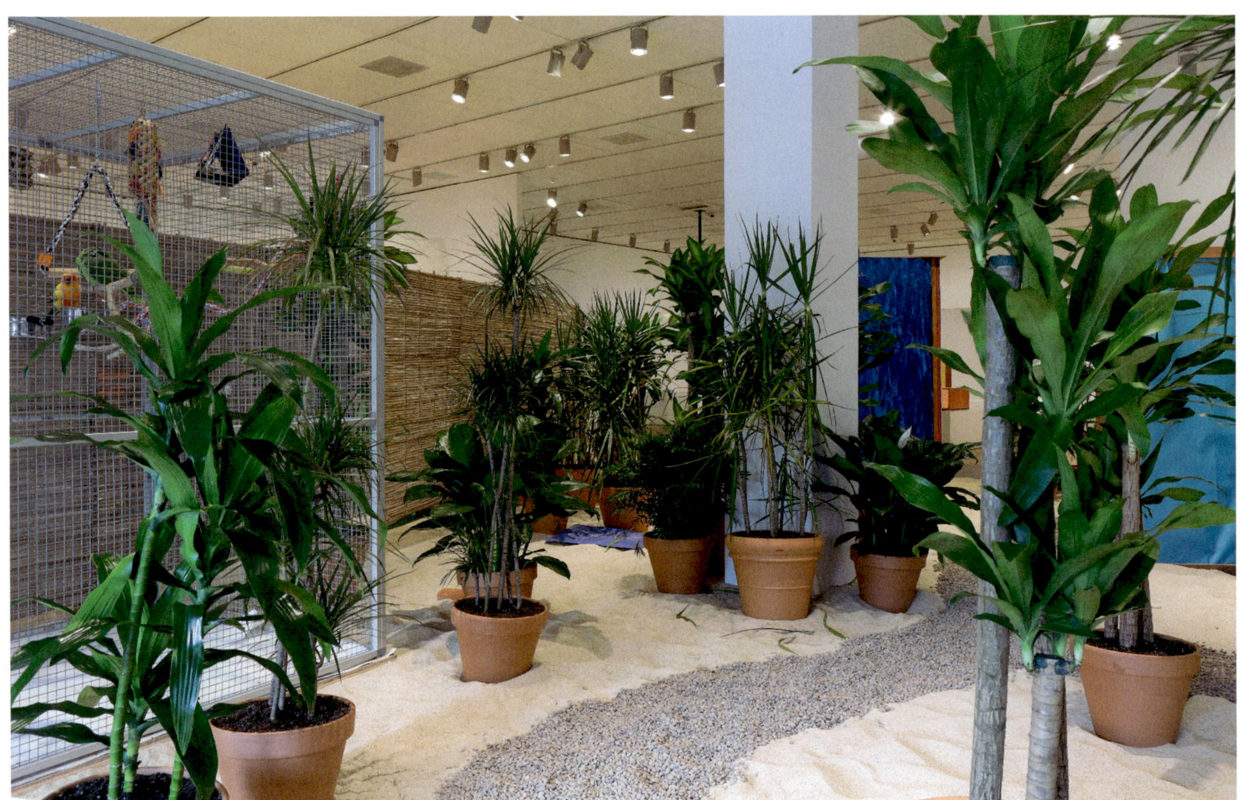

Installation view of *Hélio Oiticica: To Organize Delirium*, Art Institute of Chicago, 2017, mixed media



permeating Brazilian life in the eyes of tourists.

In a similar vein, palm trees often filled the installations of Conceptual artist Marcel Broodthaers, posing as colonial relics, promises of capitalist wealth, and exotic symbols of vacuous popular escapism. Cacti, ficuses, and palms also appeared prominently in Joseph Kosuth's iconic mid-1960s installation *One and Three Plants*—an assemblage comprising an actual plant, a photograph of it, and its description—which emphasizes representation and reality as fundamentally linguistic productions. Plants transformed our conception of the exhibition space in the latter half of the twentieth century by exposing and challenging its semantic constraints and by subverting the very notion of art as static, unalterable, and quiescent.

Beginning in the late 1960s, the politically charged provocations of conceptualism gave rise to environmentally committed art. In this case, too, plants were at the forefront of an ecological revolution, their livingness providing tangible proof of the urgency and fragility of an increasingly vulnerable planet. In an effort to express the cultural and ecological trauma caused by the vast urbanization that rapidly changed Italy after World War II, Arte Povera (literally "poor art") proponent Giuseppe Penone attempted to symbolically reverse industrialization by fashioning trees out of manufactured beams.[10] In the 1970s, Lois Weinberger and artist duo Helen and Newton Harrison were among the first to incorporate plants in outdoor and indoor installations designed to raise awareness of the impending climate crisis and evidence our interdependency with the vegetal world. The Harrisons' *Portable Orchard* (1972–73) was intended to warn of a not-too-distant future when air pollution and other apocalyptic calamities would only allow for indoor cultivation. It enlisted assorted citrus varieties and an avocado tree to test the efficacy of new grow-light technology. Some trees fared well, and others didn't. Unbeknownst to them, the artists were staging the first techno-evolutionary art experiment of the Anthropocene.[11]

In March 1982, German artist and activist Joseph Beuys began to plant seven thousand oak trees in (the particularly green-deprived town of) Kassel, Germany, as part of the seventh edition

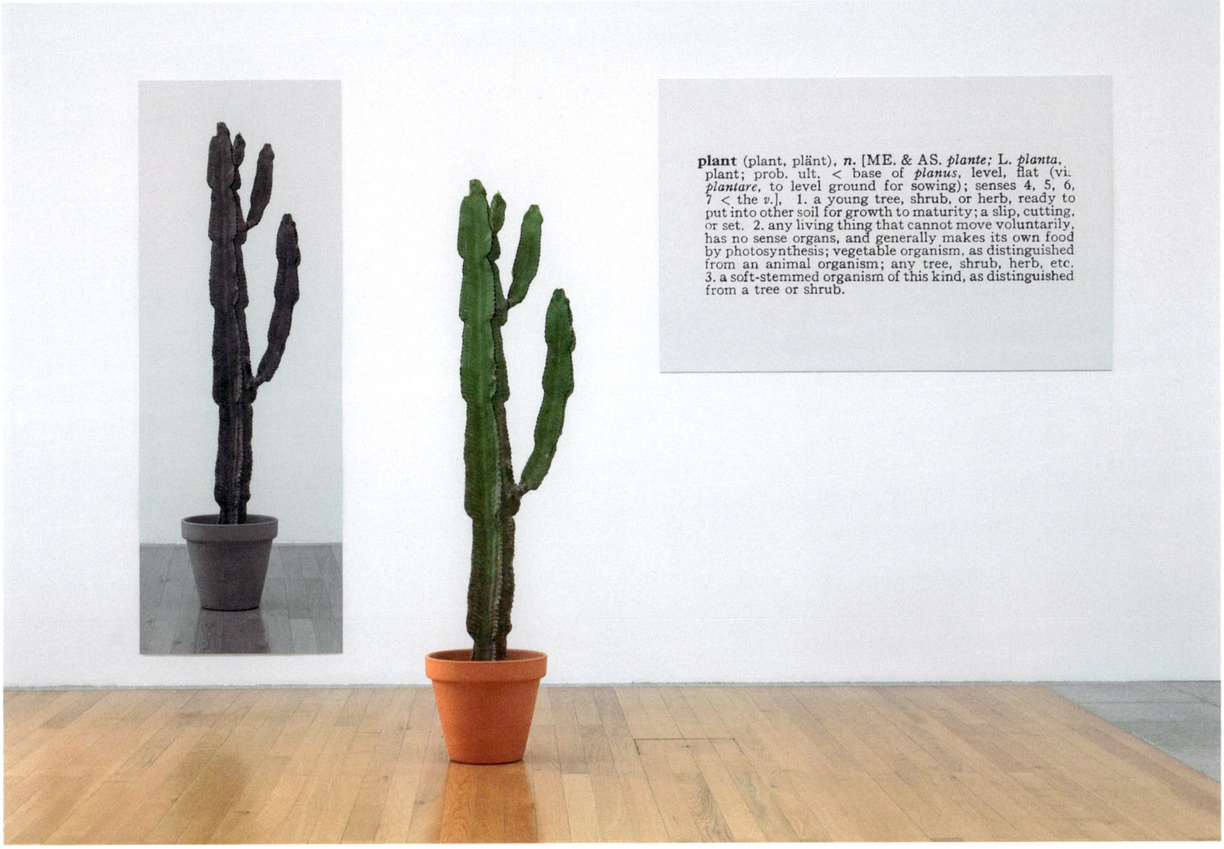

Joseph Kosuth, *One and Three Plants*, 1965, mixed media



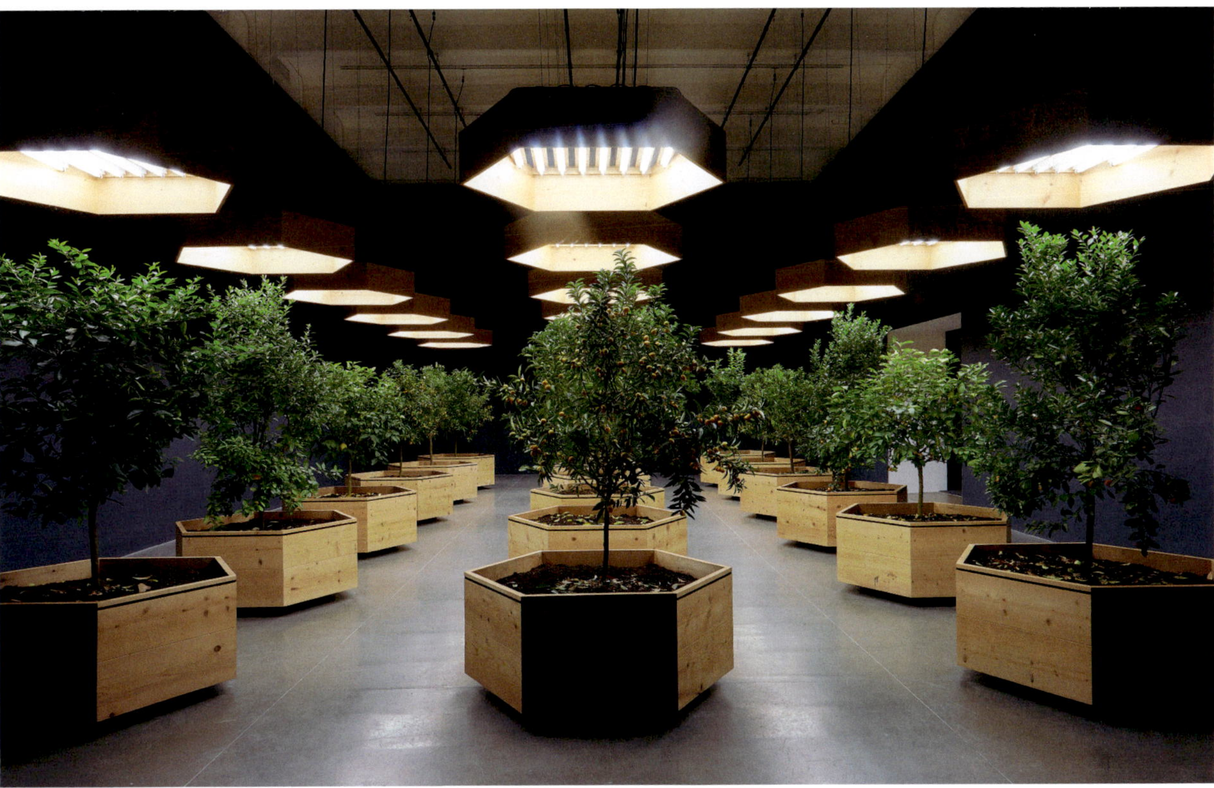

Newton Harrison and Helen Mayer Harrison, Installation view of *Portable Orchard*, Walker Art Center, Minneapolis, 1972–73, mixed media

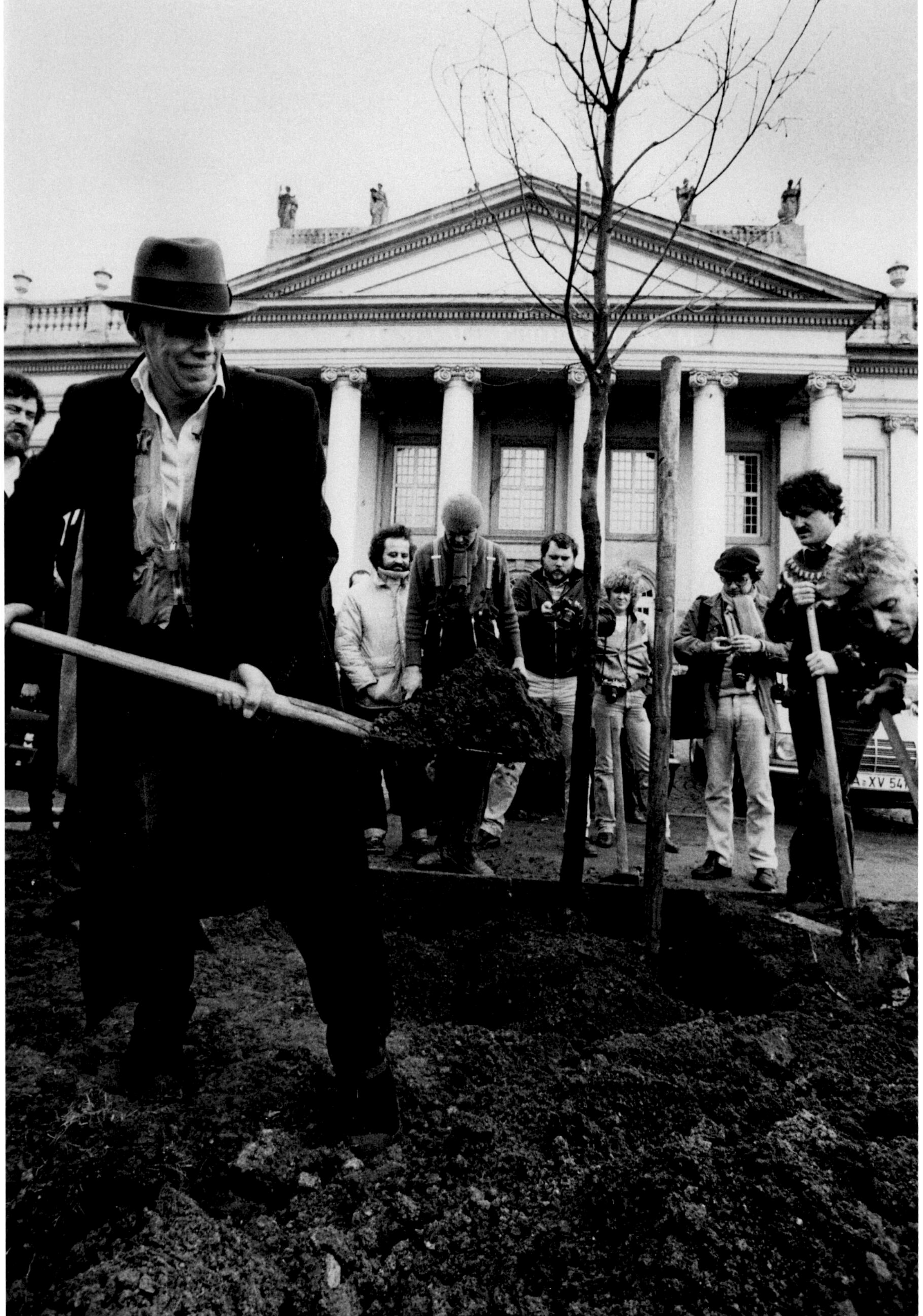

Dieter Schwerdtle, Joseph Beuys plants the first tree at the edge of Friedrichsplatz in front of the Museum Fridericianum (Kassel, Germany) as part of his project *7000 Oaks*, March 3, 1982, photograph

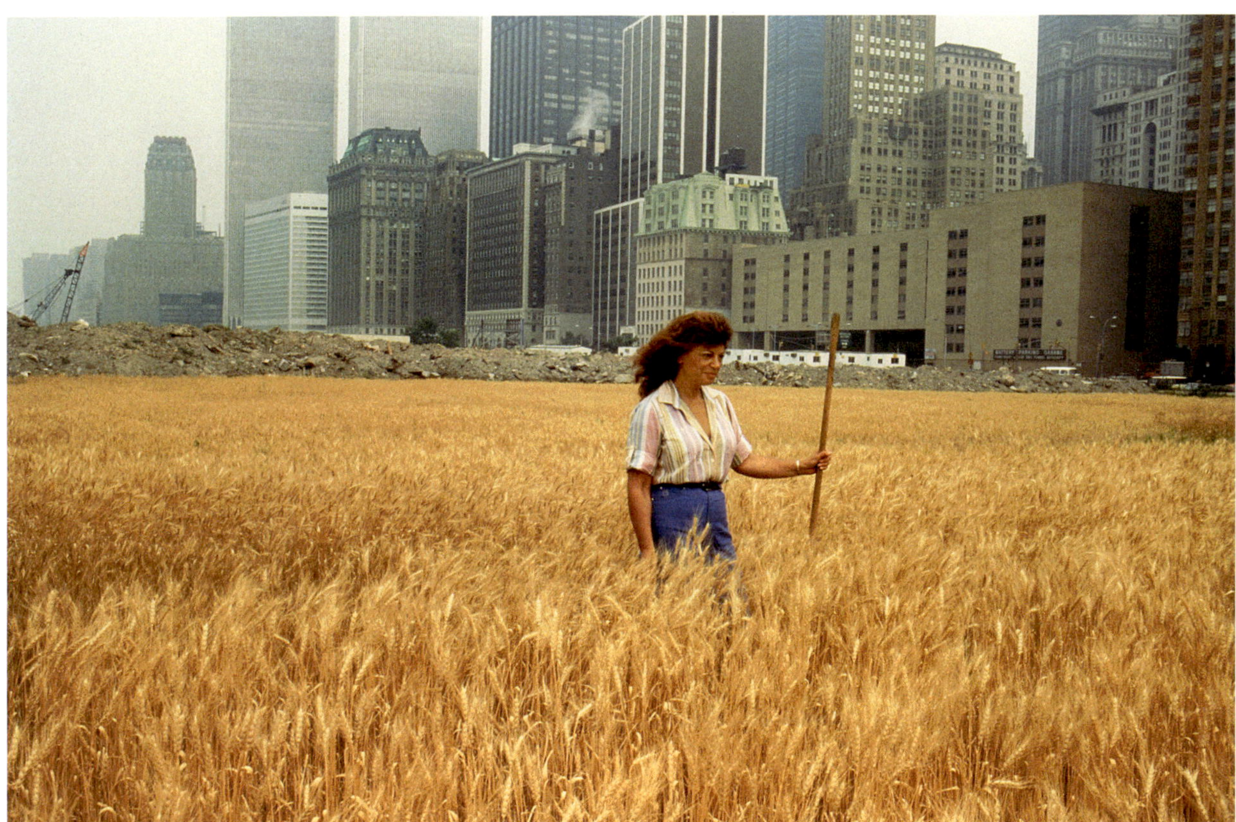

Agnes Denes pictured with her work *Wheatfield — A Confrontation: Battery Park Landfill*, downtown Manhattan, 1982, photograph



of the contemporary art event Documenta. The project changed our conception of urban spaces and foregrounded the importance of plants for healthy city living for humans as well as other creatures.[12] The same year, Land Art pioneer Agnes Denes planted two acres of wheat in downtown Manhattan, in the heart of New York's Financial District, on a temporarily vacant lot worth $4.5 billion. Denes's now-legendary *Wheatfield* was tended by the community and provided food for disadvantaged groups. Her project placed plants at the center of an urban revolution based on ecological and agricultural self-sustenance, and demonstrated that rethinking our urban realities from the ground up is indeed possible.

No longer just symbols or metaphors, as was often the case with conceptualism, during the second half of the last century plants in art began instead to offer concrete opportunities to remediate our damaged Earth. Mel Chin's iconic *Revival Field* (1991), a circular garden filled with grasses and other plants, functioned as an experimental case study for evaluating the efficiency of vegetal absorption of toxins from polluted soil.[13] In a similar vein, Frances Whitehead's *Slow Cleanup* project, which ran between 2008 and 2012 in Chicago, enlisted the help of plants to regenerate polluted soil surrounding abandoned gas stations. Petroleum and other heavy metals can be absorbed by microbes attracted to phenols and sugars exuded by the roots of some plants. Rather than simply providing recreational spaces for disadvantaged communities, Whitehead's urban gardens instilled a sense of ownership and empowerment by inviting locals to learn about plants and ecology.[14]

More recently, artist-scientist Andrea Conte, whose work focuses on the detrimental effects of climate change, has experimented with a variety of plants, including ferns and hemp, to repair damaged soil. His 2019 *Future Landscape* exhibition productively complicated notions of plant nativeness and conservation in the context of compromised landscapes that require urgent healing. Which plants can grant this planet a future? And, as our understanding of the tight connectivity that has characterized life on Earth increases, it is not

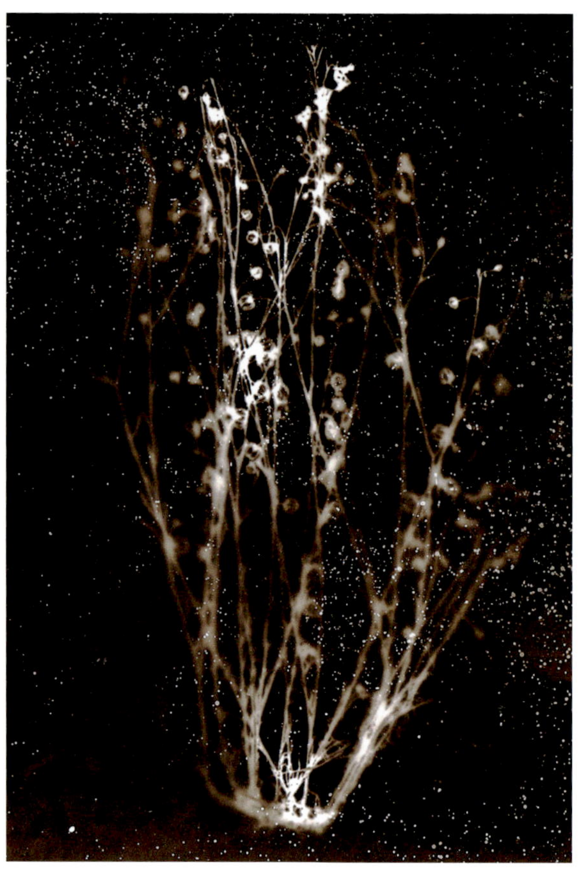

Anaïs Tondeur, *Linum strictum, Exclusion Zone, Chernobyl, Radiation level: 1.7 μSv/h*, 2011–ongoing, pigment print on rag paper

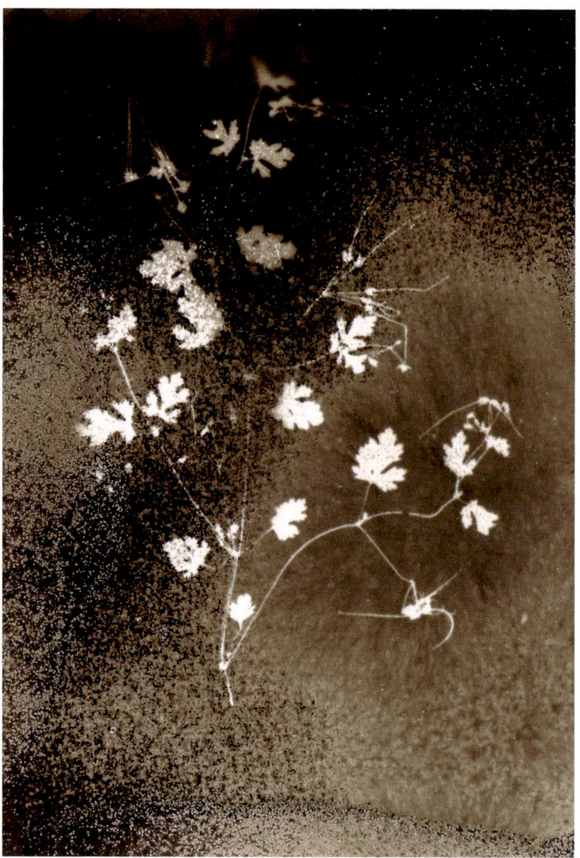

Anaïs Tondeur, *Geranium chinum, Exclusion Zone, Chernobyl, Radiation level: 1.7 μSv/h*, 2011–ongoing, pigment print on rag paper

surprising that ecological discourses in the arts should reach far and wide across lands and seas, connecting difficult pasts to precarious presents.[15]

This is certainly the case with the work of Australian artist Linda Tegg, who for the installation *Grassland* (2014) grew native grasses on the once Indigenous-owned soil upon which the State Library Victoria in Melbourne is today situated. Her temporary installation simultaneously embraced plants as metaphors as well as true ecological remediators for the Indigenous people who, like weeds, have been eradicated or pushed to the margins. An interior library of books and an outdoor library of plants were made to temporarily coexist, juxtaposing distinct but equally valid bodies of knowledge that have been kept apart for centuries. Tegg's work shows how today, through plants, we must think of ecological and cultural engagements as intimately entwined realities.

In light of the threats posed by climate change and the incommensurable enormity of scientific data, plants help us visualize both destruction and hope. Artist Anaïs Tondeur's postapocalyptic herbarium for the Anthropocene comprises more than thirty photograms, one for each year that has passed since the explosion that destroyed part of the Chernobyl nuclear power station in April 1986. The images are direct imprints of radioactive plant specimens growing within the thirty-kilometer exclusion zone around the now-decommissioned facility. Tondeur's herbarium records ghostly radioactive traces of flowers, leaves, stems, and roots, serving as an unsettling reminder of the ecological catastrophe, its destructive reverberation through time, as well as humans' capacity to alter vegetal life. Hauntingly beautiful and somewhat terrifying, Tondeur's work shows that plants still thrive in Chernobyl, although they are not quite the same as they used to be. How radiation will continue to impact them and the land in decades to come remains impossible to fully know.[16]

Resilience and memorialization in the face of devastation are also central to the work of

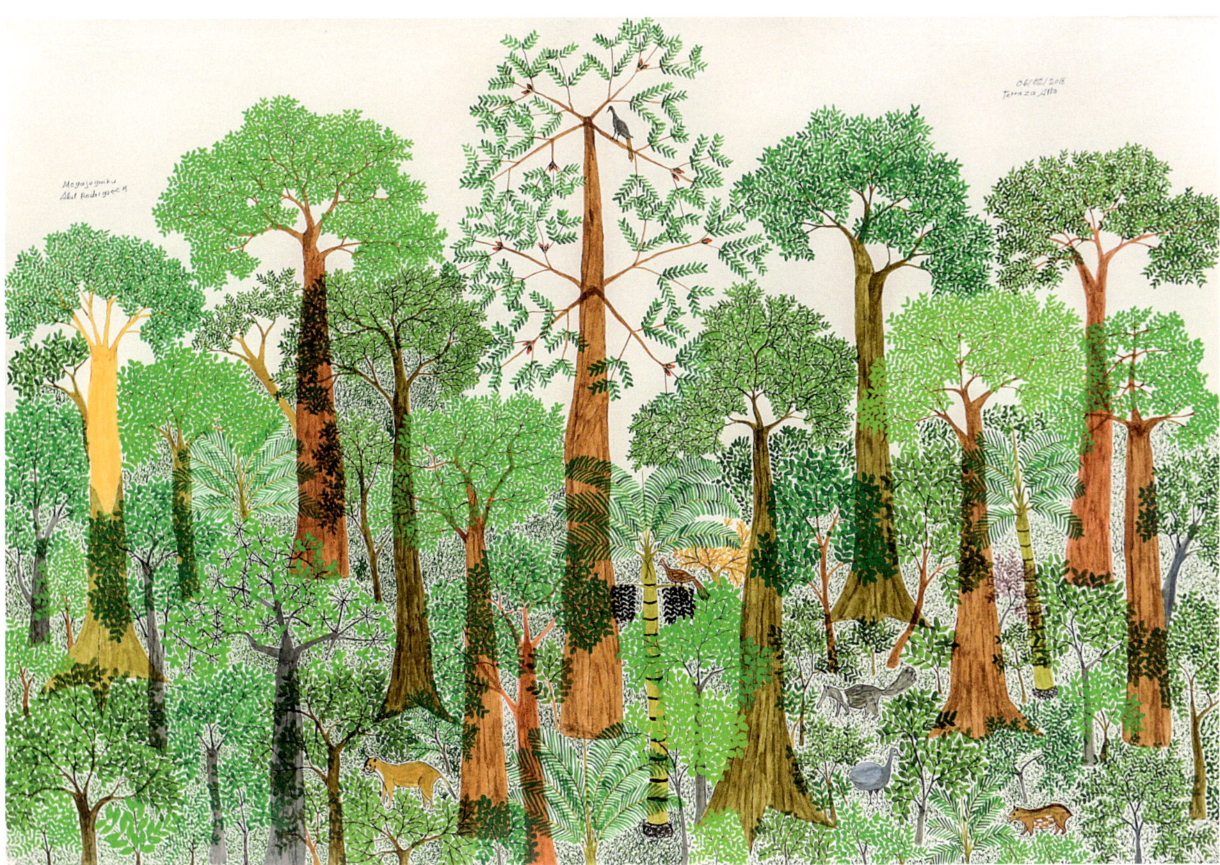



**Abel Rodríguez, *Terraza Alta II*, 2018, ink on paper**

Indigenous Amazonian artist Abel Rodríguez, who has inherited his ecological wisdom from Muinane elders as well as from the tribe of his birth, the Nonuya. Rodríguez began to work as a local guide for scientific expeditions during the 1980s. By the 1990s, faced with loss and grief as his community was displaced by political turmoil and environmental devastation, he began to transfer his knowledge onto paper in the form of extremely detailed and dense forest drawings in which every leaf and living being is of equal importance. Far from the objectifying aesthetics of Western botanical illustrations, and painted entirely from memory, Rodríguez's drawings evince the forest as a living organism in which everything is interconnected.[17]

The social-justice thread that links plants to people and the soil is also the underpinning principle behind the plant-filled installation by Nigerian American artist Precious Okoyomon, *To See the Earth before the End of the World*, which filled the unforgettable last gallery of *The Milk of Dreams*, the main exhibition at the 59th Venice Biennale in 2022. Kudzu and sugarcane grew unchecked throughout the run of the event, eventually nearly smothering the monolithic figures made of soil and straw—ancestral guardians? pantheistic deities? future incarnations?—that Okoyomon had arranged around the space. Their stern postures and enigmatic silence suggested that they might be witnesses of a future renaissance in which humans no longer are the center of all things.[18] Okoyomon's installation was simultaneously present in its overwhelmingly sensual livingness—the humidity, the fragrance of the soil—and anchored in the past. Kudzu and sugarcane share different yet intimately related histories of displacement, domestication, and ecological devastation. Kudzu was brought to the United States from its native Japan in 1876 for the Centennial Exposition in Philadelphia. Many decades later, in the 1930s, the US government used it to combat the severe soil erosion caused by the intensive cultivation of sugarcane on slave

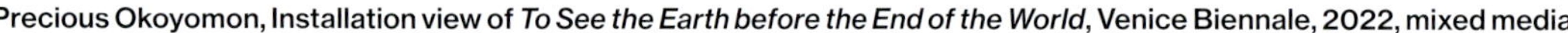



Precious Okoyomon, Installation view of *To See the Earth before the End of the World*, Venice Biennale, 2022, mixed media

plantations throughout the South. The disastrous ecological and cultural histories entangled in the roots of these two plants, both forcibly displaced Asian natives, became indissolubly intertwined upon US soil.

Further expanding the conceptual and metaphorical analogies that tie plant histories to people, artists have also turned to lowly weeds, igniting a contemporary art revolution that is changing our relationship with nature and conceptions of ecology as well as social justice. It is through art that weeds can finally express their full agential potential. No longer just plants out of place, they actively invite us to rethink our position in the world. Weeds thrive in the shadow of power. As a concept, they emerge from colonialist logics of order, Enlightenment taxonomies, boundaries, perimeters—ultimately arbitrary designations of desired versus undesirable. For some weeds, no right place can ever exist, because total eradication is the majority's desired outcome. Some species are indigenous; others have been forcefully imported or unintentionally displaced. A vast number have been brought to places that initially seemed right but quickly turned out to be wrong. There's a powerful uncontainability to weeds that deeply unsettles. They often instill fear of corruption and contamination—that once they take hold, it will be impossible to get rid of them.

More than any other plant category, weeds in art serve as monuments of resilience, constantly quivering, agitated by a relentless wind of change. They invite us to craft new registers of resistance modeled on ecological practices of tenacity and dissidence grounded in past injustices that still haunt the present. Their ability to survive and thrive despite deliberate neglect or outright oppression by institutions, governments, and law enforcement makes them profound symbols of self-perpetuation and defiance.

Our understanding of art's social function, expressive potential, and cultural significance is currently undergoing a major revolution that may, at least in part, be attributed to artists' increased interest in plants. Today across the arts, plants are essentially instigating a thorough decentralization of the human in form, content, and processes,

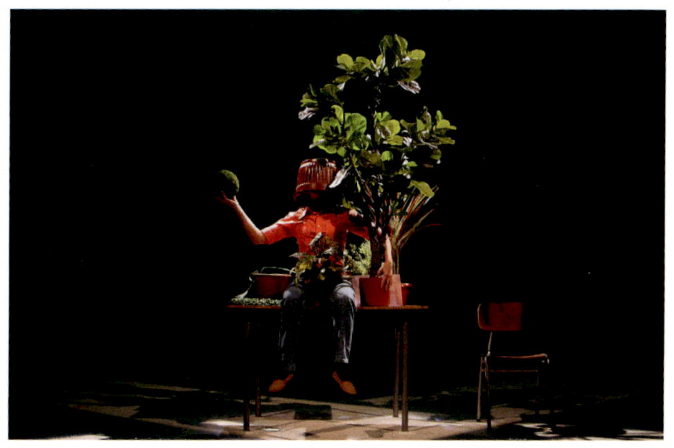

Manuela Infante, *Estado Vegetal*, 2019, still from performance

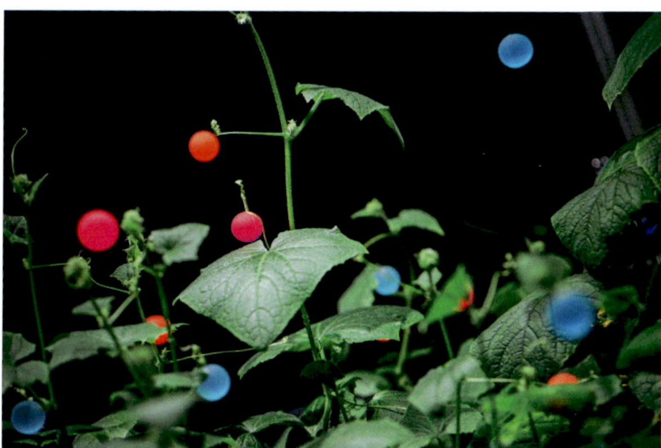

Špela Petrič, *Pl'ai*, 2020, plants and AI robot

pointing at unprecedented opportunities for charting unmapped territory. The work of philosophers Michael Marder and Emanuele Coccia, and plant vegetal neurobiologists Stefano Mancuso, Alessandra Viola, Paco Calvo, and Monica Gagliano, has led to a substantial reconsideration of vegetal being, intelligence, sentience, and agency.[19] Among others, Chilean playwright Manuela Infante has found fertile ground in their work to develop a new form of speculative theater based on forms of plant-thinking. Infante's award-winning performance *Estado Vegetal* (Vegetative State, first staged in 2016) casts plants as protagonists, charged with agency capable of uprooting culturally grounded conceptions of the world in the face of incommensurable trauma and loss.[20] Other artists have more directly aimed to evidence the overlooked reality of plant intelligence. The intricate arabesques of plant roots mapped by artist Diana Scherer rekindle the interest in Charles Darwin's controversial root-brain hypothesis that envisioned plants as upside-down animals.[21]

Bio artist and scientist Špela Petrič has conducted extensive research into the concept of plant agency and intelligence through the utilization of technology interfaces. In her most recent endeavors, Petrič has shifted her attention toward the hypothesis that plants possess the capacity to partake in playful activities.[22] Whether or not readers of this volume are ready to allow that much, it is undeniable that today more than ever before, plants are being considered active subjects rather than passive or merely attractive objects, as they were for centuries. Through different media, and new perspectives and approaches, artists are helping us to overcome the plant blindness that has largely contributed to the current climate crisis and the sixth mass extinction. Art's innovative and multidisciplinary reconnections with the vegetal world are profoundly modifying not only the content of works of art but also our conception *of* art—how artists approach their work, and how they conceive of themselves as creative individuals. The most recent botanical revolution is all-encompassing; greater by far than the many others that preceded it, it has the potential to radically change for the better the course of art as well as the destiny of our planet.

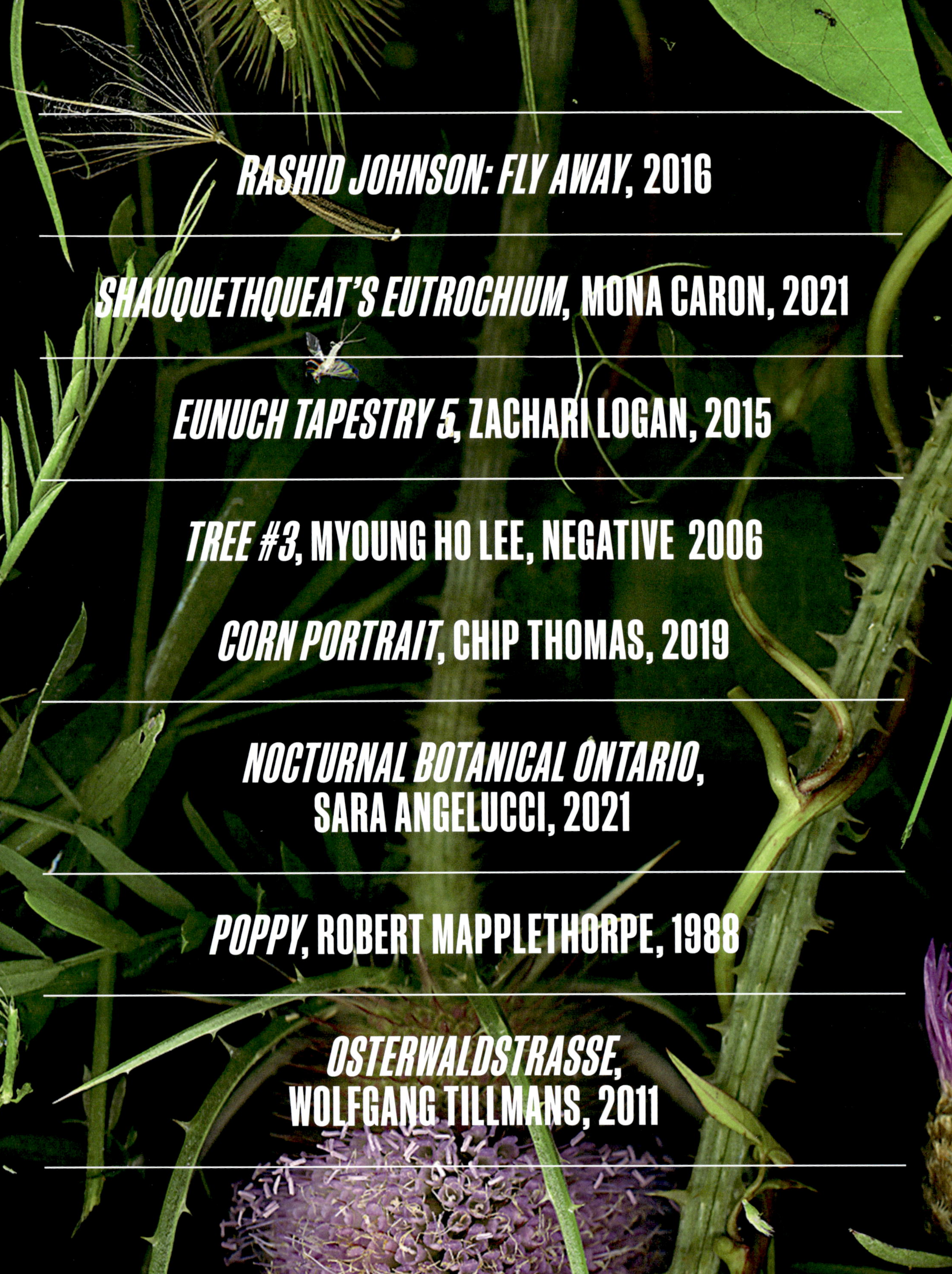

*RASHID JOHNSON: FLY AWAY*, 2016

*SHAUQUETHQUEAT'S EUTROCHIUM*, MONA CARON, 2021

*EUNUCH TAPESTRY 5*, ZACHARI LOGAN, 2015

*TREE #3*, MYOUNG HO LEE, NEGATIVE 2006

*CORN PORTRAIT*, CHIP THOMAS, 2019

*NOCTURNAL BOTANICAL ONTARIO*,
SARA ANGELUCCI, 2021

*POPPY*, ROBERT MAPPLETHORPE, 1988

*OSTERWALDSTRASSE*,
WOLFGANG TILLMANS, 2011

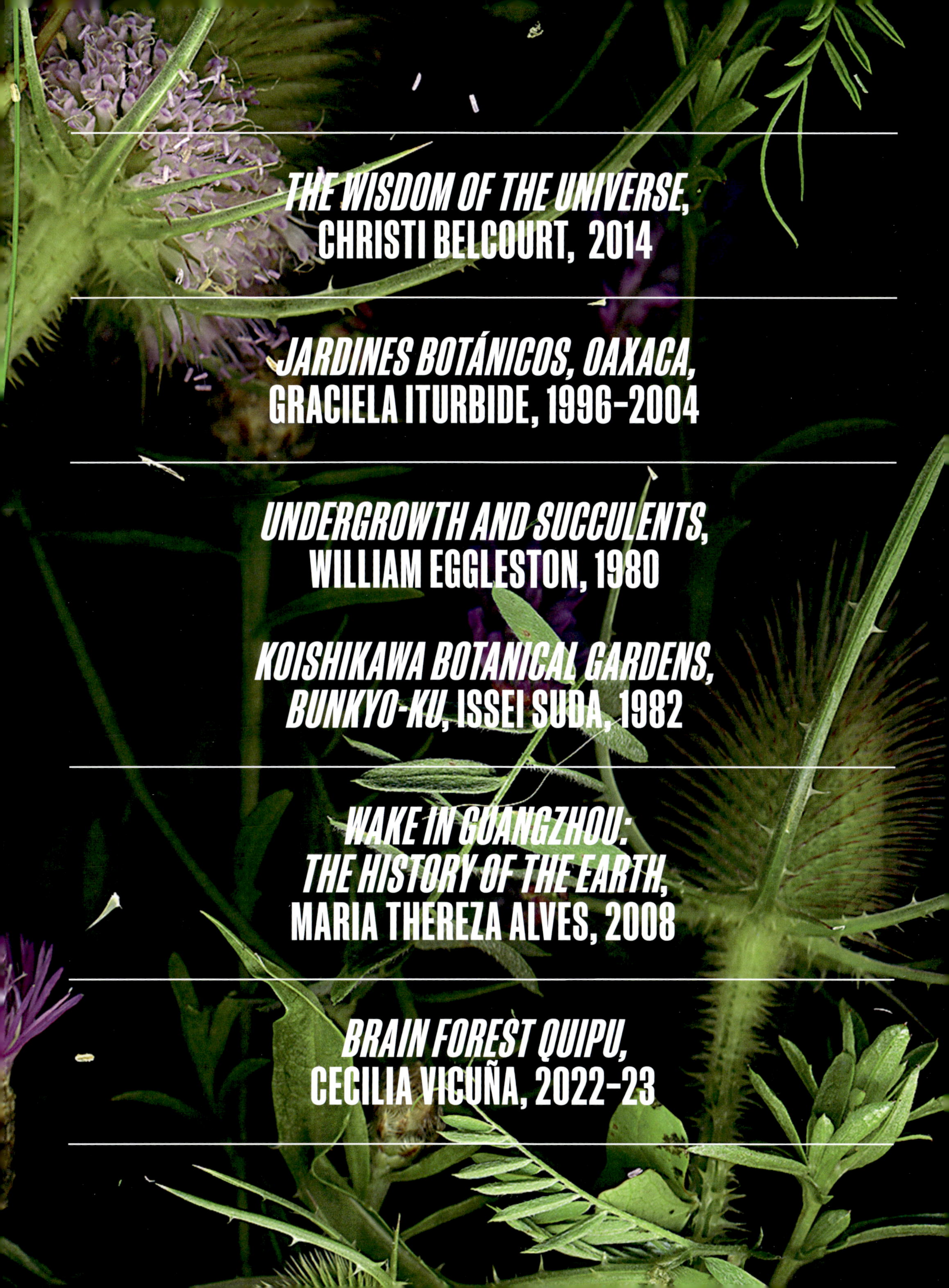
*THE WISDOM OF THE UNIVERSE,*
CHRISTI BELCOURT, 2014
*JARDINES BOTÁNICOS, OAXACA,*
GRACIELA ITURBIDE, 1996–2004
*UNDERGROWTH AND SUCCULENTS,*
WILLIAM EGGLESTON, 1980
*KOISHIKAWA BOTANICAL GARDENS,*
*BUNKYO-KU*, ISSEI SUDA, 1982
*WAKE IN GUANGZHOU:*
*THE HISTORY OF THE EARTH,*
MARIA THEREZA ALVES, 2008
*BRAIN FOREST QUIPU,*
CECILIA VICUÑA, 2022–23

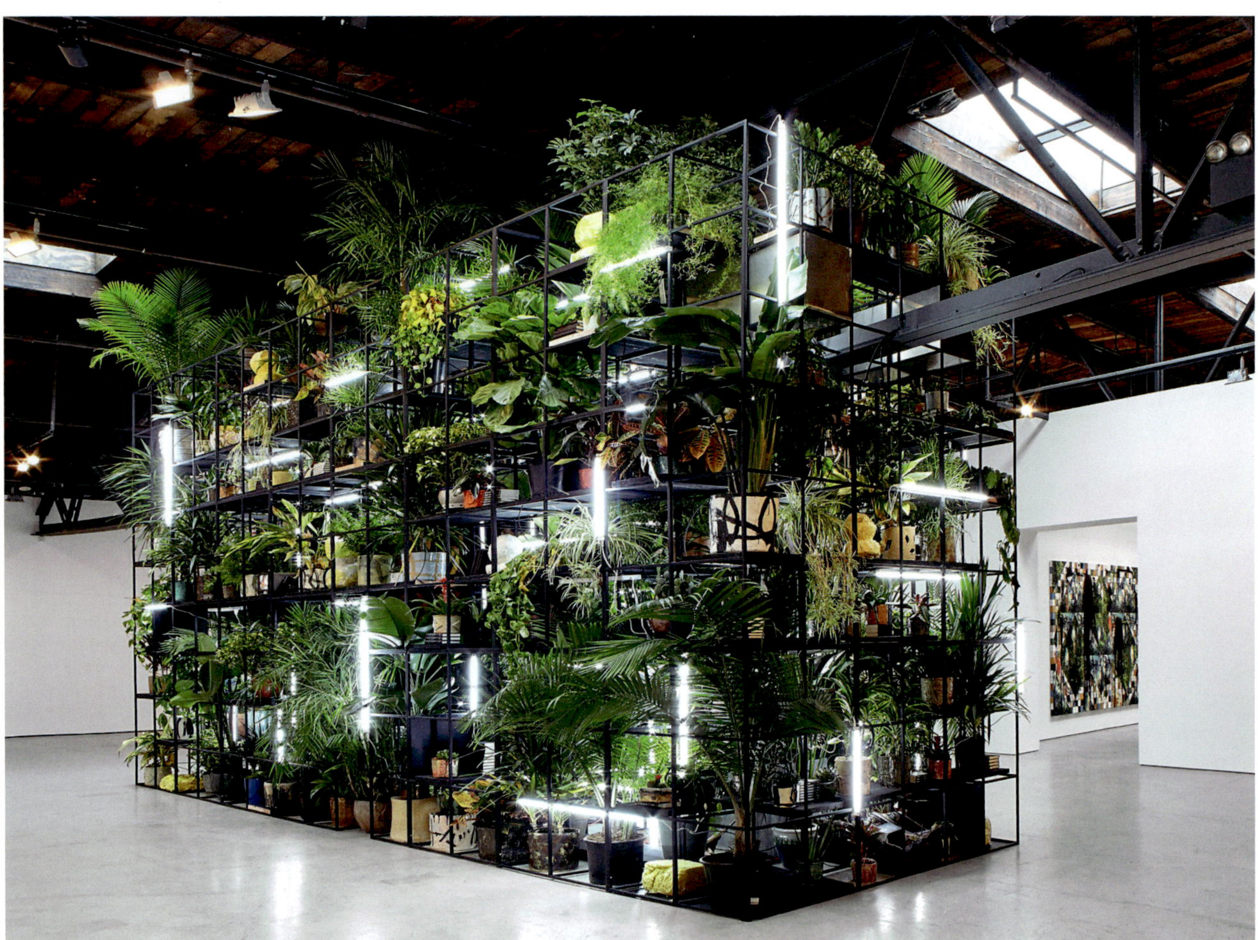

Rashid Johnson, Installation view of *Rashid Johnson: Fly Away*, Hauser & Wirth, New York, 2016

More than other outdoor shrubs or weeds, potted plants are dependent on our care and regular scrutiny. In this sense, they constitute an invitation to be present, to live in the moment, to be observant, and to care. Rashid Johnson's plant philosophy invites us to ponder: how can plant-specific qualities help us craft a model through which we might reconsider other relationships we establish in our immediate world? In Johnson's view, plants invite us to be attentive to those who are most vulnerable in our communities. They emphasize the need to learn to recognize subtle indicators of malaise and dissatisfaction, especially when individuals who are suffering do so in silence. Yet despite the slightly symbolic subtext, Johnson's plants are not anthropomorphized. They in fact bypass classical symbolism and remain wholly vegetal, branching off into an ecological dimension in which "to care" also means to be an active part of a non-hierarchical and fluid relationship of naturecultures.

## *RASHID JOHNSON: FLY AWAY*

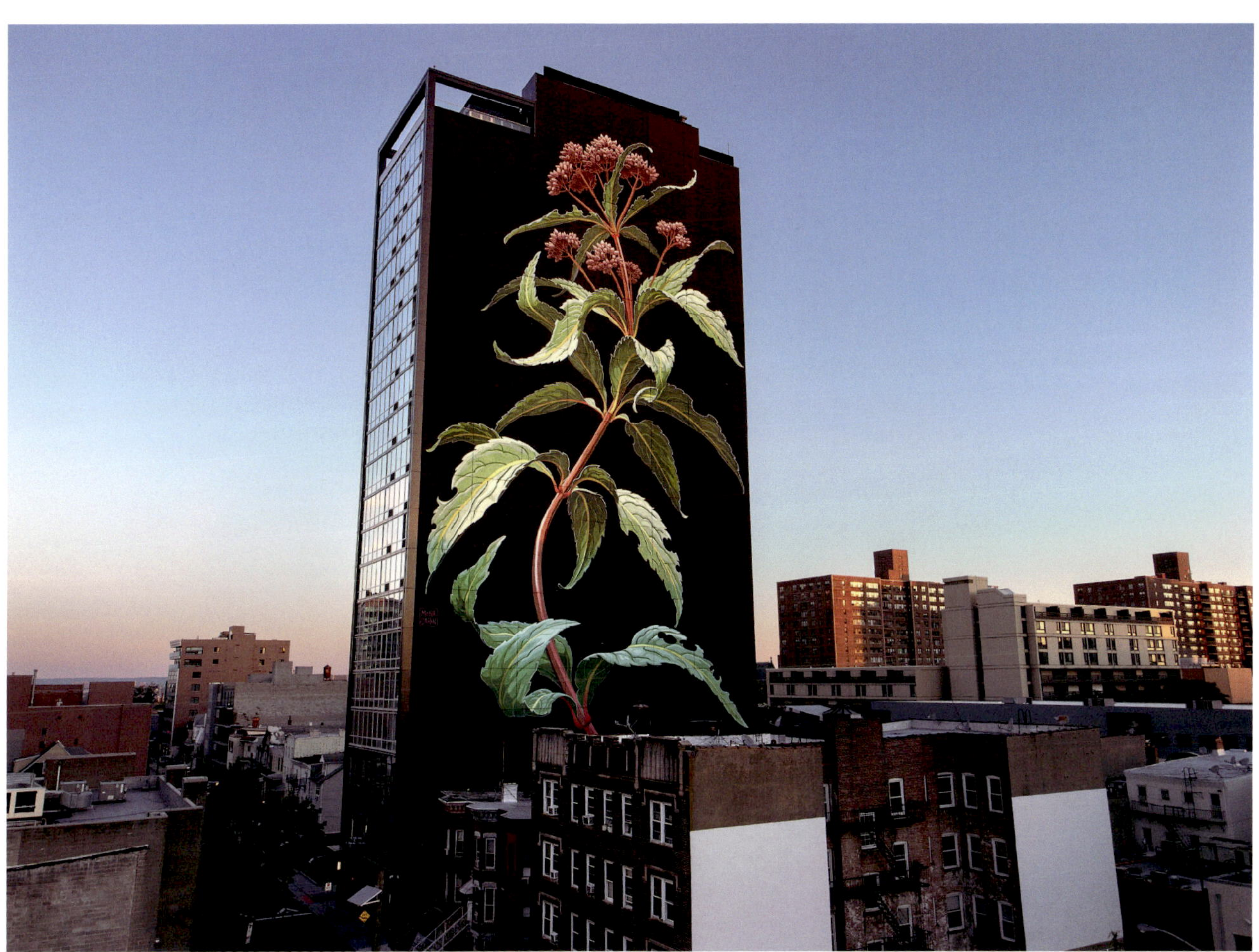



Mona Caron, *Shauquethqueat's Eutrochium*, 2021, mural

A massive weed facing the Manhattan skyline emerges imperiously from a black background. Twenty-three stories tall and painted in the style of an eighteenth-century botanical illustration, it is an astounding representation of *Eutrochium purpureum*. Street artist Mona Caron has developed a worldwide urban macro-herbarium visible across New York and San Francisco; Mumbai; Porto Alegre, Brazil; Quito, Ecuador; Vigo, Spain, and beyond. To the artist, painting weeds is a form of resistance. Her phytograffiti, as she calls them, are accessible landmarks of social and ecological resilience. *Eutrochium purpureum*, commonly known as Joe-Pye weed, derives its name from the Mohican (an Eastern Algonquian Native American tribe) healer who first utilized it in plant-based therapy. The roots of Caron's mural thus reach deep into the fraught histories of cultural subjugation and forced eradication upon which the foundations of the United States were laid. It proudly stands as a prayer for cultural healing, its bold visibility at once a vivid reminder of the erasure of Indigenous cultures and a celebration of the intimate relationship that for thousands of years these cultures have shared with the vegetal world.

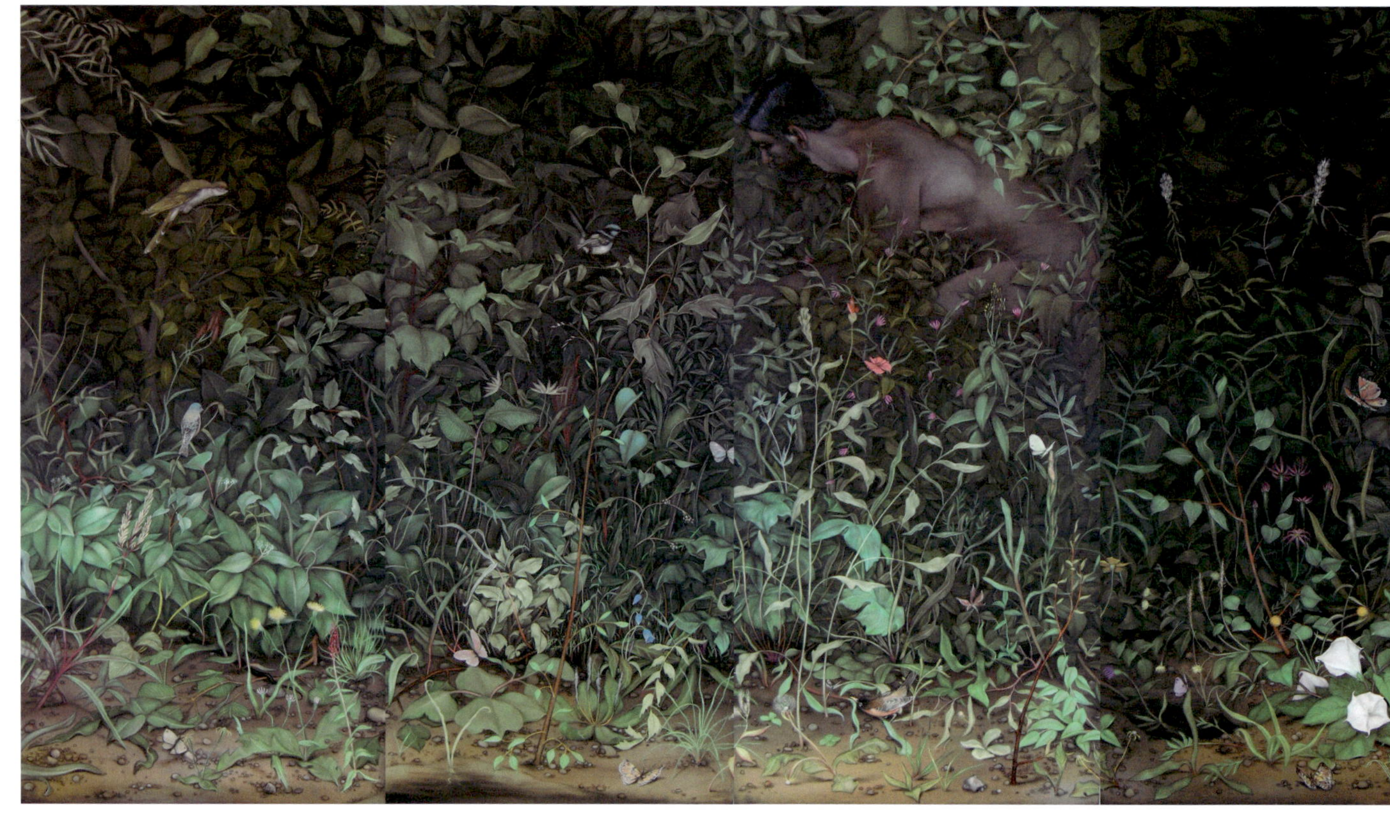

Zachari Logan, *Eunuch Tapestry 5*, 2015, pastel on eight sheets of black wove paper

# EUNUCH TAPESTRY 5

It is impossible to think of weeds outside human-conceived geographies and economies. Conflict, in the new millennium, is more than ever grounded in new conceptions of territory, invasion, and appropriation. And some weeds in contemporary art emerge from present-time interactions with local people and specific places. Their blooms unfurl to remind us that the power of dissidence is a natural element that all ecosystems require to thrive.

In this context, weeds represent the power to unsettle cultural normativity. The ditch—a weed-infested space of liminality—is a recurring motif in the work of Canadian artist Zachari Logan. Traditionally perceived as the unattractive and unwieldy-looking edge of institutionally neglected land, the ditch is a gutter with no other function than to serve as a drain or landfill. But left undisturbed, ditch weeds can reclaim their right to thrive, far from sight. In Logan's

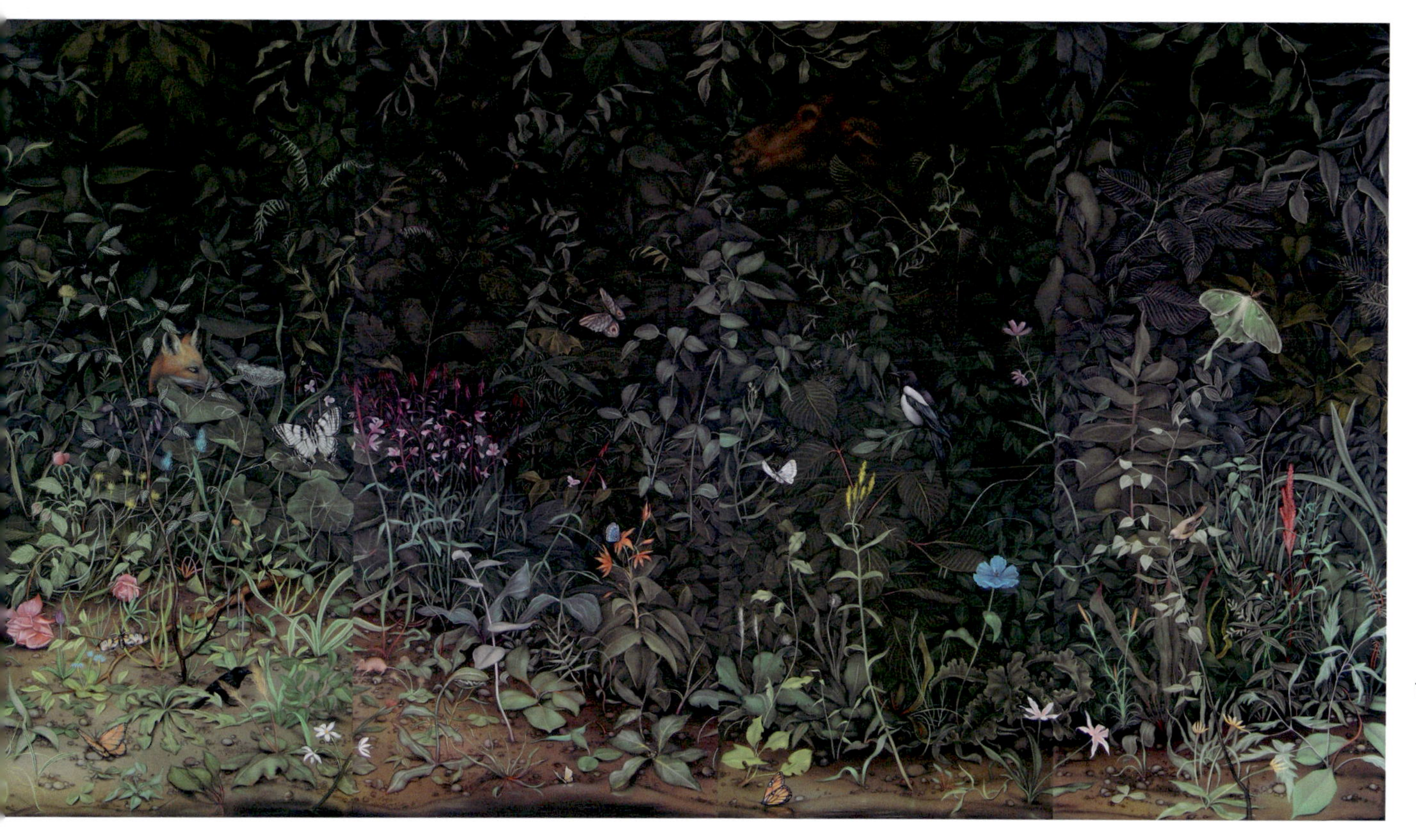



work, the ditch is neither a right nor a wrong place but "the site of the unwanted"—the marginalized, overlooked cultural fringe to which the LGBTQIA+ community has been historically relegated. And at once, this is also a site of attraction and desire: a provider of nectar and pollen for insects as well as a sheltered site for gay encounters. There is sheer beauty of an unconventional kind in Logan's vision. Far from the tidy splendor of well-tended plants and the normalized banality of formal gardens, in his work, tendrils, leaves, petals, and stems foreground the essence and importance of diversity across culture as well as ecology.

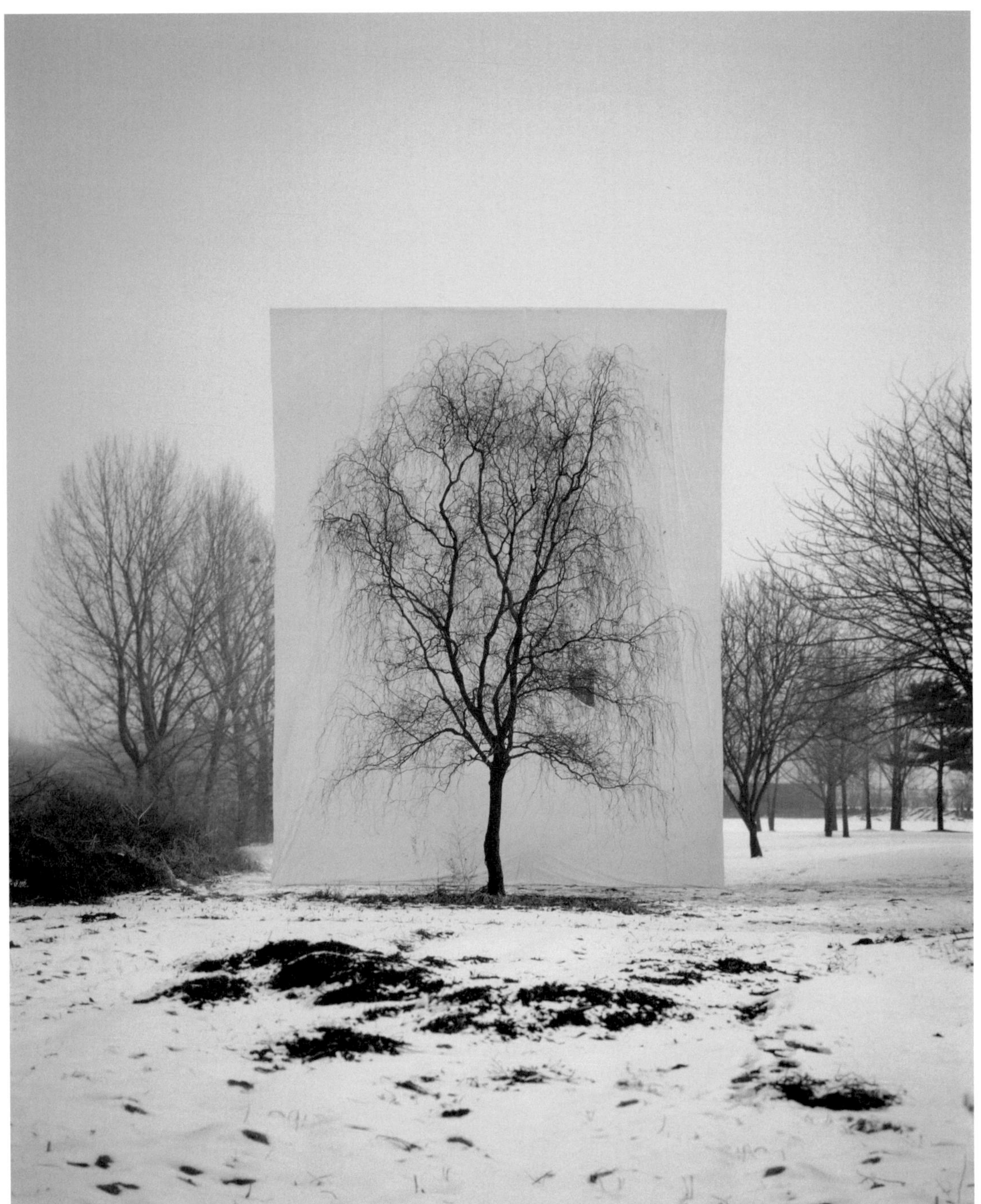

**Myoung Ho Lee, *Tree #3*, negative 2006, printed 2009, inkjet print**

Classical Western painting was founded on strict hierarchical organization of the picture plane: important subjects occupied the foreground while less-worthy ones populated the background. In the eighteenth and nineteenth centuries, the art of botanical illustration broke with that tradition by bringing leaves and stems front and center, and mercilessly exposing every part against a plain background. But that radical shift also removed the plant from the ecological networks upon which its life depends. When something is made visible, something else recedes from sight; this is an inescapable epistemic imposition that all disciplines must negotiate. Independently of each other, Myoung Ho Lee

# TREE #3

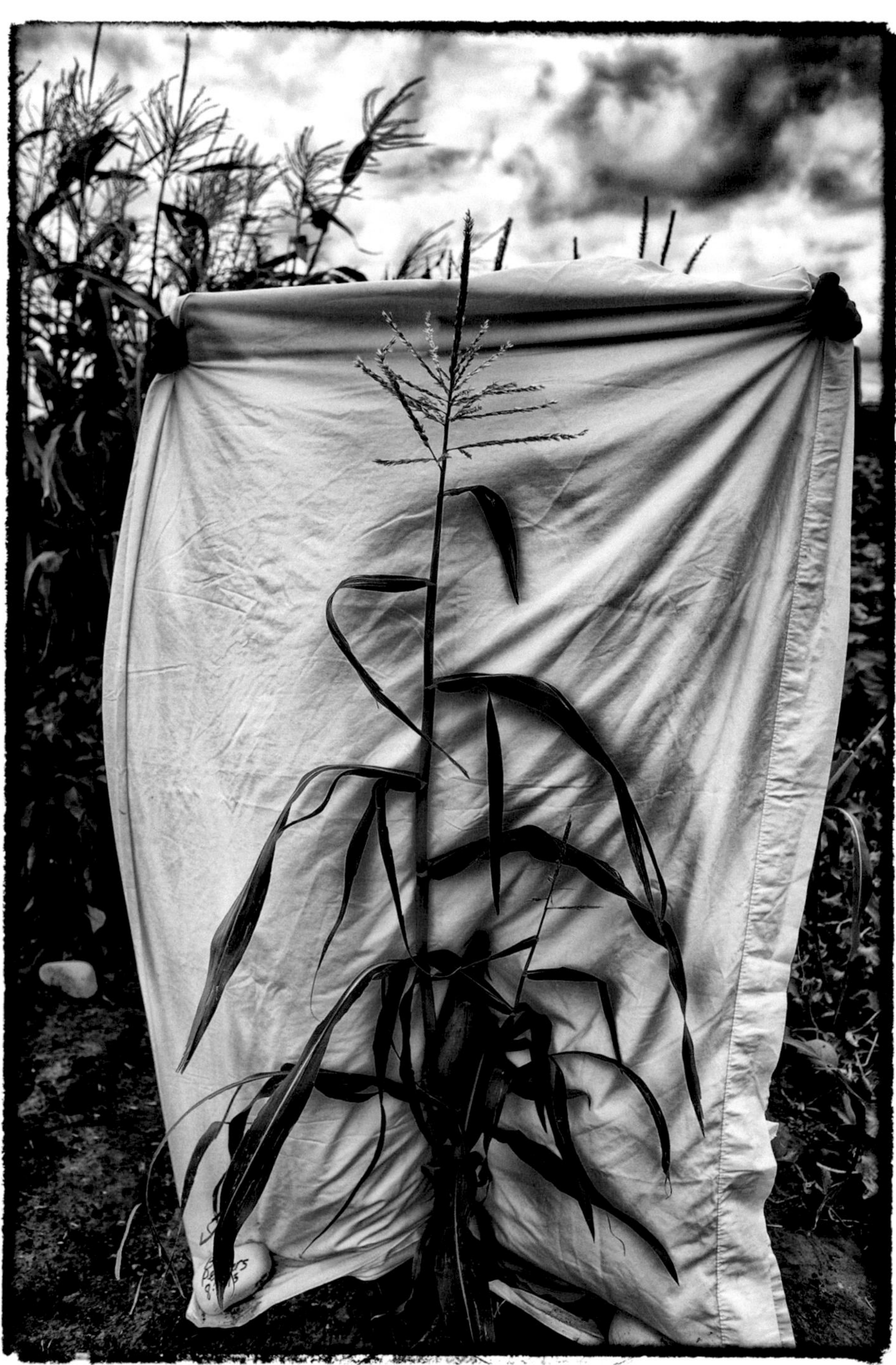

Chip Thomas, *Corn Portrait*, January 2019, screenprint



and Chip Thomas have used the photographic medium to critically address the impact of this condition by placing a white sheet of fabric behind their vegetal subjects. This practice was commonly used in nineteenth-century portraiture to make the subject stand out from background visual noise. But contra the aesthetic conventions of that time, neither of these contemporary photographers attempt to disguise their artifice. Their images own their conceptual and practical constructions—never attempting to pass themselves off as natural or transparent—and also remind us that with plants, crafting a non-objectifying, conceptual middle ground is a difficult balancing act.

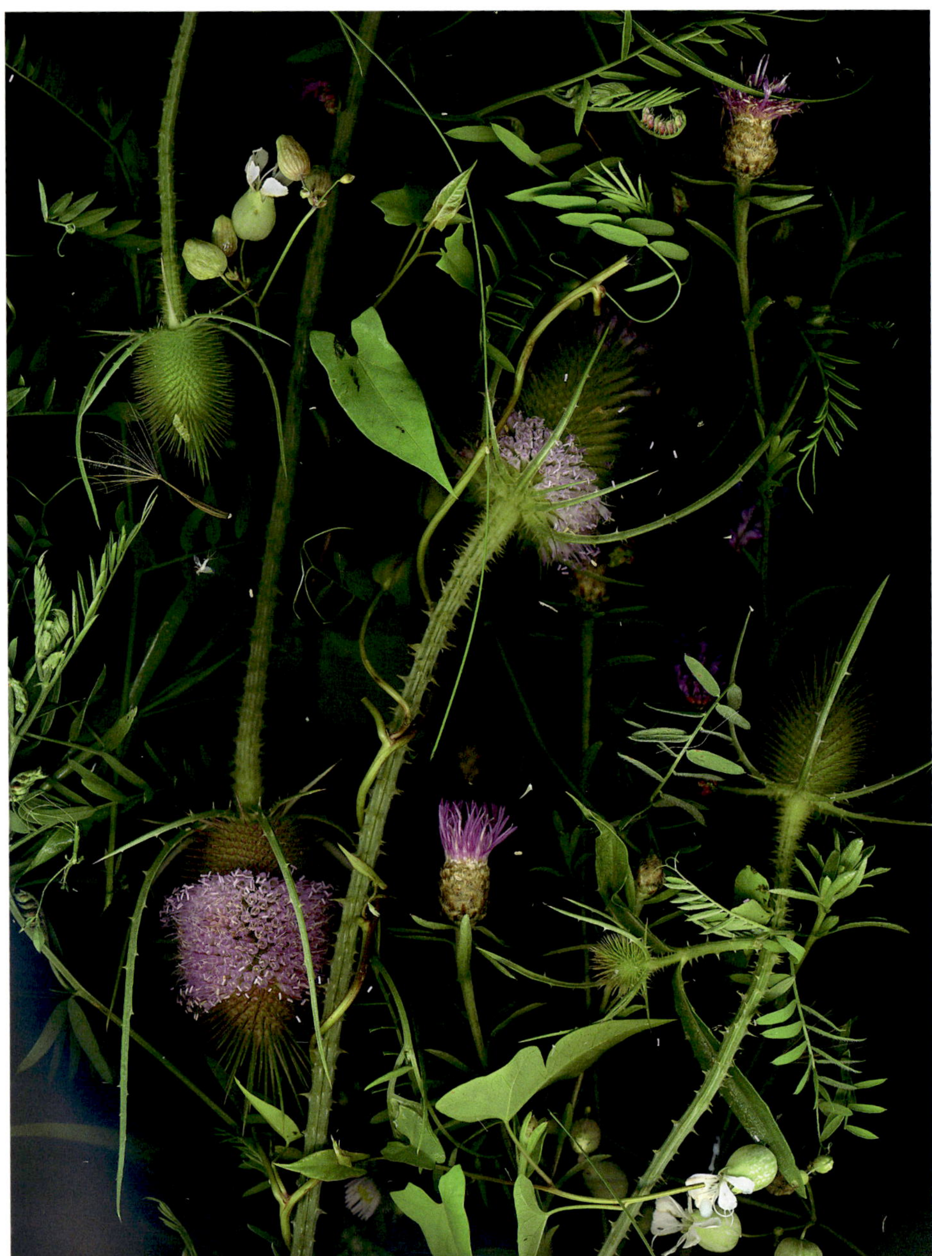

**Sara Angelucci, *Nocturnal Botanical Ontario* (showing bladder campion, teasel, bindweed, vetch, daisy fleabane, aster), July 30, 2021, inkjet print**

Sara Angelucci's images grapple with the aesthetic and conceptual legacy of traditional botanical illustration. Instead of a camera, the artist uses a scanner to envision tangled compositions of local flora. Heads down, randomly crisscrossing, overlapping, and obstructing one another, the plants in Angelucci's images outline a different kind of vegetal knowledge—neither strictly botanical nor simply decorative. Even the traditional paradigms that once underpinned the classical Dutch still-life genre fail to apply. Angelucci is keen to let plants guide her into a world of unpredictable exuberance and disorderly beauty. How does the point of view impact the encounter? How does it alter the power relation between object and subject? Are we simply caught in a seemingly purposeless vegetal swirl that foregrounds its own indifference to our gaze? Not posing for us, not endeavoring to show us their best side, not concerned with looking full or bold—this could be the ultimate statement of vegetal independence from the shackles of representation. Still realistic but ungovernable, and wholly unbound.

## NOCTURNAL BOTANICAL ONTARIO

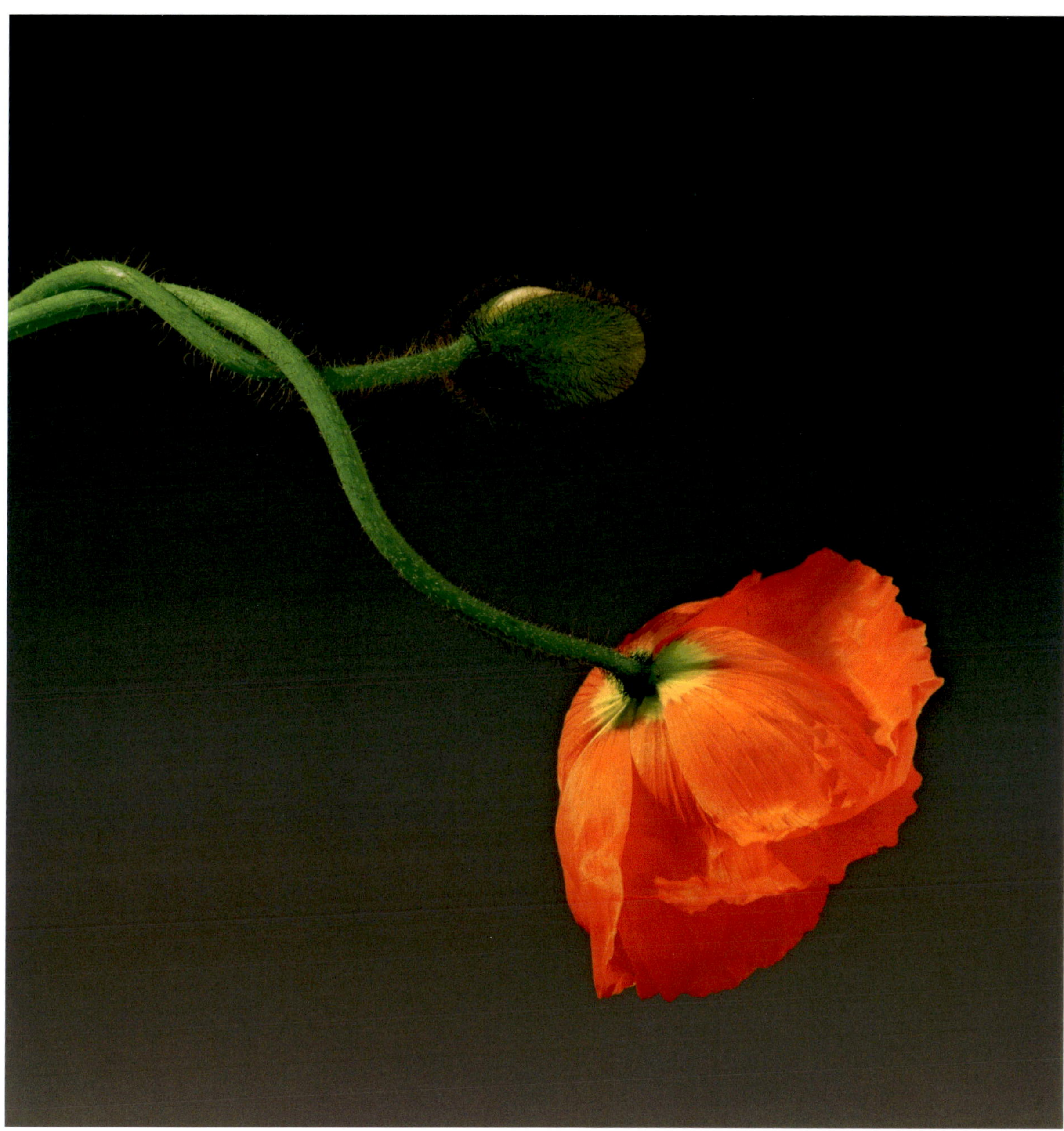

**Robert Mapplethorpe, *Poppy*, 1988, dye imbibition print**



The irreverent and nonconformist artist Robert Mapplethorpe shocked the world with his sexually explicit body of work. Toward the end of his life, as HIV/AIDS strengthened its grip on his health, the artist turned to flowers, and Mapplethorpe's blooms were among the most vividly seductive in the history of photography. No other photographer has accentuated the sexual nature of flowers quite as he did. His subjects are never obvious or bold in a horticultural aesthetic sense, but instead vacillate between an insatiable need to live their lives, to flourish, and to accept the inevitability of impending death. In this sense, Mapplethorpe's flowers reinvented the paradigm of the memento mori (a reminder of death's incumbency) in a way truer and closer to plant nature than to theology. There is no symbolism to crack, no hidden meaning to uncover. Often cropped in creative and unconventional ways, and pictured against plain or colorful backgrounds, Mapplethorpe's flowers are stripped bare—vegetal sexual organs determined to fulfill their intended purpose in the most elegantly beautiful of ways despite the limited time at their disposal. His blooms have nothing to say about Christian morals and ethics. They are wholly silent in the face of unquenchable desire.

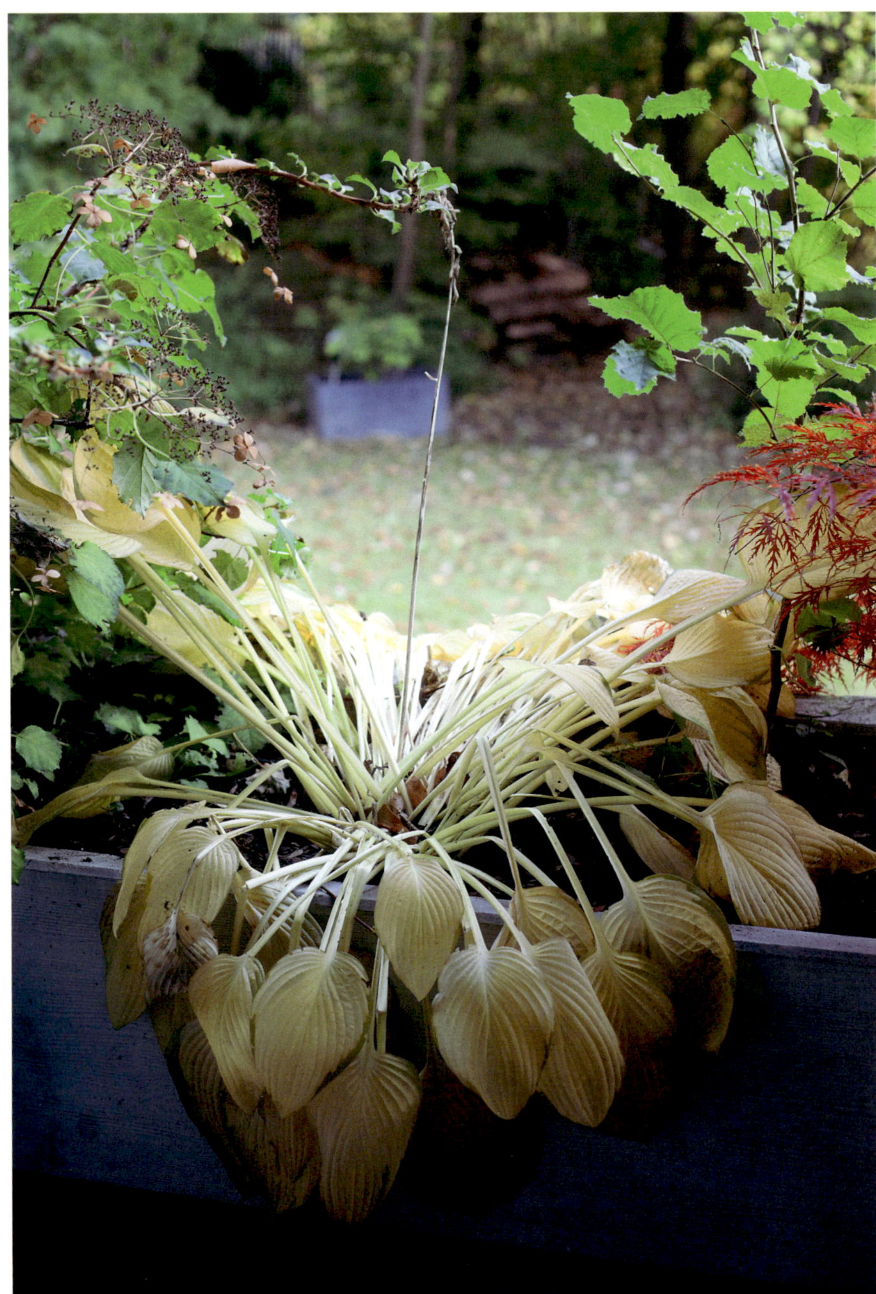

**Wolfgang Tillmans, *Osterwaldstrasse*, 2011, inkjet print on aluminum in artist's frame**

Over time, in one photograph after another, Wolfgang Tillmans has crafted a queer gaze in which everything matters—a sort of flat visual ontology underpinned by a deep, often visceral existentialism. Queer individuals of all kinds face the same challenges: to reconsider and reassess the value of everything from a personal standpoint in order to survive. From this contingency, Tillmans has established a distinctive visual vocabulary according to which plants frequently play major roles. The artist often privileges weeds or plants growing against all odds, in makeshift containers or forgotten nooks and crannies. Bold, classical beauties rarely if ever catch his eye—there are no coiffed rosebushes or generous mounds of petunias. Even when a garden favorite, in this example a hosta, is deemed a worthy subject for a photograph, it is caught in an unexpected manner—the type of image that would never be published in a gardening catalog or a scientific tome.

The ghostly solemnity of this plant and the otherworldly, translucent, golden color of its leaves are signs of an ending autumnal cycle. Tillmans's photograph thus raises crucial issues about the essence of beauty, the force of perseverance, and the courage required to overcome adversity and tragedy.

# OSTERWALDSTRASSE

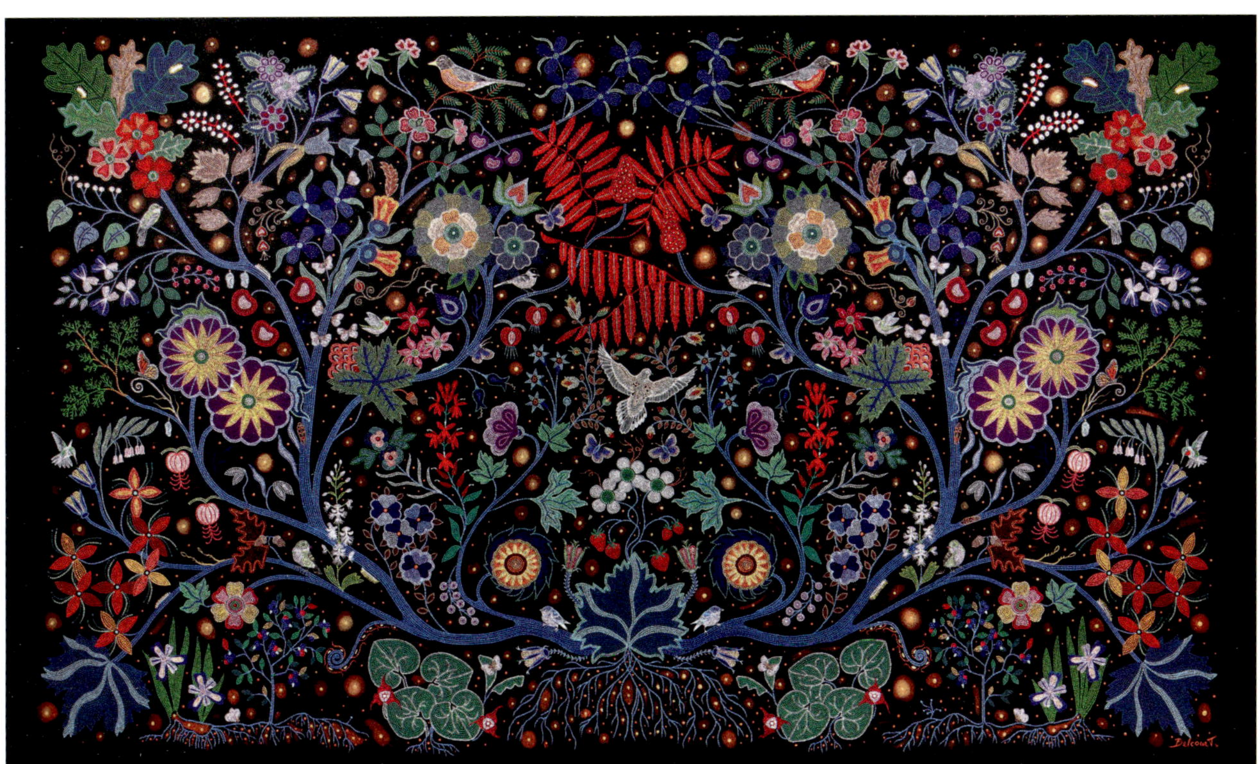

Christi Belcourt, *The Wisdom of the Universe*, 2014, acrylic on canvas



Christi Belcourt is a Métis artist living and working in Canada. Like many Native communities, the Métis Nation has become a landless people in the sense that they no longer legally own territory. Belcourt's large-scale paintings are inspired by the traditional beadwork patterns made by Métis women and celebrate the beauty of the natural world as seen through traditional Indigenous spiritual worldviews and natural medicine. The depicted scenarios promote an understanding of the land as a living, sacred being. Belcourt's compositions are often symmetrical and show vegetal and animal life intertwined in harmonious ways—pieces of a larger, perfectly fitting ecosystemic puzzle. Underlining this conception is the "reflection" of the astral plane underneath the ground: a cosmological view of unity between the earthly and the celestial spheres.

# THE WISDOM OF THE UNIVERSE

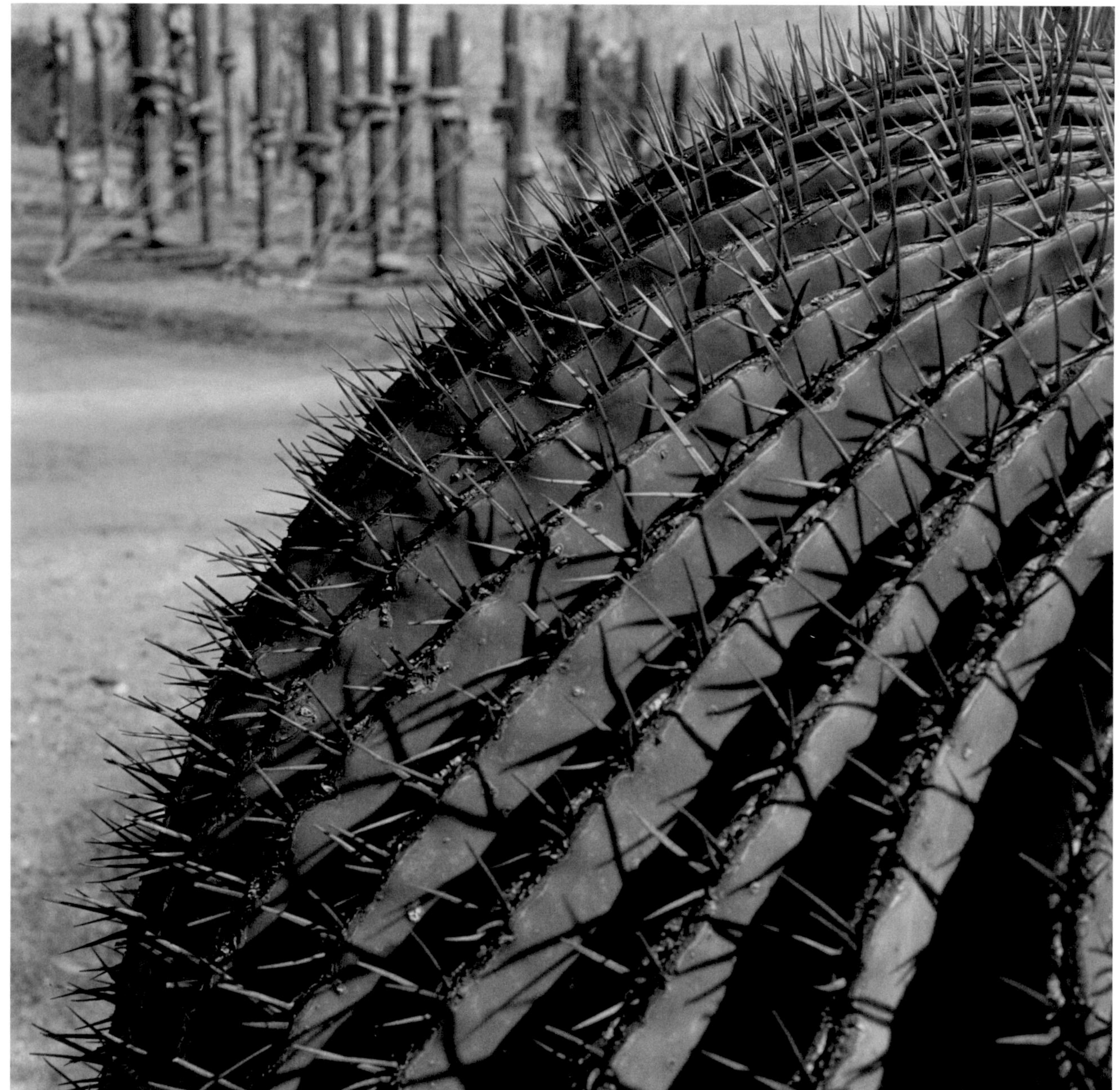

Graciela Iturbide, *Jardines botánicos, Oaxaca*, 1996–2004, chromogenic print

Graciela Iturbide photographed the Jardín Etnobotánico in Oaxaca, Mexico, around 1996. As with all of her photographs, the images provoke us to rethink our empathic positioning toward others, in this case plants. At first glance, the composition of this photograph seems to invite us to appreciate the architectural structure of a young saguaro. But a second look reveals more. In the background, numerous young saguaro cacti are supported by ropes, with cloth wrappings to prevent damage to their flesh. This practice of care is common when trees need bracing against strong winds. The photograph works on two levels: the documentary and the metaphorical. On the one hand, it exposes us to an unfiltered reality that most botanical garden visitors don't want to view since it deviates from the ideals of perfection that define these institutions' exhibits. On the other hand, the picture portrays a community and the constant tending needed to keep it alive.

## JARDINES BOTÁNICOS

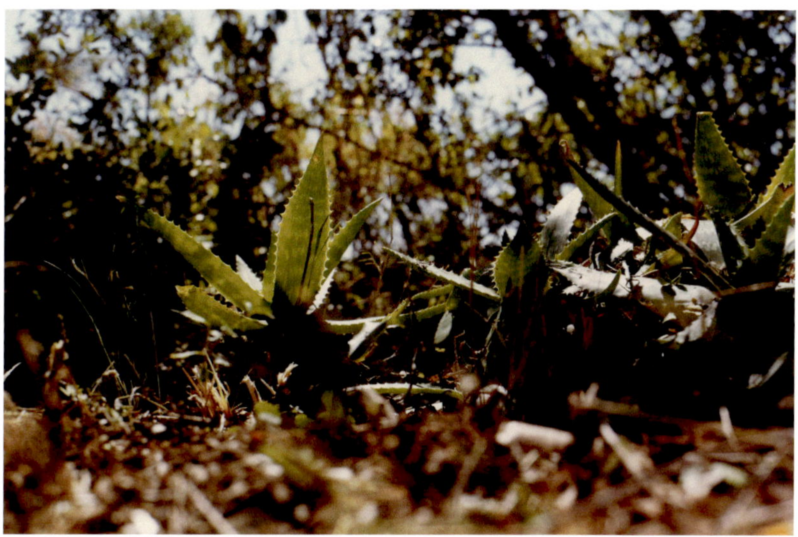

William Eggleston, *Undergrowth and Succulents*, 1980, chromogenic print

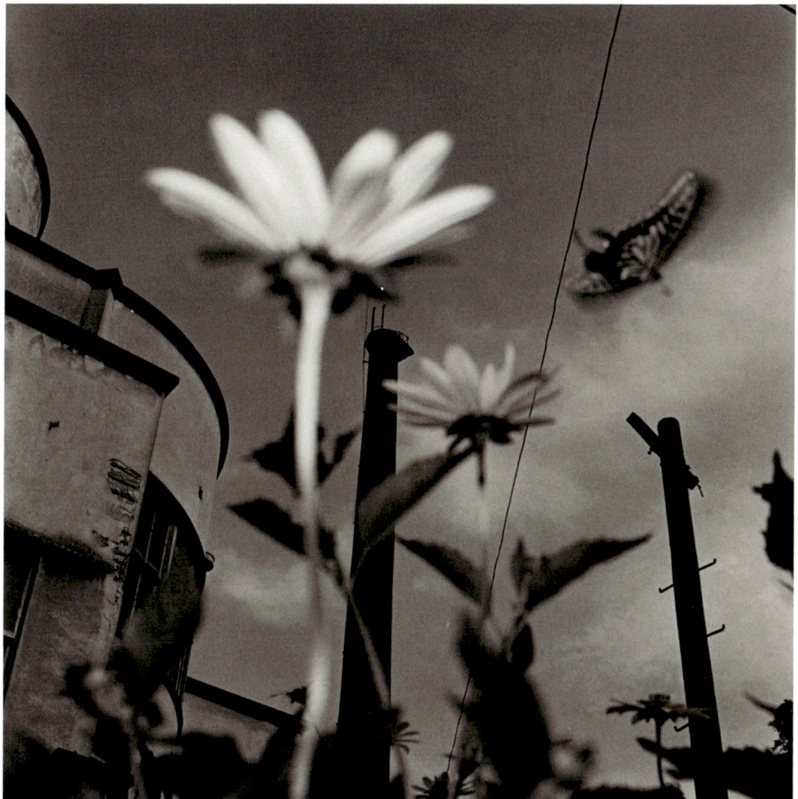

Issei Suda, *Koishikawa Botanical Gardens, Bunkyo-ku*, 1982, gelatin silver print



Pioneering photographers Issei Suda and William Eggleston persistently experimented with unusual points of view to show the world from new perspectives. But when plants are involved, what might at first glance seem like a simple destabilizing strategy takes on a more profound meaning. In these two images, by positioning our point of view near to the earth, the photographers subtly alter our anthropocentric self-conception. In the space outlined by the photograph, we are momentarily transformed into just another earthling. From here, plants look wondrous and mysterious, close and yet impenetrable as vegetal form is thrust into the realm of the uncanny. We may do a double take — our perceptual responses slow down, and our desire to find classical beauty in the plants is irremediably frustrated. Once on their level, the plants invite us to reenvision the objective-subjective relationship we have established through new forms of being with them, and among them.

## *UNDERGROWTH AND SUCCULENTS*

## *KOISHIKAWA BOTANICAL GARDENS*

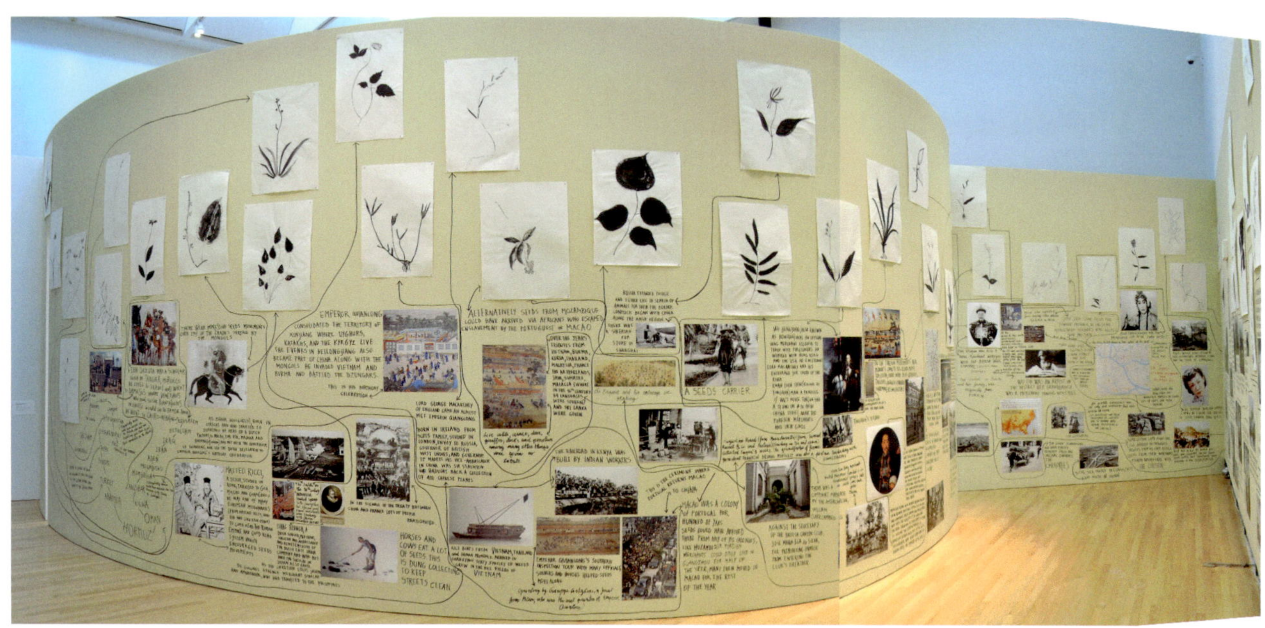

Maria Thereza Alves, Installation view of *Wake in Guangzhou: The History of the Earth*, 2008, mixed media



Since the beginning of the new millennium, contemporary artists have reshaped the boundaries of history, geography, anthropology, sociology, and, of course, art history, by following and foregrounding the agential power of plants. No longer a passive background for human vicissitudes or simply a resource to exploit, plants are being reappraised as, for better or worse, active coproducers of our world. Recovering the pivotal roles plants have played in shaping the history of humanity and that of other earthlings, artists often retrace erased or concealed narratives of subjugation and stories of ecological and cultural transformation, loss, and regrowth. In *Seeds of Change* (2017), a twenty-year investigation that spawned multiple works, Maria Thereza Alves—an environmentalist, playwright, writer, and art historian—reveals previously overlooked stories embedded in the seeds that ended up in ballast: the soil used to balance ships that traveled colonial routes connecting Marseilles, Reposaari, Dunkirk, Exeter, Topsham, Liverpool, and Bristol. The ballast would be offloaded upon arrival at the destination, thus contributing to the dissemination of what, on both sides of the Atlantic, often went by the name "invasive species." For *Seeds of Change*, Alves located historical ballast sites and flora. The artist asks: At what moment do seeds become "native"? Which sociopolitical histories of place outline the frameworks of belonging?

Can poetry help us more fully grasp the importance of ecological interconnectedness? How might contemporary art broaden the reach of poetry through multimedia encounters that root and establish existing and new communities? These questions have for decades been central to the practice of Chilean artist Cecilia Vicuña, an Indigenous eco-pioneer whose body of work is finally being better understood and appreciated by institutions and audiences worldwide. *Brain Forest Quipu* was exhibited in the prestigious Turbine Hall at London's Tate Modern in fall 2022. It comprised sound, music, and video components as well as two spectacular twenty-seven-meter-tall hanging quipu sculptures. The quipu is an ancient South American communication system made of knotted threads, and Vicuña sees in them an ecological model that non-hierarchically entwines vegetal, human, and animal forms. The world, in her perspective, is an enormous forest – a collective thinking, breathing, feeling organism of which we are all part. Her vertical, tubular quipus incorporate a range of organic materials, including found objects, unspun wool, plant fibers, rope, and cardboard. Their predominantly bleached colors evoke a ghostly presence, the memory of ancestral vegetal loss: the forests once home to Indigenous cultures, and the loss of cultural groundedness that comes with deforestation. The death of one causes the inexorable collapse of the other. Vicuña's art is both a message of optimism and a prayer for a more sustainable future in which we can all work together to restore and safeguard our health and the health of our planet.

## WAKE IN GUANGZHOU: THE HISTORY OF THE EARTH

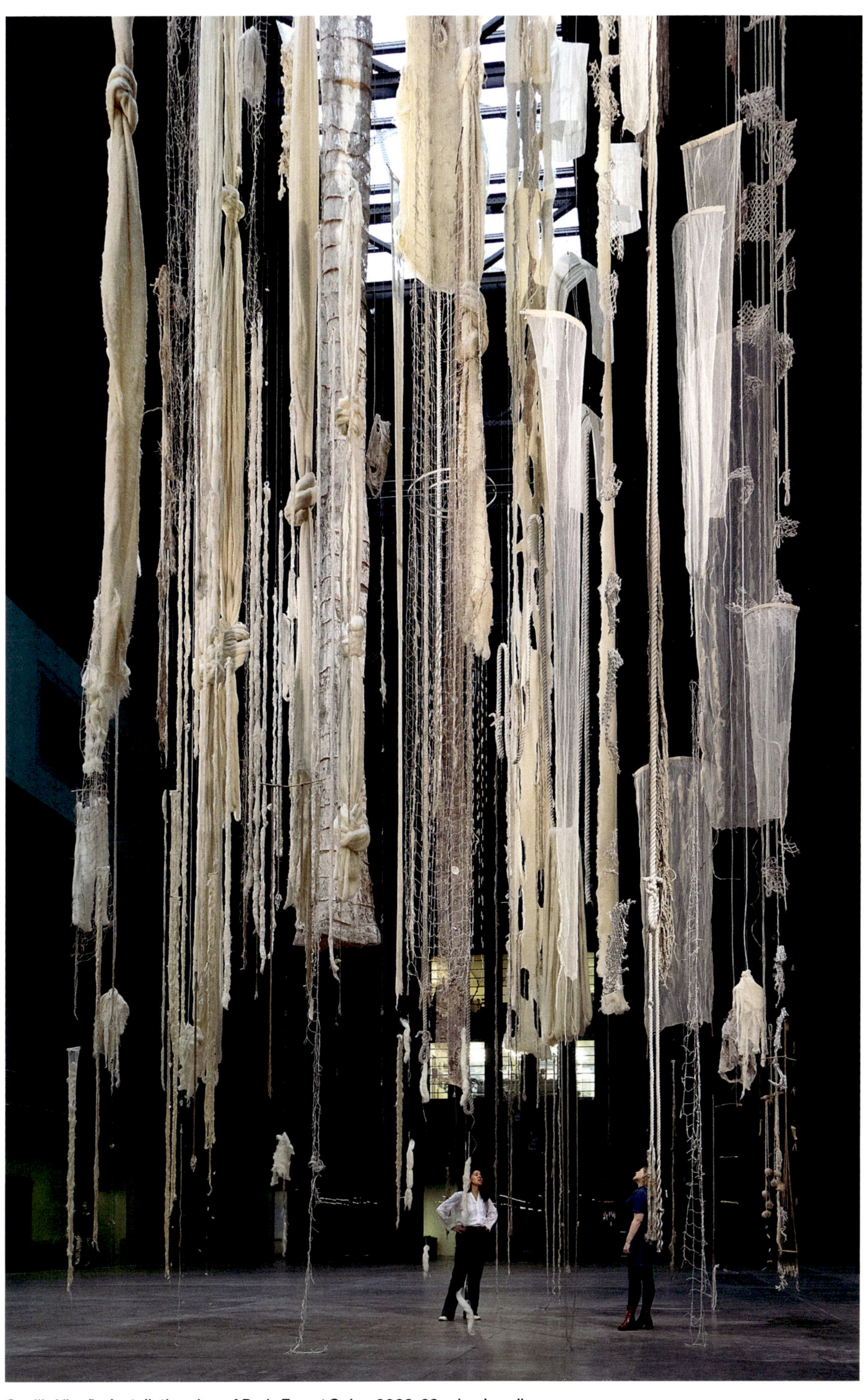

Cecilia Vicuña, Installation view of *Brain Forest Quipu*, 2022–23, mixed media

# NOTES

## INTRODUCTION

1 Plant neurobiologists Stefano Mancuso, Alessandra Viola, Monica Gagliano, and Paco Calvo have led groundbreaking research on plant intelligence, demonstrating that plants actively problem solve. See Stefano Mancuso and Alessandra Viola, *Brilliant Green: The Surprising History and Science of Plant Intelligence* (Washington, DC: Island Press, 2015); Monica Gagliano, *Thus Spoke the Plant: A Remarkable Journey of Groundbreaking Scientific Discoveries and Personal Encounters with Plants* (Berkeley: North Atlantic Books, 2018); Paco Calvo, *Planta Sapiens: The New Science of Plant Intelligence* (Washington, DC: National Geographic Books, 2023).



2 J. David Archibald, *Aristotle's Ladder, Darwin's Tree: The Evolution of Visual Metaphors for Biological Order* (New York: Columbia University Press, 2014).

3 See Jesse L. Preston and Adam Baimel, "Towards a Psychology of Religion and the Environment," *Current Opinion in Psychology* 40 (2021): 145–49.

4 Ole Jørgen Benedictow, *The Complete History of the Black Death* (Martlesham, England: Boydell and Brewer, 2021).

5 The field of new materialism has more recently foregrounded the idea that materials of all kinds are never passive, but indeed engage us in agential relations. See Karen Michelle Barad, *Meeting the Universe Halfway* (Durham, NC: Duke University Press, 2007); Jane Bennett, *Vibrant Matter: A Political Ecology of Things* (Durham, NC: Duke University Press, 2010); Zakiyyah Iman Jackson, *Becoming Human* (New York: New York University Press, 2020); Dianna Coole and Samantha Frost, eds., *New Materialisms: Ontology, Agency, and Politics* (Durham, NC: Duke University Press, 2010).

6 Eduardo Kohn, *How Forests Think: Toward an Anthropology beyond the Human* (Berkeley: University of California Press, 2013).

7 Giovanni Aloi, *Why Look at Plants? The Botanical Emergence in Contemporary Art* (Leiden, Netherlands: Brill, 2018).

8 Martin Holbraad and Morten Axel Pedersen, *The Ontological Turn: An Anthropological Exposition* (Cambridge, UK: Cambridge University Press, 2017).

9 Giovanni Aloi and Susan McHugh, eds., *Posthumanism in Art and Science: A Reader* (New York: Columbia University Press, 2021).

10 James H. Wandersee and Elisabeth E. Schussler, "Preventing Plant Blindness," *American Biology Teacher* 61, no. 2 (1999): 82–86.

## CHAPTER 1

1 Ovid, *Ovid: Metamorphoses,* trans. David Raeburn (New York: Penguin Random House, 2004), 32–33.

2 Ovid, *Metamorphoses*, 33.

3 See Agustín Villagra Caleti, *Pinturas rupestres "Mateo A. Saldaña," Ixtapantongo, Estado de México* (Mexico City: Instituto Nacional de Antropología e Historia / Secretaría de Educación Pública, 1954).

4 Ann Bingham and Jeremy Roberts, *South and Meso-American Mythology A to Z* (New York: Infobase, 2010), 84.

5 Mary Ellen Miller and Karl Taube, *An Illustrated Dictionary of the Gods and Symbols of Ancient Mexico and the Maya, with 260 Illustrations* (London: Thames & Hudson, 1997), 111.

6 Ana G. Valenzuela-Zapata and Gary Paul Nabhan, *Tequila* (Tucson: University of Arizona Press, 2004).

7 Robert Hoogenraad and George Jampijinpa Robertson, "Seasonal Calendars from Central Australia," in *Windows on Meteorology: An Australian Perspective*, ed. Eric Kenneth Webb (Collingwood, Australia: CSIRO, 1997), 34–41.

8 Paul G. Zolbrod, *Diné Bahane': The Navajo Creation Story* (Albuquerque: University of New Mexico Press, 1988).

## CHAPTER 2

1 Younes Adam Tabi et al., "Vividness of Visual Imagery Questionnaire Scores and Their Relationship to Visual Short-Term Memory Performance," *Cortex* 146 (January 1, 2022): 186–99, available at https://doi.org/10.1016/j.cortex.2021.10.011.

2 Peter Veth et al., "Plants before Farming: The Deep History of Plant Use and Representation in the Rock Art of Australia's Kimberley Region," *Quaternary International* 489 (September 2018): 26–45.

3 See Steven Roger Fischer, *History of Writing* (London: Reaktion Books, 2020).

4 See part II, devoted to organic materials, in Paul T. Nicholson and Ian Shaw, eds., *Ancient Egyptian Materials and Technology* (Cambridge, UK: Cambridge University Press, 2009).

5 Cassiodorus, *The Letters of Cassiodorus*, trans. Thomas Hodgkin (London: Henry Frowde, 1886), 483.

6 D. G. Suryawanshi, M. V. Nair, and P. M. Sinha, "Improving the Flexibility of Palm Leaf," *Restaurator* 13, no. 1 (1992): 37–46.

7 D. Udaya Kumar, G. V. Sreekumar, and U. A. Athvankar, "Traditional Writing System in Southern India—Palm Leaf Manuscripts," *Design Thoughts*, July 2009, 2.

8 James Raven, *The Oxford Illustrated History of the Book* (Oxford: Oxford University Press, 2020), 28.

9 See Nicholas A. Basbanes, *On Paper: The Everything of Its Two-Thousand-Year History* (New York: Vintage Books, 2014).

10 Maya Shatzmiller, "The Adoption of Paper in the Middle East, 700–1300 AD," *Journal of the Economic and Social History of the Orient* 61, no. 3 (2018): 461–90.

11 I use the term "nature-culture" as a concept coined by Donna Haraway in 2003 to overcome the nature-culture dichotomy typical of humanist thinking. The term encompasses a synthesis of nature and culture that recognizes their inseparability in ecological relationships as well as biological and material dimensions. Donna J. Haraway, *The Companion Species Manifesto: Dogs, People, and Significant Otherness*, vol. 1 (Chicago: Prickly Paradigm Press, 2003).

12 See Feisal Alkazi, *Srinagar: An Architectural Legacy* (New Delhi: Lotus Collection, 2014).

13 Michael Baxandall, *The Limewood Sculptors of Renaissance Germany* (New Haven, CT: Yale University Press, 1980), 28–29.

14 Christina Pratt, *An Encyclopedia of Shamanism*, vol. 1 (New York: Rosen, 2007).

15 See Manuel Aguilar-Moreno, *Handbook to Life in the Aztec World* (Oxford: Oxford University Press, 2007).

16 Dotun Oyejide, *Gelede Mask of Egbado-Yoruba* (Bloomington, IN: Dotson Creative, 2008).

17 Babatunde Lawal, *The Gẹ̀lẹ̀dé Spectacle: Art, Gender, and Social Harmony in African Culture* (Seattle: University of Washington Press, 1996), 84–85, 190.

18 Gary Edson, *Masks and Masking: Faces of Tradition and Belief Worldwide* (Jefferson, NC: McFarland, 2009), 17–20.

19 A. Azeez Olaomo, "Indigenous Art of West Africa in Wood," *Global Journal of Human Social Science* 11, no. 2 (March 2011): 63–70.

20 Ladislas Segy, *African Sculpture* (New York: Dover, 1958), 14–15.

21 Pauline Hillaire and Gregory P. Fields, *A Totem Pole History: The Work of Lummi Carver Joe Hillaire* (Lincoln: University of Nebraska Press, 2013), 5–6.

22 Kathleen Dardes and Andrea Rothe, eds., *The Structural Conservation of Panel Paintings: Proceedings of a Symposium at the J. Paul Getty Museum, 24–28 April 1995* (Los Angeles: Getty Conservation Institute, 1998), 113–14.

23 Maria Clelia Galassi and Raffaella Bruzzone, "Wood Species in Italian Panel Paintings of the Fifteenth and Sixteenth Centuries: Historical Investigation and Microscopical Wood Identification," in *Studying Old Master Paintings: Technology and Practice: National Gallery Technical Bulletin 30th Anniversary Conference Postprints*, ed. Marika Spring (London: Archetype Publications in association with the National Gallery, 2011), 253–59.

24 Maria Bazzi, *The Artist's Methods and Materials* (London: Pitman, 1960), 288.

25 See Annemarie Weyl Carr et al., *Imprinting the Divine: Byzantine and Russian Icons from the Menil Collection* (Houston: Menil Collection, 2011).

26 Yuqin Sun and Xu Chang, *A General History of China's Foreign Trade* (Singapore: World Scientific Publishing Company 2023), 6.

27 Anthea Callen, *The Art of Impressionism: Painting Technique and the Making of Modernity* (New Haven, CT: Yale University Press, 2000), 30.

28 Rutherford J. Gettens and George L. Stout, *Painting Materials* (New York: Dover, 1966), 333.

29 See Victoria Finlay, *Color: A Natural History of the Palette* (London: Random House, 2002).

30 Gettens and Stout, *Painting Materials*, 115.

31 Sallie P. Kierstead, *Natural Dyes* (Boston: Bruce Humphries, 1950).

## CHAPTER 3

1 Michael F. Suarez and H. R. Woudhuysen, *The Book: A Global History* (Oxford: Oxford University Press, 2013), 4.

2 See Tsuen-Hsuin Tsien, *Collected Writings on Chinese Culture* (Hong Kong: Chinese University Press, 2011).

3 Wen Fong and Maxwell K. Hearn, "Silent Poetry: Chinese Paintings in the Douglas Dillon Galleries," *Metropolitan Museum of Art Bulletin* 39, no. 3 (Winter 1981–82): 28, 77.

4 A 1988 PBS TV series by Joseph Campbell titled *The Power of Myth* went so far as claiming that shamanism links all artists across time, and that contemporary artists are descendants of shamans.

5 José Manuel Rodríguez Arce and Michael James Winkelman, "Psychedelics, Sociality, and Human Evolution," *Frontiers in Psychology* 12 (September 2021): https://www.frontiersin.org/articles/10.3389/fpsyg.2021.729425/full.

6 See Ahmad Ansari, Bengu Turkyilmaz Unal, Munir Ozturk, and Gary Owens, *Plants as Medicine and Aromatics* (Boca Raton, FL: CRC Press, 2023).

7 Cyril P. Bryan, *The Papyrus Ebers: Ancient Egyptian Medicine* (Eastford, CT: Martino Fine Books, 2021).

8 Shou-Zhong Yang, *The Divine Farmer's Materia Medica: A Translation of the Shen Nong Ben Cao Jing* (Boulder, CO: Blue Poppy Press, 1998). *Shennong bencao jing* (Shennong's Canon of Materia Medica) tells how he tasted all plants to distinguish between poisonous and edible ones.

9 Edward Sandford Burgess, "Studies in the History and Variations of Asters," *Torrey Botanical Society Memoirs* 10 (1902): iii, v, vii–xii, 1–5, 7, 9–93, 95–447.

10 Bernardino de Sahagún, *Historia general de las cosas de Nueva España* (Mexico City: Editorial Porrúa, 2006).

11 Ricardo Reyes-Chilpa et al., "On the First Book of Medicinal Plants Written in the American Continent: The *Libellus Medicinalibus Indorum Herbis* from Mexico, 1552. A Review," *Boletín Latinoamericano y del Caribe de Plantas Medicinales y Aromaticas* 20, no. 1 (2021): 1–27.

12 Brian W. Ogilvie, *The Science of Describing* (Chicago: University of Chicago Press, 2008).

13 M. W. Dols, "Herbs, Middle Eastern," in *Dictionary of the Middle Ages*, vol. 6, ed. Joseph R. Strayer (New York: Charles Scribner's Sons, 1980), 184–87.

14 Ikhwan al-Safa', *Rasa'il Ikhwan al-Safa'* [Epistles of the Brethren of Purity], 4 vols. (Beirut: Dar Sadir, 1957), 2:107.

15 G. Mangani and L. Tongiorgi Tomasi, *Gherardo Cibo, dilettante di botanica e pittore di "paesi" arte, scienza e illustrazione botanica nel XVI secolo* (Vicenza, Italy: Il Lavoro Editoriale, 2013).

16 Jeffrey Ashcroft, "Art in German: Artistic Statements by Albrecht Dürer," *Forum of Modern Language Studies* 48, no. 4 (2012): 386.

17 Martin Kemp, "Naturally Natural, Albrecht Dürer's Studies of Animals Have a Life of Their Own," *Science in Culture* 420 (2002): 744.

18 Wilfrid Blunt and William T. Stearn, *The Art of Botanical Illustration: An Illustrated History* (New York: Dover, 1994), 164.

19 Blunt and Stearn, *The Art of Botanical Illustration*, 162.

20 Kuo Hsi quoted in Blunt and Stearn, *The Art of Botanical Illustration*, 162.

21 See Kristen L. Chiem, *Hua Yan (1682–1756) and the Making of the Artist in Early Modern China* (Leiden, Netherlands: Brill, 2020).

22 For a concise history detailing the careers of this and other important Chinese female artists see Marsha Weidner, "Women in the History of Chinese Painting," in *Views from Jade Terrace: Chinese Women Artists, 1300–1912* (Indianapolis: Indianapolis Museum of Art; New York: Rizzoli, 1988), 13–29.

## CHAPTER 4

1 Leonhart Fuchs, *The New Herbal* (1543; repr., Cologne: Taschen, 2016).

2 Marieke van Delft, Kay Etheridge, and Hans Mulder, *Maria Sibylla Merian: Changing the Nature of Art and Science* (Tielt, Belgium: Lannoo, 2022).

3 Ann B. Shteir, *Cultivating Women, Cultivating Science: Flora's Daughters and Botany in England, 1760–1860* (Baltimore: Johns Hopkins University Press, 1999); Elsa H. Fine, *Women and Art: A History of Women Painters and Sculptors from the Renaissance to the 20th Century* (Waterville, ME: Thorndike, 1978); Lincoln Taiz and Lee Taiz, *Flora Unveiled: The Discovery and Denial of Sex in Plants* (New York: Oxford University Press, 2017), 411.

4 Paul Duro, "Imitation and Authority: The Creation of the Academic Canon in French Art 1648–1870," in *Partisan Canons*, ed. Anna Brzysky (Durham, NC: Duke University Press, 2007), 95–113.

5 Lucia Impelluso, *Nature and Its Symbols*, trans. Stephen Sartarelli (Los Angeles: J. Paul Getty Museum, 2004).

6 Anne Goldgar, *Tulipmania: Money, Honor, and Knowledge in the Dutch Golden Age* (Chicago: University of Chicago Press, 2008).

7 Diana Donald and Jane Munro, eds., *Endless Forms: Charles Darwin, Natural Science and the Visual Arts* (New Haven, CT: Yale University Press, 2009).

8 John G. T. Anderson, *Deep Things Out of Darkness: A History of Natural History* (Berkeley: University of California Press, 2013).

9 Naela Aamir, "From Divinity to Decoration: The Journey of Lotus Symbol in the Art of Subcontinent," *Pakistan Social Sciences Review* 1 (2017): 201–25.

10 Hokky Situngkir, "Deconstructing Javanese Batik Motif: When Traditional Heritage Meets Computation," October 7, 2008, https://ssrn.com/abstract=1312789, http://dx.doi.org/10.2139/ssrn.1312789.

11 Gill Saunders, *Picturing Plants: An Analytical History of Botanical Illustration* (Berkeley: University of California Press; London: Victoria and Albert Museum, 2009).

12 See Kax Wilson, *A History of Textiles* (London: Routledge, 2021).

13 Some of the most notable works in this genre include the Dutch botanical twelve-volume masterpiece *Hortus Indicus Malabaricus* (1678–93), commissioned by Hendrik Van Reede; Carl Linnaeus's *Species Plantarum* (1753); the French *Jardin de Lorixa* or the Garden of Orissa (1698–1725), compiled by Nicolas L'Empereur; William Roxburgh's *Plants of the Coast of Coromandel* (1793); Robert Wight's *The Wight Collection* (1826–28); Alexander Gibson's *The Dapuri Collection* (1846–50); and Hugh Francis Clarke Cleghorn's *The Cleghorn Collection* (1845–47).

14 Molly Peacock, *The Paper Garden: An Artist (Begins Her Life's Work) at 72* (New York: Bloomsbury, 2011).

15 Louise K. Barnett, *Jonathan Swift in the Company of Women* (Oxford: Oxford University Press, 2007), 94.

16 Martha L. Crump and Michael J. Lannoo, *Women in Field Biology* (Boca Raton, FL: CRC Press, 2022).

# CHAPTER 5

1 Peter F. Stone, *Oriental Rugs: An Illustrated Lexicon of Motifs, Materials, and Origins* (Clarendon, VT: Tuttle, 2013).

2 Enza Milanesi, *The Carpet: Origins, Art and History* (London: Firefly Books, 1999).

3 Anne Leonard, *Arabesque without End: Across Music and the Arts, from Faust to Shahrazad* (London: Routledge, 2021).

4 Charles Montgomery Skinner, *Myths and Legends of Flowers, Trees, Fruits, and Plants, in All Ages and in All Climes* (New Haven, CT: Yale University Press, 1915), 35–36.

5 See Charles Pickering, *Chronological History of Plants* (Boston: Little, Brown, 1879).

6 Syeda Munazza Gilani and Kiran Shahid Siddiqui, "Acanthus Leaves in Gandhara Art: A Symbol or a Decorative Pattern," *Historicus Journal of the Pakistan Historical Society* 68, no. 3 (2020): 7–34.

7 Emily Byrne Curtis, *Chinese-Islamic Works of Art, 1644–1912* (London: Routledge, 2022); Zakaria Ali, *Malaysian Art* (Berkeley: University of California Press, 2010).

8 See J. Nigro Sansonese, *The Body of Myth: Mythology, Shamanic Trance, and the Sacred Geography of the Body* (Rochester, VT: Inner Traditions, 1994).

9 Fiona MacCarthy, *William Morris: A Life for Our Time* (London: Faber, 2010).

10 William Morris, *The Collected Works of William Morris* (Cambridge, UK: Cambridge University Press, 2012).

11 William Morris and Norman Kelvin, *The Collected Letters of William Morris* (Princeton, NJ: Princeton University Press, 1987).

12 Jenny Balfour-Paul, *Indigo: Egyptian Mummies to Blue Jeans* (Richmond Hill, ON: Firefly Books, 2012), 207–8.

13 See Lu Pu, *Chinese Indigo Batik Designs* (North Chelmsford, MA: Courier Corporation, 2012).

14 Jamieson Boyd Hurry and Warren Royal Dawson, *The Woad Plant and Its Dye* (Oxford: Oxford University Press, 1930), 257; Cennino Cennini and Daniel V. Thompson, *The Craftsman's Handbook: The Italian "Il Libro Dell'arte"* (New York: Dover, 2018).

15 Michel Pastoureau, *Blue: The History of a Color* (Princeton, NJ: Princeton University Press, 2001), 49, 64.

16 Hurry and Dawson, *The Woad Plant and Its Dye*, 54.

17 Balfour-Paul, *Indigo*, 259.

18 Prakash Kumar, *Indigo Plantations and Science in Colonial India* (Cambridge, UK: Cambridge University Press, 2012).

19 Alexander Kraft, "The History of Prussian Blue," in *Prussian Blue-Type Nanoparticles and Nanocomposites*, ed. Yannick Guari and Joulia Larionova (Dubai: Jenny Stanford, 2019), 1–26.

20 Alyssa Couture, *Healthy Fashion* (New York: John Hunt, 2021).

21 MacCarthy, *William Morris*.

22 David Roberts, *The Total Work of Art in European Modernism* (Ithaca, NY: Cornell University Press, 2011).

# CHAPTER 6

1 Sir Ghillean Prance and Mark Nesbitt, *The Cultural History of Plants* (London: Routledge, 2012), 205–8.

2 Bradley C. Bennett, "Doctrine of Signatures: An Explanation of Medicinal Plant Discovery or Dissemination of Knowledge?" *Economic Botany* 61, no. 3 (September 2007): 246–55.

3 Roderick Cave and British Library, *Impressions of Nature: A History of Nature Printing* (London: British Library, 2010).

4 Dioscorides Pedanius (of Anazarbos), *Dioscorides de Materia Medica: Being an Herbal*

*with Many Other Medicinal Materials,* trans. Tess Anne Osbaldeston and Robert P. A. Wood (Johannesburg: Ibidis, 2000).

5 Marco Navoni and Franco Buzzi, *Leonardo da Vinci and the Secrets of the Codex Atlanticus* (Vercelli, Italy: White Star, 2015).

6 Andrea DiNoto and David L. Winter, *The Pressed Plant: The Art of Botanical Specimens, Nature Prints, and Sun Prints* (New York: Abrams, 1999).

7 Leo Lemay, *The Life of Benjamin Franklin* (Philadelphia: University of Pennsylvania Press, 2006).

8 Richard Buckley Litchfield, *Tom Wedgwood, the First Photographer; an Account of His Life, His Discovery and His Friendship with Samuel Taylor Coleridge, Including the Letters of Coleridge to the Wedgwoods and an Examination of Accounts of Alleged Earlier Photographic Discoveries* (London: Duckworth and Co., 1903; repr., Palala Press, 2015).

9 Dan Leers and Larry J. Schaaf, eds., *William Henry Fox Talbot and the Promise of Photography* (Pittsburgh: Carnegie Museum of Art, 2017).

10 Peter Boyd, "Pteridomania: The Victorian Passion for Ferns," *Antique Collecting* 28, no. 6 (1993): 9–12, available at http://www.peterboyd.com/pteridomania.htm.

11 Li Zhou, "Orchidelirium, an Obsession with Orchids, Has Lasted for Centuries," *Smithsonian Magazine*, January 29, 2015, https://www.smithsonianmag.com/smithsonian-institution/orchidelirium-obsession-orchids-lasted-centuries-180954060/.

12 Kazumasa Ogawa, *Some Japanese Flowers: Photographs by Kazumasa Ogawa* (Los Angeles: Getty Trust Publications, 2013).

13 Bertrand Lavédrine et al., *The Lumière Autochrome: History, Technology, and Preservation* (Los Angeles: Getty Conservation Institute, 2013).

14 Lionel Nathan, *The Colours of Another Age* (London: Rothschild Archive, 2007), 14; "Photographing Flowers," *British Journal of Photography*, May 20, 1887, 484.

15 Colour Supplement, *British Journal of Photography*, July 7, 1922, 28.

16 Robert Hooke, *Micrographia or Some Physiological Descriptions of Minute Bodies* (New York: Cosimo Classics, 2007).

17 Derek Bousé, *Wildlife Films* (Philadelphia: University of Pennsylvania Press, 2011).

18 Max Long, "The Ciné-Biologists: Natural History Film and the Co-Production of Knowledge in Interwar Britain," *British Journal for the History of Science 53*, no. 4 (2020): 535.

## CHAPTER 7

1 Ann Temkin et al., *Claude Monet: Water Lilies* (New York: Museum of Modern Art, 2009).

2 See Gabriele Crepaldi, *The Impressionists* (New York: Collins, 2002).

3 Vivian Russell, *Monet's Water Lilies: The Inspiration of a Floating World* (London: Frances Lincoln, 2011).

4 Ross King, *Mad Enchantment: Claude Monet and the Painting of the Water Lilies* (New York and London: Bloomsbury, 2017).

5 Monet quoted by Katharine Lochnan in Lilly Greenblatt, "How Buddhism Inspired Monet's Masterpieces," *Lion's Roar*, December 2, 2016, https://www.lionsroar.com/how-buddhism-inspired-monets-masterpieces/.

6 Hilma af Klint et al., *Hilma af Klint: Notes and Methods* (Chicago: University of Chicago Press, 2018)

7 Rudolf Steiner, "The Plant-World and the Elemental Nature-Spirits," Lecture VII, November 2, 1923, in *Nature Spirits: Selected Lectures by Rudolf Steiner* (Forest Row, England: Rudolf Steiner Press, 2016), 109.

8 MoMA Press Release, *Steichen Delphiniums*, June 1936, MoMA Archives, https://www.moma.org/momaorg/shared/pdfs/docs/press_archives/331/releases/MOMA_1936_0027_1936-06-18_18636-17.pdf.

9 Christopher Dunn, *Brutality Garden: Tropicália and the Emergence of a Brazilian Counterculture* (Chapel Hill: University of North Carolina Press, 2002).

10 Elizabeth Mangini and Giuseppe Penone, *Seeing through Closed Eyelids: Giuseppe Penone and the Nature of Sculpture* (Toronto: University of Toronto Press, 2021).

11 Helen and Newton Harrison, "Portable Orchard, 1972–73," https://www.theharrisonstudio.net/portable-orchard-1972-73.

12 Johannes Stüttgen, *Joseph Beuys' 7000 Oaks: Portrait of an Art Performance* (Düsseldorf, Germany: Free International University, 1982).

13 Mel Chin et al., *Mel Chin: Rematch* (Ostfildern, Germany: Hatje Cantz, 2014).

14 See Sacha Kagan, *Culture and Sustainable Development in the City* (New York: Taylor & Francis, 2022).

15 See Andreco Studio, "Future Landscape," https://www.andreco.org/portfolio/future-landscape/.

16 Anaïs Tondeur and Michael Marder, *The Chernobyl Herbarium* (London: Open Humanities Press, 2020).

17 "Abel Rodríguez," *Documenta14.de*, 2010, https://www.documenta14.de/en/artists/13538/abel-rodriguez.

18 Alex Greenberger, "Artist Precious Okoyomon Brings Lush Flora and Live Butterflies to Venice Biennale," *ARTnews.com*, April 20, 2022, https://www.artnews.com/art-news/news/precious-okoyomon-venice-biennale-installation-1234625947/.

19 Michael Marder, *Plant-Thinking: A Philosophy of Vegetal Life* (New York: Columbia University Press, 2013); Michael Marder, *Grafts* (Minneapolis: University of Minnesota Press, 2016); Mancuso and Viola, *Brilliant Green*; Calvo, *Planta Sapiens*; Gagliano, *Thus Spoke the Plant*.

20 Lucy Cotter, "Plants as Other: Manuela Infante's *Estado Vegetal*," *Mousse*, May 17, 2019, https://www.moussemagazine.it/magazine/manuela-infante-lucy-cotter-2019/.

21 Diana Scherer artist website, https://dianascherer.nl.

22 Špela Petrič artist website, 2023, https://www.spelapetric.org/.

# LIST OF ILLUSTRATIONS

## CHAPTER 1

**Page 12**
Gian Lorenzo Bernini (Italian, 1598–1680), *Apollo and Daphne*, 1622–25. White Carrara marble, H: 243 cm (95⅝ in.). Rome, Galleria Borghese. Photo: Scala / Luciano Romano / Art Resource, NY

**Page 14**
K. Günther, Bay laurel or sweet bay tree, *Laurus nobilis*, 1887, in Hermann Adolph Köhler, *Köhler's Medicinal Plants* (Gera, Germany: Franz Eugen Köhler, 1914). Chromolithograph. St. Louis, Missouri Botanical Garden, Peter H. Raven Library, Rare Books Collection, QK99.A1 K63 1883–1914

**Page 15**
Illustration of Mayahuel (detail), in *Codex Ríos*, Italian, sixteenth century. Vatican City, Vatican Library, Vat.lat.3738, fol. 21v. Image © Biblioteca Apostolica Vaticana

**Page 16**
Abie Loy Kemarre (Australian Aboriginal, b. 1972), *Bush Medicine Leaves*, 2020. Acrylic on linen, 110 × 200 cm (43⅜ × 78¾ in.). © Abie Loy Kemarre, licensed by Aboriginal Artists Agency Ltd

**Page 20**
Circle of Gillis van Coninxloo (Flemish, 1544–1607), *Forest Scene*, ca. 1595–1610. Brush and gouache on toned paper on prepared paper, 54.6 × 42.1 cm (21½ × 16½ in.). Los Angeles, J. Paul Getty Museum, 87.GG.12

**Page 21**
Titian (Italian, ca. 1485/90?–1576), *Bacchus and Ariadne*, ca. 1520–30. Oil on canvas, 176.5 × 191 cm (69½ × 75⅛ in.). London, National Gallery, NG35. Photo: © The National Gallery, London

**Page 22**
Unknown artist, *The Ya-te-veo, or Man-Eating Plant*, 1887. In James William Buel (American, 1849–1920), *Sea and Land: An Illustrated History of the Wonderful and Curious Things of Nature Existing before and since the Deluge* (Philadelphia: Historical Publishing Company, 1887), p. 476. Storrs, University of Connecticut Libraries, QL50.B93 1887

**Page 23, top**
Carl Ludwig Friedrich Becker (German, 1820–1900), *Hypsipyle Finds Opheltes Killed by a Snake*, ca. 1850. Photograph of mural (since destroyed), 1943/1945. Munich, Germany, Zentralinstitut für Kunstgeschichte, München, Photothek, ZI0260_0042. Photo: Otto Cürlis

**Page 23, bottom**
Nicolas-René Jollain (French, 1739–1804), *Apollo and Hyacinthus*, ca. 1768–79. Oil on canvas, 95 × 130 cm (37⅜ × 51⅛ in.). France, Palace of Versailles, MV 8342. © RMN-Grand Palais / Art Resource, NY

**Page 24**
Maize god, Maya, ca. 715. Limestone, 89 × 56.5 × 30 cm (35 × 22¼ × 11⅞ in.). London, British Museum, Am1923,Maud.8. © The Trustees of the British Museum / Art Resource, NY

**Page 25**
Shakambhari, *Navaratri Grand Celebrations at Sri Parashakthi Temple*, Friday, October 4, 2013

**Page 26**
Kumashiro Yūhim (Japanese, 1712–1772/1773), *Xi Wangmu's Peaches of Immortality*, ca. 1750. Hanging scroll, 133.5 × 63.1 cm (52½ × 24⅞ in.). Japan, Kobe City Museum

**Page 27**
Unknown French artist (early sixteenth century), "Do Not Eat Beans," ca. 1512/1514. Pen and brown ink with watercolor on laid paper, 16.3 × 10.7 cm (6⅜ × 4¼ in.). Washington, DC, National Gallery of Art, Woodner Collection, gift of Andrea Woodner, 2006.11.45, fol. 25r. Photo: Courtesy National Gallery of Art, Washington

**Pages 28–29**
Salvador Dalí (Spanish, 1904–1989), *Metamorphosis of Narcissus*, 1937. Oil on canvas, 51.1 × 78.1 cm (51⅛ × 30¾ in.). London, Tate Gallery, T02343. © 2024 Salvador Dalí, Fundació Gala-Salvador Dalí, Artists Rights Society / © Tate, London / Art Resource, NY

**Page 29**
Maria Sibylla Merian (German, 1647–1717), *Cassava Root with Garden Tree Boa, Sphinx Moth and Treehopper*, 1705. In *Metamorphosis insectorum Surinamensium* (Amsterdam: Gerard Valck, 1705). Engraving. Washington, DC, Smithsonian Libraries and Archives, QL466.M57X

**Page 30**
Unknown artist and Rudolf von Ems (Austrian, ca. 1200–1252), *Abimelech Gathering Support; Jotham's Comparison; The Trees Choosing a King; Troops Lying Down under the Trees*, ca. 1400–1410. Tempera colors, gold, silver paint, and ink, leaf 33.5 × 23.5 cm (13⅛ × 9¼ in.). Los Angeles, J. Paul Getty Museum, Ms. 33 (88.MP.70), fol. 135v

**Page 31**
*Druids being converted to Christianity*, 1758. In David Hume (Scottish, 1711–1776) and Tobias Smollett (Scottish, 1721–1771), *Complete History of England*, 1758–60. Engraving. London, Middle Temple Library / Science Photo Library, C007/8547. Photo: British Library / Science Photo Library

**Pages 32–33**
Main panel at Crow Canyon Archaeological District, northwest New Mexico, sixteenth–eighteenth century. Petroglyphs. Photo: camerafiend, 2006, via commons.wikimedia.org / CC BY-SA 3.0

## CHAPTER 2

**Page 36**
Water lilies (possibly), Drysdale River, Balangarra Country (left); Wandjina-style water lily, King George River, Balanggarra Country (right), approximately 50,000 years old. Petroglyphs. In P. Veth et al., "Plants before Farming: The Deep History of Plant-Use and Representation in the Rock Art of Australia's Kimberley Region," *Quaternary International* (2016), http://dx.doi.org/10.1016/j.quaint.2016.08.036. Photos: Images courtesy Balanggarra Aboriginal Corporation and University of Western Australia's Centre for Rock Art Research + Management

**Page 37**
Fragmentary hieratic letter, Egyptian, ca. 1200–1085 BCE. Ink on papyrus, 32.4 × 21.9 cm (12¾ × 8⅝ in.). Malibu, California, J. Paul Getty Museum, Villa Collection, gift of Mr. and Mrs. H. P. Kraus, 83.AI.46.1

**Page 38**
Katsushika Hokusai (Japanese, 1760–1849), *The Invention of Paper, Publishing and Ink*, ca. 1820s–1840s. Ink on paper, preparatory drawing (*hanshita-e*) for an illustrated book, mounted on card, 10.5 x 15.2 cm (4⅛ × 6 in.), in the series Banmotsu ehon daizen zu (Illustrations for the Great Picture Book of Everything). The scene shows Ke Dao, Cai Lun, and Li Chao and his son Ting Zhi engaged in tasks associated with publishing (carving woodblocks,

making paper). London, British Museum, 2020,3015.55. Photo: © The Trustees of the British Museum / Art Resource, NY

**Page 39**
Walnut wood carving from Kashmir, nineteenth century. Sri Pratap Singh Museum, Srinagar, Kashmir, India. Photo: Ivan Vdovin / Alamy Stock Photo

**Page 41**
Aubert-Henri-Joseph Parent (French, 1753–1835), Carved relief, 1789. Limewood, 69.5 × 47.9 × 6 cm (27⅜ × 18⅞ × 2⅜ in.). Los Angeles, J. Paul Getty Museum, 84.SD.76

**Page 42**
Xochipilli, "God of Flowers," Aztec, ca. 1450–1500. Pigment on volcanic rock, 118 × 52 cm (46½ × 20½ in.). Mexico City, National Museum of Anthropology. Photo: flickr / Dennis Jarvis / CC BY-SA 2.0

**Page 43**
Yoruba Gelede mask, Republic of Benin, Anago Region, early twentieth century. Wood, pigment, H: 38 cm (15 in.). Private collection. Photo: Courtesy Pace African & Oceanic Art, New York

**Page 44**
Totem poles in Stanley Park, Vancouver, British Columbia, Canada, 2017. Photograph. Photo: flickr / Bob n Renee / CC BY 2.0

**Page 45**
Mummy portrait of a young woman, Romano-Egyptian, ca. 170–200 CE. Tempera on wood, 34.9 × 21.3 cm (13¾ × 8⅜ in.). Los Angeles, J. Paul Getty Museum, 81.AP.29

**Page 46**
Andrey Rublyov (Russian, ca. 1360–1430), *Trinity*, ca. 1411/1425–27. Tempera on wood, 142 × 114 cm (56 × 44⅞ in.). Moscow, Cathedral of Christ the Savior. Photo: The Artchives / Alamy Stock Photo

**Page 47**
Diego Velázquez (Spanish, 1599–1660), *Las Meninas*, 1656. Oil on canvas, 320.3 × 279.1 cm (126⅛ × 109⅞ in.). Madrid, Museo del Prado, P001174. Photo: © Museo Nacional del Prado / Art Resource, NY

**Page 50**
Adinkra cloth, Ashanti region, Ghana, ca. 1825. Cotton and dye, 271 × 212 cm (106⅝ × 83½ in.). Rotterdam, the Netherlands, Nationaal Museum van Wereldculturen, coll. no. RV-360-1700. Creative Commons, CC BY-SA 4.0 / Collection Nationaal Museum van Wereldculteren

**Page 51**
Attributed to Walipurru (member of the Milingimbi people, d. 1971), Milingimba, Crocodile Island, North Arnhem Land, Australia, Four human figures and a kangaroo, 1960s. Bark painting, 64.8 × 38.7 cm (25½ × 15¼ in.). Eugene, Oregon, Museum of Natural and Cultural History, cat. #6-39. © Estate of the artist, licensed by Aboriginal Artists Agency Ltd / Courtesy of University of Oregon Museum of Natural and Cultural History, photo by Steve Wilkinson

**Page 52**
Unknown Mbuti artist, Epulu, Ituri Forest, Democratic Republic of the Congo, Display cloth, 1955. Bark cloth, raffia cloth, and dye, 208.3 × 134.6 cm (82 × 53 in.). Washington, DC, National Museum of African Art, gift of Robert McGregor, 77-44-1. © Musée du quai Branly – Jacques Chirac, Dist. RMN-Grand Palais / Art Resource, NY / Photo: Michel Urtado / Thierry Ollivier

**Page 53**
Kalamkari, attributed to India, nineteenth century. Cotton textile, 201.9 × 129.5 cm (79½ × 51 in.). New York, Metropolitan Museum of Art, Rogers Fund, 1908, 08.108.3. Photo: www.metmuseum.org/CC0

**Page 54**
Luo Ping (Chinese, 1733–1799), *Landscapes, Flowers and Birds: Orchid*, 1780. Ink on paper, 22 × 27 cm (8⅝ × 10⅝ in.). Washington, DC, National Museum of Asian Art, F1980.112c. Photo: Luo Ping / National Museum of Asian Art, Smithsonian Institution, Freer Collection, Transfer from the United States Custom Service, Department of the Treasury

**Page 55**
Unknown Burmese artist, *Parabaik* illustrating scenes from the life of the Buddha, eighteenth century. Watercolor on paper. University of Oxford, Bodleian Libraries, MS. Burm. a. 12, folds 3–12. Photo: © Bodleian Library, University of Oxford

**Page 56**
*Eighteen Arhats (Lohans)*, Qing dynasty, China, 1644–1911. Ink and colors on eighteen Bodhi leaves, each 28 × 17.8 cm (11 × 7 in.). Asian Art Museum of San Francisco, The Avery Brundage Collection, B65D4.1–.18. Photo: © Asian Art Museum of San Francisco

**Page 57**
Johannes Vermeer (Dutch, 1632–1675), *Girl with a Wine Glass*, ca. 1658/59. Oil on canvas, 77.6 × 66.9 cm (30½ × 26⅜ in.). Braunschweig, Germany, Herzog Anton Ulrich-Museum, inv. GG 316. Photo: bpk Bildagentur / Herzog Anton Ulrich-Museum / Braunschweig / C. Cordes / Art Resource, NY

**Page 58**
Sculpture in the Osun-Osogbo Sacred Grove, Yoruba, n.d. Iron and mud, dimensions variable. UNESCO World Heritage Site. Osogbo, Nigeria. Photo: robertharding / Alamy Stock Photo / Michael Runkel

**Page 59**
Elephant and Ayyanar deities, Ilangudippatti village guardian temple near Pudukkottai, Tamil Nadu, India. Dimensions variable. Photo: imageBROKER.com GmbH & Co. KG / Alamy Stock Photo / Muthuraman V

## CHAPTER 3

**Page 62**
Unknown artist, *Narcissus*, Southern Song Dyansty, 1127–1279. Fan mounted as an album leaf; ink and color on silk, 23.8 × 24.4 cm (9⅜ × 9⅗ in.). New York, Metropolitan Museum of Art, John Stewart Kennedy Fund, 1913. 13.100.112. Photo: metmuseum.org

**Page 63**
Unknown Franco-Flemish artist, A Lion (Panther) and a Dragon, ca. 1277 or after, in Hugh of Fouilloy (French, ca. 1110–1173/1174) and William of Conches (French, ca. 1080–before 1154), *De Natura Avium; De Pastoribus et Ovibus; Bestiarium; Mirabilia Mundi; Philosophia Mundi; On the Soul*. Tempera colors and ink, 23.3 × 16.4 cm (9⅛ × 6½ in.). Los Angeles, J. Paul Getty Museum, Ms. Ludwig XV 4, 83.MR.174, fol. 93v

**Page 64**
*Salvia* (sage), *Coriandrum* (coriander), *Portulaca* (purslane), *Cerefolium* (chervil), *Sisimbrium* (water mint), *Oleastrum* (alexanders), *Lilium* (lily), *Tytimallum* (spurge), ca. 1070–1100, in copy of Pseudo-Apuleius, *Herbarium Apulei Platonici*. Colored drawings on parchment. University of Oxford, Bodleian Libraries, MS. Ashmole 1431, fols. 26v–27r. © Bodleian Library, University of Oxford

**Page 65**
Katsushika Hokusai (Japanese, 1760–1849), *Shennong in a coat of leaves with blades of rice in his mouth, seated on a rock, his* takara-no-tsuba (treasure jar) before him, ca. 1820s. Woodblock print. London, British Museum, 1906,1220,0.478. Photo: POL/BT / Alamy Stock Photo

**Page 66–67**
Unknown Northern Italian artist (Lombardy), Illustration in *Tractatus de Herbis*, ca. 1440. Parchment. London, British Library, MS. Sloane 4016, fols. 039v–039r. Photo: From the British Library archive / Bridgeman Images

**Page 68**
Martín de la Cruz (Mexican, active sixteenth century), translated by Juan Badiano (Mexican, 1484–1560), Illustration in *Libellus de Medicinalibus Indorum Herbis*, 1552. Mexico City, Mexican National Institute of Anthropology and History, fols. 38v–39r. Photo: Svintage Archive / Alamy Stock Photo

**Page 70**
Ḥunayn b. Isḥāq al-ʿIbādī, Abū Zayd and Stephanus b. Bāsīl, Illustration in *Kitāb al-Ḥašaʾiš fī hāyūlā al-ʿilāǧ al-ṭibbī*, ca. 847–861 CE. Arabic translation of Dioscorides's *De materia medica*. Originally translated from the Greek into Arabic by Ḥunayn b. Isḥāq al-ʿIbādī, Abū Zayd (810–873) with Stephanus b. Bāsīl between 847–861 CE. Leiden University Libraries, Or. 289, F011v-012r. Photo: Leiden University Libraries

**Page 71**
Gherardo Cibo (Italian, 1512–ca. 1600), *Plantain*, in *Extracts from Dioscorides's* De materia medica, ca. 1564–84. Watercolor and gouache on paper. London, British Library, Add MS 22333, fol. 050r. Photo: British Library / Science Photo Library



**Page 72**
Albrecht Dürer (German, 1471–1528), *The Great Piece of Turf*, 1503. Watercolor, 40.8 × 31.5 cm (16 × 12⅜ in.). Vienna, Albertina Museum, 3075. Photo: The Albertina Museum, Vienna

**Page 73**
Ustad Mansur (Indian, active ca. 1551–1630), *Red Tulip*, ca. 1620–21. Opaque watercolor, gold, ink, and paper, dimensions unknown. Photo: Harvard Fine Arts Library, Special Collections SCW2016.07911 / CC BY 4.0

**Page 74**
Hu Zhengyan (Chinese, ca. 1584–1674), *Red Bamboo*, 1663. Woodblock print, ink and color on paper, book: 24.8 × 28.6 cm (9 ¾ × 11¼ in.). The Huntington Library, Art Museum, and Botanical Gardens. Purchased with funds from June and Simon K. C. Li, Fong Liu, Mei-Lee Ney, and Anne and Jim Rothenberg, in honor of Steven S. Koblik, 2014.7.1.81. © Courtesy of the Huntington Art Museum, San Marino, California

**Page 75**
Guan Daosheng (Chinese, 1262–1319), *Bamboo and Stone*, Yuan Dynasty, ca. 1262–1319. Ink on paper, 87.1 × 28.7 cm (34.2 × 11.2 in.). Photo: Archivah / Alamy Stock Photo

**Page 78, top**
Hans Hoffmann (German, ca. 1545/1550–1591/1592), *A Hare in the Forest*, ca. 1585. Oil on panel, 62.2 × 78.4 cm (24½ × 30⅞ in.). Los Angeles, J. Paul Getty Museum, 2001.12

**Page 78, bottom**
Abraham Bloemaert (Dutch, 1564–1651), *Studies of a Marrow Plant and Cabbages*, ca. 1605–14. Ink, wash, and gouache, 24.8 × 36.8 cm (9¾ × 14½ in.). Los Angeles, J. Paul Getty Museum, 96.GA.332

**Page 79**
Otto Marseus van Schrick (Dutch, ca. 1619/1620–1678), *Forest Still Life with Great Morning Glory and Toad*, 1660. Oil on canvas, 53.7 × 68 cm (21⅛ × 26¾ in.). Germany, Staatliches Museum Schwerin, 2459, inv. G154. Photo: bpk Bildagentur / Staatliches Museum / Schwerin / Germany / Elke Walford / Art Resource, NY

**Pages 80–81**
Trompe l'oeil garden from the Villa Livia, Roman, ca. 40–20 BCE. Fresco, dimensions variable. Rome, Museo Nazionale Romano—Palazzo Massimo alle Terme. Photo: AGTravel / Alamy Stock Photo

**Page 82**
Unknown Byzantine artist, Illustration of the cottony blackberry plant (*Rubus tomentosus*), with roots, leaves, and fruits, ca. 512, in the *Vienna Dioscorides*. Parchment, 36 × 30 cm (14⅛ × 11⅞ in.). Vienna, Österreichische Nationalbibliothek, Codex Vindobonensis Med. gr. 1, fol. 83r. Photo: © ÖNB Vienna

**Page 83, left**
Bramble, ca. 1090–1100, in Pseudo-Apuleius, *Herbarium Apulei Platonici*. Parchment. University of Oxford, Bodleian Libraries, MS. Bodl. 130, fol. 26r. Photo: © Bodleian Library, University of Oxford

**Page 83, right**
Abū Jaʿfar al-Ghāfiqī (Andalusian, twelfth century). Illustration in *Kitāb fī al-adwiyah al-mufradah*, twelfth century. Thick wove Oriental paper. Montreal, McGill University Library. Photo: Courtesy of the Osler Library of the History of Medicine, McGill University Libraries

**Page 84**
Unknown Tibetan artist. Illustration in *Tibetan materia medica: A Selection of Substances Used for the Production of Medicine Based on the Teaching of the Four (Medical) Tantras*, twelfth century. London, Wellcome Collection. Photo: wellcomecollection.org / CC BY 4.0

**Page 85**
Mandrake (*Mandragora officinarum*), in *Tacuinum sanitatis in medicina*, ca. 1380–99. Parchment, 33.5 × 23 cm (13⅛ × 9 in.). Vienna, Österreichische Nationalbibliothek, Codex Vindobonensis ser. nov. 2644, fol. 40r

**Page 86**
Chikusai Kato (Japanese, active late nineteenth century), Illustration of *Ginkgo biloba*, 1878. Artwork on board made of ginkgo wood. Kew, England, Royal Botanic Gardens, Economic Botany Collection, 39979. Photo: © The Board of Trustees of the Royal Botanic Gardens, Kew

**Page 87**
Shin Saimdang (Korean, 1504–1551), *The Embroidered Grass and Insects*, ca. 1540. Embroidery on black satin, eighth panel of eight-panel folding screen, 65 × 320 cm (25$\frac{9}{16}$ × 126 in.). Collection of Dong-A University Seokdang Museum

**Page 88**
Bandolier (shoulder bag), Anishinaabe (Ojibwe) People, ca. 1880s. Plain weave cotton, twill weave wool, velvet, plaited wool binding, wool tassels, and glass beads, 107.3 × 33 cm (42¼ × 13 in.). The Cleveland Museum of Art, James Albert and Mary Gardiner Ford Memorial Fund, 1982.61. Photo: The Cleveland Museum of Art, CC0

**Page 89**
Kono Bairei (Japanese, 1844–1895), *Cannabis sativa*, in *Senshu no Hana (One Thousand Varieties of Flowers)*, Bunkyudo, Kyoto, 1900. Woodblock print. Photo: Album / Alamy Stock Photo

# CHAPTER 4

**Page 92**
Maria Sibylla Merian (German, 1647–1717), Branch of sweet orange tree (*Citrus sinensis*) with metamorphosis of *Rothschildia hesperus* moth, 1719. In *Metamorphosis insectorum Surinamensium* (Amsterdam: G. Valck, 1705). Transfer engraving, hand colored. Washington, DC, Smithsonian Libraries and Archives, QL466 .M57X. Photo: Penta Springs Limited / Alamy Stock Photo / Artokoloro

**Page 93**
Unknown Dutch artist, *Two tulips* (recto) and *One Tulip* (verso), ca. 1633–37 (recto shown). Watercolor and wash (drawing) and ink (inscriptions) on laid paper, 17.8 × 21.6 cm (7 × 8½ in.). Los Angeles, J. Paul Getty Museum, 2020.5

**Page 94**
Jan Brueghel the Younger (Flemish, 1601–1678), *Satire of Tulipmania*, 1640. Oil on panel, 31 × 49 cm (12¼ × 19¼ in.). Haarlem, the Netherlands, Frans Hals Museum, acquired with support from the Rembrandt Society. Photo: René Gerritsen

**Page 95**
Clara Peeters (Flemish, ca. 1594–before 1657), *Flowers in a Vase with a Nibbling Mouse*,

seventeenth century. Oil on wood, 26 × 20.9 cm ($10\frac{1}{4}$ × $8\frac{1}{4}$ in.). Antwerp, Belgium, Museum Mayer van den Bergh. Photo: Bart Huysmans / Michel Wuyts

**Page 96**
Giovanna Garzoni (Italian, 1600–1670), *Still Life with Bowl of Citrons*, late 1640s. Tempera on vellum, 27.6 × 35.6 cm ($10\frac{7}{8}$ × 14 in.). Los Angeles, J. Paul Getty Museum, 2001.29

**Page 97**
Fede Galizia (Italian, 1578–ca. 1630), *Pedestal Plate with Southern Fruit*, 1600–25. Oil on canvas, 49.5 × 66 cm ($19\frac{1}{2}$ × 26 in.). Warsaw, National Museum, M.Ob.2517

**Page 99**
Jan van Huysum (Dutch, 1682–1749), *Vase of Flowers*, 1722. Oil on panel, 80.3 × 61 cm ($31\frac{5}{8}$ × 24 in.). Los Angeles, J. Paul Getty Museum, 82.PB.70

**Page 100**
Raghunandan Sharma (Indian, active early twenty-first century) and artists from Nathdwara, *Kamal Kunj*, 2019–2020. Nathdwara pichwai painting on textile, H: 1,706.9 cm (672 in.). Mumbai, Nita Mukesh Ambani Cultural Centre, Art House. © Nita Mukesh Ambani Cultural Centre (NMACC)

**Page 101**
Panel, Pekalongan, Indonesia, ca. 1920s (detail). Cotton, 255.9 × 105.4 cm ($100\frac{3}{4}$ × $41\frac{1}{2}$ in.). New York, Metropolitan Museum of Art, gift of Delia Tyrwhitt, 1965, 65.38.1. Photo: robertharding / Alamy Stock Photo / Luca Tettoni

**Page 103**
Vishnupersaud (Indian, active early nineteenth century), *Potentilla fulgens*, ca. 1821. Drawing. Edinburgh, Royal Botanic Gardens, Wallich Collection. Photo: Lynsey Wilson, used with Permission of the Trustees, Royal Botanic Garden Edinburgh

**Page 106**
Pieter Withoos (Dutch, 1654–1692), *Purple Oleander*, 1691. Watercolor with applied gum on laid paper, 35.2 × 25.2 cm ($13\frac{7}{8}$ × $9\frac{15}{16}$ in.). Los Angeles, J. Paul Getty Museum, 2020.53

**Page 107, left**
Luca Forte (Italian [Neapolitan], ca. 1610/1615–ca. 1670), *Still Life with Grapes and Other Fruit*, 1630s. Oil on copper, 31.4 × 25.9 cm ($12\frac{3}{8}$ × $10\frac{3}{16}$ in.). Los Angeles, J. Paul Getty Museum, purchased with funds provided by the Disegno Group, 86.PC.517

**Page 107, right**
Jan van Huysum (Dutch, 1682–1749), *Fruit Piece*, 1722. Oil on panel, 80 × 61 cm ($31\frac{1}{2}$ × 24 in.). Los Angeles, J. Paul Getty Museum, 82.PB.71

**Page 108**
Louise Moillon (French, ca. 1610–ca. 1696), *Still Life with a Basket of Fruit and a Bunch of Asparagus*, 1630. Oil on panel, 53.3 × 71.3 cm (21 × $28\frac{1}{2}$ in.). Art Institute of Chicago, Wirt D. Walker Fund, 1948.78

**Page 109, left**
Philipp Otto Runge (German, 1777–1810), *Poppy*, ca. 1800–1803. Paper cutout affixed to paper, 25 × 10 cm ($9\frac{13}{16}$ × $3\frac{15}{16}$ in.). Los Angeles, J. Paul Getty Museum, purchased with funds provided by the Disegno Group, 2013.58

**Page 109, right**
Barbara Regina Dietzsch (German, 1706–1783), *Dandelion*, ca. 1755. Watercolor and gouache on vellum bordered in gold, 29 × 21 cm ($11\frac{7}{16}$ × $8\frac{1}{4}$ in.). Los Angeles, J. Paul Getty Museum, 2004.147

**Page 110**
Mary Delany (British, 1700–1788), *Paeonia tenuifolia*, 1778. Paper collage with bodycolor and watercolor on ink background, 34.1 × 22 cm ($13\frac{7}{16}$ × $8\frac{5}{8}$ in.). London, British Museum, 1897,0505.644. Photo: © The Trustees of the British Museum

**Page 111**
Marianne North (British, 1830–1890), *Nepenthes northiana, a Pitcher Plant from the Limestone Mountains of Sarawak, Borneo*, 1876. Oil on board, 50.4 × 34.8 cm ($19\frac{4}{5}$ × $13\frac{7}{10}$ in.). Kew, England, Royal Botanic Gardens, gift from the artist, MN561. Photo: © The Board of Trustees of the Royal Botanic Gardens, Kew

**Page 112**
Giuseppe Castiglione (Italian, 1688–1766), *Vase of Flowers*, eighteenth century. Ink on silk, 113.4 × 59.5 cm ($44\frac{3}{5}$ × $23\frac{1}{5}$ in.). Photo: The Picture Art Collection / Alamy Stock Photo

**Page 113**
Sheikh Zain al-Din (Indian, active late eighteenth century), Brahminy starling with two *Antheraea* moths, caterpillar, and cocoon on Indian jujube tree, 1777. Opaque colors and ink on paper, 76.2 × 96.5 cm (30 × 38 in.). Minneapolis Institute of Art, gift of Elizabeth and Willard Clark, 2018.53.4. Photo: Minneapolis Institute of Art (MIA)

**Pages 114–15**
Saitō Ippo (Japanese, active early nineteenth century), *Flowers of the Four Seasons*, early nineteenth century. Ink and colors on gold leaf, six-fold screen, 93.3 × 242 cm ($36\frac{3}{4}$ × $95\frac{1}{4}$ in.). Minneapolis Institute of Art, Gift of the Clark Center for Japanese Art & Culture, 013.29.3. Photo: Minneapolis Institute of Art (MIA)

**Page 115**
Utagawa Hiroshige (Japanese, 1842–1894), *Morning Glory and Oriental Greenfinch*, 1871–73, in the album *New Selection of Birds and Flowers*. Color woodcut on Japanese paper, 23.5 × 17.5 cm ($9\frac{1}{4}$ × $6\frac{7}{8}$ in.). Amsterdam, Van Gogh Museum, n0111-003V1962. Photo: Van Gogh Museum, Amsterdam (Vincent van Gogh Foundation)

**Page 116**
Marianne North (British, 1830–1890), *Flowers of Datura and Humming Birds, Brazil*, ca. 1873. Oil on board, 45 × 35 cm ($17\frac{7}{10}$ × $13\frac{7}{10}$ in.). Kew, England, Royal Botanic Gardens, gift from the artist, MN561. Photo: © The Board of Trustees of the Royal Botanic Gardens, Kew

**Page 117**
Johanna Helena Herolt (German, 1668–ca. 1723), *Maltese cross (*Lychnis chalcedonica*), Monkshood (*Aconitum napellus*), and insects*, date unknown. Watercolor and bodycolor on vellum, 37.1 × 30.2 cm ($14\frac{5}{8}$ × $11\frac{7}{8}$ in.). Upperville, Virginia, Oak Spring Garden Foundation

**Page 118**
F. Sansom Jr. (dates unknown), Garden balsam, (*Impatiens balsamina*), 1810, in *Curtis' Botanical Magazine*, vols. 31/32, plate 1256 (London and New York: Academic Press). Hand-colored copperplate engraving. Photo: Florilegius / Alamy Stock Photo

**Page 119**
Attributed to Kano Shôei (Japanese, 1519–1592), *Birds and Flowers*, late sixteenth century. Ink, color, gold leaf, and gold fleck on paper, unfolded overall 174.6 × 375.2 cm ($68\frac{3}{4}$ × $147\frac{11}{16}$ in.). New York, Brooklyn Museum, Gift of Dr. and Mrs. John Fleming, 83.183.1. Photo: Brooklyn Museum / CC BY-SA 3.0

## CHAPTER 5

**Page 122**
Isfahan carpet. Hand-knotted carpet, dimensions unknown. Photo: Massimo Pizzotti / Alamy Stock Photo

**Page 123**
Various artists, *Acanthus mollis*, in *Les dix livres d'Architecture de Vitruve, corrigez et traduits nouvellement en François, avec notes & de figures*, 1684. Printed book with woodcut illustrations and engraved plates and frontispiece, 44.2 × 30.7 × 4 cm ($17\frac{3}{8}$ × $12\frac{1}{16}$ × $1\frac{9}{16}$ in.). New York, Metropolitan Museum of Art, Bequest of W. Gedney Beatty, 1941, 41.100.388. Photo: metmuseum.org/CCO

**Page 124**
Buddha within acanthus-leaf

capital, Gandhara, ca. third or fourth century CE. Stucco, 23.9 × 38.9 × 13 cm (9 7/16 × 15 5/16 × 5 1/8 in.). Paris, Musée Guimet. Photo: © RMN-Grand Palais / Art Resource, NY / Mathieu Ravaux

**Page 125**
William Morris (British, 1834–1896), *Acanthus*, 1875. Block print in distemper colors on paper, 68 × 52.3 cm (26 3/4 × 20 5/8 in.). London, Victoria & Albert Museum, E.441-529-1919. Photo: Historia Graphica / Heritage Image Partnership Ltd / Alamy Stock Photo

**Page 126, left**
John Gerard (British, 1545–1612), *Potato of Virginia*, in *The Herball or, Generall Historie of Plantes* (London: E. Bollifant for B. & John Norton, 1597). Woodcut. London, Wellcome Collection

**Page 126, right**
John Gerard (British, 1545–1612), Title page, in *The Herball, or, Generall Historie of Plantes* (London: Adam Islip, Joice Norton and Richard Whitakers, 1633). Engraving. Washington, DC, Library of Congress, QK41 .G3 1633. Photo: Library of Congress, Rare Book and Special Collections Division

**Page 127**
William Morris (British, 1834–1896), Carpet, ca. 1881–83. Hand-knotted wool on cotton warps with jute bindings, 570.3 × 303.3 cm (224 1/2 × 119 7/16 in.). London, Victoria & Albert Museum, Bequeathed by Miss Aglaia Ionides, CIRC .458-1965. Photo: © Victoria and Albert Museum, London

**Page 128**
Unknown artist, *Isatis tinctoria* (common woad) and *Crambe maritima* (smooth sea caule), 1792, in Joshua Hamilton (British, active late eighteenth century), *Culpeper's English Family Physician*, vol. 3, plate 168 (London: W. Locke, 1792). Hand-colored copperplate engraving. London, Royal College of Physicians. Photo: Florilegius / Alamy Stock Photo

**Page 129**
Hendrik van Rheede tot Draakenstein (Dutch, 1637–1691), *Indigofera tinctoria*, 1678–79, in *Hortus Indicus Malabaricus*, vol. 1, fig. 54, ca. 1678–93. Copperplate engraving, 34 × 43 cm (13 3/8 × 16 15/16 in.). St. Louis, Missouri Botanical Garden, Peter H. Raven Library. Photo: Well/ BOT / Alamy Stock Photo

**Page 130, top**
Oscar Mallitte (British, ca. 1829–1905), *Cutting Indigo Plant in the Field and Loading Carts*, 1877. Albumen silver print, image 18.7 × 23.4 cm (7 3/8 × 9 3/16 in.), mount 27.8 × 44.2 cm (10 15/16 × 17 3/8 in.). Los Angeles, J. Paul Getty Museum, 84.XO.876.8.5

**Page 130, bottom**
Barry Lewis (British, b. 1948), *Dye Making in the City of Jaipur, Rajasthan, India*, 2018. Digital photograph. Photo: Barry Lewis / In Pictures via Getty Images

**Page 131**
Jean-Baptiste Chapuy (French, ca. 1760–1814), *Vue des 40. jours d'incendie des habitations de la plaine du Cap Français*, ca. 1791. Etching, color print, 64 × 94.5 cm (25 3/16 × 37 3/16 in.). Paris, Musée Carnavalet, G.29486. Photo: Paris Musées / Musée Carnavalet – Histoire de Paris, CC0

**Page 132**
Katsushika Hokusai (Japanese, 1760–1849), *Peonies and Canary*, ca. 1834. Woodblock print (*nishiki-e*), ink and color on paper, 25.4 × 18.7 cm (10 × 7 3/8 in.). Published by Nishimuraya Yohachi (Eijudō) (1760–1849). Minneapolis Institute of Art, bequest of Richard P. Gale, 74.1.205. Photo: Minneapolis Institute of Art (MIA)

**Page 133, top**
Frank Lloyd Wright (American, 1867–1959), Dana-Thomas House, Springfield, Illinois, 1902. Photograph showing the architect's geometric abstraction of the native prairie sumac, which is a prominent motif in the house. Photo: Courtesy of Doug Carr, Dana-Thomas House Foundation

**Page 133, bottom**
Frank Lloyd Wright (American, 1867–1959), Avery Coonley House, Riverside, Illinois, 1908–12. Photo: Anthony V. Thompson

**Pages 136–37**
Alessandro Magnasco (Italian, 1667–1749), *The Triumph of Venus*, ca. 1720–30. Oil on canvas, 118.1 × 148.6 cm (46 1/2 × 58 1/2 in.). Los Angeles, J. Paul Getty Museum, 78.PA.2

**Page 138**
Johannes Janson (Dutch, 1729–1784), *A Formal Garden*, 1766. Oil on canvas, 53.3 × 73 cm (21 × 28 3/4 in.). Los Angeles, J. Paul Getty Museum, 78.PA.202

**Page 139**
Leonardo da Vinci (Italy, 1452–1519), Sala delle Asse, ca. 1498. Fresco. Milan, Castello Sforzesco. Photo: Castello Sforzesco, Milan. © Comune di Milano, all rights reserved / Saporetti, ca. 1990

**Page 140**
Unknown artist, Paradise garden mural in the Augustine convent at Malinalco, Mexico, sixteenth century. Photo: Album / Alamy Stock Photo

**Page 141**
Wat Arun temple, Bangkok, likely before 1656 (main prang completed in 1851). Porcelain tile. Photo: Parichart Thongmee / Alamy Stock Photo

**Page 142**
Rayonnant Gothic rose window (north transept), Notre-Dame de Paris Cathedral, Paris, ca. 1250. Stained glass. Photo: Julia Anne Workman / CC BY-SA 3.0

**Page 143**
Hector Guimard (French, 1867–1942), Gate of Castel Béranger, Paris, 1895/1898. Dressed stone, millstone, red brick, glazed brick, ironwork, ornamental cast iron, and architectural ceramics. Photo: B. O'Kane / Alamy Stock Photo

**Page 144**
After designs by Alexandre-François Desportes (French, 1661–1743), Savonnerie Manufactory (French, active 1627–present), Four-Panel Screen (Paravent), knotted between 1719–84. Wool, linen, wood frame, modern cotton-twill gimp, modern silk velvet, modern brass nails, 185.4 × 254 cm (73 × 100 in.). Los Angeles, J. Paul Getty Museum, 75.DD.1

**Page 145**
Savonnerie Manufactory (French, active 1627–present), after cartoons by Jean-Baptiste Belin de Fontenay (French, 1653–1715) and Alexandre-François Desportes (French, 1661–1743), Three-Panel Screen (Paravent), ca. 1714–40. Wool, linen, cotton-twill gimp, wooden interior frame, modern velvet lining, object (overall): 273.6 × 194.2 cm (107 11/16 × 76 7/16 in.). Los Angeles, J. Paul Getty Museum, 83.DD.260

## CHAPTER 6

**Page 149**
Leonardo da Vinci (Italian, 1452–1519), Nature printing of a leaf of *Salvia*, ca. 1500, in *Codex Atlanticus*, 64.5 × 43.5 cm (25 3/8 × 17 1/8 in.). Milan, Biblioteca Ambrosiana, Cod. atl., fol. 197v. Photo: © Veneranda Biblioteca Ambrosiana / Metis e Mida Informatica / Mondadori Portfolio / Codice Atlantico

**Page 150**
Benjamin Franklin (American, 1706–1790), Nature-printed American currency, 1779. From Hall and Sellers, printed front and back. 1779 uncut continental currency. Printed in Philadelphia, Hall and Sellers. Reproduced from the original held by the Department of Special Collections of the Hesburgh Libraries of Notre Dame

**Page 151**
William Henry Fox Talbot (British, 1800–1877), Botanical Specimen, 1840. Direct positive photogenic drawing, 17.8 × 11.1 cm (7 × 4 3/8 in.). Los Angeles, J. Paul Getty Museum, 85.XM.150.12

**Page 152**
Anna Atkins (British, 1799–1871), *Laurencia pinnatifida*, 1846–47. Cyanotype, 26.4 × 21 cm (10⅜ × 8¼ in.). Los Angeles, J. Paul Getty Museum, 84.XA.1107.6

**Page 153**
Artist unknown, Wardian case with plants, 1856. Engraving. Photo: Chronicle / Alamy Stock Photo

**Page 154**
Kazumasa Ogawa (Japanese, 1860–1929), *Group of Azaleas*, 1896. Colored collotypes, closed book 39.2 × 28.3 × 1.6 cm ($15\frac{7}{16}$ × 11⅛ × ⅝ in.). Los Angeles, J. Paul Getty Museum, 84.XB.759.6.13

**Page 158**
Ernestine Eberhardt Zaumseil (American, 1828–1904), *Branches and Vines*, ca. 1875. Cotton, silk, and wool quilt, 223.5 × 218.4 cm (88 × 86 in.). New York, Metropolitan Museum of Art, Gift of George E. Schoellkopf, 2013.958. Photo: metmuseum.org/CC0

**Page 159, left**
William Henry Fox Talbot (British, 1800–1877), *Erica mutabilis*, March 1839. Photogenic drawing negative, salt fixed, 14 × 6.8 cm (5½ × $2\frac{11}{16}$ in.). Los Angeles, J. Paul Getty Museum, 85.XM.150.13

**Page 159, right**
Sir John Frederick William Herschel (British, 1792–1871), *Ravine in the Simplon Opposite Isella*, September 1, 1821. Graphite drawing made with the aid of a camera lucida, 29.7 × 20.5 cm ($11\frac{11}{16}$ × $8\frac{1}{16}$ in.). Los Angeles, J. Paul Getty Museum, Gift of the Graham and Susan Nash Collection, 91.GG.98.48

**Page 160**
Claude Monet (French, 1840–1926), *Still Life with Flowers and Fruit*, 1869. Oil on canvas, 100.3 × 81.3 cm (39½ × 32 in.). Los Angeles, J. Paul Getty Museum, 83.PA.215

**Page 161**
Gustave Courbet (French, 1819–1877), *Bouquet of Flowers in a Vase*, 1862. Oil on canvas, 100.3 × 73.3 cm (39½ × 28⅞ in.). Los Angeles, J. Paul Getty Museum, 85.PA.168

**Page 162**
Vincent van Gogh (Dutch, 1853–1890), *Irises*, 1889. Oil on canvas, 74.3 × 94.3 cm (29¼ × 37⅛ in.). Los Angeles, J. Paul Getty Museum, 90.PA.20

**Page 163**
Paul Cézanne (French, 1839–1906), *Still Life with Apples*, 1893–94. Oil on canvas, 65.4 × 81.6 cm (25¾ × 32⅛ in.). Los Angeles, J. Paul Getty Museum, 96.PA.8

**Page 164**
Unknown photographer, Henri Matisse in his studio, Hotel Regina, Nice, 1948. New York, The Morgan Library & Museum, Pierre Matisse Gallery Archives, MA 5020: 212.48, Department of Literary and Historical Manuscripts. Photo: The Morgan Library & Museum, New York

**Page 165**
Henri Matisse (French, 1869–1954), *La Gerbe*, 1953. Ceramic tile embedded in plaster, 274.3 × 396.2 cm (108 × 156 in.). Los Angeles County Museum of Art, Gift of Frances L. Brody in honor of the museum's twenty-fifth anniversary, M.2010.1. Digital image © 2024 Museum Associates / LACMA / Licensed by Art Resource, NY. © 2024 Succession H. Matisse / Artists Rights Society (ARS), New York

**Page 166**
Possibly Frances Elizabeth Jocelyn, Viscountess Jocelyn (British, 1820–1880), *Sandringham*, ca. 1850–60. Albumen silver print, 7.9 × 7.5 cm (3⅛ × $2\frac{15}{16}$ in.). Los Angeles, J. Paul Getty Museum, 84.XA.876.2.34

**Page 167**
Arnold Eagle (American, 1909–1992), *Three men stand in a greenhouse*, ca. 1940–42. Gelatin silver print, 33.6 × 26.3 cm (13¼ × 10⅜ in.). Los Angeles, J. Paul Getty Museum, 84.XB.204.68

**Page 168**
Karl Blossfeldt (German, 1865–1932), *Thistle* (*Dipsacus lacinatus*), plate from *Urformen der Kunst I*, 1928. Pigment prints, each page 40 × 28.9 cm (15¾ × 11⅜ in.). Photo: Courtesy Robert Klein Gallery

**Page 169**
J. D. Möller (German, 1844–1907), Diatom arrangement, ca. 1870–90. Glass slide. Belgium, Meise Botanic Garden. Photo: Courtesy of Jef Schoors

**Page 170**
Ansel Adams (American, 1902–1984), *Oak Tree, Snowstorm, Yosemite National Park, California*, negative 1948, print 1981. Gelatin silver print, 49.8 × 39.1 cm (19⅝ × 15⅜ in.). Los Angeles, J. Paul Getty Museum, 2011.83.18. © The Ansel Adams Publishing Rights Trust

**Page 171**
Ansel Adams (American, 1902–1984), *Redwoods, Bull Creek Flat, Northern California*, negative ca. 1960, print 1980. Gelatin silver print, 38.7 × 48.6 cm (15¼ × 19⅛ in.). Los Angeles, J. Paul Getty Museum, gift of Carol Vernon and Robert Turbin in Memory of Marjorie and Leonard Vernon, 2011.83.22. © The Ansel Adams Publishing Rights Trust

**Page 172**
Graciela Iturbide (Mexican, b. 1942), *Sahuaro* [Saguaro], *Los Seris, Desierto y Mar, Estado de Sonora, México*, negative 1979, print later. Gelatin silver print, 25.5 × 30 cm ($10\frac{1}{16}$ × $11\frac{13}{16}$ in.). Los Angeles, J. Paul Getty Museum, gift of Susan Steinhauser and Daniel Greenberg, 2007.65.41. © Graciela Iturbide

**Page 173**
Jacques-Henri Lartigue (French, 1894–1986), *Field of Poppies*, ca. 1960–78. Chromogenic print, 29.5 × 39.7 cm (11⅝ × 15⅝ in.). Los Angeles, J. Paul Getty Museum, 84.XP.463.16. Photo: Jacques-Henri Lartigue / © Ministère de la Culture – France / AAJHL

## CHAPTER 7

**Page 176**
Photographer unknown, Claude Monet in the garden of his home at Giverny, France, April 10, 1905. Photo: Chronicle / Alamy Stock Photo

**Page 178**
Hilma af Klint (Swedish, 1862–1944), *Group IV, The Ten Largest, No. 2, Childhood*, 1907. Tempera on paper mounted on canvas, 315 × 234 cm (124 × 92⅛ in.). Stockholm, the Hilma af Klint Foundation, HaK 103. Photo: Courtesy of The Hilma af Klint Foundation

**Page 179**
Hilma af Klint (Swedish, 1862–1944), *The W Series, Tree of Knowledge, No. 1*, 1913. Watercolor, gouache, graphite, metallic paint, and ink on paper, 45.7 × 29.5 cm (18 × 11⅗ in.). Stockholm, the Hilma af Klint Foundation. Photo: Courtesy of The Hilma af Klint Foundation

**Pages 180–81**
Installation view of the exhibition *Edward Steichen's Delphiniums*, Museum of Modern Art, New York, June 1936. Gelatin silver print, 18.1 × 33.8 cm (7⅛ × $13\frac{5}{16}$ in.). Los Angeles, J. Paul Getty Museum, 84.XP.459.15. © 2024 The Estate of Edward Steichen / Artists Rights Society (ARS), New York

**Page 182**
Installation view of *Hélio Oiticica: To Organize Delirium*, Art Institute of Chicago, 2017, showing Hélio Oiticica (Brazilian, 1937–1980), *Tropicália*, 1966–67. Sand, plants, birds, and poems by Roberta Camila Salgado, dimensions variable. © César and Claudio Oiticica / Courtesy Projecto Hélio Oiticica and Lisson Gallery / Photo: The Art Institute of Chicago / Art Resource, NY

**Page 183, top**
Joseph Kosuth (American,

b. 1945), *One and Three Plants*, 1965. Cardboard, photograph, and plant (cactus), dimensions variable. © Joseph Kosuth / Artists Rights Society (ARS), New York / Image courtesy of the artist and Sean Kelly Gallery

**Page 183, bottom**
Newton Harrison (American, 1932–2022) and Helen Mayer Harrison (American, 1929–2018), Installation view of *Portable Orchard*, Walker Art Center, Minneapolis, 1972–73. Mixed media, dimensions variable. © Harrison Family / Photo: Courtesy of the Helen and Newton Harrison Family Trust / Gene Pittman for Walker Art Center

**Page 184**
Dieter Schwerdtle (German, 1952–2009), Joseph Beuys plants the first tree at the edge of Friedrichsplatz in front of the Museum Fridericianum (Kassel, Germany) as part of his project *7000 Oaks*, March 3, 1982. Photograph, 23.4 cm × 16.8 cm ($9\frac{1}{4} \times 6\frac{5}{8}$ in.). Kassel, Germany, Documenta Archiv, MS, d07, dA_DSchwerdtle_607. © 2024 Artists Rights Society (ARS), New York / VG Bild-Kunst, Bonn. / © documenta archiv / Photo: Dieter Schwerdtle

**Page 185**
Agnes Denes (American, b. 1938) pictured with her work *Wheatfield — A Confrontation: Battery Park Landfill*, downtown Manhattan, 1982. Photograph. © Agnes Denes. Photo: John McGrail, Courtesy Agnes Denes and Leslie Tonkonow Artworks + Projects

**Page 186, left**
Anaïs Tondeur (French, b. 1985), *Linum strictum, Exclusion Zone, Chernobyl, Radiation level: 1.7 μSv/h*, 2011–ongoing. Pigment print on rag paper, 36 × 24 cm ($14\frac{3}{16} \times 9\frac{7}{16}$ in.). Chernobyl, Ukraine. © Anaïs Tondeur

**Page 186, right**
Anaïs Tondeur (French, b. 1985), *Geranium chinum, Exclusion Zone, Chernobyl, Radiation level: 1.7 μSv/h*, 2011–ongoing. Pigment print on rag paper, 36 × 24 cm ($14\frac{3}{16} \times 9\frac{7}{16}$ in.). Chernobyl, Ukraine. © Anaïs Tondeur

**Page 187**
Abel Rodríguez (Colombian, b. 1941), *Terraza Alta II*, 2018. Ink on paper, 50 × 70 cm ($19\frac{11}{16} \times 27\frac{9}{16}$ in.). © Abel Rodriguez (Mogaje Guihu) / Image courtesy of the artist and Instituto de Visión / Photo: Maria Paula Bastidas

**Page 188**
Precious Okoyomon (Nigerian American, b. 1993), Installation view of *To See the Earth before the End of the World*, Venice Biennale, 2022. Mixed media, dimensions variable. © Precious Okoyomon / Photo: Clelia Cadamuro, courtesy of La Biennale di Venezia

**Page 189, left**
Manuela Infante, *Estado Vegetal*, 2019. Still from performance. © Manuela Infante / Photo: Isabel Ortiz

**Page 189, right**
Špela Petrič (Slovenian, b. 1980), *Pl'ai*, 2020. Plants and AI robot. © Špela Petrič / Photo: Hana Marn

**Page 192**
Rashid Johnson (American, b. 1977), Installation view of *Rashid Johnson: Fly Away*, Hauser & Wirth, New York, 2016. Black steel, grow lights, plants, wood, shea butter, books, monitors, rugs, and piano, dimensions variable. © Rashid Johnson / Courtesy the artist and Hauser & Wirth / Photo: Martin Parsekian

**Page 193**
Mona Caron (American, active 1998–present), *Shauquethqueat's Eutrochium*, 2021. Mural, 65.8 × 33.8 m (216 × 111 ft.). Jersey City, New Jersey, commissioned by the Jersey City Mural Arts Program, of the City of Jersey City's Office of Cultural Affairs, with additional support by Namdar Group. © Mona Caron / Photo: Mona Caron

**Pages 194–95**
Zachari Logan (Canadian, b. 1980), *Eunuch Tapestry 5*, 2015. Pastel on eight sheets of black wove paper, installation 213.3 × 731.5 cm (84 × 288 in.). Ottawa, National Gallery of Canada, 47546. © Zachari Logan / Photo: Courtesy of the artist

**Page 196**
Myoung Ho Lee (South Korean, b. 1975), *Tree #3*, negative 2006, printed 2009. Inkjet print, 40 × 32 cm ($15\frac{3}{4} \times 12\frac{5}{8}$ in.). Los Angeles, J. Paul Getty Museum, purchased with funds provided by the Photographs Council, 2009.97.2. © Myoung Ho Lee / Courtesy Yossi Milo Gallery, New York

**Page 197**
Chip Thomas (American, active 1987–present), *Corn Portrait*, January 2019. Screenprint, 28 × 43 cm (11 × 17 in.). © jetsonorama

**Page 198**
Sara Angelucci (Canadian, b. 1962), *Nocturnal Botanical Ontario* (showing bladder campion, teasel, bindweed, vetch, daisy fleabane, aster), July 30, 2021. Inkjet print, 85.3 × 118.8 cm ($33\frac{1}{2} \times 46\frac{4}{5}$ in.). © Sara Angelucci / Courtesy of Stephen Bulger Gallery

**Page 199**
Robert Mapplethorpe (American, 1946–1989), *Poppy*, 1988. Dye imbibition print, 50.3 × 47.5 cm ($19\frac{13}{16} \times 18\frac{11}{16}$ in.). Los Angeles, J. Paul Getty Museum, 2011.9.39. © Robert Mapplethorpe Foundation. Used by permission

**Page 200**
Wolfgang Tillmans (German, b. 1968), *Osterwaldstrasse*, 2011. Inkjet print on aluminum in artist's frame, 87 × 70.3 cm ($32\frac{1}{5} \times 27\frac{7}{10}$ in.). Riehen/Basel, Fondation Beyeler, Inv.FB.14.24. © Wolfgang Tillmans / Photo: Robert Bayer

**Page 201**
Christi Belcourt (Canadian, b. 1966), *The Wisdom of the Universe*, 2014. Acrylic on canvas, 171 × 282 cm ($67\frac{5}{16} \times 111$ in.). Art Gallery of Ontario, purchased with funds donated by Greg Latremoille, 2014/6. © Christi Belcourt / Photo: AGO

**Page 202**
Graciela Iturbide (Mexican, b. 1942), *Jardines botánicos, Oaxaca*, 1996–2004. Chromogenic print, 76.2 × 76.2 cm (30 × 30 in.). Los Angeles, J. Paul Getty Museum, Gift of the artist and Rose Gallery, 2007.24.8. © Graciela Iturbide

**Page 203, top**
William Eggleston (American, b. 1939), *Undergrowth and Succulents*, 1980. Chromogenic print, 22.2 × 32.9 cm ($8\frac{3}{4} \times 12\frac{15}{16}$ in.). Los Angeles, J. Paul Getty Museum, gift of Caldecot Chubb, 2001.90.154. © Eggleston Artistic Trust

**Page 203, bottom**
Issei Suda (Japanese, 1940–2019), *Koishikawa Botanical Gardens, Bunkyo-ku*, 1982. Gelatin silver print, 22 × 21.4 cm ($8\frac{11}{16} \times 8\frac{7}{16}$ in.). Los Angeles, J. Paul Getty Museum, 2008.51.8. © SUDA ISSEI Works

**Page 204**
Maria Thereza Alves (Brazilian, b. 1961), Installation view of *Wake in Guangzhou: The History of the Earth*, 2008, in the exhibition *The Way Things Go: A Special Curatorial Project with Rirkrit Tiravanija*, Yerba Buena Center for the Arts, San Francisco, 2015. Mixed media, dimensions variable. © Maria Thereza Alves / Photo: John Foster Cartwright, courtesy of Yerba Buena Center for the Arts, San Francisco

**Page 205**
Cecilia Vicuña (Chilean, b. 1948), Installation view of *Brain Forest Quipu*, Hyundai Commission 2022, Turbine Hall, Tate Modern, London, 2022–23. Plant matter, wool, and other mixed media, dimensions variable. © 2024 Cecilia Vicuña / Artists Rights Society (ARTS), New York. Courtesy of the artist and Lehmann Maupin, New York, Hong Kong, Seoul, and London / Photo: © Tate (Matt Greenwood) 2022

# INDEX

## D



## E



## F



## G



## H

# ACKNOWLEDGMENTS

First and foremost, I'd like to thank the plants in my garden. It has been in their company, summer after summer, that this book has come to life. I have a special writing place nestled among the towering elephant ears and cannas, where I prop my chair and table, surrounded by the plants that have brought so much joy and meaning to my life since I was a child in the south of Italy. It was important to me that this book should be written next to them; that every time I raised my eyes away from the computer screen or someone else's book, I could see them; that their stoicism, determinacy, and wholesomeness could ground every one of sentences into some kind of vegetal dignity or pride. Thank you, my dear companions, for sticking with me through thick and thin and teaching me what truly matters in life. This book would not have been feasible without your contributions, both conceptually and materially.

My thanks also go to the several plant-loving friends, students, and colleagues who have reminded me at every turn, over the last four years, that loving plants entails cultivating knowledge, wisdom, diversity, and empathy. Your voices have filled the silence of plants with important lessons, observations and considerations that in one way or another have radically shaped my perspectives on vegetal relations. In no order or ranking: Paul Moss, Manuela Infante, Prudence Gibson, Tessa Laird, Mandy-Suzanne Wong, and Randy Malamud, the students who took my Botanical Revolutions class at SAIC between 2021 and 2024; D. Denenge Duyst-Akpem, Michael Marder, Diana Scherer, Anicka Yi, Jenny Kendler, Zachari Logan, Linda Tegg, Lynn Turner, Maria Thereza Alves, Cecilia Vicuña, Sara Angelucci, Anaïs Tondeur, Uriel Orlow, Alessandra Viola, Annie Freud, Harry Smith, and David Goyder; Anna Haigh at Kew Botanical Gardens, London; and Yota Batsaki and Anatole Tchikine at Dumbarton Oaks, Washington, DC. Heartfelt thanks to my manuscript reviewers, whose constructive criticism strengthened the book's narrative. Many thanks also to the dedicated editorial, design, rights, and production teams at Getty Publications for their support and determination: Ruth Evans Lane and Rachel Barth, Dani Grossman, Victoria Gallina, Danielle Brink, Kate Justement, Lindsey Westbrook, Anne Canright, Jane Friedman, Diana Murphy, Nola Butler, Clare Davis, Kara Kirk, and Karen Levine.

Finally, thanks to my wonderful partner, Chris Hunter, for providing critical insights and never-ending support, and for tirelessly helping me to haul roughly two hundred potted plants into our basement every October. I know our knees will give in well before our enthusiasm for plants might even begin to quaver.

# ABOUT THE AUTHOR

Dr. Giovanni Aloi is an author, educator, and curator specializing in the representation of nature and the environment in art. He is the editor in chief of *Antennae: The Journal of Nature in Visual Culture*. Aloi is the author of *Art & Animals* (2011), *Speculative Taxidermy: Natural History, Animal Surfaces, and Art in the Anthropocene* (2018), *Why Look at Plants? The Vegetal Emergence in Contemporary Art* (2019), *Lucian Freud—Herbarium* (2019), and the editor of *Posthumanism in Art and Science* (2020), *Vegetal Entwinements in Philosophy and Art* (2023), *Estado Vegetal: Performance and Plant-Thinking* (2023), *I'm Not an Artist: Reclaiming Creativity in the Age of Infinite Content* (2025), and *Lawn* (2025). Aloi has contributed to BBC Radio and PBS TV, worked at Whitechapel Art Gallery and Tate Galleries in London, and currently is USA correspondent for *Esse Magazine*. He has curated exhibitions in the US and Europe and is co-editor of the University of Minnesota Press series Art after Nature.

© 2025 J. Paul Getty Trust
Text © Giovanni Aloi

**Published by Getty Publications, Los Angeles**
1200 Getty Center Drive, Suite 500
Los Angeles, CA 90049-1682
getty.edu/publications

Rachel Barth and Ruth Evans Lane with Kate Justement, *Project Editors*
Lindsey Westbrook, *Manuscript Editor*
Dani Grossman, *Designer*
Victoria Gallina, *Production*
Danielle Brink and Pauline Lopez, *Image and Rights Acquisition*

Distributed in the United States and Canada by the University of Chicago Press
Distributed outside the United States and Canada by Yale University Press, London

Printed in China

Library of Congress Cataloging-in-Publication Data
Names: Aloi, Giovanni, author.
Title: Botanical revolutions : how plants changed the course of art / Giovanni Aloi.
Description: Los Angeles : Getty Publications, [2025] | Includes bibliographical references and index. | Summary: "This lush volume unearths plants' representation in and impact on art, advocating for the botanical world's rightful place in art history"—Provided by publisher.
Identifiers: LCCN 2024032837 (print) | LCCN 2024032838 (ebook) | ISBN 9781606069479 (hardback) | ISBN 9781606069486 (adobe pdf)
Subjects: LCSH: Plants in art. | Botany in art. | Botanical illustration. | Plants—Symbolic aspects. | Art—History.
Classification: LCC N7680 .A49 2025 (print) | LCC N7680 (ebook) | DDC 704.9/434—dc23/eng/20240821
LC record available at https://lccn.loc.gov/2024032837
LC ebook record available at https://lccn.loc.gov/2024032838

The complete manuscript of this work was peer reviewed through a single-masked process in which the reviewers remained anonymous.

Illustration Credits
Every effort has been made to contact the owners and photographers of illustrations reproduced here whose names do not appear in the captions or in the illustration credits listed at the back of this book. Anyone having further information concerning copyright holders is asked to contact Getty Publications so this information can be included in future printings.

Notes on the Type
The book's body text is set in the 2010 revival of Neue Haas Grotesk, designed by Christian Schwartz. The display type in this book is set in Mānuka, designed by Kris Sowersby of Klim Type Foundry in 2021. Sowersby describes Mānuka as "new growth from old wood," a reference to moveable wood type, a predominant production method of the 1800s from which the font's design originated. The designer writes, "Tight spacing, closed apertures, and sharp joins make a compelling texture, like sunlight sparkling through a forest canopy. Vertical slivers of light shimmering amongst acute arcs planted the roots for Mānuka." To read more about Mānuka, visit www.klim.co.nz/blog/manuka-design-information.

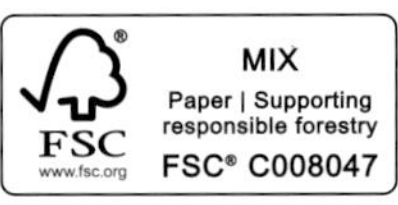


Front cover, inside letters: **B:** Possibly Frances Elizabeth Jocelyn, *Sandringham*, ca. 1850–60 (detail, page 166); **O:** Jan van Huysum, *Fruit Piece*, 1722 (detail, page 107); **T:** Hans Hoffmann, *A Hare in the Forest*, ca. 1585 (detail, page 78); **A:** After designs by Alexandre-François Desportes, Savonerrie Manufactory, Four-Panel Screen (Paravent), knotted 1719–84 (detail, page 144); **N:** Abraham Bloemaert, *Studies of a Marrow Plant and Cabbages*, ca. 1605–14; **I:** Unknown artist and Rudolf von Ems, *Abimelech Gathering Support; Jotham's Comparison; The Trees Choosing a King; Troops Lying Down Under the Trees*, ca. 1400–1410 (detail, page 30); **C:** Jan van Huysum, *Vase of Flowers*, 1722 (detail, page 99); **A:** Barbara Regina Dietzsch, *Dandelion*, ca. 1755 (detail, page 109); **L:** Arnold Eagle, *Three men stand in a greenhouse*, ca. 1940–42 (detail, page 167); **R:** Gustave Courbet, *Bouquet of Flowers in a Vase*, 1862 (detail, page 161); **E:** Johannes Janson, *A Formal Garden*, 1766 (detail, page 138); **V:** Aubert-Henri-Joseph Parent, Carved relief, 1789 (detail. page 41); **O:** Alessandro Magnasco, *The Triumph of Venus*, ca. 1720–30 (detail, page 136); **L:** Claude Monet, *Still Life with Flowers and Fruit*, 1869 (detail, page 160); **U:** Jan van Huysum, *Vase of Flowers*, 1722 (detail, page 99); **T:** Jan van Huysum, *Fruit Piece*, 1722 (detail, page 107); **I:** Pieter Withoos, *Purple Oleander*, 1691 (detail, page 106); **O:** Johannes Janson, *A Formal Garden*, 1766 (detail, page 138); **N:** Circle of Gillis van Coninxloo, *Forest Scene*, ca. 1595–1610 (detail, page 20); **S:** William Henry Fox Talbot, Botanical Specimen, 1840 (detail. page 151)
Pages 1–2: Jan van Huysum, *Fruit Piece*, 1772 (detail, page 107); pages 9–10: Nicolas-René Jollain, *Apollo and Hyacinthus*, ca. 1768–79 (detail, page 23); pages 18–19: Circle of Gillis van Coninxloo, *Forest Scene*, ca. 1595–1610 (detail, page 20); pages 34–35: *Eighteen Arhats (Lohans)*, Qing Dynasty, 1644–1911 (detail, page 56); pages 48–49: Unknown Mbuti artist, Display cloth, 1955 (detail, page 52); pages 60–61: Otto Marseus van Schrick, *Forest Still Life with Great Morning Glory and Toad*, 1660 (detail, page 79); pages 76–77: Hans Hoffmann, *A Hare in the Forest*, ca. 1585 (detail, page 78); pages 90–91: Jan Brueghel the Younger, *Satire of Tulipmania*, 1640 (detail, page 94); pages 104–5: Giovanni Garzoni, *Still Life with Bowl of Citrons*, ca. late 1640s (detail, page 96); pages 120–21: Johannes Janson, *A Formal Garden*, 1766 (detail, page 138); pages 134–35: Alessandro Magnasco, *The Triumph of Venus*, ca. 1720–30 (detail, page 136); pages 146–47: Jacques-Henri Lartigue, *Field of Poppies*, ca. 1960–78 (detail, page 173); pages 156–57: Gustave Courbet, *Bouquet of Flowers in a Vase*, 1862 (detail, page 161); pages 174–75: Precious Okoyomon, Installation view of *To See the Earth before the End of the World*, 2022 (detail, page 188); pages 190–91: Sara Angelucci, *Nocturnal Botanical Ontario*, 2021 (detail, page 198)